# Psychopharmacology of Aging

AGING

Series Editor: *Carl Eisdorfer, Ph.D., M.D.*

---

**Psychopharmacology of Aging**

Edited by *Carl Eisdorfer, Ph.D., M.D.* and *William E. Fann, M.D.*

# Psychopharmacology of Aging

Edited by

**Carl Eisdorfer, Ph.D., M.D.**
Professor and Chairman
Department of Psychiatry and Behavioral Sciences
School of Medicine
University of Washington, Seattle

and

**William E. Fann, M.D.**
Professor of Psychiatry
Associate Professor of Pharmacology
Baylor College of Medicine
and Chief, Psychiatry Service
Veterans Administration Hospital
Houston, Texas

**SP MEDICAL & SCIENTIFIC BOOKS**

New York

SPECTRUM PUBLICATIONS, INC.
175-20 Wexford Terrace, Jamaica, N.Y. 11432

**Library of Congress Cataloging in Publication Data**
Main entry under title:

The psychopharmacology of aging.

Includes index.
1. Geriatric psychopharmacology.    I. Eisdorfer, Carl.    II. Fann, William.
[DNLM:    1. Aging—Drug effects.    2. Psychopharmacology in old age.
WT150 P9745]
RC451.4.A5P779        615′.78        80-19944
ISBN 0-89335-117-2

# Contributors

**S. ABDEL'AL, Ph.D.**
Sandoz Medical Research Institute
Basel, Switzerland

**ROBERT J. BARRETT, Ph.D.**
Department of Psychology
Vanderbilt University
Nashville, Tennessee

**JOHN M. DAVIS, M.D., Ph.D.**
Illinois State Psychiatric Institute
Department of Psychiatry
Pritzker School of Medicine
University of Chicago
Chicago, Illinois

**CARL EISDORFER, Ph.D., M.D.**
Department of Psychiatry and
    Behavioral Sciences
University of Washington School of
    Medicine
Seattle, Washington

**A. ENZ, Ph.D.**
Sandoz Medical Research Institute
Basel, Switzerland

**WILLIAM E. FANN, M.D.**
Departments of Psychiatry and
    Pharmacology
Baylor College of Medicine
Psychiatry Service
Veterans Administration Medical
    Center
Houston, Texas

**H. FREY, Ph.D.**
Sandoz Medical Research Institute
Basel, Switzerland

**ALEXANDER H. GLASSMAN,
M.D.**
Department of Psychiatry
Columbia University College of
    Physicians and Surgeons
New York, New York

**P. GYGAX, Ph.D.**
Sandoz Medical Research Institute
Basel, Switzerland

**ROBERT HICKS, M.D.**
Department of Psychiatry
University of Texas Medical Branch
Houston, Texas

**O. HUNZIGER, Ph.D.**
Sandoz Medical Research Institute
Basel, Switzerland

**P. IWANGOFF, Ph.D.**
Sandoz Medical Research Institute
Basel, Switzerland

**SHEPARD J. KANTOR, M.D.**
Department of Psychiatry
Columbia University College of
    Physicians and Surgeons
New York, New York

**WILLIAM MEIER-RUGE, M.D.**
Sandoz Medical Research Institute
Basel, Switzerland

**G.C. PALMER, Ph.D.**
Department of Pharmacology
University of South Alabama School
    of Medicine
Mobile, Alabama

**PATRICIA N. PRINZ, Ph.D.**
Department of Psychiatry and
    Behavioral Sciences
University of Washington School of
    Medicine
Seattle, Washington

**OAKLEY S. RAY, Ph.D.**
Department of Psychology
Vanderbilt University
Nashville, Tennessee

**K. REICHLMEIER, Ph.D.**
Sandoz Medical Research Institute
Basel, Switzerland

**G. ALAN ROBISON, Ph.D.**
Department of Pharmacology
University of Texas Medical
    Branch
Houston, Texas

**T. SAMORAJSKI, Ph.D.**
Texas Research Institute of Mental
    Sciences
Houston, Texas

**M.J. SCHMIDT, Ph.D.**
Eli Lilly Laboratories
Indianapolis, Indiana

**ROBERT C. SMITH, M.D., Ph.D.**
Texas Research Institute of Mental
    Sciences
Department of Pharmacology
Baylor College of Medicine
Houston, Texas

**J. RANDOLPH STRONG, B.A.**
Texas Research Institute of Mental
    Sciences
Houston, Texas

**JANET STRONG, B.A.**
Texas Research Institute of Mental
    Sciences
Houston, Texas

**M.J. VETEAU, Ph.D.**
Sandoz Medical Research Institute
Basel, Switzerland

**N. WIERNSPERGER, Ph.D.**
Sandoz Medical Research Institute
Basel Switzerland

# Introduction

The "aging" of the world population is by now a well-recognized phenomenon. It has become a matter of concern to the social planner and deliverer of services, as well as to the clinician. On a per capita basis, the aged—that is those 65 and older—appear in outpatient health care facilities at a rate which is approximately fifty percent greater than their adult peers, stay about three times as long in general medical and surgical facilities, and represent more than 90 percent of the long-term-care beds in the United States. In addition, at a time when they represented approximately 10 percent of the total population, the aged were the recipients of 25 percent of all prescriptions for medication. Thus, an understanding of the drug use consequences, misuse and abuse of drugs among older persons, has become a salient issue for the scientist, clinical physician, and other health care professionals.

The aged are a group at heightened risk for a number of disorders and often present with clinical problems not usually encountered in an aging population. Many such problems are the direct consequence of multiple, concurrent, and complicating disorders; drug/drug interactions, compliance with physician prescription, the use of concurrent non-prescribed substances such as alcohol or over-the-counter medication, and a variety of other behaviors.

There is also a growing interest in the well recognized, but poorly understood, pattern of organic changes which occur in later maturity. Somatic changes in later life lead to consequent changes in pharmacokinetics of drugs administered. As we learn more about pharmacodynamics, the scientific study of drug action, we appreciate that advancing age is an important variable to be considered in the *in vivo* effects of therapeutically active substances. Changes in the ratio of adipose to protein and water in the older individual have long been recognized, in that this has considerable consequence for the storage of psychoactive drugs, most of which are lipophilic. Even greater effects, however, may be the result of cell loss in specific organ systems, impaired feedback linkages, changes in end organ sensitivity, and changes in circulating hormone levels. It is particularly noteworthy that it is not always simple to predict on any *ad hominem* basis whether a specific substance or reaction may decrease or increase with advancing age. Often, the changes occurring with aging may have effects upon the various aspects of the pharmacokinetics which may proceed in opposite directions; thus, absorption from the gut and consequent blood level may be decreased for a particular substance while end organ sensitivity, therefore reactivity, may be increased for that same substance. The relationship between central and peripheral measures is another complicating factor, particularly germane to our focus on psychoactive drugs. Thus, while norepinephrine (Nor Epi) levels may decrease in the brain, Nor Epi and Epinephrine levels may increase in serum collected peripherally. The implication of such changes for peripheral autonomic nervous system and central nervous system activity and interaction remains less clear. A neurotransmitter may decrease because it is not being produced, or because of the metabolic consequences of another enzyme, e.g. MAO. The changes with age in those organ systems which are responsible for elimination of medication, e.g. lungs and kidney, may significantly alter the half life of a circulating medication, while the changes in cell permeability or end organ action may shift the drug action in an entirely opposite direction. It is with these and a variety of other factors in mind, that the editors organized this volume on basic issues in the *Psychopharmacology of Aging*.

This collection of works was developed in an initial effort to focus the attention of the scientific and clinical community on emerging data and to identify foci of scientific activity in this developing area. The authors in this volume are all distinguished scientists, experienced in some aspect of the interaction between aging and psychoactive medication. The chapters incorporate not only the newly emerging data, but many of the issues involved in a range of topics relevant to the discipline.

The impact of age itself as a variable must be reviewed. We can no longer be content with a simple late-life category of 65 or older. Social scientists have recognized the existence of the "young-old" and the "old-old" among the aged. Individuals at 60 to 75 appear to have very similar social and psychological patterns. At age 75 and beyond, these patterns appear to change significantly. It is of some interest that the study of intelligence has shown that there is little or no evidence of generalized intellectual decline among physically healthy older persons in the decade from age 65 to 75, but that decline following age 75 does occur. The possible impact of this for the clinician is clear. For the scientist, it may mean that a process of change is not linear, but, rather, that with later age the change may be accelerated and assume different mathematical functions. Similarly, in studying the epidemiology of dementia, there is a relative doubling of the prevalence rate with advancing age beyond 60. Whether this information has some analogy to the dynamics of drug activity is as yet unstudied, but represents an important area for future investigation. Do physical changes occur at a rate accelerating with age but not recognized until a much later stage, or is it a differing function with certain thresholds beyond which changes are more manifest?

The purpose of this book is, then, to focus examinations upon a set of phenomena, i.e. the effects of later life on medication. Not accidentally, there will also be interest in the effects of medication on adaptation in later life. The pattern of relationships often speculated upon is as yet relatively uncharted and *terra incognita* for the scientist and clinician but one that can ultimately affect the lives of tens of millions of persons.

# Contents

# CHAPTER 1

# *Sleep Changes With Aging*

## P.N. PRINZ

This chapter will describe sleep changes in later life and discuss the nature of sleep alterations in the context of the other neurobiological changes typical of old age. The influence of general health factors on neurobiological aging processes and on sleep will be examined, as will the possible influence of sleep per se on age-related changes in the nervous system. Lastly, we will focus on clinical implications for the physician who is called upon to treat sleep disturbances in elderly patients.

## PSYCHOBIOLOGICAL SUBSTRATES OF ABNORMAL SLEEP

As summarized by Feinberg and Carlson,[1] these sleep variables follow trends that are comparable to life-span curves for brain weight, neuronal population density, brain metabolic rate (oxygen utilization) and cerebral blood flow.

### Cerebral Blood Flow and Metabolism

Of all the physiological indices that decline with advanced age, only cerebral blood flow (CBF) can be measured nontraumatically in intact subjects. For this reason, and because CBF is physiologically linked to brain metabolic rate,[2,3] CBF has often been used in human multidisciplinary studies of aging. In a recent preliminary study, CBF levels were compared with sleep-pattern variables measured in the same elderly community volunteer subjects. It was observed that individuals having greater amounts of REM sleep also had more slow-wave sleep[4] and in general maintained CBF levels closer to the norm for young adults.[5] In addition, dominant alpha frequencies were found to be higher in those elderly with greater amounts of REM and slow-wave sleep.[5] Thus, there is limited preliminary evidence that sleep variables may correlate with brain blood flow and metabolism, as well as EEG alpha frequency. These relationships may depend upon underlying minor alterations in cerebral physiology, since the CBF levels in most of the subjects were observed to be reduced by varying degrees from young adult norms.

## Structural Changes in the Aged Brain

The recent findings of Brody and associates[6] are of particular interest in any consideration of a possible neurobiological basis for age-related sleep changes: he observed a sizable (40 to 50 percent) age-related depopulation of neurons in the locus ceruleus, a brain-stem site thought to be involved in wakefulness behavior,[7] although probably not involved in generating REM sleep.[8] Other brain-stem areas have been more clearly implicated in regulating sleep and wakefulness. There is a large literature describing the role of midbrain reticular neurons in achieving arousal responses and maintained wakefulness.[9] Opposing mechanisms that induce sleep are thought to arise from reticular (gigantocellularis) neurons in pontine regions of the brain stem.[10] Although midbrain reticular neurons are reported to show degenerative changes in senescence,[11] evidence regarding alterations in pontine neurons is not available. Additional morphologic studies of these brain regions in senescence could provide useful anatomic correlates of sleep-pattern changes in senescence.

## Psychometric Correlates of Sleep

It has been observed that sleep-pattern variables in elderly groups parallel mental-function test scores. Feinberg et al.,[12] in an NIH study of aged men selected for good health, observed that time spent in REM sleep was correlated positively with WAIS performance and with Wechsler Memory scores. Moreover, this relationship was improved when REM sleep intensity (as inferred from summed scores for the amount of rapid eye movements) was compared with psychometric scores.[13] Subsequent studies have confirmed the finding that amount of REM sleep and psychometric scores are correlated in typical elderly subjects.[14,15]

Correlations between sleep variables and psychometric scores are not observed in healthy young subject groups; however, there is some evidence that psychological functions are influenced by the quantity of sleep in young adults.[16] In a study comparing young adults with restless or sound sleep patterns, Williams and Williams[17] observed that restless sleepers had more awakenings and more transitions from stage to stage and less slow-wave sleep; although their performance on psychological tests is similar to that for sound sleepers, restless sleepers appeared to be more sensitive to the effects of sleep loss, as indicated by their poorer performance following a night of sleep deprivation. Recovery sleep on the night following sleep deprivation was similar for both groups.

Sleep-pattern characteristics of elderly individuals are similar in many respects to the restless sleepers in this study; hence, it is possible that sleep deprivation would be particularly disruptive of psychological function in elderly subjects. It is not known whether recovery sleep following deprivation is as efficient in elderly subjects as in younger ones.

Since the available studies on sleep in the aged did not employ extremely rigorous subject selection procedures of the sort utilized in the NIH study of Birren at al.,[18] it is possible that these relationships depend upon impaired cerebral physiology and imperfect health.

## LONGITUDINAL STUDIES OF SLEEP CHANGES

Modern measurements of sleep and wakefulness patterns are based on eye-movement monitoring and all-night polygraphic recordings of the electrical signals generated by the brain and the postural muscles. Because the brain's electrical activity undergoes changes relating to the process of aging, our discussion of sleep stage changes will include electroencephalographic (EEG) changes with age.

### The Transition from Wakefulness to Sleep

In the transition period from wakefulness to sleep, the adult EEG pattern typically undergoes notable changes (Figure 1-1).

The alpha rhythm during quiet wakefulness slows in frequency as drowsiness sets in and is gradually replaced by low-voltage theta and fast desynchronized activity as the individual enters stage 1 sleep.[19] At the same time, the individual's responsiveness to the environment becomes unpredictable or slowed.[20] In addition, postural muscle tonus declines as measured from chin electromyogram (EMG) electrodes, and the rapid eye

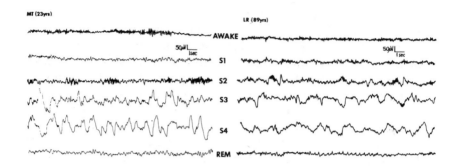

Figure 1-1. REM Sleep/NREM Sleep Relationship Throughout Human Life.

movements characteristic of the alert state disappear as indicated by electroculogram (EOG) electrodes placed at the outer canthus of each eye. The sleep pattern which follows is conventionally defined according to changing activities in these EEG, EOG and EMG electrodes.[21]

## The Sleep Stages

Normal sleep is divided into two main categories comprising a total of five stages.[21] Nonrapid eye movement (NREM) sleep includes stages 1, 2, 3 and 4. Rapid eye movement (REM) sleep is the fifth stage (also called active sleep or paradoxical sleep).

In NREM sleep, eye movements are absent and muscle tonus is moderately reduced from the waking levels. In stage 1 sleep there is an absence of rapid eye movements (REMs). The EEG pattern is of low amplitude, irregular, fast-frequent activity (shown in Figure 2). In stage 2 sleep, synchronous waves of 12 to 16 Hz (spindles) occur against a background of low-amplitude, fast-frequency activity. In stage 3 sleep, high-amplitude (75 $\mu$V or more), slow (0.5 to 2.5 Hz) delta waves become more frequent than in stage 2, comprising 20 to 50 percent of the EEG record; stage 4 is reached when 50% or more of the EEG record is comprised of delta waves.

REM sleep is characterized by low-amplitude, fast-frequency EEG activity, similar to the EEG during wakefulness. Bursts of rapid eye movements are present. Just prior to or at the onset of a REM sleep period, muscle tonus undergoes a marked decrease which is sustained throughout the REM period except for brief, phasic activity. Figure 1-1 depicts the appearance of the EEG trace during all the sleep stages, as well as wakefulness in a typical young and aged subject.

## Changes in Sleep EEG with Age

Several prominent changes in the sleep EEG have been found in elderly as compared with young adults (Figure 1-1). The delta waves characterizing stages 3 and 4 are greatly attenuated in amplitude.[12,14] In a study of 12 healthy elderly (aged 75 to 92), the largest slow-wave amplitudes rarely exceeded 150 $\mu$V, whereas 200 $\mu$V or larger waves are commonly seen in young adults[4] (see Figure 2). Possibly as a result of amplitude changes, there is an overall decreased amount of typical delta-wave activity (75 $\mu$V or larger), in the all-night EEG record.[4] It should be noted that the focal or diffuse EEG slow waves seen during wakefulness in some elderly subjects are independent phenomena unrelated to the slow waves of sleep, since the former reflect tissue injury or other pathological process,[22] while the latter represent a normal physiological state attained during sleep. Further evidence that these are distinct phenomena derives from the observations that diffuse slow activity during waking is associated with a greatly reduced cerebral metabolism and blood flow[23] that does not occur during sleep.[24,25]

In addition, changes in spindle activity have also been observed in the sleep records of elderly subjects; as compared with young adults, senescent sleep spindles are often poorly formed and of lower amplitude,[12] resulting in an infrequent occurrence of typical spindling activity. Moreover, spindle frequencies of the elderly often are slower than those of young adults.[12,26] As originally noted by Feinberg,[12] these changes are analogous to the changes in alpha activity, which also decreases in frequency, amplitude and overall amount in senescence. Similarly, the changes in sleep-related EEG slow waves with advanced age also decrease in both amplitude and overall amount.

## Changes in Sleep Patterns with Age

Coincident with altered EEG characteristics during sleep, there are also changes in the amounts and patterning of the various sleep stages (stages 1 through 4 and stage REM). As illustrated in Figure 1-2, sleep undergoes considerable change across the human lifespan. Total sleep, stage 4 and REM sleep are at maximum levels in childhood and drop to more stable adult levels after puberty, followed by a further decline in senescence.[25,28] Probably because of the reduced amplitude of sleep-related EEG slow waves that characterize stage 4 sleep, this stage is greatly reduced or absent in senescence.[4,12,14,26] At the same time, there is a significantly increased wakefulness. Only minor nonsignificant changes have been observed for sleep stages 1, 2 and 3.

6

PRINZ

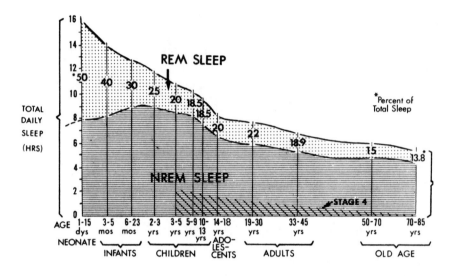

Figure 1-2.

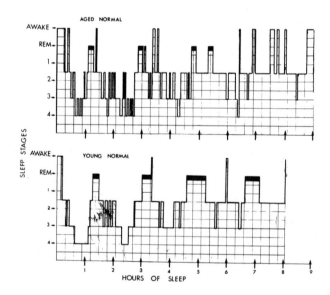

Figure 1-3.

In addition, time spent in REM sleep has been observed to be consistently diminished in studies of senescent sleep patterns.[4,12,14,26] There is, moreover, a decline in the intensity of the REM sleep state, as inferred from the diminution of the REM activity that normally accompanies this state.[13] The available studies of senescent sleep patterns are all consistent in finding decreased stage 4 and REM sleep, together with increased wakefulness.

Human sleep stages are known to cycle in characteristic fashion, as illustrated in Figure 1-3. After falling asleep, the individual descends from stage 1 into stages 2, 3 and then 4, after which a REM period generally occurs. This sequence of sleep stages terminating in REM sleep is repeated four to five times across the night's sleep. In general, a similar cycling pattern is observed in elderly subjects; however, some differences have been observed. The first cycle of the night is often shorter, perhaps reflecting the fact that stage 4, which in young adults occurs predominantly in the first cycle, is reduced (Figure 1-3). It has also been noticed that the length of the REM periods, which in young adults increases with each successive cycle, remains more constant in senescent sleep recordings.[29]

Perhaps the most striking change visible in the all-night sleep pattern, however, is the more frequent interruption of sleep by long periods of wakefulness (Figure 1-3). In addition, more frequent shifts between stages are observed, particularly for REM sleep, which is often interrupted by stage 2 sleep.[14]

These changes are generally taken as evidence that sleep is impaired in the elderly. The changes are essentially similar in both men and women.[28,30] Both increased wakefulness and decreased slow-wave sleep are subjectively experienced as less-sound sleep, which may account for more frequent complaints of poor sleep and the greater usage of drugs to promote sleep among elderly individuals. In addition, the more frequent daytime naps taken by many elderly probably represent an attempt to compensate for impaired sleep. Studies of daytime napping in elderly are scarce; nevertheless, there are indications that allowing elderly subjects to nap ad lib does not alter the overall finding of reduced stage 4 and REM sleep.[15]

Although there are many differences among individuals in sleep variables, sleep-pattern characteristics are generally stable from night to night, provided adaptation to the experimental setting has been achieved and other temporary factors have been ruled out. The studies of sleep in the aged summarized here are all based on stable measurements obtained over multiple nights of sleep recordings.

Because depressive illnesses, anxiety or poor health are commonly associated with sleep impairments that resemble the sleep changes of the elderly (less slow-wave sleep, more time spent awake), an accurate evaluation of aging influences on sleep requires that studies be based on relatively healthy subjects, selected to be as free as possible from depressive symptoms and anxiety. Both the Feinberg[12] and the Prinz[15] studies employed such selection procedures, but nevertheless, they observed increased wakefulness and decreased stage 4 and REM sleep. Hence, these alterations in sleep are probably independent of the effects of depression, anxiety or clinically identifiable disease processes. As such, they may represent the effects of some age-dependent alteration in the nervous system.

## INFLUENCES OF SLEEP CHANGES ON BIOLOGICAL SYSTEMS

The biological implications of age-related changes in sleep and wakefulness remain unclear. Among young adult subjects, both REM and stage 4 sleep are considered to be homeostatically regulated, since experimentally induced sleep losses are followed by compensatory increases in stage 4, followed by REM sleep on recovery nights.[31,32] It is not clear whether such homeostatic influences on sleep are altered in the aged. While deprivation of REM or stage 4 sleep appear to be tolerated by the organism without notable pathological change,[29,33] there are several reports that prolonged total sleep loss is accompanied by neuronal degenerative changes and ultimate death in animals.[34,25] The time-honored notion that sleep serves restorative functions for the organism have been reexamined[36] in the light of recent findings that human growth hormone (known to promote protein synthesis in many body tissues, including the brain) is released into the plasma in large amounts during slow-wave sleep stages[37] and could presumably influence processes of tissue maintenance and repair. In fact, the reduced slow-wave sleep in aged individuals is associated with reduced growth hormone levels in plasma across the night.[38]

There are numerous theories of neuronal aging that invoke the malfunction and/or malformation of cellular elements, including neurotubules, neurofilaments,[39] genetic material (DNA) or the associated RNA that transcribes genetic instructions into cellular proteins, dendritic membranes and synaptic vesicles containing neurotransmitter substances [recently reviewed in Brody[6]]. Because the neuron does not divide and reproduce, and because of its greater workload (its oxygen consumption is much greater than that of the somatic cell), neuronal systems are likely to be particularly sensitive to factors that either cause malfunction of neuronal elements or impede the normal repair processes in the cell.

Factors such as immunologic, endocrine, nutritional, viral, radiation or toxic environmental pollutants are among the influences that have been proposed in theories of senescence. To the extent that sleep serves a restorative function for brain tissue, we can also theorize that the sleep losses sustained with advancing age may serve as an additional factor capable of influencing the physiologic and morphologic systems under decline with age.[40] Multidisciplinary studies of the effects of prolonged total and partial sleep loss on neuronal tissue in animals are needed in order to evaluate this possibility.

## SLEEP AND HEALTH

Sleep patterns are known to be impaired by chronic diseases that affect the nervous system, including neurologic, cardiovascular, renal, respiratory, nutritional and endocrine disorders [recently reviewed by Williams et al.[28]]. Generally speaking, these diseases are more prevalent in older populations. In addition, disturbed sleep is a common concomitant of malfunction in the control mechanisms regulating breathing or cardiovascular function during sleep. It has been estimated[41] that sleep apnea syndromes are much more prevalent in the older patient. Cardiovascular irregularities during sleep are in need of greater study in the older patient.

In addition, organic brain damage of all types tends to impair sleep. Although the sleep patterns of "normal" elderly individuals appear impaired by young-adult standards, they are not so disturbed as the sleep of elderly patients suffering from dementias of varying etiologies [i.e., organic brain syndrome (OBS)]. In a study comparing three subject groups, Feinberg and coworkers[12] observed significantly greater decrements in stage 4, REM and total sleep among OBS patients than for normal elderly or young-adult groups. In addition, OBS patients exhibited more exaggerated decreases in eye-movement rates during REM sleep. The lowered times spent in REM sleep in OBS patients were observed to correlate with psychometric test scores. In another study[4] using selected senile dementia patients of the Alzheimer's type (thus excluding cerebrovascular and other types of dementia), these observations were confirmed: REM and stage 4 sleep were greatly reduced or absent; nighttime and daytime sleep were greatly fragmented by wakening.

The increased wakefulness in dementia patients during the night is much more prominent than in normal elderly, a fact that is of some practical concern in the management of demented patients, since such patients sometimes hallucinate or wander about following nighttime awakenings, necessitating institutionalization or usage of psychoactive drugs.

## SOME CONSIDERATIONS IN TREATING SLEEP DISTURBANCES
## IN THE ELDERLY

It has been estimated that older patients (above age 60) consume more than one-third of the sleeping medications prescribed annually. Nevertheless, the sleep literature does not contain a single well-controlled polygraphic study of drug effects on sleep in this age group of patients. In the many clinical trials of various drugs conducted in recent years,[42] there has been a general policy either to exclude the older patient from the study or to overlook the age factor and combine treatment groups irrespective of age.

It is difficult to adequately evaluate sleep-promoting drugs in elderly individuals. The older patient is more likely to be influenced by medical conditions that affect his sleep: he is also more likely to be taking other medications that could confound the clinical evaluation. In addition, the pharmacokinetics of drug action are likely to be altered in the older patient,[43] whose kidney and liver may metabolize and excrete drugs differently. Hence, dose levels may need adjustment in some older patients to achieve the expected blood levels of the drug.

In approaching this complex issue, it would be useful to distinguish the various types of sleep disturbance in the aged patient. For example, a drug that improves sleep in the anxious or depressed older patient may not affect the patient whose sleep disturbance arises from mild organic brain syndrome or from other medical conditions. Since age per se is such a prominent factor altering sleep, one would ideally like to see clinical evaluations in individuals with an age-related onset of insomnia, who have no evidence of other conditions affecting sleep.

## REFERENCES

1. Feinberg I, Carlson V: Sleep variables as a function of age in man. *Arch Gen Psychiatry* 18:239–250, 1968.
2. *Brain Work.* Edited by Ingvar DH, Lassen NA. New York, Academic Press, 1975.
3. Obrist WD: Cerebral blood flow and its regulation. *Clin Neurosurg* 22, 1975.
4. Prinz PN, Andrews-Kulis M, Storrie M, Bartol M, Raskind M, Gerber C: Sleep waking pattern in normal aging and in dementia. *Sleep Res,* 1978, in press.
5. Prinz P, Obrist W, Wang H: Sleep patterns in healthy elderly subjects: Individual differences as related to other neurobiological variables, in Chase M, Stern W, Walters (eds.): *Sleep Research.* Los Angeles, Brain Information Service/Brain Research Institute, UCLA, 1975.
6. Brody H, Harmon D, Ordy J: *Aging.* New York, Raven Press, 1975, vol 1.
7. Korf J, Aghajanian G, Roth R: Increased turnover of norepinephrine in the rat cerebral cortex during stress: Role of the locus coeruleus. *Neuropharmacology* 12:933–938, 1975.

8. Henley K, Morrison A: A re-evaluation of the effects of lesions of the pontine tegmentum and locus coeruleus on phenomena of paradoxical sleep in the cat. *Acta Neurobiol Exp* 34:215–232, 1974.

9. Magoun HW: *The Waking Brain.* Springfield, Ill, Charles C Thomas, 1958.

10. Jouvet M: Neurophysiology of the states of sleep. *Physiol Rev* 47:117–177, 1967.

11. Yakovlev PI, Lecours A: The myelogentic cycles of regional maturation of the brain, in Minowski A (ed.): *Regional Development of the Brain in Early Life.* Philadelphia, FA Davis, 1967, pp 3–70.

12. Feinberg I, Koresko, R Heller N: EEG sleep patterns as a function of normal and pathological aging in man. *J Psychiatr Res* 5:107–144, 1967.

13. Feinberg I, Braun M, Koresko R: Vertical eye-movement during REM sleep: Effects of age and electrode placement. *Psychophysiology* 5:556–561, 1969.

14. Kahn E, Fisher C: The sleep characteristics of the normal aged male. *J Nerv Ment Dis* 148:477–505, 1969.

15. Prinz PN: Sleep and intellectual function in the aged. *J Gerontol* 32:279–286, 1977.

16. Johnson LC: The effect of total, partial and stage sleep deprivation on EEG patterns and performance, in Burch NR, Altschuler H (eds.): *Behavior and Brain Electrical Activity.* New York, Plenum Press, 1975, pp 1–30.

17. Williams HL, Williams CL: Nocturnal EEG profiles and performance. *Psychophysiology* 3:164–175, 1966.

18. Birren JE, Butler RN, Greenhouse SW: Interdisciplinary relationships: Interrelations of physiological, psychological and psychiatric findings in healthy elderly men, in *Human Aging: A Biological and Behavioral Study.* Washington, DC, US Government Printing Office (USPHS Pub No 986).

19. Johnson L, Lubin A, Naitoh P: Spectral analysis of the EEG of dominant and non-dominant alpha subjects during waking and sleeping. *Electroencephalogr Clin Neurophysiol* 26:361–370, 1969.

20. Williams HL, Granda H, Jones R: EEG frequency and finger pulse volume as predictions of reaction time during sleep loss. *Electroencephalogr Clin Neurophysiol* 14:65–70, 1962.

21. Rechtschaffen A, Kales A: *A Manual of Standardized Terminology, Techniques, and Scoring Systems for Sleep Stages of Human Subjects.* USPHS Pub No 204, US Government Printing Office, Washington, DC, 1968.

22. Gibbs FA, Gibbs EL: *Medical Electroencephalography.* Reading, Mass, Addison-Wesley, 1967.

23. Obrist WD: Cerebral physiology of the aged: Influence of circulatory disorders, in Gaitz CM (ed.): *Aging and the Brain.* New York, Plenum Press, 1972, pp 117–133.

24. Mangold R, Sokoloff L, Conner E: The effects of sleep and lack of sleep on the cerebral circulation and metabolism of normal young men. *J Clin Invest* 34:1092–1100, 1955.

25. Townsend RE, Prinz PN, Obrist WD: Human cerebral blood flow during sleep and waking. *J Applied Physiol* 35:620–625, 1973.

26. Kales A, Wilson T, Kales J: Measurements of all-night sleep in normal elderly persons: Effects of aging. *J Am Geriatr Soc* 15:405–414, 1967.

27. Roffwarg HP, Munzio JN, Dement WC: Ontogenic development of the human sleep-dream cycle. *Science* 152:604–619, 1966.

28. Williams RL, Karacan I, Hursch CJ: *Electroencephalography (EEG) of Human Sleep: Clinical Applications.* New York, John Wiley and Sons, 1974.

29. Feinberg I: Changes in sleep cycle patterns with age. *J Psychiatr Res* 10:283–306, 1974.

30. Kahn E, Fisher C, Lieberman L: The sleep characteristics of the human aged female. *Compr Psychiatry* 11:274–278, 1970.

31. Agnew H, Webb W, Williams R: The effect of stage four sleep deprivation. *Electroencephalogr Clin Neurophysiol* 17:68–70, 1964.
32. Berger R, Oswald I: Effects of sleep deprivation on behavior, subsequent sleep and dreaming. *Br J Psychiatry* 108:457–465, 1962.
33. Freemon F: *Sleep Research: A Critical Review.* Springfield, Ill, Charles C Thomas, 1972.
34. Karadzic V: Physiological changes resulting from total sleep deprivation, in Koella W, Levin P (eds.): *Sleep: Physiology, Biochemistry, Psychology, Pharmacology, Clinical Implications.* Basel, S Karger, 1973, pp 165–174.
35. Kleitman N: *Sleep and Wakefulness.* Chicago, Ill, Chicago Press, 1963.
36. Oswald I: Is sleep related to synthetic purpose? in Koella W, Levin P (eds.): *Sleep: Physiology, Biochemistry, Psychology, Pharmacology, Clinical Implications.* Basel, S Karger, 1973, pp 225–239.
37. Honda Y, Takahashi E, Takahashi S: Growth hormone secretion during nocturnal sleep in normal subjects. *J Clin Endocrinol Metab* 29:20–29, 1969.
38. Prinz P, Blenkarn D, Linnoila M, Weitzman E: Nocturnal growth hormone secretion during sleep in elderly men. *Sleep Res* 5:87, 1976.
39. Wisniewski H, Terry RD: An experimental approach to the morphogenesis of neurofibrillary degeneration and the argyrophilic plague, in Wolstenholme J, O'Conner M (eds.): *Alzheimer's Disease and Related Conditions.* 1970, pp 167–186.
40. Prinz N: EEG during sleep and waking states, in *Experimental Aging Research,* Special Review. Bar Harbor, Ear, 1976, pp 135–163.
41. Dement WC, Laughton M (eds.): *Sleep and Aging,* in Proceedings of the NIA Conference. June 1–2, 1978, in press.
42. Williams RL, Karacan I (eds.): *The Pharmacology of Sleep.* New York, Wiley & Sons, 1976, p 354.
43. Friedel R: Pharmacokinetics of Aging, in Elias et al. (eds.): *Special Rev Exp Aging Res,* 1976.

# CHAPTER 2

# Enzymatic Changes In The Aging Brain And Some Aspects Of Its Pharmacological Intervention With Ergot Compounds

K. REICHLMEIER
P. IWANGOFF
A. ENZ

The process of aging involves a series of physiological changes such as reduced memory functions, shortened sleep span, flattening of mood, decreasing tolerance and altered endocrine functions. The brain seems to function as a pacemaker in the process of aging. In its unique position as a communication and regulation system between environment and body, the brain represents the body's most important control function.

Important physiological variations occur during the lifespan, which are often superposed or masked by alterations originating from diseases. This makes a characterization of the natural aging process more difficult. On the other hand, aging may result in an increased susceptibility to diseases. A separation of the normal or intrinsic aging process from processes which may be influenced by external effects is complicated and nearly impossible to achieve.

One of the most important prerequisites in the neurochemistry of aging research is the investigation of age-dependent parameters. Alterations in enzyme activities, enzyme properties or substrate concentrations in the

13

brain during aging provide us with information about functional contexts. Knowledge of such changes, in comparison with pathological alterations due to diverse neurological or psychiatric diseases, is the basis for any pharmacological intervention in brain metabolism during aging.

This basic information can enable us to set up research into the pharmacology of the aging brain and to work out the requirements for a beneficial drug action.

Drugs claimed to be active on age-dependent disturbances in the human brain must be able to compensate or to interact with age-impaired functions. To obtain some basic information about the action of different drugs, it is essential to introduce experimental animal models which are suitable for special pharmacological tests. At the same time, animal colonies with old animals should be available to compare the abovementioned age-dependent parameters directly with possible compensatory activities of certain drugs. But such studies are limited, owing to the high costs of aging animals and the restriction to some rodent species.

Enzymes are especially suitable for working out basic parameters of the influence of age. They already represent an "in vivo matrix," and they are linked among themselves and dependent on each other. Primarily, knowledge about influence of age on regulatory enzymes within a coherent chain of enzymes is of great interest. For instance, age-dependent disturbances in the pattern of the enzymes involved in energy metabolism of the brain affect all the energy-dependent systems, such as neurotransmitter systems and enzymes related to neurotransmitter function.

The following sections describe the age dependency of a series of enzymes in animal and human brains. First, the effect of age on enzymes of the glycolytic pathway and on ATPases is described. Then, some transmitter-related enzymes belonging to the cyclic AMP system are also considered.

Some effects of a class of substances, dihydrogenated ergot alkaloids, on the cyclic AMP system and on energy metabolism in in vitro assays are described, and their possible intervention in the aging process is discussed.

## NEUROCHEMICAL FINDINGS IN AGING ANIMAL AND HUMAN BRAINS

Aging has serious consequences for membrane function, synaptic transmission, enzyme activities, substrate concentrations and accessibility, neurotransmitter turnover and function, availability of energy and economy of energy turnover. As already pointed out, the question of cerebral enzymes demonstrating changes in their activities and kinetic parameters with increasing age is of significant importance. This section concentrates on enzymes involved in transmitter function, on those regulating the synthesis and breakdown of energy-rich compounds, and on those responsible for interrelated reactions within these fields.

Attempts to study the neurochemistry of aging are hampered by the fact that the brain is a very complex organ. It is not only composed of a variety of cell types, but also shows a highly organized structural and functional differentiation from region to region. This complexity increases when the human brain is chosen for studies of aging, as many more variables are added that can interfere with the effects due to aging. These include premortem conditions, drug therapy, underlying diseases, postmortem delay and genetic factors. These difficulties are reflected in the scarcity of papers describing the influence of age on enzyme activities of the human brain.

We report here the results of a study of nearly 50 human brains. According to the clinical records, all cases were free of neurological or psychiatric diseases. The principal intention was to study the effects of "normal" aging on different enzyme systems. Postmortem delay was from four to 24 hours, and the age of the donors ranged from 19 to 92 years. The evaluation of the results with regard to aging was performed by linear regression analysis and by comparison of individual age groups. Factors such as premortem influences and postmortem effects on enzyme activities will be discussed.

## The Problem of Energy Supply in the Aging Brain

The brain is dependent on a constant supply of glucose for normal function. The human brain, for example, utilizes about 100 grams of glucose per day. Glucose is metabolized by the aerobic glycolytic pathway combined with the citric-acid cycle and the respiratory chain. This reaction sequence provides for the synthesis of the energy-rich compound ATP. Glycolytic regulation has a predominant importance for the total energy metabolism. However, the possibility cannot be excluded that there also exist other regulatory mechanisms in the biochemical chain of ATP production.

The influence of aging on enzymes of the glycolytic pathway is reported by Iwangoff et al.[1] According to this study, several glycolytic enzymes of the autoptic human brain are influenced by age (Table 2-1). A substantial and significant decrease of activity was observed in the case of phosphofructokinase (Figure 2-1) in both cortex and putamen. The

Table 2-1: The effect of age on enzymes of the glycolytic pathway in human brain. Cases with neurological diseases are excluded from this investigation. According to the clinical records, a separation of cases with sudden death (short agony) was performed. Results of linear regression analysis, coefficients of correlation and significances are given (* $2\alpha < 0.05$, ** $2\alpha < 0.01$, *** $2\alpha < 0.001$). X means the age in years, and Y is the level of activity dependent on age.

| Enzyme | | FRONTAL CORTEX | | | | PUTAMEN |
|---|---|---|---|---|---|---|
| | n | All Cases | n | Short Agony | n | All Cases |
| Hexokinase | 48 | Y = 0.6336 + 0.0132 X<br>r = 0.4393 ** | 28 | Y = 0.4475 + 0.0135 X<br>r = 0.5281 ** | 48 | Y = 1.0694 + 0.0133 X<br>r = 0.3880 ** |
| Phosphoglucose isomerase | 32 | Y = 81.2659 − 0.0954 X<br>r = 0.110 | | | 32 | Y = −95.8485 − 0.0339 X<br>r = 0.02 |
| Phosphofructokinase | 48 | Y = 4.4220 − 0.0441 X<br>r = 0.4442 ** | 28 | Y = 6.1502 − 0.0592 X<br>r = 0.610 *** | 48 | Y = 4.8554 − 0.0438 X<br>r = 0.3537 * |
| Fructose-1.6-diphosphate aldolase | 32 | Y = 5.4818 − 0.0195 X<br>r = 0.387 * | | | 32 | Y = 5.0389 − 0.0026 X<br>r = 0.044 |
| Triose-phosphate isomerase | 32 | Y =1344.7009 −<br>1.1415 X r=0.100 | | | 32 | Y = 1488.4526 +<br>0.910 X r=0.064 |
| Glyceraldehyde-3-phosphate dehydrogenase | 32 | Y =85.7966 + 0.0916 X<br>r = 0.158 | | | 32 | Y = 112.6276 + 0.3054 X<br>r = 0.459 ** |
| 3-Phosphoglycerate kinase | 32 | Y =78.2522 − 0.0309 X<br>r = 0.067 | | | 32 | Y =90.7555 + 0.0873 X<br>r = 0.148 |
| Phosphoglycerate mutase | 48 | Y=69.4492 − 0.3206 X<br>r = 0.3257 * | 28 | Y =71.9456 − 0.2608 X<br>r = 0.4768 * | 48 | Y =72.2198 − 0.2278 X<br>r = 0.1536 |
| Enolase | 32 | Y =41.5685 − 0.0342 X<br>r = 0.126 | | | 32 | Y =49.6762 + 0.0712 X<br>r = 0.176 |
| Pyruvate kinase | 32 | Y=65.1493 + 0.0178 X<br>r = 0.320 | | | 32 | Y =91.3478 + 0.3264 X<br>r = 0.411 * |
| Lactate dehydrogenase | 32 | Y=76.5879 + 0.0200 X<br>r = 0.052 | | | 32 | Y =103.9220 + 0.1903 X<br>r = 0.329 |

| Enzyme | n | All Cases | n | Short Agony | n | All Cases |
|---|---|---|---|---|---|---|
| Glucose-6-phosphate dehydrogenase | 48 | $Y = 0.8781 - 0.0027\,X$<br>$r = 0.2701$ | 28 | $Y = 0.9196 - 0.0028\,X$<br>$r = 0.3679$ | 48 | $Y = 0.6421 + 0.0021\,X$<br>$r = 0.1732$ |
| Glycerol-3-phosphate dehydrogenase | 32 | $Y = 1.3350 - 0.0015\,X$<br>$r = 0.105$ | | | 32 | $Y = 2.1198 - 0.0055\,X$<br>$r = 0.285$ |

**Table 2-2: The effect of age on different enzymes of the human brain. The details are the same as described for Table 2-1.**

| | FRONTAL CORTEX | | | | PUTAMEN | |
|---|---|---|---|---|---|---|
| Enzyme | n | All Cases | n | Short Agony | n | All Cases |
| $Mg^{2+}$-ATPase | 31 | $Y = 9.4479 - 0.0106\,X$<br>$r = 0.0964$ | | | 30 | $Y = 12.1533 - 0.0130\,X$<br>$r = 0.130$ |
| $Na^{+}\,K^{+}$-ATPase | 30 | $Y = 3.4084 - 0.0030\,X$<br>$r = 0.0671$ | | | 30 | $Y = 5.8394 - 0.0084\,X$<br>$r = 0.2154$ |
| Carbonic anhydrase | 44 | $Y = 7.7430 - 0.0394\,X$<br>$r = 0.5486$ *** | | | 44 | $Y = 9.0388 - 0.0430\,X$<br>$r = 0.4427$ ** |
| Protein kinase: basal activity | 48 | $Y = 32.3806 - 0.1208\,X$<br>$r = 0.2417$ | 28 | $Y = 37.1340 - 0.1477\,X$<br>$r = 0.4362$ * | 44 | $Y = 21.3261 - 0.0252\,X$<br>$r = 0.0627$ |
| Activation by $5\,\mu M$ cAMP | 48 | $Y = 86.1610 - 0.3942\,X$<br>$r = 0.3595$ * | 28 | $Y = 96.7203 - 0.4946\,X$<br>$r = 0.5541$ ** | 44 | $Y = 65.8524 - 0.1942\,X$<br>$r = 0.1789$ |

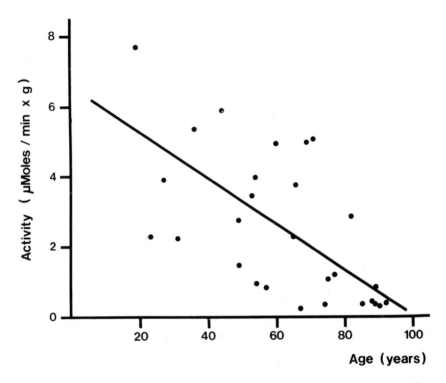

Figure 2-1:    Influence of age on phosphofructokinase activity in human brain cortex. All cases investigated are free of neurological diseases. In this figure, the activity of cases with short agony (n=28) is presented.[4] A significant age-dependent decrease of phosphofructokinase activity is observed (see also Table 2-1).

activity increased significantly with age for soluble hexokinase in cortex and putamen, and to a substantial degree in putamen for glyceraldehyde-3-phosphate dehydrogenase and glucose-6-phosphate dehydrogenase, an enzyme related to the pentose phosphate shunt. Phosphoglycerate mutase showed a significant negative correlation with age in the cortex. All the other enzymes of the glycolytic pathway in the human brain demonstrated negligible changes in activity with age. Interestingly, these findings could not be confirmed in rat 'brain investigated at a maximum age of 120 weeks.[95]

Bird et al.[2] found no correlation of human brain phosphofructokinase with age, but owing to a lack of detailed description of the determination, it is not possible to make any direct comparison with the values described here.[1,95]

The autolytic behavior of most glycolytic enzymes and the ATPases was checked in human and cat brain.[1,3] A more refined study of the different autoptic cases, which differentiated between age, postmortem delay, sudden death and prolonged agonal state, demonstrated a higher significant negative correlation of phosphofructokinase activity with age (Figure 2-1) in the group of sudden death cases in comparison with the total of all cases.[1,4] This is a clear sign that "normal aging" is better reflected in brains that are not impaired by agonal state or underlying disease.[5] Postmortem studies of hexokinase and the ATPases also suggest that these enzymes maintain substantial levels of activity long after death.[2,6]

ATP, one of the energy-rich end products after entry of glucose into the glycolytic pathway, is used for the maintenance of ionic gradients and for their restoration after electrical activity of the cell. The enzyme involved in this process is $Na^+/K^+$-ATPase, which represents the cationic pump system. It is often closely connected with $Mg^{2+}$-ATPase. Both ATPases are presumably involved in transport processes of catecholamines and neurotransmitters.[7] A more detailed description of their function is given in the section on ATPases. Total ATPases are roughly indicative of consumption of cellular energy.

In the studies on aging, too, the ATPases were differentiated into total ATPases, $Mg^{2+}$-ATPase, and $NA^+/K^+$-ATPase. With none of the ATPases investigated was a significant effect of age observed in either human or rat brain.[1,95]

Another paper[8] describes the effects of age on ATPases of human brain as shown by the fact that ethanol is able to produce a higher inhibition of synaptosomal $Na^+/K^+$-ATPase in older subjects than in young ones.

Some remarks on the relationship between availability and consumption of energy in the form of ATP in the aging human brain seem to be justified. Hexokinase and phosphofructokinase are reported to be key enzymes in glycolytic regulation.[9] The first of these, hexokinase, shows a higher degree of soluble activity in old age, which, it has been suggested, may be an inactivation of the mitochondrial enzyme.[10] The second enzyme, which follows hexokinase at a later stage in the glycolytic pathway, decreases with age. This implies a decline of the maximal glycolytic capacity. These results suggest that, with increasing age, the regulation mechanism of the glycolytic chain is impaired, and that, as a consequence, the synthesis of ATP is limited. No obvious change with age was seen in the ATP-degradation process.

The end product of glucose degradation, namely $CO_2$, has to be eliminated from the brain. Carbonic anhydrase regulates this process by catalyzing the decarboxylation of either carbonic acid or bicarbonate.[11] This is a very important process for the maintenance of tissue pH.[12]

Carbonic anhydrase seems to be involved in ionic transport processes coupled with other enzymatic systems.[13,14] It is also suggested that this enzyme influences acid-base equilibrium in the brain, which implies a possible feedback action on glycolytic regulation.

In the human brain, an age-dependent decline of carbonic anhydrase activity was observed.[15,16,17] This decrease was significant in cortex and putamen (Table 2-2) with a loss of activity of about 30 percent between 20 and 90 years of age. In an investigation with rats it was seen[18] that brain carbonic anhydrase showed a significant decrease from the adult level in 27-week-old animals in the group aged 78 weeks.

The postmortem behavior of carbonic anhydrase studied in rat brain shows a marked loss of activity, of about 50 percent in the first 30 minutes after death, and then no more change in activity up to 24 hours. The possibility cannot be excluded that one form of the enzyme (isoenzyme) is lost after death in the human brain. The observed activity, however, in autoptic human brain is nonsignificantly correlated with the postmortem delay.

The decrease in the activity of carbonic anhydrase in the aging human brain may be relevant to an impairment of $CO_2$ exchange with a consequent influence on the pH optimum of other enzyme activities, including those of the glycolytic pathway. The reduced capacity for $CO_2$ transportation in the aged central nervous system bears additional risks under metabolic hyperactive conditions.

### The cAMP System of the Aging Human Brain

The formation of the second messenger cAMP is the expression of a stimulus exerted by a neurohormone such as norepinephrine or dopamine at its specific receptor. Essentially, this chapter deals with the effects of age on adenylate cyclase and phosphodiesterase, the two enzymes responsible for synthesis and degradation of cAMP, and on protein kinase, the enzyme that mediates the effects of cAMP in the cell (Figure 2-2).

Nothing is known about the age dependency of adenylate cyclase and phosphodiesterase in human brain. There is, however, some information available on the levels of these enzymes there.[19,20,21,22,23] According to these studies, phosphodiesterase is detected in human[23] and rat brains[24] with two different affinity constants ($K_m$-values) for its substrate cAMP.

The significance of different phosphodiesterase forms and its implications for pharmacological intervention are discussed in the section on ergot alkaloid effects on the cAMP system.

The adenylate cyclase system of the human brain was shown to be stimulated in vitro by different putative neurotransmitters.[19,21,22] Nor-

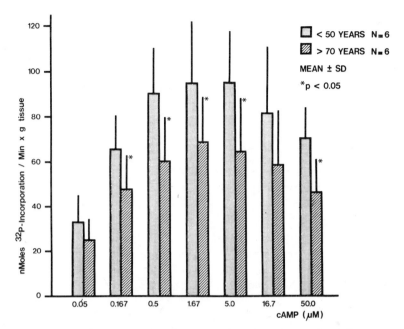

Figure 2-2: Schematic representation of the transmitter-dependent cyclic AMP system. Possible points of interaction by different drugs at the receptor and on enzymes of the cAMP system are shown.

epinephrine in particular exerted a clearly stimulating effect on cAMP production in cortical brain slices.[19,21]

Concerning the effects of age in rat brain cortex,[25,26,27] striatum[28,29] and hippocampus,[26,27] no age-related changes in the basal activity of adenylate cyclase were observed. Levels of cAMP after stimulation by norepinephrine are reported to be lower in the cortex of old rats,[27,30] but these findings were not confirmed by Schmidt and Thornberry.[26] A significant reduction of dopamine-sensitive adenylate cyclase activity[26,29] was found in the striatum of senescent rats. Other authors[27,28] reported no further significant activation of adenylate cyclase by dopamine in the striatum of 2-year-old rats.

High $K_m$-phosphodiesterase was not found to change with age in the cortex[25] and in the striatum[28] of rat brain. The low $K_m$-enzyme, however, decreased to a slight extent in the cortex[27] and significantly in the striatum of 30-month-old rats in comparison to 4- and 12-month-old animals.[28] These results suggest an alteration of striatal dopaminergic neurons with aging.

A lot of our work was concentrated on the protein kinase system, which is an indirect parameter of hormonal action.[31] Protein kinases mediate intracellularly the information carried by the second messenger. They catalyze the transfer of phosphate groups from ATP to different proteins in the cell, such as membrane proteins,[32,33] nuclear proteins[34] or enzymes which are altered in their activity state by phosphorylation.[35,36]

Protein kinases are composed of regulatory and catalytic subunits. In

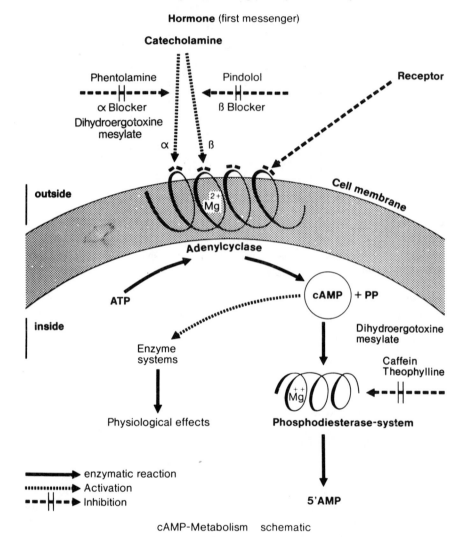

Figure 2-3:  Effect of age on cAMP-dependent protein kinase activity in human brain cortex. Significantly less cAMP-dependent protein kinase activity was found in the brain cortex of old persons (>70 years, n=6) than in younger subjects (<50 years, n=6) over a broad range of cAMP concentrations (0.05 to 50.0 μM).[40]

the basal state, protein kinases show a rather low activity, owing to blockade of the active site by the regulatory subunit. Activation occurs by binding of cAMP to the regulatory subunit and a consequent release of the catalytic unit. This process which reflects hormonal action is dependent on the intracellular concentration of cAMP, reaching maximum in vitro phosphorylation at 5 $\mu$M.[37]

First results on the influence of aging on the cerebral protein kinase describe a decrease of cAMP-dependent activity in bovine brain without a change in basal activity.[37] In the human brain, protein kinase demonstrated a gradual decline of cAMP-dependent activity with increasing age, this being more pronounced in the cortex than in the putamen.[15,16,17] The decreasing activity in the cortex was significantly correlated with the age of the donors (Table 2-2). The same result was obtained also from comparison of different age groups, with a loss of about 30 percent between young and aged.[1] In both cortex and putamen, basal protein kinase activity did not change significantly with age.

Postmortem studies in bovine,[15] rat and human brains[38,39] did not reveal any loss of activity during the first 24 hours after death. The occurrence of a few very low values for basal and cAMP-stimulated protein kinase activity, both in cortex and putamen and independent of age, was attributed to premortem conditions and a prolonged agonal state.[5] Indeed, the separation of cases with sudden death resulted in a higher significant correlation of decreasing activity with increasing age,[38] and a significant decrease of basal protein kinase activity in the cortex became also evident (Table 2-2).

Diminished activation in the human brain cortex in old age was observed at all cAMP concentrations studied, covering a broad range from 0.05 to 50.0 $\mu$M cAMP (Figure 2-3).[17,40] The effect of age on the cortical cAMP-activated protein kinase was seen with different protein substrates for the enzyme, such as various histones, protamine, or the endogenous substrate contained in the homogenate.[40]

Studies with subcellular fractions of the human brain cortex[40] revealed that membrane-bound protein kinase showed a remarkable decrease in cAMP-dependent activity with increasing age. In the soluble fraction, however, a significant age-dependent increase in cAMP-activated protein kinase was observed. Obviously, two independent age effects are present: a general decline of the cAMP response in total protein kinase and, in addition, a possible release of membrane-bound enzyme into the soluble compartment due to neuronal membrane defects occurring in old age, as was suggested for the brain[8,41,42] and the liver.[43] The latter idea of age-related membrane disturbances is especially attractive for pharmacological intervention, in that drugs with membrane-protecting properties could prove to be helpful in geriatric indications for the treatment of the symptoms of aging.[44,45]

The protein kinase system in the human brain cortex seems to be regulated by noradrenergic transmission.[19,21] Norepinephrine was found to increase the phosphorylation rate in slices of guinea-pig cerebral cortex.[46] In rat striatal slices, which include the putamen, norepinephrine and dopamine had similar stimulatory effects on protein phosphorylation.[47]

It is also reported that dopaminergic and beta-adrenergic receptors are present in the caudate nucleus.[48] Thus, the dissimilarities observed between the age dependencies of protein kinase in cortex and putamen may be explicable by differing neurotransmitter systems.

The protein kinase system and phosphorylation steps are involved in a series of nerve-cell functions[49] such as synaptic transmission,[50] catecholamine biosynthesis[35,36] and learning and memory formation.[51] Glycolysis in the brain, too, is probably influenced by cAMP-dependent mechanisms,[52,53] as some glycolytic enzymes may serve as substrates for a cAMP-dependent protein kinase. Thus, the observed age-dependent decrease in the cAMP-regulatory capacity of the protein kinase system may have far-reaching consequences for normal nerve-cell function in the aging human brain.

## BIOCHEMICAL EFFECTS OF ERGOT COMPOUNDS IN THE CNS

In this section, some aspects of ergot alkaloid interaction on the cAMP system and the ATPase system in the brain are presented. The same biochemical systems have already been discussed with respect to aging. Some details will be repeated or explained more thoroughly, whenever it is believed to be necessary for the clarification and the significance of the results.

### The cAMP System

A great step forward in the understanding of the mechanism of action of many hormones and drugs at the cellular level was the "second messenger" concept introduced by Sutherland.[54] According to this concept (see also Figure 2-3), hormones as "first messengers" bind to specific receptor sites on or in the cell membrane of their target cells, and induce the activation of the enzyme adenylate cyclase. As a result, the second messenger cAMP is formed. A second enzyme, phosphodiesterase, is responsible for the degradation of cAMP. The intracellular concentration of cAMP, dependent on synthesis and degradation, regulates the activation of protein kinases, the enzyme system, which ultimately gives rise to physiological effects by protein phosphorylation.[55]

It is important that the enzymes of the cAMP system have higher activity levels in nervous tissue than in other organs.

Many putative neurotransmitters, such as norepinephrine, dopamine, serotonin and histamine, increase the cAMP concentration in several parts of the brain, and there is convincing evidence that cAMP is involved in the modulation of transmission of nerve impulses.[49,56]

The process of formation and limitation of information taken up by the cell in the form of cAMP is a rather complex biological mechanism. Analogous to a feedback control system, differences in cAMP concentration may originate from a change in the activities of both adenylate cyclase and phosphodiesterase. Under normal conditions, the activity in the brain can be considered as the result of a coordinated, dynamic interplay of inhibition and excitation among several neuronal systems. Disturbances of such an interplay are a possible cause in the etiology of diseases like Parkinson's or schizophrenia, because they are associated respectively with an under- and overactivity of dopaminergic neurons in the striatum or the limbic system. Impairment of cerebral functions is frequently found in elderly people, in whom among other symptoms disturbances of behavior may occur. At present it is unclear if these disturbances are due to an imbalance of neuronal activity or a general degeneration of nerve cells in the brain.

Dihydrogenated ergot alkaloids are a group among the substances which interact with the cAMP system. DH-ergotoxine has been used successfully in the treatment of many symptoms characteristic of cerebral disturbances of old age,[57,58] but the exact mechanism of its action remains unclear although a number of biochemical and pharmacological properties of this drug are known.[59,60]

Sutherland and his group[61] could show that the antiadrenergic effect of ergotamine, known since 1905,[62] is associated with the cAMP system. In experiments with dog heart and liver, these authors found an inhibition by ergotamine of the norepinephrine-dependent activation of adenylate cyclase.

In 1975, Markstein and Wagner[63] demonstrated that DH-ergotoxine interferes with the neurotransmitter action of norepinephrine on cerebral adenylate cyclase of the rat. These in vitro experiments showed that DH-ergotoxine at low concentrations antagonizes the norepinephrine-induced activation of adenylate cyclase at the receptor level, whereas it does not interfere with the activation of this enzyme due to isoproterenol.

In contrast to the beta-blocker pindolol, the ergot compound did not totally abolish the norepinephrine-induced activation of adenylate cyclase. The antagonistic effect of ergot alkaloids on catecholamine-stimulated adenylate cyclase in the CNS was also verified in several other studies.[64,65,66,67] Recent studies[68] demonstrated an accumulation of DH-ergotoxine in vivo in the brain. Repeated oral application of the drug over several weeks led to a decreased stimulatory effect of norepinephrine on adenylate cyclase of rat cerebral cortex. Incorporation studies with tritiated ergot compound, too, confirmed the accumulation of these substances preferentially in several brain regions ([69,70,96]; for a more detailed description, see following section).

To limit the information taken up by the cell in the form of cAMP and to restore the original state ready for the uptake of new signals, the nerve cells contain a further enzymatic system, the cAMP-phosphodiesterase, which decomposes cAMP. The phosphodiesterase is not a uniform enzyme.[24,71,72] One part of the enzyme exists in a soluble form, and the other is associated with membranous structure.[73,74] Both enzymatic activities split off cAMP. Whereas the soluble enzyme with a hundredfold weaker substrate affinity ($K_m \approx 10^{-4}$M), also called high $K_m$-phosphodiesterase, shows normal kinetic behavior according to Michaelis and Menten,[104] the membrane-bound enzyme (low $K_m$-phosphodiesterase, $K_m \approx 10^{-6}$ M) shows anomalous kinetic properties which can be expressed as negative cooperativity.[75,76,77] The possible physiological role of this behavior is described by Russel et al.[75] as "kinetic buffering." When negative cooperativity is very pronounced, the enzyme has no great influence on the turnover of cAMP. Thus, an increase in the substrate concentration at a high steady-state level would not accelerate the breakdown of cAMP. On the other hand, an enzyme whose activity cannot be regulated by a cooperativity, according to Michaelis and Menten, would show too great a change in substrate turnover to be able to guarantee a certain level for a definite time. An enzyme which possesses negative cooperativity between the extremes has in this model a physiological significance for "kinetic buffering." The physiological role for phosphodiesterase implies a maintenance of a certain cAMP level for a limited time.

Iwangoff and coworkers[78,79] described a moderate inhibition by DH-ergot alkaloids of cAMP-phosphodiesterase originating from cat and rat brains. As observed with DH-ergotoxine, this inhibition is brain-specific[79] and it is stronger at low substrate concentrations, reflecting a higher inhibitory effect on low $K_m$-phosphodiesterase than on the high $K_m$-enzyme. This result, which is similar for DH-ergotoxine and DH-ergotamine, is shown in Figure 2-4. After separation of the brain homogenate into low and high $K_m$-phosphodiesterase, DH-ergot com-

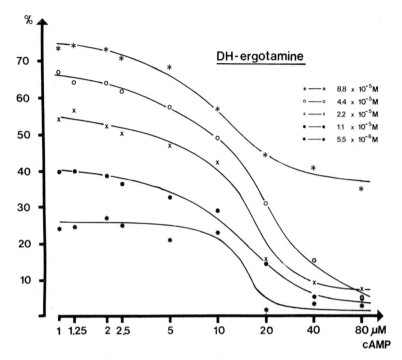

Figure 2-4:    Influence of DH-ergotamine on low $K_m$-phosphodiesterase activity after purification on agarose gel. The inhibition of activity at different substrate concentrations (cAMP) is given in % of the control. The inhibition due to DH-ergotamine at low cAMP concentrations (1-10 $\mu$M) is considerably higher than that at high substrate concentrations.

pounds showed not only a more pronounced inhibition, but also a change in the kinetic properties of the low $K_m$-enzyme.[76,77] This change results in a lowering of the negative cooperativity. If, by their influence on the kinetics of the low $K_m$-enzyme, dihydrogenated ergot alkaloids tend to decrease the affinity of the low $K_m$-enzyme for its substrate cAMP, they can intervene in the regulation of cAMP metabolism at low substrate concentrations.

The pharmacological consequence of the interaction of DH-ergot compounds on the low $K_m$-phosphodiesterase is of particular importance for the regulation of basal cellular cAMP levels. The DH-ergots thus prevent a drop of cAMP to unphysiologic levels but do not interfere at high cAMP concentrations induced by hormonal stimulation. This results in a more quickly attained threshold for further hormonal stimulation. In other words, the postsynaptic responsiveness is increased.

Little information is available about the influence of dihydrogenated ergot alkaloids on the cAMP-dependent protein kinase system in the brain.[59,80] During in vitro experiments, DH-ergot compounds exerted a nonsignificant but slightly activating effect on the basal protein kinase activity of both cat and bovine brains. Homogenates, soluble and synaptosomal fractions were used as a source of enzyme. An inhibition was observed with several DH-ergot compounds of the protein kinase activated by different concentrations of cAMP. This inhibitory effect increased with the concentration of cAMP added in vitro, being greatest at the highest cAMP stimulation. DH-ergotoxine and DH-ergonine clearly demonstrated this effect at rather high drug concentrations, whereas at concentrations lower than the micromolar range the inhibition approached zero. DH-ergotamine was a very weak inhibitor under all conditions tested, and behaved more like the strong phosphodiesterase inhibitor papaverine, which exerted no influence on protein kinase activity. Similar results were obtained with DH-ergotoxine on protein kinase of human brain homogenate and synaptosomal fractions.

These results are complementary to the observations on DH-ergot alkaloid effects on adenylate cyclase and phosphodiesterase systems. Basal protein kinase function is activated rather than inhibited, which parallels the maintenance of the basal cAMP level by inhibition of the low $K_m$-phosphodiesterase. There is a strong effect on cAMP production by inhibition of the catecholamine-stimulated adenylate cyclase and, to a lesser degree, a limitation of the cAMP signal by inhibition of the cAMP-dependent protein kinase, whereas the degradation of high cAMP levels by high $K_m$-phosphodiesterase is not significantly influenced by ergot compounds.

Dihydrogenated ergot compounds can thus be considered as regulators of the second messenger system in that there is not only a limitation of too high a response of cAMP production and function to a neurohormone, but also a maintenance of the basal cAMP levels important for basal neuronal function and its subsequent postsynaptic transmitter response.

## The ATPase System

The principal splitting of ATP is performed biologically by the ATPases. The part of this enzymatic system which is not inhibited by $10^{-3}$M ouabain is called $Mg^{2+}$-ATPase.

A recent report[81] suggests that this enzyme is involved in the accumulation of calcium by synaptic vesicles. In other studies,[82,83] neurotransmitter release and uptake are described as being partially dependent on $Mg^{2+}$-ATPase. The other main part of the ATPases, inhibited by $10^{-3}$M ouabain, is $Na^+/K^+$-ATPase, the so-called $Na^+$-pump. It represents about 60 percent of the total brain ATPases.

$Na^+/K^+$-ATPase is involved in the coupled transport of $Na^+$ and $K^+$ ions against concentration gradients of both ions, an energy-dependent process which consumes ATP. The enzyme occurs in the CNS mostly bound to cellular membranes and often associated with $Mg^{2+}$-ATPase. Several theories about the molecular mechanisms of the $Na^+/K^+$-ATPase reaction exist.[84,85] An important step in the reaction sequence of the ATPase is the $K^+$-dependent dephosphorylation of the phosphorylated $Na^+/K^+$-ATPase, performed by the so-called $K^+$-dependent p-nitrophenyl-phosphatase ($K^+$-p-NPPase).[86]

The physiological function of $Na^+/K^+$-ATPase has been elucidated in more detail than that of $Mg^{2+}$-ATPase. The separated ional charges represent the energy immediately available at the nerve cells. Among other cellular processes, $Na^+/K^+$-ATPase is involved in the transportation of biologically active substances against concentration gradients. Evidence has now accumulated that both ATPases contribute to the passive transportation of biogenic amines.[7] Ouabain, known to inhibit $Na^+/K^+$-ATPase, also antagonizes the depressant action of catecholamines on cerebral, cerebellar and caudate neurons.[87] Today, the maintenance of $Na^+$ and $K^+$ gradients at cellular membranes and the transport of catecholamines are regarded as the main direct operations of $Na^+/K^+$-ATPase in the CNS.

An interesting finding is that the ATPases are activated in vitro by relatively high concentrations of catecholamines. The activation of $Na^+/K^+$-ATPase[88,89,90,91,92] and of $K^+$-p-NPPase[90,93] is similar in extent, but is considerably less for $Mg^{2+}$-ATPase.[88,91] Norepinephrine and epinephrine exhibited a stronger activation effect on both $Na^+/K^+$-ATPase and $K^+$-p-NPPase than dopamine. The effect was not found to be stereo-specific, giving rise to the idea that it is an unspecific transport phenomenon not directly associated with adrenergic receptors.

The activation of $Na^+/K^+$-ATPase and $K^+$-p-NPPase can be reversed by suitable blockers. In the case of norepinephrine, the activated state of both enzymes is reduced by alpha- and beta-adrenergic blockers and by dihydrogenated ergot alkaloids (Tables 2-3, 2-4). The degree of deactivation of $Na^+/K^+$-ATPase by DH-ergot compounds[90] is less than that by a beta-blocker (propranolol) but greater than that by an alpha-adrenergic antagonist (phentolamine). Concerning the effects on $K^+$-p-NPPase, DH-ergotoxine reduces the activation of the enzyme to an extent similar to alpha- or beta-blockers or even greater, depending on the norephinephrine concentration.

In analogy to the ergot alkaloid effects on the cAMP system, it is certainly of some importance that ergot compounds may exert their regulatory influences also on the ATPase system: a reduction of the

**Table 2-3: The effect of $\alpha$- and $\beta$-blockers and of DH-ergotoxine on the norepinephrine-activated Na$^+$-K$^+$-ATPase activity of cat brain.**

| Treatment | n | I μM | NE μM | Activity of Na$^+$-K$^+$-ATPase | Significancy to activation | − % reduced activation |
|---|---|---|---|---|---|---|
| Control | 18 | — | — | 33.9 ± 0.80 | — | — |
| Activation by NE | 9 | — | 330 | 52.5 ± 1.09 | — | — |
| | 3 | — | 100 | 44.8 ± 0.82 | — | — |
| Activation by NE | 6 | 88 | 330 | 46.0 ± 0.34 | xx | −34.9 |
| +DH-ergotoxine | 6 | 44 | 330 | 50.6 ± 0.72 | ns | −10.2 |
| | 3 | 44 | 100 | 38.9 ± 0.55 | xx | −54.2 |
| | 3 | 11 | 100 | 42.6 ± 0.21 | x | −20.2 |
| Activation by NE | 6 | 88 | 330 | 46.3 ± 0.48 | xx | −33.5 |
| + Propranolol | 6 | 44 | 330 | 48.1 ± 1.74 | x | −23.6 |
| | 3 | 44 | 100 | 34.8 ± 0.58 | xx | −91.6 |
| | 3 | 11 | 100 | 39.8 ± 0.44 | xx | −45.8 |
| Activation by NE | 6 | 88 | 330 | 47.5 ± 0.92 | xx | −27.3 |
| + Phentolamine | 6 | 44 | 330 | 50.5 ± 1.81 | ns | −11.1 |
| | 3 | 44 | 100 | 42.7 ± 0.48 | x | −19.0 |
| | 3 | 11 | 100 | 43.5 ± 0.68 | ns | −11.8 |

Table 2-4: The effect of α- and β-blockers and of DH-ergotoxine on the norepinephrine-activated K⁺-pNPPase activity of cat brain.

| Treatment | n | I μM | NE μM | Activity of K⁺-pNPPase | Significancy to activation | − % reduced activation |
|---|---|---|---|---|---|---|
| Control | 12 | — | — | 83.5 ± 1.77 | — | — |
| Activation by NE | 6 | — | 1000 | 128.6 ± 3.16 | — | — |
|  | 6 | — | 330 | 120.8 ± 5.11 | — | — |
| Activation by NE + DH-ergotoxine | 6 | 88 | 1000 | 108.5 ± 5.33 | xx | −44.0 |
|  | 6 | 88 | 330 | 97.6 ± 3.21 | xx | −73.7 |
|  | 6 | 44 | 1000 | 109.4 ± 1.33 | xx | −42.5 |
|  | 6 | 44 | 330 | 100.5 ± 3.97 | xx | −54.3 |
| Activation by NE + Propranolol | 3 | 88 | 1000 | 118.8 ± 0.44 | x | −21.7 |
|  | 3 | 88 | 330 | 104.4 ± 2.48 | x | −44.0 |
|  | 3 | 44 | 1000 | 130.6 ± 1.90 | ns | — |
|  | 3 | 44 | 330 | 102.2 ± 2.65 | xx | −50.0 |
| Activation by NE + Phentolamine | 3 | 88 | 1000 | 125.0 ± 2.73 | ns | − 8.0 |
|  | 3 | 88 | 330 | 97.8 ± 0.44 | xx | −73.7 |
|  | 3 | 44 | 1000 | 123.2 ± 5.73 | ns | −13.7 |
|  | 3 | 44 | 330 | 101.7 ± 1.57 | xx | −51.3 |

norepinephrine-induced activation of $Na^+/K^+$-ATPase and $K^+$-p-NPPase, but not a total reversal of this effect, and further, no influence on the basal activity of both enzymes.[90]

The role of norepinephrine and its antagonists in relation to the regulation of the ATPase system in the brain is not yet clear. Under typical conditions of stress characterized by an increased release of catecholamines, a high metabolic activity is induced, owing to the activation exerted by catecholamines.

Most of these processes need energy in the form of ATP, which is consumed for the formation and maintenance of ional gradients at cellular membranes or for the active transport of catecholamines. In any case, the supply of additional energy in the form of ATP has to be guaranteed by an increased activity of the glycolytic chain. If, however, the activation of ATPases rises under metabolic overstimulation to produce an excess need for glucose decomposition and consequently the formation of metabolically undesired lactate, the cell reaches a critical point with an ATP breakdown exceeding that of ATP synthesis.

This situation may occur under conditions of disturbed brain functions characteristic for old age, owing either to a reduced glucose and oxygen supply of the aging brain or to metabolic disturbances of the energy turnover as a consequence of the aging process.

The function of adrenergic blockers and also of DH-ergot alkaloids is to limit the energy consumption under hyperactive conditions. As has been pointed out, the ergots do not totally suppress the regulatory function of norepinephrine, but they can indeed help to avoid critical situations of excessive ATP turnover by economizing the energy available.

## INCORPORATION STUDIES WITH TRITIATED ERGOT COMPOUNDS IN THE BRAIN

In the preceding sections, some effects of DH-ergot alkaloids on different enzyme systems and on neurotransmitter-related processes are described. DH-ergot compounds need minimum threshold concentrations to be able to interact with metabolic processes in the brain. The in vivo levels should be comparable with the in vitro concentrations which are needed to influence an enzymatic system. To obtain information on whether these threshold concentrations are reached, the incorporation and distribution of radioactively labeled DH-ergot alkaloids in brain tissue was studied.[69,70,94]

DH-ergotoxine and DH-ergotamine show a rather similar pattern of incorporation into different regions of cat brain after intracarotid infusion

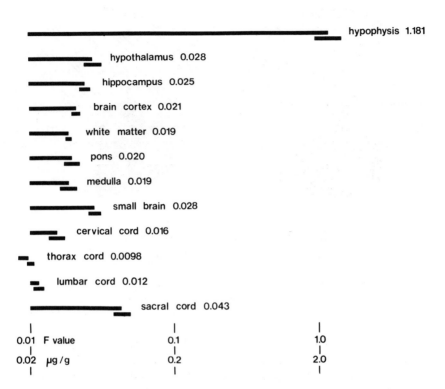

F—Values (average values ± SEM) $^3$H-DHE (cat n = 10)

hypophysis 1.181

hypothalamus 0.028

hippocampus 0.025

brain cortex 0.021

white matter 0.019

pons 0.020

medulla 0.019

small brain 0.028

cervical cord 0.016

thorax cord 0.0098

lumbar cord 0.012

sacral cord 0.043

| 0.01 F value | 0.1 | 1.0 |
| 0.02 μg/g | 0.2 | 2.0 |

Figure 2-5: Distribution of $^3$H-DH-ergotamine in different parts of the cat brain. The distribution factor F is defined by the ratio of the specific activity of the single organ in relationship to the specific activity of the whole animal under the condition of a homogenous distribution of the substance investigated.

(Figure 2-5).[69,94] Microhistoautoradiographic investigation of the incorporation of $^3$H-DH-ergotoxine revealed a high accumulation of radioactivity in the neuronal cells of the reticular formation in pons and medulla,[69] similar to that found in the neurons of the dentate nucleus and the inferior olivary nucleus. A more refined study demonstrated that $^3$H-DH-ergot alkaloids show a specific pattern of distribution at the subcellar level.[69]

$^3$H-DH-ergotoxine and $^3$H-DH-ergotamine are accumulated to a considerable extent in the synaptosomal and myelin fractions of cat cerebral cortex and cerebellum (Figure 2-6). The possibility cannot be ruled out that the radioactivity associated with the soluble fraction is partly due to $^3$H-$H_2$O, originating from metabolized $^3$H-ergot derivative.

In a further series of experiments,[70] the time course after a single

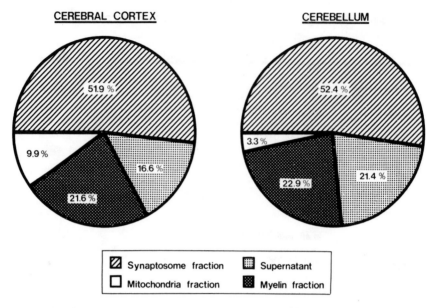

Figure 2-6:    Subcellular distribution of $^3$H-DH-ergotamine in cerebral cortex and cerebellum of the cat after intracarotid infusion. The percentage incorporation of radioactivity into the different fractions separated by density gradient centrifugation is given.

injection of $^3$H-DH-ergocornine and $^3$H-DH-ergonine into the vena cephalica was studied. The maximum incorporation of both drugs was much lower in several regions of the brain than in the visceral organs and was observed about one hour after application. Its temporal latency, however, was longer in the CNS than in the visceral tissues. After the maximum had been reached, a logarithmic clearance occurred in all tissues, the slope of the clearance being considerably flatter in the brain structures.

According to clinical publications,[57,58] DH-ergot alkaloids such as DH-ergotoxine need about four weeks of oral application to be effective in the human brain. During this time, an accumulation of the drug apparently takes place. To test the relevance of these effects, some studies with repeated application of $^3$H-DH-ergot compounds were performed.[70]

The repeated application of $^3$H-DH-ergot alkaloids increased the incorporation rate into most tissues of the cat as compared to a single injection. Most organs of the cat seem to be saturated more quickly by $^3$H-DH-ergonine than by $^3$H-DH-ergocornine. The retention of radioactivity after repeated application of $^3$H-DH-ergot alkaloids is higher in the brain than in most visceral organs. This effect is demonstrated for $^3$H-DH-ergotoxine in Figure 2-7.

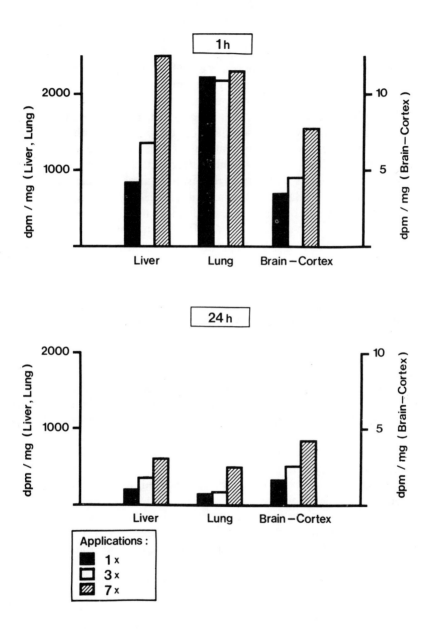

Figure 2-7:  Incorporation of $^3$H-DH-ergotoxine (0.25 mCi per mg) in different organs of the cat, 1 hour and 24 hours after single or repeated application. The drug was given 1, 3 and 7 days with doses of 2 mg/kg i.v. once a day (n=2, each group).

The average concentration of incorporated $^3$H-DH-ergot alkaloids was calculated to be in the range of $10^{-7}$M in most structures of the brain. Even when a partial metabolization of the ergot compounds is taken into consideration, levels of about 1 to 5 x $10^{-8}$M of incorporated DH-ergot seem to be realistic. These values agree well with results from Markstein and Wagner,[68] who derived an in vivo concentration of $10^{-8}$M after feeding DH-ergotoxine to rats for several weeks.

The significance of the incorporation and distribution studies with $^3$H-DH-ergot alkaloids lies in the fact that these drugs show a higher retention in brain structures than in visceral organs. The half-life of the ergot compounds is increased, in particular after repeated application of the substances, with levels still very high 24 hours after application.

A great deal of $^3$H-DH-ergotoxine and $^3$H-DH-ergotamine is accumulated in the fraction of the nerve endings, where high levels of the ATPases and the enzymes of the cAMP system are located. All these results are also in favor of a brain-specific site of action of dihydrogenated ergot alkaloids.


## ENZYMATIC CHANGES DUE TO AGING AND ERGOT ALKALOID EFFECTS: IMPLICATIONS AND CONSEQUENCES

In our group, ergot alkaloids were studied primarily in physiological models of energy deprivation[59,97] and then extended to biochemical models related to energy metabolism and neurotransmitter function represented by the cyclic AMP system. From these studies, a concept of experimental pharmacology to test drugs active on symptoms of the aging brain was built up.

It is now well documented that metabolic disturbances are of principal importance in the aging process. In this section, an outline of the links between the models on one side, represented by physiological and biochemical studies, and the real changes found in the aged human and animal brain on the other side, is attempted. The difficulties encountered in this trial are manifold, but some agreement does exist on the interactions of the symptoms of aging and a possibly effective pharmacological treatment.

The integrity and the functional capacity of the energy-converting enzyme systems in old age need special consideration. The glycolytic pathway is the functional compartment for the synthesis of energy-rich compounds. It has been shown that most enzymes of the glycolytic chain do not reveal age-dependent changes in their activity in the human brain.

However, the key enzymes of the glycolytic pathway demonstrate significant changes in their activities with increasing age, which represents an increasing dysregulation of glycolysis.

It also has to be considered that the different enzymes of the human brain were measured in vitro under optimal biochemical conditions. Under normal physiological conditions of the living organism, the brain can probably meet the energy-supply requirements even in old age. It is conceivable that under metabolic stress conditions, accompanied by a release of catecholamines, the energy-providing enzyme machinery of the aging human brain cannot compensate for a constant higher ATP requirement. This situation is worsened by the fact that the ATPases do not slow down ATP consumption in the human brain, as there is no decrease of their activities during the life span. Thus, the consequences for the aging human brain imply an impairment of the balance between ATP synthesis and consumption, becoming critical under high energy demand.

As already mentioned, ATPases are activated in vitro by various catecholamines.[90,93] Dihydrogenated ergot compounds cause in vitro a reduction of the norepinephrine-activated ATPase system. These effects may be interpreted as an economizing of the energy available: a reduced energy supply due to aging is met by a drug-induced lowered energy consumption. Thus, the adrenergic effect of ergot alkaloids may result in reduced ATP decomposition under excessive metabolic conditions. This hypothesis, though not elucidated in all details, points to the close connection between disturbances of energy supply occurring in the aged human brain and their compensation as a result of drug influence.

A similar situation is found in the cAMP system. In a series of investigations, an interaction between dihydrogenated ergot alkaloids and the cAMP system in the brain was demonstrated.[63,64,65,66,67,68,76,77,79] According to these studies, the catecholamine activation of adenylate cyclase in different parts of the brain is antagonized by various ergot compounds. Norepinephrine-stimulated adenylate cyclase, for example, is reduced dose-dependently by DH-ergotoxine in rat cerebral cortex.[63] Moreover, an in vivo effect after application of DH ergotoxine could be demonstrated,[68] as seen in a decreased norepinephrine activation of adenylate cyclase.

On the cAMP degradation side, high $K_m$-phosphodiesterase only is weakly inhibited by DH-ergots. The low $K_m$-enzyme shows significantly stronger inhibition by ergot compounds such as DH-ergotoxine and DH-ergotamine.[76,77,79] In addition, the kinetic properties of the low $K_m$-phosphodiesterase are changed by the ergots, influencing in this way the cAMP turnover at very low substrate concentrations. The ergot compounds thus prevent a decrease of the receptor response of the postsynaptic membrane, which depends on the basal cAMP level of the resting metabolism of the nerve cell.

The activity of protein kinase, the mediator of the cAMP information, is reduced by ergots such as DH-ergotoxine and DH-ergonine, especially in the region of high cAMP stimulation. Basal activity often is nonsignificantly and slightly elevated. The in vitro effects are, however, rather slight and disappear at drug concentrations of $10^{-7}$M and less.

Thus, a common feature of the dihydrogenated ergot compounds is that they can be considered as regulators of the second messenger system in that they not only limit an excessively high response of cAMP production and function to a neurohormone, but they also maintain the basal function of the corresponding neurohormone at its receptor and of cAMP in the cell. All these effects together fit well into the concept of "regulation and economizing."

The significance of these results is increased by studies giving evidence that the ergots really reach the brain regions where they are supposed to have an action. These include the already mentioned in vivo application experiments of DH-ergotoxine[68] and in vivo incorporation and distribution studies of radioactively labeled ergot compounds. The localization of a high degree of radioactivity in the fraction of nerve endings gives clear evidence of CNS effect of dihydrogenated ergots, as the enzymes of the cAMP system and the ATPases have high levels of activity in synaptic membranes.

The results obtained with ergot compounds in the cAMP system cannot be brought into direct connection with the effect of age on these enzyme systems. At first glance, it might even appear that there is something like a contradiction. There are on one side reduced norepinephrine and dopamine levels[98,99] and a lowered dopamine sensitivity of adenylate cyclase in the striatum of old rat brains;[26,27,28,29] on the other side is a reduction of the catecholamine-stimulated adenylate cyclase by different DH-ergot compounds. However, ergot compounds are considered to demonstrate both agonistic and antagonistic behavior with respect to dopaminergic and alpha-adrenergic receptors in the CNS.[103]

A similar problem exists for protein kinase: an inhibition by ergots of the cAMP-dependent activity, and a decrease of cAMP-stimulated activity in old age. Here, another aspect has to be cited. In vivo application of the phosphodiesterase inhibitors aminophylline and 1-methyl-3-isobutyl-xanthine caused an activation of cAMP-dependent protein kinase,[100] whereas in vitro addition of theophylline and 1-methyl-3-isobutylxanthine resulted in an inhibition of protein phosphorylation.[101] Preliminary results from our group after in vivo application of ergots also show the tendency to increasing protein kinase activity.

One aspect of the age-dependent fate of protein kinase in the human brain cortex deserves further consideration. There are several papers which show that aging affects membrane function and, as a consequence, the activity of membrane-bound enzymes.

The findings with protein kinase point in this direction: there is an age-dependent decrease of cAMP activation of the membrane-bound enzyme and an increase of the soluble enzyme activity.[40] This points to an exchange of protein kinase from the membranous form into the soluble compartment, as a consequence of age-dependent disturbances of the neuronal membrane. Changes in the membranes of neurons may represent specific or nonspecific effects of aging. But this is an important point for a pharmacological intervention. Drugs which bind to membranes might be effective in reversing the membrane leakages that arise in the aging brain, in the sense of establishing a membrane stabilization. Chlorpromazine and Gerovital H3 are reported to interact with membranes.[44] DH-ergot compounds might also have a similar action, because of their lipophilic properties. It is clear that their efficacy in geriatric indications has to be tested in this model, but the action of DH-ergotoxine (HYDERGINE®) in the treatment of symptoms of aging may be explained partly by membrane interactions.

This model of age-dependent membrane disturbances and possible drug effects on membrane stabilization is not primarily related to the intrinsic aging process, but to consequences resulting from alterations of several parameters as a function of age.

The pharmacological intervention on aging is interested in improving or reversing particular symptoms that are the consequence of the aging process. Basic gerontological research in the brain provides the information which is necessary as a basis for any pharmacological intervention.

One way is to find empirically drugs that are effective in the treatment of symptoms of aging. To this category belong the dihydrogenated ergot compounds, and especially DH-ergotoxine, which has become clinically rather well established in geriatric indications. For this drug, hypotheses, concepts and models have been developed to reveal its mode of action. The other way is the deductive method: to investigate key factors of the aging process as a basis for pharmacological intervention, and on this basis to work out by the introduction of suitable animal models the preliminaries for the treatment of symptoms of aging.

The combination of both methods should enable us to find more new drugs which can serve as effective geriatric agents. Dihydrogenated ergot alkaloids represent a class of substances for which this difficult task has been undertaken, and with the results obtained, the models described and the proposals made, new ways may be opened up in the pharmacology and gerontology of brain research in the future.

## SUMMARY AND CONCLUSIONS

In this paper, a survey has been presented on experimental gerontology coupled with pharmacological brain research. This approach is based on the investigation of neurochemical parameters of the aging process and on the evaluation of drug effects in biochemical models. The results due to aging serve as a background for the establishment of pharmacological concepts for the selection of drugs as potential geriatric agents, as was attempted with dihydrogenated ergot compounds as an example.

The normal function of energy performance and neuronal regulation processes represented by neurotransmitters belongs to the most important features of the brain for the regulation of physiological processes. Neurotransmitter function and related processes are dependent on energy supply. The enzymes of the cAMP system are involved in the mediation of the information given by a neurotransmitter, which regulates such important processes as nerve-cell transmission, formation of short-term memory and other physiological processes.

Since an effect of age on the systems mentioned, as well as on energy supply, cannot be excluded, the basic enzymatic parameters were investigated with respect to aging in human and animal brains. In addition, the effects of a class of substances, dihydrogenated ergot alkaloids, were tested in biochemical in vitro and in vivo models related to energy turnover and neurotransmitter function. It was checked to see if there is a relationship between changes due to aging and ergot alkaloid effects in the sense of a normalization of age-related disturbances or relief of the symptoms of aging. This was reported to take place with DH-ergotoxine in a series of clinical double-blind studies.[57,58,102]

Ergot compounds manifest themselves as regulators of stress-induced metabolic situations characterized by a reduction of catecholamine-stimulated enzyme systems such as the ATPases, adenylate cyclase, and to a lesser extent also of cAMP-activated protein kinase. The dihydrogenated ergots investigated do not exhibit an inhibition of basal activity of the enzymes mentioned; there is rather a slight to moderate stimulating effect.

DH-ergotoxine and DH-ergotamine show interesting effects on phosphodiesterase, the cAMP degrading enzyme: a significant inhibition of the low $K_m$-enzyme, which regulates basal neuronal cAMP metabolism, together with a change in the kinetic properties of the low $K_m$-enzyme, and only a slight inhibition of the high $K_m$-enzyme, which is active at high cAMP-concentrations.

With respect to the energy situation, the effects of ergot alkaloid action can be directly connected with the consequences of alterations due to aging. A possible impairment of the energy supply under metabolic stress conditions, as demonstrated in age-related changes of the key enzymes of the glycolytic pathway in the human brain, is met by a DH-ergot-alkaloid-induced reduction of energy consumption, by the way of partial inhibition of catecholamine-stimulated ATPase activity.

All these results of dihydrogenated ergot alkaloid effects work toward a limitation of a maximal response caused by a stressor but a maintenance of basal metabolic function. The DH-ergot compounds can thus be regarded as regulators or modulators of functionally important neuronal systems at the synaptic level, and their action results in an economizing effect.

On the side of the cAMP system, there is a lack of investigations of the influence of age on adenylate cyclase and phosphodiesterase systems in the human brain. The cAMP-dependent activity of protein kinase in the human brain decreases significantly with age, which is a clear sign of a decline in adaptation to metabolic stress situations in old age. A direct connection between the effects of age and the ergot alkaloid effects on this system cannot be drawn but, owing to their influence on kinetic parameters of enzymes, the regulatory effects of DH-ergot compounds are certainly of significant importance for the mediation of hormonal information, even under altered conditions caused by aging.

The aspect of age-related membrane disturbances, indicated by protein kinase in the human brain cortex, can also be regarded in the light of ergot alkaloid interaction. At the moment, no direct studies can be presented to show the protective effect of ergot alkaloids on membrane instability in this model. The lipophilic properties of ergot compounds, however, are in favor of a positive effect of these substances on membrane stabilization. An influence of DH-ergotoxine on membrane function, different from a possible interaction with receptors, could also help to explain its clinically approved value in the treatment of symptoms of aging.

## REFERENCES

1. Iwangoff P, Reichlmeier K, Enz A, Meier-Ruge W: Neurochemical findings in physiological aging of the brain. *Interdiscipl Topics Geront,* 15:13–33, 1979.
2. Bird ED, Gale JS, Spokes EG: Huntington's chorea: Post mortem activity of enzymes involved in cerebral glucose metabolism. *J Neurochem* 29:539–545, 1977.

3. Iwangoff P, Armbruster R, Enz A: Glycolytic enzymes in human brain: Effects of ageing and autolytic stability. *Z Physiol Chem* 358:254, 1977.

4. Iwangoff P, Armbruster R, Enz A, Sandoz P: Influence of ageing, post-mortem delay and agonal state on phosphofructokinase (PFK) in human brain tissue obtained at autopsy. *IRCS Medical Science* 6:83, 1978.

5. McGeer PL, McGeer EG: Enzymes associated with the metabolism of catecholamines, acetylcholine and GABA in Human Controls and patients with Parkinson's disease and Huntington's chorea. *J Neurochem* 26:65–76, 1976.

6. Samaha FJ: Studies on $Na^+$-$K^+$-stimulated ATPase of human brain. *J Neurochem* 14:333–341, 1967.

7. Lee SL, Phillis JW: Stimulation of cerebral cortical synaptosomal Na-K-ATPase by biogenic amines. *Can J Physiol Pharmacol* 55:961–964, 1977.

8. Sun AY, Samorajski T: The effects of age and alcohol on $(Na^+ + K^+)$-ATPase activity of whole homogenate and synaptosomes prepared from mouse and human brain. *J Neurochem* 24:161–164, 1975.

9. Lowry OH, Passonneau JV: The relationships between substrates and enzymes of glycolysis in brain. *J Biol Chem* 239:31–42, 1964.

10. Bielicki L, Krieglstein J: Solubilization of brain mitochondrial hexokinase by thiopental. *Arch Exp Path Pharmakol* 298:61–65, 1977.

11. Severinghaus JW, Hamilton FN, Cotev S: Carbonic acid production and the role of carbonic anhydrase in decarboxylation in brain. *Biochem J* 114:703–705, 1969.

12. Annau Z: The effect of carbonic anhydrase inhibition on electrical self stimulation of the brain during hypoxia. *Life Sci* 20:1043–1050, 1977.

13. Bourke RS, Kimelberg HK, Nelson LR: The effects of temperature and inhibitors on $HCO_3$-stimulated swelling and ion uptake of monkey cerebral cortex. *Brain Res* 105:309–323, 1976.

14. Garg, LC, Mathur PP: Effect of ouabain on cerebrospinal fluid formation after carbonic anhydrase inhibition. *Arch Int Pharmacodyn* 213:190–194, 1975.

15. Reichlmeier K, Ermini M, Schlecht HP: Altersbedingte enzymatische Veranderungen im menschlichen Grosshirncortex. *Akt Geront*, 8:441–448, 1978.

16. Reichlmeier K, Enz A, Iwangoff P, Meier-Ruge W: Age-related changes in human brain enzyme activities: A basis for pharmacological intervention, in *Pharmacological Intervention of the Aging Process*. New York, Plenum Press, 1978, pp 251–252.

17. Reichlmeier K, Schlecht HP, Iwangoff P: Enzyme activity changes in the aging human brain. *Experientia* 33:798, 1977.

18. Koul O, Kanungo MS: Alterations in carbonic anhydrase of the brain of rats as a function of age. *Exp Geront* 10:273–278, 1975.

19. Kodama T, Matsukado Y, Shimizu H: The cyclic AMP system of human brain. *Brain Res* 50:135–146, 1973.

20. Williams RH, Little SA, Ensinck JW: Adenyl cyclase and phosphodiesterase activities in brain areas of man, monkey and rat. *Am J Med Sci* 258:190–202, 1969.

21. Fumagalli R, Bernareggi V, Berti F, Trabucchi M: Cyclic AMP formation in human brain: An *in vitro* stimulation by neurotransmitters. *Life Sci* 10:1111–1115, 1971.

22. Duffy MJ, Wong J, Powell D: Stimulation of adenylate cyclase activity in different areas of human brain by substance P. *Neuropharmacology* 14:615–618, 1975.

23. Hidaka H, Shibuya M, Asano T, Hara F: Cyclic nucleotide phosphodiesterase of human cerebrospinal fluid. *J Neurochem* 25:49–53, 1975.

24. Thompson WI, Appleman MM: Characterization of cyclic nucleotide phosphodiesterase of rat tissue. *J Biol Chem* 246:3145–3150, 1971.

25. Zimmerman ID, Berg AP: Phosphodiesterase and adenyl-cyclase activities in the cerebral cortex of the aging rat. *Mech Ageing Develop* 4:89–96, 1975.
26. Schmidt MJ, Thornberry JF: Cyclic AMP and cyclic GMP accumulation in vitro in brain regions of young, old and aged rats. *Brain Res* 139:169–177, 1978.
27. Walker JB, Walker JP: Properties of adenylate cyclase from senescent rat brain. *Brain Res* 54:391–396, 1973.
28. Puri SK, Volicer L: Effect of aging on cyclic AMP levels and adenylate cyclase and phosphodiesterase activities in the rat corpus striatum. *Mech Ageing Develop* 6:53–58, 1977.
29. Govoni S, Loddo P, Spano PF, Trabucchi M: Dopamine receptor sensitivity in brain and retina of rats during aging. *Brain Res* 138:565–570, 1977.
30. Berg A, Zimmerman ID, Effects of electrical stimulation and norepinephrine on cyclic-AMP levels in the cerebral cortex of the aging rat. *Mech Ageing Develop* 4:377–383, 1975.
31. Nimmo HG, Cohen PH: Hormonal control of protein phosphorylation. *Adv Cyclic Nucleotide Res* 8:145–266, 1977.
32. Ueda T, Greengard P: Adenosine 3':5'-monophosphate-regulated phosphoprotein system of neuronal membranes. *J Biol Chem* 252:5155–5163, 1977.
33. Routtenberg A, Ehrlich YH: Endogenous phosphorylation of four cerebral cortical membrane proteins: Role of cyclic nucleotides, ATP and divalent cations. *Brain Res* 92:415–430, 1975.
34. Johnson EM: Cyclic AMP-dependent protein kinase and its nuclear substrate proteins. *Adv Cyclic Nucleotide Res* 8:267–309, 1977.
35. Goldstein M, Bronaugh RL, Ebstein B, Roberge C: Stimulation of tyrosine hydroxylase activity by cyclic AMP in synaptosomes and in soluble striatal enzyme preparations. *Brain Res* 109:563–574, 1976.
36. Morgenroth VH III, Hegstrand LR, Roth RH, Greengard P: Evidence for involvement of protein kinase in the activation by adenosine 3':5'-monophosphate of brain tyrosine 3-monooxygenase. *J Biol Chem* 250:1946–1948, 1975.
37. Reichlmeier K: Age related changes of cyclic AMP-dependent protein kinase in bovine brain. *J Neurochem* 27:1249–1251, 1976.
38. Reichlmeier K, Citherlet K, Sandoz P, Meier-Ruge W: Das Proteinkinase-System des menschlichen Gehirns: Ein Beitrag zum Studium des "normalen" Alterns. *Akt Geront* 9:351–358, 1979.
39. Schmidt MJ, Truex LL, Thornberry JF: Cyclic nucleotides and protein kinase activity in the rat brain postmortem. *J Neurochem* 31:427–431, 1978.
40. Reichlmeier K, Citherlet K, Ermini M: Some aspects of the protein kinase system in the ageing human brain cortex. *Z Physiol Chem* 359:308–309, 1978.
41. Sun AY, Seaman RN: The effect of aging on synaptosomal $Ca^{2+}$ transport in the brain. *Exp Ageing Res* 3:107–116, 1977.
42. Sun AY, Ordy JM, Samorajski T: Effect of alcohol on aging in the nervous system, in Ordy JM, Brizzee KR (eds): *Neurobiology of Aging*. New York, Plenum Press, 1975, pp 505–520.
43. Kalish MI, Katz MS, Pineyro MA, Gregerman RI: Epinephrine- and glucagon-sensitive adenylate cyclases of rat liver during aging. Evidence for membrane instability associated with increased enzymatic activity. *Biochem Biophys Acta* 483:452–466, 1977.
44. Samorajski T, Sun A, Rolsten C: Effects of chronic dosage with chlorpromazine and gerovital $H_3$ in the aging brain, in: Nandy K, Sherwin I (eds): *The Aging Brain and Senile Dementia*. New York, Plenum Press, 1977, pp 141–156.

45. Samorajski T, Strong JR, Sun A: Dihydroergotoxine (hydergine) and alcohol-induced variations in young and old mice. *J Gerontol* 32:145–152, 1977.
46. Williams M, Rodnight R: Protein phosphorylation in respiring slices of guinea-pig cerebral cortex. *Biochem J* 154:163–170, 1976.
47. Williams M: Protein phosphorylation in rat striatal slices. Effects of noradrenaline, dopamine and other putative transmitters. *Brain Res* 109:190–195, 1976.
48. Forn J, Krueger BK, Greengard P: Adenosine 3', 5'-monophosphate content in rat caudate nucleus: Demonstration of dopaminergic and adrenergic receptors. *Science* 186:1118–1120, 1974.
49. Greengard P: Possible role for cyclic nucleotides and phosphorylated membrane proteins in postsynaptic actions of neurotransmitters. *Nature* 260:101–108, 1976.
50. Greengard P, Kebabian JW: Role of cyclic AMP in synaptic transmission in the mammalian peripheral nervous system. *Fed Proc* 33:1059–1067, 1974.
51. Ehrlich YH, Rabjohns RR, Routtenberg A: Experimental input alters the phosphorylation of specific proteins in brain membranes. *Pharmacol Biochem Behav* 6:169–174, 1977.
52. Leonard BE: A study of neurohumoral control of glycolysis in the mouse brain in vivo: Role of noradrenaline and dopamine. *Z Naturforsch* 30c:385–391, 1975.
53. Anchors JM, Garcia-Rill E: Dopamine, a modulator of carbohydrate metabolism in the caudate nucleus. *Brain Res* 133:183–189, 1977.
54. Sutherland EW: Fractionation and characterisation of a cyclic adenine ribonucleotide formed by tissue particles. *J Biol Chem* 232:1077–1091, 1958.
55. Greengard P: Phosphorylated proteins as physiological effectors. *Science* 199:146–152, 1978.
56. Nathanson JA: Cyclic nucleotides and nervous system function. *Physiol Rev* 57:157–256, 1977.
57. Gaitz CM, Varner R, Overall JE: Pharmacotherapy for organic brain syndrome in late life. *Arch Gen Psychiatry* 34:839–845, 1977.
58. Rosen HJ: Mental decline in the elderly: Pharmacotherapy (ergot alkaloids versus papaverine). *J Am Geriatr Soc* 23:169–174, 1975.
59. Meier-Ruge W, Enz A, Gygax P, Hunziker O, Iwangoff P, Reichlmeier K: Experimental pathology in basic research of the aging brain, in Gershon S, Raskin A (eds): *Aging,* vol 2. New York, Raven Press, 1975.
60. Meier-Ruge W (ed): Workshop on advances in experimental pharmacology of hydergine. *Gerontology* 24 (suppl 1): 1–153, 1978.
61. Murad F, Chi YM, Rall TW, Sutherland EW: Adenyl cyclase. III. The effect of catecholamines and choline esters on the formation of adenosine 3', 5'-phosphate by preparations from cardiac muscle and liver. *J Biol Chem* 237:1233–1238, 1962.
62. Sollman T, Brown ED: Intravenous injection of ergot. *JAMA* 45:229–240, 1905.
63. Markstein R, Wagner H: The effect of dihydroergotoxine, phentolamine and pindolol on catecholamine-stimulated adenyl-cyclase in rat cerebral cortex. *FEBS Letters* 55:275–277, 1975.
64. Govoni S, Iuliano E, Spano PF, Trabucchi M: Effect of ergotamine and dihydroergotamine on dopamine-stimulated adenylate cyclase in rat caudate nucleus. *J Pharm Pharmacol* 29:45–47, 1977.
65. Sawaya MChB, Dolphin A, Jenner P, Marsden CD, Meldrum BS: Noradrenaline-sensitive adenylate cyclase in slices of mouse limbic forebrain: Characterisation and effect of dopaminergic agonists. *Biochem Pharmacol* 26:1877–1884, 1977.
66. Sundquist H, Anttila M, Nieminen L, Urpo K, Kalliomaki L: The effect of dihydroergotoxine on the adenylcyclase activity in homogenates of rat cerebral cortex. *Acta Pharmacol Toxicol* 40:589–592, 1977.

67. Schmidt MJ, Hill LE: Effects of ergots on adenylate cyclase activity in the corpus striatum and pituitary. *Life Sci* 20:789–798, 1977.

68. Markstein R, Wagner H: Effect of dihydroergotoxine on cyclic-AMP-generating systems in rat cerebral cortex slices. *Gerontology* 24 (suppl 1): 94–105, 1978.

69. Iwangoff P, Meier-Ruge W, Schieweck Ch, Enz A: The uptake of DH-ergotoxine by different parts of the cat brain. *Pharmacology* 14:27–38, 1976.

70. Iwangoff P, Enz A, Meier-Ruge W: Incorporation, after single and repeated application of radioactive labeled DH-ergot alkaloids in different organs of the cat, with special reference to the brain. *Gerontology* 24 (suppl 1): 126–138, 1978.

71. Monn E, Christiansen RO: Adenosine 3', 5'-monophosphate phosphodiesterase multiple forms. *Science* 173:540–542, 1971.

72. Uzunov P, Shein HW, Weiss B: Multiple forms of cyclic 3', 5'-AMP phosphodiesterase of rat cerebrum and cloned astrocytoma and neuroblastoma cells. *Neuropharmacology* 13:377–391, 1974.

73. Adinolfi AM, Schmidt SY: Cytochemical localization of cyclic nucleotide phosphodiesterase activity at developing synapses. *Brain Res* 76:21–31, 1974.

74. Florendo NT, Barnett RI, Greengard P: Cyclic 3', 5'-nucleotide phosphodiesterase: Cytochemical localization in cerebral cortex. *Science* 173:745–747, 1971.

75. Russel TR, Thompson WI, Schneider FW, Appleman MM: 3', 5'-cyclic adenosine monophosphate phosphodiesterase: Negative cooperativity. *Proc Nat Acad Sci* 69:1791–1795, 1972.

76. Enz A, Chappuis A, Iwangoff P: Kinetic studies on the low $K_m$-phosphodiesterase inhibition by DH-ergot-alkaloids. *Experientia* 32:767, 1976.

77. Enz A, Iwangoff P, Chappuis A: The influence of dihydroergotoxine mesylate on the low $K_m$-phosphodiesterase of cat and rat brain in vitro. *Gerontology* 24 (suppl 1): 115–125, 1978.

78. Iwangoff P, Enz A: The influence of various dihydroergotamine analogues on cyclic adenosine 3', 5'-monophosphate phosphodiesterase of the gray matter of cat brain in vitro. *Agents Action* 2:223–230, 1972.

79. Iwangoff P, Enz A, Chappuis A: Inhibition of cAMP phosphodiesterase of different cat organs by DH-ergotoxine in the micromolar substrate range. *IRCS Medical Science* 3:403, 1975.

80. Reichlmeier K, Iwangoff P: Influence of phosphodiesterase inhibitors on brain protein kinases in vitro. *Experientia* 3:691, 1974.

81. Kendrick NC, Blaustein MP, Fried RC, Ratzlaff RW: ATP dependent calcium storage in presynaptic nerve terminals. *Nature* 265:246–248, 1977.

82. Yamamoto H, Harris RA, Loh HH, Way EL: Effects of morphine tolerance and dependence on $Mg^{2+}$ dependent activity on synaptic vesicles. *Life Sci* 20:1533–1540, 1977.

83. Philippu A, Becke H, Burger A: Effect of drugs on the uptake of noradrenaline by isolated hypothalamic vesicles. *Europ J Pharmacol* 6:96–101, 1969.

84. Albers RW, Koval GJ, Siegel GJ: Studies on the interaction of ouabain and other cardioactive steroids with sodium-potassium activated adenosine triphosphatase. *Mol Pharmacol* 4:324–336, 1968.

85. Goldmann SS, Albers RW: Sodium-potassium activated adenosine-triphosphatase. IX. The role of phospholipids. *J Biol Chem* 248:867–874, 1973.

86. Formby B, Clausen J: Phosphatase activity in particulate fraction of rat brain. *J Physiol Chem* 349:349–356, 1968.

87. Sastry BSR, Phillis JW: Antagonism of biogenic amine-induced depression of cerebral cortical neurones by $(Na^+K^+)$-ATPase inhibitors. *Can J Physiol Pharmacol* 55:170–179, 1977.

88. Logan JG, O'Donovan DJ: The effects of ouabain and the activation of neural membrane ATPase by biogenic amines. *J Neurochem* 27:185–189, 1976.

89. Hexum TD: The effect of catecholamines on transport (Na+K+)-ATPase. *Biochem Pharmacol* 26:1221–1227, 1977.

90. Chappuis A, Enz A, Iwangoff P: The influence of adrenergic effectors on the cationic pump of brain cell membrane. *Triangle* 14:93–98, 1975.

91. Iwangoff P, Chappuis A, Enz A: The influence of catecholamines on the ATPase in the cat's brain cortex. *IRCS Medical Science* 73-8:3–10–19, 1973.

92. Iwangoff P, Chappuis A, Enz A: Dependence of noradrenaline activated ATPase activity on monovalent and bivalent ions in the brain cortex of the cat. *IRCS Medical Science* 2:1182, 1974.

93. Iwangoff P, Enz A: Effects of some biogenic amines on the (Na+K+)-ATPase system (K+-pNPPase, Step 3). *Experientia* 32:771, 1976.

94. Meier-Ruge W, Schieweck Ch, Iwangoff P: The distribution of ($^3$H)-hydergine in the cat brain. *IRCS Medical Science* 73-4:7–10–3, 1973.

95. Iwangoff P, Enz A, Armbruster R, Emmenegger H, Pataki A, Sandoz P: Der Einfluss von Alter, Zeitspanne bis zur postmortalen Isolierung des Gewebes sowie der Agonie auf einige glycolytische Enzyme in autoptischen Gehirnproben des Menschen. *Akt Geront*, 1980, in press.

96. Meier-Ruge W, Emmenegger H, Enz A, Gygax P, Iwangoff P, Wiernsperger N: Pharmacological aspects of dihydrogenated ergot alkaloids in experimental brain research. *Pharmacology* 16 (suppl 1):45–62, 1978.

97. Gygax P, Wiernsperger N, Meier-Ruge W, Baumann T: Effect of papaverine and dihydroergotoxine mesylate on cerebral microflow, EEG, and $pO_2$ in oligemic hypotension. *Gerontology* 24 (suppl 1):14–22, 1978.

98. Finch CE: Catecholamine metabolism in the brains of ageing male mice. *Brain Res* 52:261–276, 1973.

99. Samorajski T: Age-related changes in brain biogenic amines, in Brody H, Harman D, Ordy JM (eds): *Aging*, vol 1. New York, Raven Press, 1975, pp 199–214.

100. Costa M, Manen C-A, Russell DH: In vivo activation of cAMP-dependent protein kinase by aminophylline and 1-methyl 3-isobutylxanthine. *Biochem Biophys Res Commun* 65:75–81, 1975.

101. Kinnier WJ, Wilson JE: Effects of some inhibitors of cyclic nucleotide phosphodiesterase on protein phosphorylation in isolated neurons and glia from rat brain. *Biochem Biophys Res Commun* 77:1369–1376, 1977.

102. Kugler J, Oswald WD, Herzfeld U, Seus R, Pingel J, Welzel D: Langzeittherapie altersbedingter Insuffizienz-Erscheinungen des Gehirns. *Dtsch Med Wschr* 103:456–462, 1978.

103. Lew JY, Hata F, Ohashi T, Goldstein M: The interactions of bromocriptine and lergotrile with dopamine and ∝-adrenergic receptors. *J Neural Transmission* 41:109–121, 1977.

104. Michaelis L, Menten ML: Die Kinetik der Invertinwirkung. *Biochem Ztschr* 49:333–369, 1913.

# CHAPTER 3

# *Assessment Of Age-Related Changes In Learning And Performance In The Rat*

OAKLEY S. RAY
ROBERT J. BARRETT

## PREVIOUS LITERATURE

### Appetitive Studies

As might be expected, virtually all the studies reported in the literature show age-related decrements in some aspect of the measured behavior. However, some of the first studies done by Stone[1,2] failed to find any systematic age-related differences in learning over a large portion of the rat's lifespan. These studies involved testing rats in a variety of appetitively motivated mazes. Much later in a study by Verzar-McDougall,[3] a marked age-related decrement in learning was found when rats were tested for rate of learning a Stone 14-unit multiple T-maze. Verzar-McDougall[3] stated that the differences were found only when young and old rats were not maintained on differential deprivation (the practice of depriving old rats more than younger rats) and suggested this difference to explain Stone's failure to show age effects on learning. In a review by Jerome,[4] the disparate finding between the Stone[1,2] experiments and the one by Verzar-McDougall was emphasized as perhaps reflecting the importance of age-related changes in motivation.

This issue was not further pursued until Goodrick[5] designed a study to compare highly motivated mature-young (6 months old) and senescent (26 months or more) rats on learning the 14-unit Stone maze where both massed and spaced trials were employed. "Highly motivated" was operationally defined as depriving the young rats to 75 percent of normal body weight and the older rats to 70 percent of *ad libitum* weight. The logic of the 5 percent differential has to do with the fact that the younger rats would still be growing. Following learning, some subjects were given a retention test 45 days after, while others were run on extinction. The results of this experiment supported the Verzar-McDougall finding in that senescent rats failed to learn the maze as quickly as young rats when four trials 60 to 80 minutes apart were given each day. Furthermore, increased spacing of trials (one per day) potentiated the difference while massed trials (12 per day) resulted in facilitation of learning. These findings, in addition to the failure to find age-related differences on the 45-day retention test, were interpreted as strongly suggestive of a short-term memory deficit associated with aging.

One further procedure of interest involved testing both young and old rats on extinction following criterion acquisition. On this test senescent rats made fewer errors and continued running faster to the goal box in comparison with younger rats. This behavior was interpreted as representing a tendency for aged rats to perseverate, which was thought to reflect a general behavioral inflexibility making it more difficult for these animals to adjust to a changing environment.

This notion — that elderly rats are less able to alter ongoing behaviors than young rats — had previously been thought relevant to understanding reported increased rigidity of human subjects of advanced age.[6] Consequently, a number of studies testing the behavioral rigidity concept had appeared in the literature.[6] The results reported by Botwinick *et al.*[6] pretty well sum up the findings from these experiments. In that study, rats from three age groups (27 months, 10 months, and 3 to 4 months) were trained to learn a left-right position response in a single-unit Y-maze, following which a series of four reversals was run. Only small age-related differences were observed on the errors to criterion measure employed to compare learning rates. Although the older rats learned more slowly, the reversal procedure failed to support the prediction that older rats would require more trials to reverse their position choice.

In a follow-up study,[7] a more complicated maze involving four serial choice points was used in the hope of obtaining a more sensitive index of age-related disruption. Indeed, impressive differences were found on original learning; however, again there was little evidence for an age-related disruption of reversal learning.

The perseveration notion attracted little interest following these reports and might explain why Goodrick's 1968 report—showing fewer errors and faster running times for aged animals tested during extinction—seems to have stimulated little interest. In fact, not until 1975, by Goodrick himself, was the only serious attempt made to rekindle the perseveration hypothesis. This experiment[8] tested mature-young (5 months) and aged (25 months) rats in a 14-unit T-maze using a forced-correct-response procedure. This involved blocking off entry to the 14 culs-de-sac for 20 trials (4 per day) at which time the barriers were removed and testing continued. For one-half of the young and old rats one trial per day (distributed trials) was run, while for the other half four (30 minutes between trials) massed trials were run. The major finding in the experiment was that the aged rats on the forced-correct procedure during early training learned in fewer trials than the young rats when the barriers were removed. This finding supported the notion that older rats tend to perseverate on previously acquired responses, which in this instance resulted in fewer errors once the forced-choice procedure was no longer in effect.

Furthermore, the massed trials resulted in greater facilitation for the aged rats, as had previously been reported by Goodrick.[5,9] The author devotes little time trying to explain failures by others, noted above, in supporting the perseveration explanation. He does say that "these results were probably due to a failure to use adequate numbers of aged rats or to use of tests inadequate in complexity for studying the learning process" ([8], p. 207). He concluded that the aging process in rats results in a deficit in short-term memory processes as well as a response perseveration tendency, both of which would be expected to retard learning in most situations. Other appetitive maze studies showed that task complexity augmented age-related differences. Goodrick,[10] for example, showed a general decline in performance with age for multiple-choice maze learning in rats of the Wistar strain, 66 to 8 months old versus 26 to 27 months. As the number of choices increased from 1 to 14, age differences were accentuated. This study illustrates the advantage of looking for behavioral change across a variety of tasks which serve to increase the sensitivity of the behavioral measure.

**Aversive Conditioning**

Since the task demands of appetitively and aversively motivated tasks are quite different, we chose to discuss separately representative studies of each type.

An early study by Denenberg and Kline[11] tested rats 20, 60 or 225 days of age in a shock-avoidance task requiring the subjects to enter a chamber adjoining the main shock chamber to successfully avoid shock. The shock was preceded by a 5-second-buzzer CS which terminated when the rat either escaped or avoided the shock by entering the shockfree chamber. Results from the acquisition phase of the experiment showed a curvilinear age-related function where the 60-day subjects learned fastest followed by the 225- and 30-day-old subjects in that order. Although this study did not use old rats, the data do agree with the general belief that rats avoid best around 60 to 90 days of age and by four months are already showing deficits.

A study by Freund and Walker[12] used mice to test for the effect of advancing age on shuttle-box avoidance acquisition and subsequent retention. Their experimental design was intended to allow for independent assessment of age and length of the acquisition-retention interval in explaining the decline in performance. C57BL/6J mice 3, 6, 9, 12 and 15 months old were given 30 trials a day for 10 days in a shuttle-box active avoidance task. All mice were tested for retention when they were 15 months old. Four additional groups of mice were all trained at 3 months of age and tested for retention at 6, 9, 12 and 15 months of age.

Results from the first condition, in agreement with Denenberg et al.[11] indicated a progressive decline in acquisition as age at acquisition increased from 3 to 15 months. When these animals were retested at 15 months of age, performance further declined in proportion to the length of the training-retest interval. However, since initial learning varied for these subjects, the performance on the retention trials is not an accurate measure of memory loss as a function of time elapsed since training. When initial acquisition was equated in the second group of mice by training them all at the age of 3 months, the resulting decline in avoidance was again found to be proportional to the retest interval length. Although no differences existed in acquisition level among these groups, the retention interval is now confounded with age. The authors dealt with this problem by comparing the retention of the animals from the second group trained at 3 months and retested 6 months later at 9 months of age, with mice from the first group which had a 6-month retention interval but had been trained when 9 months old and consequently were 15 months old when retested. Since these two groups showed equal retention decrements, the authors concluded, "the decline in performance is not attributable to performance changes related to age *per se* because it is demonstrable even when all animals are of the same age at the time of retention testing" ([12], p. 23). This conclusion is in conflict with the previously cited Denenberg et al.[11] study as well as one reported by Oliverio and Bovet.[18]

These latter two authors reported a decline with age of shuttle-box acquisition in 60- to 360-day-old mice which they interpreted as reflecting a short-term memory deficit associated with aging. Of the three studies, the data from the Freund and Walker[12] experiment are least supportive of the conclusions drawn. In that experiment it was initially shown that 9-month-old mice do not acquire the avoidance task as well as 3-month-old mice. Thus, if indeed these groups no longer differ on the 6-month retention test, even though they differ in chronological age (9 and 15 months), not only would age not be a factor in explaining the *equal* decrement resulting in both groups following the six-month retest interval, but rather age must have proportionally facilitated the 15-month-old animals, since they apparently were *inferior* to the 9-month-old mice in acquiring the avoidance task six months previously. It would seem that Freund et al.[12] are saying that there are age-related deficits in learning but apparently not in either retention or performance. We will return to this controversy at a later point in the paper.

A paper by Doty[13] emphasizes the desirability of having a variety of tasks differing in complexity as a means of detecting age-related changes. He employed three levels of complexity with rats aged 1, 5 and 25 months and also varied the intertrial interval (10 seconds, 1 hour or 4 hours) during acquisition of an avoidance response. The results showed that although performance declined for all age groups with increasing task complexity, the effect of age was most pronounced on the more difficult tasks. Interestingly, the trials at four-hour intervals eliminated age differences on one of the tasks. It will be recalled that Goodrick[5] found that *massed* trials had a positive effect on aged rats in learning an appetitively motivated complex maze. More recent evidence regarding the nature of avoidance learning[14] supports the Doty finding with respect to the facilitation produced by spacing in avoidance learning. It is quite possible that spacing versus massed trials will have quite different effects depending on whether the task is motivated by aversive or appetitive stimuli.

## RECENT CONTRIBUTIONS

In a series of studies on aging, some of which were previously reported,[14] we were initially concerned with simply identifying and describing age-related behavioral changes in a variety of situations. In the first study,[15] we tested young (1 month) and old (12 months) rats of both sexes from four different commercial suppliers in an open-field-activity situation 5 minutes a day for five days. Animals used were albinos from Zivic-Miller Laboratories in Pittsburgh, black hooded from Simonsen

Laboratories, albinos from Holtzman Laboratories, and the inbred Fischer
strain, CDF from Charles River Laboratory. The most important effect of
aging on activity was an increased rate of habituation which occurred
across days in the old rats. This was most pronounced in male rats and
varied greatly depending on the strain. The strain differences are
interesting not only because they emphasize the importance of genetic
factors in determining some aspects of aging, but also because they
illustrate the need to consider this factor when comparing results across
studies. Thus, even in an environment where there were no specific
demands on the rats, older animals behaved quite differently from young
rats.

   In another part of this study, additional rats from the same groups were
compared on rate of learning a Lashley III maze. Interestingly, although
the young rats had no difficulty in learning the maze, few of the old
subjects except for some of the Holtzman animals showed significant
learning during the 16 training trials. This failure to learn was directly
related to the performance observed in the old rats on open-field activity.
Essentially, the old rats discontinued exploring the maze if they failed to
solve it on the initial trials and would remain in the start compartment for
the duration of the 5-minute interval allowed for each trial. Finally,
independent groups of the same four strains were compared on learning in
a shuttle-box and Sidman avoidance task. No age-related differences were
found on Sidman avoidance, but age did significantly disrupt shuttle-box
avoidance learning. Again, this task-specific nature of the age deficit in
avoidance demonstrates the need to test behavior in a wide variety of tasks
to optimize finding measures sensitive to age-induced changes.

   In addition to illustrating the importance of genetic determinants of
age-related changes in behavior, the Barrett and Ray[15] study emphasizes
the importance of evaluating the specific demands of the behavioral task
and assessing how these demands would interact with changes in the rats'
response hierarchy brought about by advancing age. Our goal in
subsequent experiments on aging involved being able to more specifically
describe and define the nature of the behavioral change. As was apparent
from the brief literature review, a question of continuing interest has been
the extent to which behavioral deficits are due to learning or performance
factors.

   In many experiments these two possible explanations are confounded
in the experimental design. Although learning and performance can be
conceptualized as separate and distinct ways of characterizing behavior, it
is not always an easy empirical distinction to achieve. The fundamental
problem is that learning is an inferred process based on quantification of
some aspect of change in the organism's performance. The performance

generally involves responding to some nominal task selected by the experimenter. The age-related changes in behavior are typically ascribed either to an organism's loss of ability to process, store or retrieve information (learning and memory) or to deficiencies in sensory-motor systems (performance), which often result in seemingly indistinguishable behavior. It is also generally implied that age-related deficiencies in "learning" reflect disruption of specific central nervous system mechanisms directly responsible for coding and storing information. It is not always clear at what level of reductionism these substrates will be found, but rather it often seems that failure to explain an age-correlated change in behavior as due to an observable performance factor requires their existence. This kind of compartmentalization of learning versus performance factors is reflected in the literature, where results are usually interpreted as supporting either one or the other explanation of behavioral change in aged subjects. The question we wish to address is whether this is a meaningful distinction which lends itself to empirical resolution. And if so, what strategy can the behavioral scientist employ to operationally define learning and performance in a meaningful noncircular manner?

For a variety of reasons, we chose active-avoidance as the behavior to concentrate on in this series of studies on age-related changes in rat behavior. Some of these reasons were practical. Food-motivated tasks present problems in equating motivational levels between young and old rats, and the tendency for old rats to rapidly habituate exploration of new environments adds another complication that has no easy solution. Eventually we would like to add other measures that meet a specific need in further describing aging.

The approach adapted in our attempt to understand age-related changes in active avoidance behavior consisted of developing a set of converging measures to operationally define and empirically distinguish learning from performance variables. As presented by Garner, Hake and Erickson,[16] "converging operations may be thought of as any set of *two* or more experimental operations which allow the selection or elimination of alternative hypotheses or concepts which could explain an experimental result. They are called converging operations because they are not perfectly correlated and thus can converge on a single concept" ([16], pp. 150–151). In order to obtain several concurrent response measures, we designed a completely automated Y-maze active avoidance apparatus which had the capacity to differentiate not only between escapes and avoidances but also between correct and incorrect discriminations, since on each trial the animal is faced with a two-choice discrimination problem. Thus, the concurrent recording of avoidance and choice behavior provides two sets of operations converging on the concepts of learning and performance. Within the same task we also provided for simultaneous, automated recording of the additional measures described below.

In order to test the usefulness of the Y-maze in interpreting differences in avoidance behavior, we compared acquisition data from two strains (ZMs and F-344) which we had previously shown to differ markedly in shuttle-box avoidance learning. We ran males and females of both strains 25 trials per day for 10 consecutive days. The trials were programmed on a constant 30-second intertrial interval and consisted of switching the light cue in a random order to one of the previously dark arms. Entry into the lighted arm within 10 seconds successfully avoided shock. Failure to avoid within 10 seconds resulted in shock (.75 ma, 60Hz ac) onset, after which only escape responses were possible. The following response measures were concurrently recorded during each session.

1. Correct discriminations: number of trials on which the initial response (whether avoidance or escape) was to run into the lighted arm.
2. Avoidances: entry into the lighted (safe) arm at any time during the 10 seconds prior to shock onset.
3. Incorrect avoidances: number of trials on which the *initial* response was entry into the dark arm during the 10 seconds prior to shock onset. An incorrect avoidance generally resulted in the animal receiving shock at the end of the CS-US interval until it entered the safe arm. On these trials the animal was not credited with an avoidance as defined above. However, occasionally an animal would initially enter the incorrect arm and subsequently enter the correct arm prior to shock onset. This sequence was recorded as one incorrect avoidance and one avoidance.
4. Incorrect escapes: a number of trials on which the initial response was entry into the dark arm following shock onset. Since shock was on in this arm, the animal continued to be shocked until it ran into the lighted arm.
5. Activity: a measure of locomotor activity within the lighted arm during the intertrial interval recorded automatically with the touch-sensitive circuit wired through the grid-floor bars.
6. Intertrial crosses: number of times the animal left the lighted (safe) arm during the intertrial interval. Since the dark arms and the center section were electrified during the intertrial interval, such responses resulted in the animal's running into shock.
7. Response latency: time elapsed between onset of a trial and the animal's entry into the lighted arm.

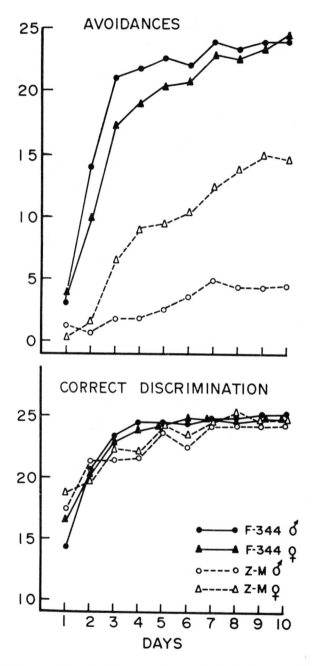

Figure 3-1:  Mean number of avoidances and correct discriminations over 25 trial sessions as a function of strain and sex.

56 RAY and BARRETT

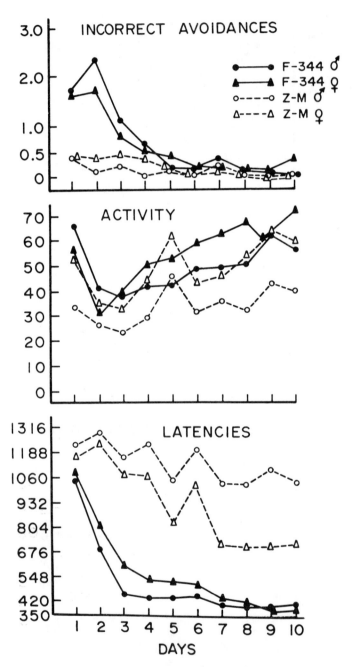

Figure 3-2: Mean number of incorrect avoidances, motor activity or response latency during daily sessions of 25 trials as a function of strain and sex.

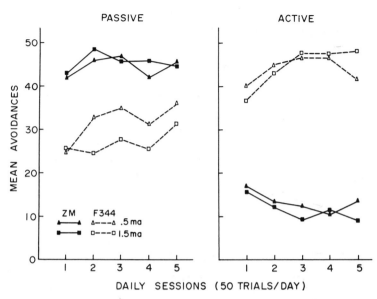

Figure 3-3:   Mean number of avoidances as a function of strain, shock intensity and whether active or passive avoidance was required to avoid shock.

The avoidance and discrimination data for male and female rats from both strains are shown in Figure 3-1. In the upper panel the basic strain difference previously reported in the shuttle box[15] is replicated in the Y-maze. F–344 rats of both sexes were clearly superior to the ZM strain in learning this response. The correct discrimination data shown in the lower panel clearly show that rats from both strains readily learned "where" to run. Thus, that measure does not converge with the avoidance data on "learning ability" differences as the explanation for the strain-specific avoidance behavior. In Figure 3-2, three additional measures are presented. Most informative are the incorrect avoidance data shown in the top panel. Early in training the F–344 rats make significantly more errors involving running at the correct time but to the incorrect place than do the ZMs. In the middle panel the motor-activity measure also shows that the F–344s are more active than the ZM rats during the intertrial interval. Taken together, these response measures suggest that the differences in rate of learning to avoid are due in large part to the fact that the F–344s' initial reaction to shock (basically increased activity) is more compatible with the response demands of this task than the decrease in activity produced by shock in the ZM rats. Thus, although this does not change the fact that the F–344 rats are more adept at learning active avoidance than the ZMs, it does provide information useful in identifying the responsible factors.

Subsequent studies further converged on this explanation of the avoidance differences between the two strains. Figure 3-3 shows the results of one study where ZM and F–344 acquisition of active and passive avoidance was compared in a shuttle-box apparatus. Shock avoidance in the passive situation required the rat to suppress motor movement during a 10-second light-on CS, while active avoidance required movement during the CS. Trials were programmed on a 30-second intertrial interval. As shown in Figure 3-3, the major source of variance is the genetically determined response to shock. Clearly the rate of learning the active and passive responses will vary for the two strains, depending on the compatibility between the task demands and the shock-elicited behavior. These studies illustrate the advantage of recording a variety of converging responses to choose between opposing interpretations of a behavioral phenomenon.

Prior to automating the discrimination measure we reported[14] results of a long-term retention study using only the avoidance measure in the Y-maze as an index of learning and retention. At each of six retest intervals (1, 15, 30, 90, 180 and 270 days), three groups of rats were tested which differed in the number of trials they had received (20, 40 and 80) on original training. The subjects were male F–344 rats 69 days old when trained and either 70, 85, 100, 160, 250 or 340 days old when retested. In order to assess the effect of age unconfounded by prior experience, separate naive control groups were assigned to each of the retention intervals. At the time when the retention animals were retested, the appropriate naive control groups (20, 40 and 80 trials) were trained and retested 24 hours later. Thus, these rats provided an index of the effects of age on learning and performing the avoidance response and were important in interpreting any decrement observed in the rats trained and subsequently retested at one of the six retest intervals. All subjects were given 150 trials during a single retest session. The results from this study showed that avoidances did gradually decline over the six retest intervals and furthermore, the decrement was inversely related to the number of training trials. However, when these data were compared to the age-control animals, it was found that age alone could account for the decrement in avoidance. Thus, rats trained one day and retested 24 hours later avoided no better than equal-aged rats which had been trained up to 9 months prior to retesting. Since age rather than time since training proved to be the major factor contributing to the avoidance decrement, this relationship is graphed in Figure 3-4 where the data are combined for rats of the same age without regard for the retest interval. These data were interpreted as indirectly reflecting little loss of memory for the avoidance response. However, it was still not clear to what extent the age-related decrement was

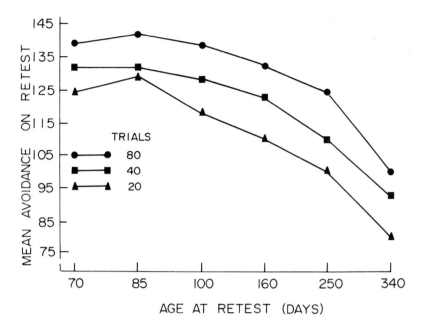

Figure 3-4:    Mean number of avoidances as a function of three levels of training and age at retention.

related to motivational-performance factors as opposed to learning and memory processes.

This question was pursued in the first study on aging which employed the automated Y-mazes with the full complement of measures. Male F-344 rats either 2, 5, 11, 16 or 19 months old were given a single 80-trial training session in the brightness discrimination Y-maze avoidance task. Although shock intensity was to have been .75 ma for all groups, a procedural error resulted in two age groups (16 and 19 months) receiving a higher intensity (1.25 ma) of shock. The results of the study are presented in Figure 3-5. Statistical analysis of the avoidance data revealed that of the groups receiving .75 ma shock, the 5- and 11-month-old rats made fewer avoidances than those 2 months old. Interestingly, the higher shock intensity used on the 17- and 20-month-old animals resulted in a considerable facilitation of avoidance acquisition. On the basis of other data, rats of this age trained on 0.75 ma for 80 trials would be expected to make about 10 to 15 avoidances. On the right of Figure 3-5, the correct choice data for the same animals are plotted. On this measure there were no significant differences among any of the age groups irrespective of the shock intensity. The avoidance and discrimination data as well as the measures of intertrial activity and intertrial crosses (not shown) indicated

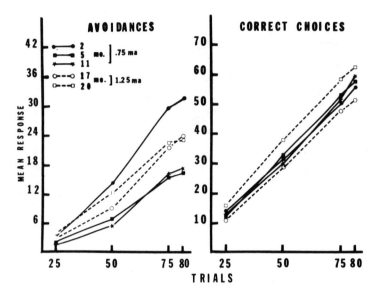

Figure 3-5:   Mean number of avoidances and correct discriminations as a function of age during 80 acquisition trials.

that the age-related decrement in avoidance acquisition reflects a performance or motivational deficit rather than a loss of ability to form and retain new associations (learning and memory). In order to further study retention loss as a function of time since learning, a second experiment was conducted in which groups of rats were all given 80 training trials when they were 70 days old and 150 retest trials either 0 (actually 24 hours), 3, 9, 15 or 18 months later. Results from these groups, presented in Figure 3-6, show the gradual decline in avoidance behavior as a function of the increasing train-retest interval. The extent to which the avoidance decrement represents performance, motivational or memory deficits, or a combination of these factors can in part be determined by the outcome on the choice measure shown on the right of Figure 3-5. Although the choice measure was not available for the 24-hour retest group, inspection of the data for the 3-, 9-, 15- and 18-month retest animals indicates there was no decrement in ability to recall the correct choice even 18 months after training. In fact, the 18-month retest group averaged no more than 5 incorrect choices out of 150 two-choice decisions. Usually these rats remembered where to run as well as if they had been trained the day before.

Age-control animals were included in this experiment to assess the extent to which the avoidance decrement was due to age-related factors rather than memory loss related to the training-retest interval. These

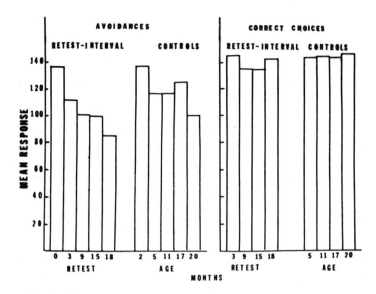

Figure 3-6:   Mean number of avoidances and correct discriminations as a function of train-retest interval and age at time of testing during 150 retention trials in the Y-maze active-avoidance task.

subjects were either 2, 5, 11, 17 or 20 months old when given 80 training trials and 150 retest trials 24 hours later. The training data for these subjects (Figure 3-5) was presented previously. The retention data for these animals are shown on the left of Figure 3-6. Recall, however, that the 17- and 20-month-old rats were inadvertently trained and tested on 1.25 ma shock rather than .75 ma. This resulted in both improved acquisition and retention scores, which although compromising to some extent the intent of the control procedure does demonstrate the potential role of motivational factors in improving performance in the aged. From the previous studies testing animals of comparable age, the 17- and 20-month-old animals would normally be expected to make approximately 105 and 90 avoidances, respectively. On the right of Figure 3-6, the choice data are presented for these animals. As can be seen, there were no differences in ability to choose the correct arm of the maze as a function of age. These rats averaged only four or five errors total. Clearly, the age-related decrement in avoidances was not due to either failure to learn or failure to recall where to run.

Taken together, the data from the above studies show that active avoidance behavior deteriorates with advancing age and that this reflects performance rather than learning and memory variables. More specifically, the multiple response measures indicate that as animals grow older they become less reactive following shock and develop a tendency to "freeze" or suppress responding in general. These response tendencies are seen as incompatible with the active response required by the avoidance task, with the result that avoidance behavior is disrupted.

The fact that in the present experiments no retention deficits were observed on the choice measures is not interpreted to mean that rats never forget anything. Clearly an appropriately selected combination of task difficulty and length of retest interval could be found which would be sensitive to memory loss. There is also little question that advancing age adversely affects learning processes in rats as it does in humans. For example, a recent experiment by Thompson and Fitzsimmons[17] used a four-unit maze to train rats on a brightness-discrimination task. They used Sprague-Dawley rats of the following ages: 3, 7, 12, 14 and 24.5 months. The subjects were required to choose the lighted exit on four consecutive two-choice discrimination units. The authors monitored whether a correct or incorrect choice was made, but not whether the rat avoided or escaped shock. Shock was presented if responding had not been initiated within 5 seconds of the start of a trial and anytime a remaining correct choice had not been made within 10 seconds of the previous choice. The subjects were run to criterion learning and retested for retention eight days later. These authors report a significant age-correlated increase in number of trials to criterion on both original learning and subsequent retention tests.

Although these findings were different from the outcome of our experiments, they are not necessarily conflicting. More likely, the four-unit maze is more sensitive than the Y-maze in detecting differences in associative learning since it is a more complex task. However, neither does this finding question the interpretation of the Y-maze data, since clearly different task demands require different capacities of an organism which are not necessarily affected equally by the aging process. For this reason we believe it is important to carefully describe age-related deficits as they relate to the specific environmental demands.

## REFERENCES

1. Stone C: The age factor in animal learning. I. Rats in the problem box and the maze. *Genetic Psychology Monographs* 5:1–130, 1929.
2. Stone C: The age factor in animal learning. II. Rats in a multiple light discrimination box and a difficult maze. *Genetic Psychology Monographs* 6:125–202, 1929.
3. Verzar-McDougall J: Studies in learning and memory in aging rats. *Gerontologia* 1:65–85, 1967.
4. Jerome EA: Age and learning-experimental studies, in Birren JE (ed): *Handbook of Aging and the Individual: Psychological and Biological Aspects.* Chicago, University of Chicago Press, 1959, pp 655–699.

5. Goodrick CL: Learning, retention and extinction of a complex maze habit for mature-young and senescent Wistar albino rats. *J Gerontol* 23:298–304, 1968.
6. Botwinick J, Brinley J, Robbin JS: Learning a position discrimination and position reversals by Sprague-Dawley rats of different ages. *J Gerontol* 17:315–319, 1962.
7. Botwinick J, Brinley J, Robbin JS: Learning and reversing a four-choice multiple Y-maze by rats of three ages. *J Gerontol* 18:279–282, 1963.
8. Goodrick CL: Behavioral rigidity as a mechanism for facilitation of problem solving for aged rats. *J Geronotol* 30:181–184, 1975.
9. Goodrick C: Maze learning of mature-young and aged rats as a function of distribution of practice. *J Exper Psychol* 98:344–349, 1973.
10. Goodrick C: Learning by mature-young and aged Wistar albino rats as a function of test complexity. *J Gerontol* 27:353–357, 1972.
11. Denenberg VH, Kline NJ: The relationship between age and avoidance learning in the hooded rat. *J Comp Physiol Psychol* 51:488–491, 1958.
12. Freund G, Walker D: The effect of aging on acquisition and retention of shuttle box avoidance in mice. *Life Sci* 10:1343–1349, 1971.
13. Doty BA: Age differences in avoidance conditioning as a function of distribution of trials and task difficulty. *J Genetic Psychol* 109:249–254, 1966.
14. Ray OS, Barrett RJ: Interaction of learning and memory with age in the rat. *Adv Behav Biol* 6:17–39, 1973.
15. Barrett RJ, Ray OS: Behavior in the open field, Lashley III maze, shuttle-box and Sidman avoidance as a function of strain, sex, and age. *Development Psychol* 3:73–77, 1970.
16. Garner WR, Hake HW, Erickson CW: Operationism and the concept of perception. *Psychol Rev* 63:149–159, 1956.
17. Thompson C, Fitzsimmons T: Age differences in aversively motivated visual discrimination learning and retentions in male Sprague-Dawley rats. *J Gerontol* 31:47–52, 1976.
18. Oliverio A, Bovet, D: Effects of age on maze learning and avoidance conditioning of mice. *Life Sciences* 5:1317–1324, 1966.

Psychopharmacology of Aging

# CHAPTER 4

# *A Synoptic View Of Pathophysiology And Experimental Pharmacology In Gerontological Brain Research*

W. MEIER-RUGE
P. GYGAX
N. WIERNSPERGER

Investigation of aging process is today one of the most challenging scientific tasks, which concerns us individually, but also, with the increasing number of retired elderly, constitutes an extraordinary challenge to human society. In this connection, aging of the brain has become a leading problem worldwide.

Two main aspects of aging must be considered:

1. Because of the postmitotic state of the neuronal cells, the brain is as old as the organism itself;
2. The brain is characterized by an extraordinarily high metabolic turnover, which makes this organ very sensitive to all kinds of disturbances of the metabolism or the oxygen supply. Therefore, aging of the brain is, at least in part, subject to secondary acceleration resulting from deteriorations due to disease and adverse environmental stimuli. A decline, however, in the high metabolic performance of the brain (either primary due to genetic expression, or secondary due to disease and/or environmental lesions) may disturb the complex balanced system of cholinergic stimulation and

catecholaminergic modulation, resulting in a series of psychomotor and endocrine disorders.

Independent of these pathophysiological aspects, problems of social life are of major consideration. With the increasing number of retired people, alterations in the social life of the elderly due to central nervous system disorders have attracted more and more interest, leading finally to a demand for effective pharmacological intervention in the aging process.

This situation gave rise to a series of questions on the part of experimental pharmacology:[1,2,3]

1. Which symptoms of aging should be treated?
2. What models are available to investigate drugs that act on symptoms of the aging process?
3. Do we want to increase life or only to compensate for the symptoms of aging?

Even today, there are more questions open than answers available. Attempts have been made to develop experimental pharmacological models and concepts to permit the development of new drugs that at least exert an effect on the symptoms of brain aging.

Aging is a complex change in function and structure. While morphological findings in the aging brain are purely descriptive, functional disorders are always a combined alteration in metabolic and physiological organ performance. These age-induced changes can be investigated on fairly different levels of the organization of the brain, extending from the molecular level up to the integrated organ. From the pharmacological point of view, only the drug effect in the integrated organ system is of final interest. This, however, presents experimental pharmacology with an extraordinarily complicated situation. Currently, models of hypoxic energy deprivation seem to offer an approach for investigations of this kind.[2,4,5,6,7,8]

This article will give a short survey of current knowledge of the aging process of the brain and will try to crystalize the essentials that are important for the development of experimental models. A series of pharmacological approaches in gerontological brain research will demonstrate the current situation in this field.

## CHARACTERISTICS OF THE CENTRAL NERVOUS SYSTEM AGING PROCESS

### Morphological Aspects of the Aging Brain

Since the early days of Virchow's "Cellular Pathology," age-dependent accumulation of lipofuscin in the perineurium of the nerve cells has been considered to be age-related.[9,10] For decades, opinions about its importance were controversial. Although its significance for the nerve-cell function is unknown, it is certain that lipofuscin increases with age.[11,12,13,14,15]

There is strong evidence that lipofuscin must be regarded as "ashes" of free radical reactions.[16] In this way, the quantity of lipofuscin seems to be an expression of the degree of minimal metabolic nerve-cell lesions. However, there is no possibility of determining the calendar age of the cell from the degree of lipofuscinosis. But all other histopathological alterations of the brain are also unspecific signs of the aging process, being only statistically correlated with the calendar age of the patient.

Recent results of morphometric studies of the brain cortex, the brain stem nuclei and the spinal cord have improved our knowledge of the nerve-cell loss in CNS aging. No correlation was found between senile dementia and nerve-cell loss in the brain cortex.[17]

We know today that only a moderate loss, approximately 25 percent, of the large neuronal cells in the brain cortex occurs with age. The large neuronal cells do not diminish in all cortical regions, and the loss is most pronounced in the temporo-parietal brain cortex.[17,18,19,20]

These findings have recently been confirmed in morphometric studies in brain cortex areas of aging rhesus monkeys (20 years), which revealed a significant decrease of the mean neuron packaging density in the fourth nerve-cell layer of the brain cortex area 3, and an increase of the glial cell density.[13]

The different cortical regions differ morphometrically with regard to age-related cell number. Most brain-stem nuclei show no changes in cell number with age—for example, facial nerve nucleus;[21] ventral cochlear nucleus;[22,23] abducens nucleus;[24] trochlear nerve nucleus.[25] Only the nucleus of the locus coeruleus shows a 25 percent decrease of nerve cells after 65 years of age,[20,25] and also in the dentate nucleus, the nerve-cell number decreases with age.[26,27]

The morphometric determination of the nerve-cell number of the main olivary nucleus in man is today controversial. Monagle and Brody[28] observed no significant alterations of the nerve-cell number, while Sandoz and Meier-Ruge[29] found a 20 percent decrease in the nerve cells between 20 and 50 years of age (Figure 4-1). In rats, the mitral cell volume of the olfactory bulb decreased significantly between 24 and 30 months of age.[30]

Far more interesting than a nerve-cell loss is an age-dependent loss of dendrites in the aged brain cortex, brain stem and spinal cord of man. This was observed mainly in the third pyramid cell layer of prefrontal and superior temporal brain cortex.[31,32]

This alteration is thought to be accompanied by a decrease of the total

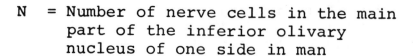

N = Number of nerve cells in the main part of the inferior olivary nucleus of one side in man

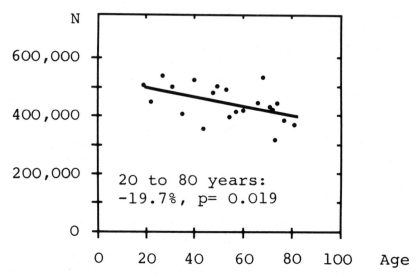

Figure 4-1: Age-related decrease of nerve cells from the human inferior olive.[29]

postsynaptic surface. But submicroscopic studies in the temporal and frontal cortex of normal and mentally defective brains showed no age-related changes in the number of neocortical synapses. On the contrary, in demented patients (n = 10), 13 percent more synapses were observed in comparison with normal brains of the same age.[33]

Similar findings were reported from aging rats (34 to 36 months). With increasing age, a decrease of the basal dendritic tree of the pyramidal cells (Layer V) was observed in the auditory cortex.[34] Another age-dependent characteristic is a loss of dendritic spines, which seems to be a continual process throughout the whole adult life of the rat and mouse.[35,36,37] In the dentate gyrus of 24-month-old Fisher rats, a 27 percent decrease in the number of synapses was observed.[38]

But the extracellular space in the gray matter of the brain also decreases. In aging rats a diminution of the extracellular space from 20.8 percent (3 months) to 9.6 percent (26 months) was observed.[39]

What general conclusion can be drawn from these morphological findings? In comparison with early adult life, aging develops only quantitative differences. This possibly reduces the functional reserve or redundancy of the brain.[40] The morphological data, however, provide no clearly defined experimental pathological approach.

## Neurochemical Characteristics of the Senescent CNS

During aging, imbalances in neurotransmitter synthesis and their metabolizing enzymes are possibly of greater importance for a functional decline of the aging brain than a decrease of any morphological parameter. Changes of enzymes of the energy metabolism may also be relevant for a reduced functional reserve of the senile brain.

To avoid any confusion, a clear distinction must be made between physiological aging and pathological aging. *Forms of pathological aging* are cerebrovascular insufficiency and organic brain syndrome with multiple infarct dementia, senile dementia, Alzheimer's disease and Pick's disease. In these diseases, aging is only a precondition of a pathological process which today is still not well understood, and is independent of normal symptoms of aging. This explains findings demonstrating that senile dementia as well as Alzheimer's disease are positively correlated with age, but decrease at ages over 75.[41]

In addition to alterations in physiological aging, senile dementia and Alzheimer's disease show a series of characteristic disturbances of metabolic turnover rates of the transmitters: Alzheimer's disease reveals a significant decrease of cholineacetyl transferase (CAT) as well as glutamic decarboxylase.[42,43,44,45]

Like Alzheimer's disease, senile dementia shows decreased CAT and glutamic decarboxylase.[42,43] Transmitter studies have demonstrated a significantly lowered level of noradrenaline, dopamine and homovanillic acid in different parts of the brain, particularly in the striatum.[46]

Huntington's chorea and Parkinson's disease are specific forms of pathological aging with focal brain disorders. This differentiates these diseases from Alzheimer's disease and senile dementia as well as from physiological aging. In Huntington's chorea, it is mainly glutamic decarboxylase that is decreased in the extrapyramidal structures, while cholinacetyl transferase activity is irregularly changed.[47,48,49] In the putamen and nucleus caudatus a significant decrease of phosphofructokinase was observed.[50] Parkinson's disease shows a significant decrease of tyrosine hydroxylase activity in substantia nigra and the striatum with a decrease in dopamine.[49,51,52] These observations of pathological aging processes are far from complete.

In contrast to the previously outlined findings, *physiological aging* seems to be characterized more by a decreased response to transmitters such as dopamine, serotonin, noradrenaline etc., or by a decreased hormonal response.[53,54,55] This decreased response may be caused by a decrease of DOPA decarboxylase, glutamic decarboxylase and tyrosine hydroxylase.[56,57]

The diminished turnover of catecholaminergic transmitters may be regarded in part as an age-dependent decline of the extracellular space. Bondareff et al.[58] demonstrated in aging rats that the intrastriatal extracellular transport of adrenaline is only half that observed in younger animals.

In mice, decreased dopamine level and catabolism in the striatum and a retarded catabolism of noradrenaline were observed in the hypothalamus.[59] Other observations were made in rhesus monkeys, showing an age-dependent decrease of noradrenaline and serotonin level in the brain,[60] but here the noradrenaline uptake was also decreased.[61] In aging rats a decrease of the serotonin-rate-limiting enzyme tryptophan hydroxylase was observed. The serotoninergic system seems to be more vulnerable than the cholinergic system.[62]

It is certain that monoamines are important modulators of cholinergic excitation in the brain. The decrease of excitation with age qualifies them as pacemakers of the aging process.[63,64] Age-induced alterations can be observed also with regard to *hypothalamic-pituitary-peripheral endocrine pathway*.[59,65,66] Not only the ovary function, together with menarche and

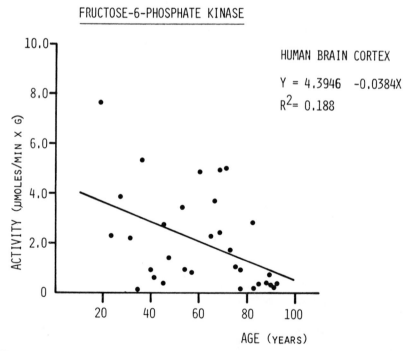

Figure 4-2:    Decrease of fructose-6-phosphate kinase in aged human brain cortex.[80]

menopause, is age-dependent and hypothalamus-controlled;[59,67,68,69] but also many other endocrine and autonomic phenomena.[64,70,71]

The decrease in transmitter response with age can also be observed at the level of second messenger regulation: the cAMP level in senescent rats (in which hormonal stimulation is carefully excluded) was observed to be four times lower than in younger animals.[72] The decreased cAMP level may be relevant to an increase of the phosphodiesterase activator potency due to aging.[73] Other investigators could not confirm this finding. They demonstrated an age-dependent decrease of low-$K_m$ phosphodiesterase and of the dopamine-sensitivity of adenylcyclase.[74] The last finding is consonant with the decreased dopamine response of the aging brain. A decrease of cAMP-stimulated proteinkinase with age[75,76,77] was observed in animal and human brains.

Similar phenomena, characteristic of the second messenger pathway and transmitter response at the synapses, are observed with enzymes that are important in energy-dependent processes. In this connection, in human-brain tissue an age-correlated increased ethanol inhibition of the membrane-bound synaptosomal $Na^+/K^+$-ATPase was shown.[78] This increase of ethanol sensitivity is an example of an age-induced decrease of adaptability of the brain to environmental stress.

The increased sensitivity of the brain to hypoxic energy deprivation with age may be at least partly caused by a decrease of phosphofructokinase activity.[76,79,80] The decline of this key enzyme of the glycolytic pathway might hinder the adaptive stimulation of the glycolytic turnover (Figure 4-2).

A considerable part of these different findings argues for a delayed cholinergic or endocrine modulation through a catecholaminergic response. These observations are also compatible with a diminished functional steady state of the brain, which is of relevance in adaptation to the environment.

## Functional Disturbances of the Brain due to Aging

Age-related EEG changes, disturbed memory and cognitive function are regarded as being correlated with decreased metabolic turnover in general and decreased synaptic performance in particular.[81,82] The decreases in catecholamine and choline turnover are particularly important for such functions. The negative correlation between age and EEG frequency was demonstrated in several EEG quantification studies. Aging is characterized by a continuous shift of the dominant alpha frequency to lower frequencies.[83,84,85,86,87,88]

Depletion of biogenic amines in the brain impairs memory formation. We have learned from animal studies that a decreased catecholamine synthesis, in particular of noradrenaline — e.g., due to antimetabolites such as puromycine, anisomycine, cycloheximide, etc. — causes a loss of memory.[89] In active and passive avoidance tests the inhibition of tyrosine hydroxylase and dopamine-beta-hydroxylase seems to be of significance in disturbing memory.[90,91] An age-related alteration of noradrenaline synthesis may therefore play an important role in the decline of cognitive function and memory.

Noradrenaline is at least as important for the hypothalamic control of the pituitary gland and its effects on other endocrine glands. In this respect, the hypothalamus has the function of a biologic clock.[59,65,66,70,92,93]

The decreased extent of adaptation to the environment was recently demonstrated in aging rats, which show a slow but permanent decline of oxygen consumption.[94] This finding was established by the observation that, after traumatic brain lesions, a significantly longer time is needed for reorganizing the disturbed brain function in aging rats than in young ones.[95]

Also, age-related adverse reactions to psychoactive drugs, caused by a decrease of dopaminergic activity (for example, Parkinsonism), are the consequence of a decreased reserve of the dopaminergic system of the brain.[63,65,96,97,98,99]

## WHICH FINDINGS ON THE PATHOGENESIS OF SYMPTOMS OF BRAIN AGING ARE USEFUL FOR THE DEVELOPMENT OF EXPERIMENTAL MODELS IN PHARMACOLOGY?

This question immediately provokes the counter-question: Is aging a disease? Of course, aging per se is not a disease entity, but a physiological phenomenon of normal life. Aging, however, is a process, as shown in the preceding pages, which decreases adaptation to environmental changes and reduces adequate response to environmental stimuli. Therefore, symptoms of adverse brain function develop (drug-induced Parkinsonism, etc.). This qualifies aging as a slow but continuous process of deviation from the situation of normal adult life,[94] disposing the organism to a series of pathological or adverse reactions to environmental changes.[93,95,100,101,102]

Discussion about the etiology of the aging process is today concentrated on the molecular level of cell mechanisms. It was strongly stimulated by the "error catastrophe theory" of Orgel[103,104] and Comfort.[105] Up to now, however, no convincing results could be presented in support of this heuristic theory. Holliday and Tarrant's observation[106] that aging fibroblasts in culture produce more faultily synthesized, heat-labile glucose-6-phosphate dehydrogenase and 6-phosphogluconate dehydrogenase[107,108] seemed to support this theory. The finding of a catalytic reduction of liver and muscle aldolase[109,110] as well as rat liver superoxide dismutase, nematode enolase and phosphoglycerate kinase,[111] with unchanged antigenic enzyme properties, argued against the error catastrophe theory and far more for a simple conformational change of the enzyme molecules. These findings were recently confirmed by the investigations of Rothstein.[112]

Normally, it might be thought that experimental pharmacology on aging is necessarily carried out in aging animals. This appears to be obvious, but experimental research with aging animals is limited to a few selected purposes. For routine pathophysiological and pharmacological work, aging animals are too expensive, the number of test animals is restricted, and the animal species are usually limited to rat and mouse.[1,2,3,71]

If we follow the mentioned disciplines involved in aging research (morphology, biochemistry and physiology), no direct experimental neuroanatomical or neuropathological approach using techniques of morphological research is available. Only in Parkinson's disease does neurochemistry offer a pharmacological approach correlated with this phenomenom of aging.

Experimental pharmacology of age-induced cerebrovascular insufficiency, transient ischemic attacks and mild symptoms of senility is mainly carried out with models of hypoxic energy deprivation of the brain.

## The Neurochemical Approach in Experimental Pharmacology of Gerontological Brain Research

Psychopharmacological treatment in geriatric medicine is today a well-established therapy.[113,114,115,116,117,118,119,120] The link between pharmacology and clinical treatment in psychiatry is extraordinarily close. It is in fact a question of definition: what is a psychiatric disease in itself, what is a latent psychiatric disease aggravated by the aging process of the brain, and what is a brain disease exclusively due to aging. This may always be an inherent problem in psychogeriatric diagnosis and therapy. At least in part, the situation in neurological aging diseases is simpler.

In Parkinson's disease, for instance, animal models with a clear neuropharmacological concept have been developed. The first important step was the finding of a decreased striatal dopamine level in Parkinson's disease.[49,51,52,121] It was postulated from these observations that the symptoms of this particular disease—rigidity, tremor and hypokinesia—

are associated with a loss of dopaminergic transmitter function. A unilateral degeneration of the dopaminergic nigrostriatal pathway by electrocoagulation[122,123] or intracerebral unilateral injection of 6-hydroxydopamine into the substantia nigra[124] causes a characteristic experimental disease, which can be used for testing drugs with dopaminergic activity. The degeneration of dopaminergic and noradrenergic neurons in the striatum causes a rotation of the animal. The supersensitive receptors of the lesioned side respond strongly to stimulation by dopaminergic agonists, causing contralateral rotations.[124,125]

Anden and coworkers[123] were the first to observe the dopaminergic effect of apomorphine and its blockade by haloperidol. A series of dopaminergic ergot compounds were studied in animals.[126] In monkeys, involuntary movements and tremor due to unilateral electrolyte-induced tegmental lesion can be effectively blocked by L-dopa.[127] More selective dopaminelike actions, different from the action of bromocriptine or levodopa, were demonstrated with a new nonpeptide ergoline derivate [a 9-10-Didehydro-6-methyl-8-beta-(2-pyridylthiomethyl)-ergoline].[128] Another dopaminergic ergoline derivate is lergotrile, which effectively inhibits prolactin release from the pituitary gland,[129,130] an effect also exerted by bromocriptine.[131,132,133] The dopaminergic effects of Hydergine (co-dergocrine) were qualified as moderate and short-lasting,[68,134] while bromocriptine has a long-lasting effect.[135]

The excellent correlation between these experimental-animal observations and clinical findings[136,137,138,139,140,141,142,143,144,145] confirmed the reliability of this model for the development of anti-Parkinsonism drugs, except for the fact that the animal model shows no symptoms characteristic of Parkinsonism.

This kind of neuropharmacological approach for the development of dopaminergic drugs is at present the one most used in the experimental pharmacology. For the other age-induced diseases of the brain, which have serious consequences for the patient as well as the community, such as pseudobulbar paralysis, Korsakow syndrome, Huntington's chorea, Alzheimer's disease and senile dementia, neither suitable animal models[146,147] nor an unambiguous pathogenesis is available.

**Neurophysiological Aspects of the Development of Experimental Models**

From the neurophysiological point of view, some interesting concepts were developed for testing pharmacological compounds, which are active in the treatment of cerebrovascular insufficiency, transient ischemic brain lesions and also diffuse symptoms of a mild deficit syndrome due to the normal aging process of the brain.[2,3]

It is obviously difficult to reproduce in an animal model the aging process in its multivarious forms. There are, however, symptoms of the aging process that can be simulated experimentally, if we accept that, generally speaking, the aging process is characterized by a decline of postsynaptic neuronal response as well as a decrease of adaptation of brain function to adverse environmental stimuli. It is certain that none of the animal models used today reproduces absolutely the complex aging situation of the brain. In this connection, hypoxic energy deprivation is an efficient way to disturb the adaptability of brain function to environmental stress.

Hypoxic energy deprivation has some features in common with aging, in particular with cerebral vascular insufficiency, transient ischemic attack and stroke. The great advantage of this model is its excellently reproducible regulation, extending from reversible up to irreversible lesions.[31,148] The most sensitive transmitters in the aging brain are serotonin, noradrenalin and dopamine.[54,55,58] Noradrenalin in particular is a highly excitable transmitter released immediately by stress or a moderate ischemic energy deprivation.[149,150,151,152]

In the near future, it will be possible to make (by the use of the microanalytical technique of mass-fragmentography) routine determinations of these transmitter metabolites in the cerebrospinal fluid.[153] The noradrenalin level and its interaction with dopamine seems to be critical for memory formation.[89,91,154,155] A disturbed neurotransmitter balance as characteristic of aging[49,56,57] is also observed under stress.[156,157]

These findings demonstrate a series of parallels between aging and hypoxic energy deprivation of the brain. They are of interest for testing drugs which are effective in treating these kinds of impairments, which are also typical of aging.

The study of transmitters, released in the cerebrospinal fluid by ischemic hypoxia, recently opened up a completely new perspective for the study of pathological transmitter release in man.[151,153,158,159,160] Today, many results on the metabolic consequences of a hypoxic energy deprivation of the brain due to anoxia, hypoxia or ischemia are available.[148,158,161,162,163,164,165] These studies improved our knowledge of the pathogenesis of cerebrovascular insufficiency, transient ischemic attack and stroke, but informed us also about the pathophysiology of such age-dependent diseases of the brain.

EXPERIMENTAL PATHOPHYSIOLOGY AND PHARMACOLOGY OF
HYPOXIC ENERGY DEPRIVATION IN THE CENTRAL NERVOUS
SYSTEM

The normal human brain, comprising only about 2 percent of the total
body weight, accounts for approximately 15 percent of the resting cardiac
output. This high rate of blood flow is required to support a comparably
high metabolic rate. Nowadays, it is generally accepted that cerebrovascular insufficiency, which leads to instability of brain circulation,[166,167] may be
at least one of the causes of senile decline in human-brain activity. This
observation, among others, has in recent years directed increasing
attention to the pathophysiology of hypoxic energy deprivation in the
brain.

The correlation of neurotransmitter function and cerebral energy
production,[153] the recovery of neuronal function after brain ischemia,[168,169,170] metabolic changes of the brain tissue due to hypoxia,[163,171,172]
and the correlation of cerebral blood flow and EEG activity[173,174,175] were
some of the most important topics in this field. Today, a great number of
models of hypoxic energy deprivation can be found in modern
pharmacological literature.[3,164]

*Temporary cerebral ischemia* represents an optimal reproducible experimental model inducing an acute energy deprivation of the central nervous
system, suitable for pharmacological studies. We used the isolated
perfused cat head[176,177] as described in 1975.[178] This model excludes effects
from other organs which are especially susceptible to ischemic conditions,
such as pituitary and suprarenal gland, heart, kidney, etc.

Biphasic ischemia in the cat brain causes a disturbance in electrical
brain activity and increases the lactate production in the brain. This
functional disturbance was improved by co-dergocrine mesylate and DH-
ergonine. The quantitative EEG evaluation demonstrated that biphasic
temporary ischemia affects chiefly the EEG alpha and beta frequency
ranges.[178,179,180] The decrease in lactate formation induced by co-dergocrine
mesylate, which indicates a decreased anaerobic metabolism, correlated
well with a significant increase in EEG activity. Similar results obtained
with DH-ergonine demonstrated that this ergot compound is about ten
times more effective than co-dergocrine mesylate (Hydergine[R]).

From the clinical point of view, the extraction of some practical
consequences from these findings seems a complicated matter. The link
between findings in animal experiments and clinical trials could be the
EEG. A fairly clear way to visualize a therapeutic drug effect on brain
lesion due to cerebral vascular insufficiency is by perspective visualization
of consecutive EEG energy plots in three dimensions. In this way, the

# Three - dimensional display of EEG - energy

## Ischaemia – experiment without DH-ergotoxine

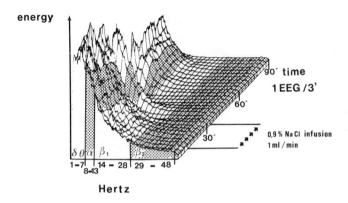

## Ischaemia – experiment with DH-ergotoxine

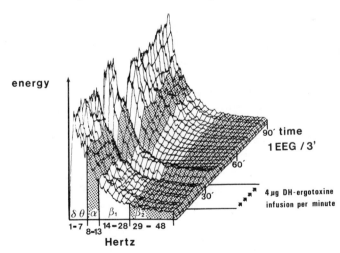

Figure 4-3: Three-dimensional representation of EEG recordings calculated every three minutes throughout the biphasic ischemic experiments in isolated perfused cat brain.[178]

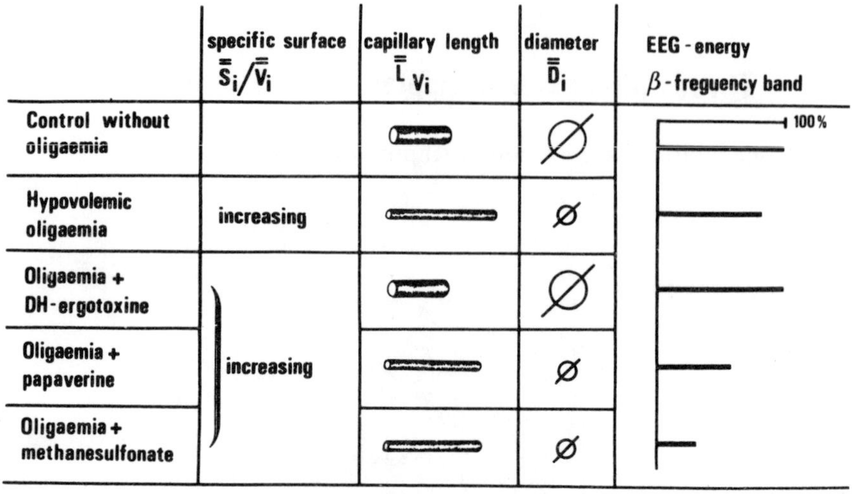

| | specific surface $\bar{S}_i/\bar{V}_i$ | capillary length $\bar{L}_{V_i}$ | diameter $\bar{D}_i$ | EEG - energy $\beta$ - frequency band |
|---|---|---|---|---|
| Control without oligaemia | | | | 100% |
| Hypovolemic oligaemia | increasing | | | |
| Oligaemia + DH-ergotoxine | increasing | | | |
| Oligaemia + papaverine | increasing | | | |
| Oligaemia + methanesulfonate | increasing | | | |

Figure 4-4: Schematic representation of morphometric parameters of the capillary network and EEG-energy under the influence of hypovolemic oligemia. Treatment with DH-ergotoxine, (co-dergocrine) papaverine and methanesulfonate shows that vasodilating compounds as papaverine or methane-sulfonate improve neither any capillary parameter nor EEG-activity.

EEG frequencies from 0 to 48 Hz are plotted in the third dimension. Figure 4-3 shows consecutive EEG energy plots computed every 3 to 6 minutes in the course of an animal experiment with and without co-dergocrine mesylate infusion. Such a perspective visualization of weekly EEG recordings, covering a period of several months, would provide the physician with an objective record of the effects of a drug therapy.

After these isolated brain perfusion studies we tried, in a second series of experiments using the *model of hypovolemic oligemia,* to show whether co-dergocrine mesylate has analogue effects on hypoxic energy deprivation in the whole animal model.

As already shown by Gygax et al.,[181,182] a 30 to 40 percent decrease of cerebral blood flow by blood-letting and subsequent lowering of blood pressure to 45mm Hg causes an initial EEG activation. This effect is due to a hypoxic transmitter release.[153,175] It is followed by progressive EEG depression.[173,182] This symptomatology has parallels in cerebrovascular insufficiency.

The particular pharmacological problems arising with vasodilators were recently discussed in a survey by Hauth and Richardson.[183] Experimental investigations by Hunziker and coworkers[184] on the effect of vasoactive drugs (papaverine) on brain activity, under condition of decreased microcirculation due to hypovolemic oligemia, have demonstrated that no

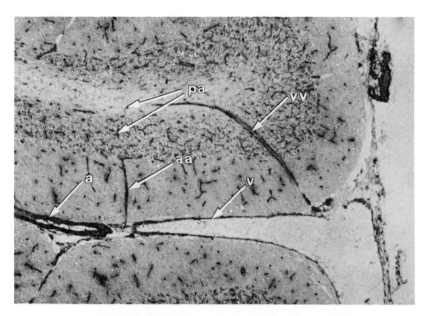

Figure 4-5: Arteriovenous shunt circulation in the cerebellum cortex caused by a vasoactive therapy with papaverine. Dilatation mainly of the venous vessels can be observed. Enzyme histochemical staining of muscle containing vessels by ATPase reaction (hemalum counterstaining). (a = leptomeningeal artery; aa = intracerebral arteries; vv = intracerebral venous vessel; v = leptomeningeal venous vessel magnif. x 58).

positive effects on EEG activity can be registered. However, under identical oligemic conditions, co-dergocrine mesylate maintained the EEG energy at a constant level (Figure 4-4). Papaverine, by increasing flow rate in the muscle-containing vessels, may induce a steal phenomenon in the capillaries, which contain no muscular elements (Figure 4-5). As shown in correlating morphometric investigations, the capillary diameter is dilated secondarily as a result of the changed blood flow and the changed metabolism of the brain tissue.[184,185]

Several authors have pointed out that, under hypoxic conditions, catecholamines are involved in the impairment of cerebral metabolic activity.[151,175,186] Since other substances which influence catecholamine turnover, such as phenoxybenzamine (alpha-blocker),[186] or barbiturates (catecholamine release),[185,187] also protect the brain against hypovolemic oligemia, it can be concluded from these experiments that the protection induced is in part due to their regulating effect on the CNS catecholamines.

Kovach and Sandor[175] demonstrated that a hypoxia-induced hyperactivity of the sympathetic system increases cerebral oxygen consumption.

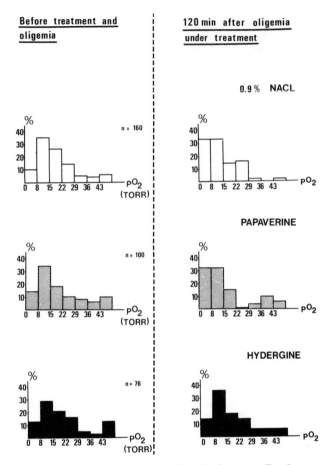

Figure 4-6:   pO$_2$ microelectrode measurements in cat brain cortex. The figure shows left
the pO$_2$ values under normotensive conditions. Right pO$_2$ values are demonstrated 120
minutes after onset of hypovolemic oligemia and 80 minutes after drug infusion.
Hypovolemic oligemia increases the incidence of low-pO$_2$ values (0–15 mm Hg pO$_2$), which
cannot be influenced by papaverine. Administration of co-dergocrine mesylate
(HYDERGINE[R]) returns pO$_2$ distribution to the initial values of the normotensive state.

Our correlating studies of EEG activity and cortical pO$_2$ demonstrated that
papaverine treatment (1mg/kg i.v.) shifts the regional cerebral blood flow to
normal values, but without improving effects on either EEG activity or
pO$_2$ distribution (Figure 4-6). The pO$_2$ histogram is dissociated into two
groups of lower and higher values, indicating the presence of uneven
perfusion in the cortical tissue. In contrast to papaverine, co-dergocrine
mesylate (0.08mg/kg i.v.) improves the cortical O$_2$ supply, returning it to
preshock conditions.[182,188] These pO$_2$ values confirm the above mentioned

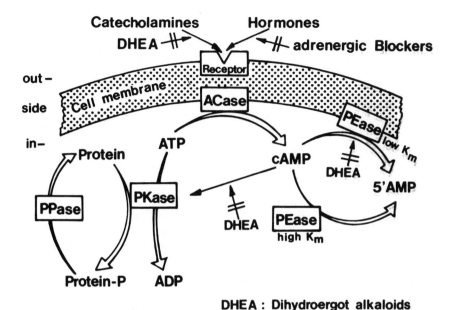

DHEA : Dihydroergot alkaloids

Figure 4-7: Schematic representation of the normalizing effect co-dergocrine mesylate (DHEA) on noradrenaline activated adenylcyclase and the inhibition of low-$K_m$ phosphodiesterase regulating basal neuronal activity.

morphometric measurements of the network of brain capillaries by Hunziker et al.[184] The pathophysiologic changes in the capillary parameters, caused by alteration of the microenvironment of the capillary bed, are restored to normal dimensions by co-dergocrine.

These pathophysiological studies have shown that co-dergocrine mesylate, as well as DH-ergonine, mitigates the deleterious effects of hypoxic energy deprivation in the brain.

Biochemical in vitro studies demonstrated that DH-ergot alkaloids require minimal threshold concentrations for interactions with enzymatic reactions as well as with specific receptor molecules.[126,189,190,191] From these investigations arose the question of the tissue level of the DH-ergot alkaloids, in particular of co-derocrine mesylate, to be expected in vivo. Distribution studies on co-dergocrine mesylate and DH-ergonine were therefore performed.

Autoradiographic and gradient centrifugation studies with $^3$H-co-dergocrine mesylate have demonstrated that this compound is accumulated at neuronal cells. Gradient centrifugation studies finally proved that 60 percent of co-dergocrine mesylate is accumulated at the synaptosomes.[192] After i.v. application of $^3$H-co-dergocrine this ergot compound attains very rapidly a maximal brain level. As shown by Iwangoff et al.,[193] DH-ergonine tissue level declines more slowly in the brain than in visceral organs. Repeated applications of DH-ergonine increase the retention of radioactivity in the brain.

These distribution studies show that a tissue level of co-dergocrine mesylate and of DH-ergonine is attained, which may possibly be related to the observed improvement of EEG activity and metabolic economy that has been disturbed by energy deprivation.

We believe that the ameliorative effect of co-dergocrine mesylate is due not to increased metabolism but to an improved metabolic economy of the brain tissue:[185,189,194,195]

1. Reduction of a catecholamine-enhanced ATP turnover.[196,197]
2. Decrease of catecholamine-activated cAMP adenylcyclase.[189,190,191]
3. Brain-specific inhibition of low-$K_m$ phosphodiesterase.[189,198]

These actions of co-dergocrine mesylate manifest themselves as a normalization of a norepinephrine-or stress-induced rise in ATP turnover as well as an improvement of the neuronal cAMP level through regulation of the synthesizing and degrading enzymes. The latter is an inhibitory alpha-receptor action.

Loew et al.,[134,135] Goldstein et al.[199] and Clemens and Fuller[68] have demonstrated that co-dergocrine mesylate also has a moderate dopaminergic effect. The mixed agonistic (dopaminergic) antagonistic (alpha-receptor inhibition) action of co-dergocrine balances the activity state of the receptors in such a way that therapeutic efficacy is achieved without major side effects.[199]

The counteraction by co-dergocrine mesylate of the antinociceptive effects of morphine is also interpreted as a dopaminergic activity.[134] The effectiveness of co-dergocrine mesylate at the receptor has been shown neurochemically.[189,190,191,199] Tissue culture studies by Gahwiler[200] have also demonstrated that co-dergocrine acts directly on the neurotransmission, synchronizing irregular spontaneous neuronal firing and at the same time increasing the amplitude of the action potential. The influence of co-dergocrine mesylate on the receptor and the energy-rich system modulates the synaptic transmission of the neuronal cell (Figure 4-7).

As a result of this mechanism of action, the alpha- and beta-frequencies of the cat brain, which are most sensitive to energy deprivation, are greatly improved.[178,185] This may be a link to clinical findings that demonstrate, in addition to an improvement of psychological variables, an increase of EEG energy particularly in the alpha-frequency range;[201,202,203] and in psychomotoric activity.[204,205,206,207,208,209] Another link between clinical data on psychomotor activity and pharmacological results may be the observation of Loew et al.[134] and Carruthers-Jones et al.,[210] who demonstrated a prolonging of wakefulness accompanied by increased EEG energy in rats treated with co-dergocrine mesylate.

Arrigo et al.[202] observed in a placebo-controlled double-blind study with co-dergocrine mesylate (Hydergine⁻R) an increase of EEG activity and a corresponding improvement of symptoms of senility. It has been shown that the beneficial effects of co-dergocrine mesylate in clinical studies are most probably the result of a drug action on neuronal cell function and not of a vasodilator effect.[117,211,212]

## FURTHER TENDENCIES IN EXPERIMENTAL PHARMACOLOGY OF GERONTOLOGICAL BRAIN RESEARCH

During recent years a series of new compounds for the treatment of CNS aging has been investigated and partly compared with co-dergocrine mesylate. Besides dihydroergonine and bromocriptine, which have already been mentioned, vincamine, piracetam and nicergoline, among others, were of major interest in experimental pharmacology.

Vincamine proved to have protective effects against cerebral ischemia in cats similar to those of co-dergocrine mesylate (Hydergine⁻R) and pyritinol.[213] In other investigations, vincamine (5mg/kg i.v.) and co-dergocrine mesylate (0.3 and 0.6mg/kg i.v.) decreased the time for the reappearance after repeated 2-minute ischemic periods of an evoked response in the pyramidal tract to ipsilateral motor cortex stimulation.[214,215] The protective action of vincamine against hypoxic brain lesions was demonstrated in rats with hypoxic amnesia; similar effects were observed with co-dergocrine piracetam, and other compounds.[7] The clinical data also present many results similar to those for co-dergocrine. With the aid of rating scales and psychometric tests, an improvement of memory and attention was determined.[216]

Piracetam, a 2-oxo-1-pyrrolidinyl-2-antamide with the promising designation "nootropic agent," is another compound considered to have an effect on symptoms of senility. The first pharmacological investigations referring to the psychotropic activity of piracetam were not very encouraging.[217] Other investigations, however, demonstrated in a multitrial learning test that this compound facilitates learning in aging rats, as well as in rats with hypoxic brain lesions.[218,219] In curarized cats piracetam increased the cortical response at electrical stimulation of the gyrus supersylvianus.[220] A survey of the piracetam psychopharmacology was given by Giurgea in 1972.

In biochemical studies, it was shown that piracetam enhances protein metabolism: it was observed that piracetam increases the total protein content of the lysosomal fraction in brain and liver from young as well as old rats.[221] These findings were in accordance with data which report an increase in the relation of polyribosomes/ribosomes by piracetam in comparison to the decreased relation in the aging rat brain.[222,223] Application of 100mg piracetam/kg resulted in a significant decrease of lysosomal brain enzymes (bound beta-glucuronidase, beta-acetylglucoseaminidase, cathepsin D) in aging rats.[221] The protection against hypoxic amnesia in rats afforded by piracetam was similar to that offered by vincamine.[7] The clinical trials available demonstrate beneficial effects in patients with head injuries,[224] chronic alcoholism[225] and psychoorganic brain syndrome.[226,227,228] In a double-blind study with 196 geriatric patients, treated with high doses of piracetam (2.4g/day), Stegnik[226] observed improvements in alertness and psychomotor behavior.

Nicergoline, a nonhydrogenated ergot alkaloid, proved to have central nervous effects similar to those of co-dergocrine mesylate and dihydroergonine. Since 1970 nicergoline has been studied in a series of pharmacological experiments. Measurements of cortical blood flow and some basic metabolic parameters in the brains of cats and pigs were inconclusive. No correlation was found between cortical blood flow on the one hand, and cortical $pCO_2$ and pH on the other.[229,230]

In cats an improvement of asphyxia-depressed EEG activity was shown.[231] In curarized dogs with hypovolemic hypotension, nicergoline caused a decrease in the lactate/pyruvate ratio and an increase of the energy charge potential.[4,5] In cats nicergoline (150$\mu$g/kg, i.v.) caused shortening of the EEG recovery time after temporary ischemia[232] and the return of cortical evoked potentials to normal values.[6]

Neurochemical studies in dogs demonstrated that nicergoline increases significantly the posthypoxic recovery of adenylcyclase activity and cAMP content of the brain.[233] In rat brain cortex slices nicergoline caused an increase of adenylcyclase activity.[234] In the same rat experiments an inhibition of cAMP phosphodiesterase was seen.[234] The prevention of an ischemic increase of free fatty acids by nicergoline (150$\mu$g/kg cat) tends in the same direction.[232]

It is obvious that experimental pharmacology in gerontological research is in the beginning stages. During recent years an increasing interest in the neuropharmacology of ergot alkaloids has developed. This interest is mainly linked to the interaction of ergot alkaloids with biogenic amines of the brain,[126,134,235,236] its specific actions on the brain stem[128,237,238,239,240] and its beneficial effects on hypoxic energy deprivation of the brain.[182,184,185,189]

Further pharmacological studies are an imperative necessity to increase our knowledge of the experimental pharmacology of gerontological brain research and to provide us with new, efficient drugs for pharmacological intervention against symptoms of the aging process.

## SUMMARY

A survey is given of the pathophysiological aspects of brain aging and its consequences in experimental pharmacology. Current knowledge of the aging process of the brain in neuroanatomy, neurochemistry and pathophysiology is considered.

Today, no morphological criterion which would permit a determination of brain age exists. In comparison with early adult life, aging develops in first-line quantitative differences. From the neurochemical point of view, imbalances in neurotransmitters and their enzymes as well as of enzymes of the energy metabolism may reduce the adaptability of the aging brain to metabolic stress. These alterations may be accompanied by a decline of adaptation to the environment. Age-related adverse reactions to psychoactive drugs, causing parkinsonism, are relevant to a decreased homeostasis of the dopaminergic system.

Consideration is given to the question: Which findings on the pathogenesis of aging symptoms may be useful in the development of models in experimental pharmacology?

Pharmacological intervention in the aging process is normally thought to be carried out in aging animals. Pathophysiological and pharmacological investigations with aging animals, however, are limited to a few selected experiments, owing to the restricted number of aging animals, high costs and limitation to rats and mice.

In Parkinson's disease, which is a pathological form of an aging disease of the brain, clear neuropharmacological models have been developed in recent years.

In experimental pharmacology of cerebrovascular insufficiency, transient ischemic attacks and the deficit syndrome in the normal aging process of the brain, models of hypoxic energy deprivation can be used. Despite the fact that the model of hypoxic energy deprivation simulates only some symptoms of the aging process, such as decline of postsynaptic neuronal response and decreased adaptation of brain function to environmental adverse stimuli; these experiments are beneficial for the better understanding of selective parameters of the pathogenesis of the aging process.

Neurotransmitter turnover is particularly sensitive to hypoxia. It is shown that acute energy deprivation in the brain, due to hypoxia, simulates symptoms typical of cerebral vascular insufficiency and of senility of the brain. Dihydrogenated ergot alkaloids such as co-dergocrine mesylate or DH-ergonine are compounds which mitigate significantly the deleterious effects of hypoxic energy deprivation in the brain, increasing EEG energy and lowering lactate production. These actions are regarded as the effects of a normalization of a norepinephrine- or stress-induced rise in energy consumption, and a normalization of the neural cAMP level, through regulation of the cAMP synthesizing adenylcyclase and the degrading low-$K_m$ phosphodiesterase.

It is shown that co-dergocrine mesylate (Hydergine$^{-R}$) has beneficial effects on neuronal cell function. Experimental as well as clinical data provide a good scientific basis for the use of this compound in the pharmacotherapy of mental symptoms of aging.

In the last section, new tendencies in experimental pharmacology in gerontological brain research are outlined. In particular, piracetam, vincamine and nicergoline are compounds that have recently attracted increasing interest in the field of pharmacological intervention in the aging process. Today, our knowledge of drug mechanisms in the treatment of central nervous symptoms of aging is limited.

The study of hypoxic energy deprivation of the brain has increased our understanding of experimental pharmacological intervention in the aging process of the brain. We need further studies to develop more reasonable models, which will finally correlate better with the complex mechanisms of the disturbed adaptability of the aging brain to adverse environmental stimuli.

## REFERENCES

1. Kormendy CG: Ageing: Can research do something about it? Pharmaceutical implications, in Platt D (ed) *Altern.* Stuttgart-New York, Schattauer-Verlag, 1974, pp 115–126.
2. Meier-Ruge W: Experimental pathology and pharmacology in brain research and aging. *Life Sci* 17:1627–1636, 1975.
3. Mitruka BM, Rawnsley HM, Vadehra DV: Animals for medical research, in *Animal Models in Gerontology.* New York, J Wiley & Sons, 1976, pp 425–431.
4. Benzi G, Arrigoni E, Manzo L, De Bernardi M, Ferrara A, Panceri P, Berte F: Estimation of changes induced by drugs in cerebral energy-coupling processes in situ in the dog. *J Pharm Sci* 62:758–764, 1973.
5. Benzi G: An analysis of the drug acting on cerebral energy metabolism. *Jap J Pharmacol* 25:251–261, 1975.
6. Boismare F, Lorenzo J: Study of the protection afforded by nicergoline against the effects of cerebral ischemia in the cat. *Arzneimittel-Forsch* 25:410–413, 1975.
7. Gouret C, Raynaud G: Utilisation du test de la boite a deux compartiments pour la recherche de substances protegeant le rat contre l'amnesie par hypoxie. *J Pharmacol* 7:161–175, 1976.

8. Meier-Ruge W, Reichlmeier K, Iwangoff P: Enzymatic and enzyme histochemical changes of the aging animal brain and consequences for experimental pharmacology on aging, in Terry RD, Gershon S (eds): *Neurobiology of Aging*. New York, Raven Press, 1976, pp 379–387.
9. Muhlmann M. *Ueber Hirnpigmente*. Inaug Diss Univ Berlin, 1892.
10. Muhlmann M: *Das Altern und der physiologische Tod G*. Fischer, Jena, 1910.
11. Mann DMA, Yates PO: Lipoprotein pigments—their relationship to ageing in the human nervous system. I. The lipofuscin content of nerve cells. *Brain* 97:481–488, 1974.
12. Siakotus AN, Armstrong D: Age-pigment: A biochemical indicator of intracellular aging, in Ordy JM, Brizzee KR (eds): *Neurobiology of Aging*. New York, Plenum Press, 1975, pp 369–399.
13. Brizzee KR, Ordy JM, Hansche J, Kaack B: Quantitative assessment of changes in neuron and glial cell packing density and lipofuscin accumulation with age in the cerebral cortex of a nonhuman primate (Macaca Mulatta), in Terry RD, Gershon S (eds): *Neurobiology of Aging*. New York, Raven Press, 1976, pp 229–244.
14. Strehler BL: Introduction: Aging and the human brain, in Terry RD, Gershon S (eds): *Neurobiology of Aging*. New York, Raven Press, 1976, pp 1–22.
15. Nandy K, Schneider H: Lipofuscin pigment formation in neuroblastoma cells in culture, in Terry RD, Gershon S (eds): *Neurobiology of Aging*. New York, Raven Press, 1976, pp 245–264.
16. Tappel AL: Protection against free radical lipid peroxidation reactions, in Roberts J, Adelman RC, Cristofalo VJ (eds): *Pharmacological Intervention in the Aging Process*. New York, Plenum Press, 1978, pp 111–131.
17. Tomlinson BE, Henderson G: Some quantitative cerebral findings in normal and demented old people, in Terry RD, Gershon S (eds): *Neurobiology of Aging*. New York, Raven Press, 1976, pp 183–204.
18. Brody H: Aging of the vertebrate brain, in Rockstein M, Sussman ML (eds): *Development and Aging in the Nervous System*. New York, Academic Press, 1973, pp 121–133.
19. Shefer VF: Absolute number of neurons and thickness of cerebral cortex during aging, senile and vascular dementia, in Pick's and Alzheimer's Disease. *Neurosci Behav Physiol* 6:319–324, 1973.
20. Brody H: An examination of cerebral cortex and brain stem aging, in Terry RD, Gershon S (eds): *Neurobiology of Aging*. New York, Raven Press, 1976, pp 117–181.
21. Van Buskirk C: The seventh nerve complex. *J Com Neurol* 82:303–333, 1945.
22. Konigsmark BW, Murphy EA: Neuronal populations in the human brain. *Nature* 228:1335, 1970.
23. Konigsmark BW, Murphy EA: Volume of ventral cochlear nucleus in man: Its relationship to neuronal population and age. *J Neuropathol Exp Neurol* 31:304–316, 1972.
24. Vijayashankar N, Brody H: Neuronal population of the human abducens nucleus. *Anat Rec* 169:447, 1971.
25. Vijayashankar N, Brody H: The neuronal population of the nuclei of the trochlear nerve and the locus coeruleus in the human. *Anat Rec* 172:421–422, 1973.
26. Treff WM, Fix JD: Ueber Korrelationen zwischen der Neokorticalisation und den Struktur-sowie Zellparametern des nucleus lateralis sive dentatus im Kleinhirn der Primaten. *Acta Anat* 86:325–352, 1973.
27. Treff WM: Das Involutionsmuster des nucleus dentatus cerebelli: Eine morphometrische Analyse, in Platt D (ed): *Altern*. Stuttgart, Schattauer FK, 1974, pp 37–54.
28. Monagle RD, Brody H: The effect of age upon the main nucleus of the inferior olive in the human brain. *J Comp Neurol* 155:61–66, 1974.

29. Sandoz P, Meier-Ruge W: Age-related loss of nerve cells from the human inferior olive, and unchanged volume of its gray matter. *IRCS Medical Science* 5:376, 1977.

30. Hinds JW, McNelly NA: Aging of the rat olfactory bulb: Growth and atrophy of constituent layers and changes in size and number of mitral cells. *J Comp Neurol* 171:345-368, 1977.

31. Schneider H, Ballowitz L, Schachinger H, Hanefeld F, Droszus JU: Anoxic encephalopathy with predominant involvement of basal ganglia, brain stem and spinal cord in the perinatal period. *Acta Neuropath* 32:287-298, 1975.

32. Scheibel MB, Scheibel AB: Structural changes in the aging brain, in Brody H, Harman D, Ordy JM (eds): *Alzheimer's Disease: Dementia and Related Disorders.* New York, Raven Press, 1975, pp 11-37.

33. Cragg BG: The density of synpases and neurons in normal, mental defective and aging human brains. *Brain* 98:81-90, 1975.

34. Vaughan DW: Age-related deterioration of pyramidal cell basal dendrites in rat auditory cortex. *J Comp Neurol* 171:501-516, 1977.

35. Feldman ML, Dowd C: Loss of dendritic spines in aging cerebral cortex. *Anat Embryol* 148:279-301, 1975.

36. Feldman ML: Aging changes in the morphology of cortical dendrites, in Terry RD, Gershon S (eds): *Neurobiology of Aging.* New York, Raven Press, 1976, pp 211-227.

37. Machado-Salas J, Scheibel ME, Scheibel AB: Neuronal changes in the aging mouse: Spinal cord and lower brain stem. *Exp Neurol* 54:504-512, 1977.

38. Bondareff W, Geinisman Y: Loss of synapses in the dentate gyrus of the senescent rat. *Am J Anat* 145:129-136, 1976.

39. Bondareff W, Narotzky R: Age-changes in the neuronal microenvironment. *Science* 176:1135-1136, 1972.

40. Strehler BL: Molecular and systemic aspects of brain aging: Psychobiology of informational redundancy, in Terry RD, Gershon S (eds): *Neurobiology of Aging.* New York, Raven Press, 1976, pp 281-311.

41. Krauss B, Sabunca N: Klinisch-morphologische Vergleichsuntersuchungen bei zerebralen Alterskrankheiten. *Akt Geront* 4:463-469, 1974.

42. Bowen DM, Smith CB, White P, Davison AN: Neurotransmitter-related enzymes and indices of hypoxia in senile dementia and other abiotrophies. *Brain Res* 99:459-496, 1976.

43. Bowen DM, Smith CB, White P, Davison AN: Senile dementia and related abiotrophies: Biochemical studies on histologically evaluated human postmortem specimens, in Terry RD, Gershon S (eds): *Neurobiology of Aging.* New York, Raven Press, 1976, pp 361-378.

44. Davies P, Maloney AJF: Selective loss of central cholinergic neurons in Alzheimer's Disease. *Lancet,* I: 1403, 1976.

45. Perry EK, Perry RH, Blessed G, Thomlinson BE: Necropsy evidence of central cholinergic deficits in senile dementia. *Lancet* 189, 1977.

46. Gottfries CG, Roos BE, Winblad B: Monoamine and monoamine metabolites in the human brain post-mortem in senile dementia. *Akt Geront* 6:429-435, 1976.

47. Bird ED, MacKay AVP, Rayner CN, Iversen LL: Reduced glutamic-acid decarboxylase activity of post-mortem brain in Huntington's chorea. *Lancet* 1:1090-1092, 1973.

48. Perry TL, Hansen S, Kloster M: Huntington's chorea: Deficiency of gamma-aminobutyric acid in brain. *N Engl J Med* 288:337-342, 1975.

49. McGeer PL, McGeer EG: Enzymes associated with the metabolism of catecholamines, acetylcholine and GABA in human controls and patients with Parkinson's disease and Huntington's chorea. *J Neurochem* 26:65-76, 1976.

50. Bird ED, Gale JS, Spokes EG: Huntington's chorea: Post-mortem activity of enzymes involved in cerebral glucose metabolism. *J Neurochem* 29:539–545, 1977.

51. Ehringer H, Hornykiewicz O: Verteilung von Noradrenalin und Dopamin (3-hydroxytryptamin) im Gehirn des Menschen und ihr Verhalten bei Erkrankungen des extrapyramidalen Systems. *Klin Wschr* 38:1236–1239, 1960.

52. Hoehn MM, Yahr MD: Parkinsonism: Onset, progression, mortality. *Neurology* 17:427–442, 1967.

53. Eleftheriou BE: Changes with age in pituitary-adrenal responsiveness and reactivity to mild stress in mice. *Gerontologia* 20:224–230, 1974.

54. Jonec V, Finch CE: Ageing and dopamine uptake by subcellular fractions of the C57BL/6J male mouse brain. *Brain Res* 91:197–215, 1975.

55. Ziegler MG, Lake CR, Kopin IJ: Plasma noradrenalin increases with age. *Nature* 261:333–335, 1976.

56. McGeer E, McGeer PL: Neurotransmitter metabolism in the aging brain, in Terry RD, Gershon S (eds): *Neurobiology of Aging*. New York, Raven Press, 1976, pp 389–403.

57. McGeer PL, McGeer EG, Suzuki JS: Aging and extrapyramidal function. *Arch Neurol* 34:33–35, 1977.

58. Bondareff W, Narotzky R, Routtenberg A: Intrastriatal spread of catecholamines in senescent rats. *J Gerontol* 26:163–167, 1971.

59. Finch CE: Catecholamine metabolism in the brains of aging male mice. *Brain Res* 52:261–276, 1973.

60. Ordy JM, Brizzee KR: Cell loss, neurotransmitters and hormones as regulators of aging, in *Age*. Am Aging Assoc Inc, 1976, no 1, abstr 25.

61. Sun AY: Aging and in vivo norepinephrine-uptake in mammalian brain. *Exp Ageing Res* 2:207–219, 1976.

62. Meek JL, Bertilsson L, Cheney DL, Zsilla G, Costa E: Aging-induced changes in acetylcholine and serotonin content of discrete brain nuclei. *J Gerontol* 32:129–131, 1977.

63. Samorajski TH: Age-related changes in brain biogenic amines, in Brody H, Harman D, Ordy JM (eds): *Clinical, Morphologic, and Neurochemical Aspects in the Aging Central Nervous System*. New York, Raven Press, 1975, pp 199–214.

64. Stein M, Schiavi RC, Camerino M: Influence of brain and behaviour on the immune system. *Science* 191:435–440, 1976.

65. Timiras PS: Decline in homeostatic regulation, in *Developmental Physiology and Aging*. New York, MacMillan, 1972, pp 542–563.

66. Finch CE: Endocrine and neural factors of reproductive aging: A speculation, in Terry RD, Gershon S (eds): *Neurobiology of Aging*. New York, Raven Press, 1976, pp 335–338.

67. Clemens JA, Amenomori Y, Jenkins T, Meites J: Effects of hypothalamic stimulation, hormones and drugs on ovarian function in old female rats. *Proc Soc Exp Biol Med* 132:561–563, 1969.

68. Clemens JA, Fuller RW: Chemical manipulation of some aspects of aging, in *Exploration in Aging*, 2nd Philadelphia Symposium on Aging. New York, Plenum Press, 1977, in press, vol 2.

69. Peng MT, Huang HO: Aging on hypothalamic-pituitary-ovarian function in the rat. *Fertil Steril* 23:535–542, 1972.

70. Everitt AV: The hypothalamic-pituitary control of aging and age-related pathology. *Exp Geront* 8:265–277, 1973.

71. Denckla WD: Minireview: A time to die. *Life Sci* 16:31–44, 1975.

72. Berg A, Zimmermann ID: Effects of electrical stimulation and norepinephrine on cyclic-AMP levels in the cerebral cortex of the aging rat. *Mech Ageing Develop* 4:377–383, 1975.

73. Zimmerman ID, Berg AP: An effect of age on the phosphodiesterase activator protein of rat cerebral cortex. *Mech Ageing Develop* 6:67-71, 1977.
74. Puri K, Volicer L: Effect of aging on cyclic AMP levels and adenylate cyclase and phosphodiesterase activities in the rat corpus striatum. *Mech Ageing Develop* 6:53-58, 1977.
75. Reichlmeier KD: Age-related changes of cyclic AMP-dependent protein kinase in bovine brain. *J Neurochem* 27:1249-1251, 1976.
76. Reichlmeier KD, Enz A, Iwangoff P, Meier-Ruge W: Age-related changes in human brain enzyme activities: A basis for pharmacological intervention, in Roberts J, Adelman RC, Cristofalo VJ (eds): *Pharmacological Intervention in the Aging Process.* 1978, pp 251-242.
77. Reichlmeier KD, Schlecht HP, Ermini M: Enzyme activity changes in the aging human brain. Abstract from 29th Meeting of the Gerontological Society (New York), 39, 1976.
78. Sun AY, Samorajski TH: The effects of age and alcohol on (Na+/K+)-ATPase activity of whole homogenate and synaptosomes prepared from mouse and human brain. *J Neurochem* 24:161-164, 1975.
79. Lowry OH, Passonneau JV: The relationships between substrates and enzymes of glycolysis in brain. *J Biol Chem* 239:31-41, 1964.
80. Iwangoff P, Armbruster R, Enz A: Glycosis and ATP-decomposition in the aged brain. VIth International Meeting of the Society for Neurochemistry, Copenhagen, abst 17, 1977.
81. Robertson-Tchabo EA, Arenberg D: Age-differences in cognition in healthy educated men: A factor analysis of experimental measures. *Exp Ageing Res* 2:75-79, 1976.
82. Thompson LW: Cerebral blood flow, EEG and behaviour, in Terry RD, Gershon S (eds): *Neurobiology of Aging.* New York, Raven Press, 1976, pp 103-119.
83. Obrist WD: The electroencephalogram of normal aged adults. *Electroencephalogr Clin Neurophysiol* 6:235-244, 1954.
84. Obrist WD, Busse EW, Eisdorfer C, Kleemeier RW: Relation of the electroencephalogram to intellectual function in senescence. *J Gerontol* 17:197-206, 1962.
85. Busse EW, Obrist WD, Wang HS: Pre-senescent electroencephalographic changes in normal subjects. *J Gerontol* 20:315-320, 1965.
86. Roubicek J: EEG in old age. *Electroencephalogr Clin Neurophysiol* 33:354, 1972.
87. Roubicek J: The electroencephalogram in the middle-aged and the elderly. *J Am Geriatr Soc* 25:145-152, 1977.
88. Shan Wang H, Busse EW: EEG of healthy old persons. *J Gerontol* 24:419-426, 1969.
89. Flexner LB, Goodman RH: Studies on memory: Inhibitors of protein synthesis also inhibit catecholamine synthesis. *Proc Nat Acad Sci* 72:4660-4663, 1975.
90. Randt CT, Quartermain D, Goldstein M, Anagnoste B: Norepinephrine biosynthesis inhibition: Effects on memory in mice. *Science* 172:498-499, 1971.
91. Dismukes RK, Rake AV: Involvement of biogenic amines in memory formation. *Psychopharmacologia* 23:17-25, 1972.
92. Hasan M, Glees P, El-Ghazzawi E: Age-associated changes in the hypothalamus of the guinea pig: Effect of dimenthylaminoethyl-p-chlorophenoxyacetate. A microscope and histochemical study. *Exp Geront* 9:153-159, 1974.
93. Samorajski TH: How the human brain responds to aging. *J Am Geriatr Soc* 24:4-11, 1976.
94. Peng MT, Peng Y, Chen FN: Age-dependent changes in the oxygen consumption of the cerebral cortex, hypothalmus, hippocampus and amygdaloid in rats. *J Gerontol* 32:517-522, 1977.
95. Stein DG, Firl AC: Brain damage and reorganization of function in old age. *Exp Neurol* 52:157-167, 1976.

96. Fann WE, Lake CR, Richman BW: Drug-induced Parkinsonism: A reevaluation. *Dis Nerv Syst* 36:91–93, 1975.
97. Iversen LL: Dopamine receptors in the brain. *Science* 188:1084–1089, 1975.
98. Sweet RD: Parkinson's disease: Current diagnosis and treatment, in Fields WS (ed): *Neurological and Sensory Disorders in the Elderly.* New York, Stratton Intercont Med Book Corp, 1975.
99. Zivkovic B, Guidotti A, Revuelta A, Costa E: Effect of thioridazine, clozapine and other antipsychotics of the kinetic state of tyrosine hydroxylase and on the turnover rate of dopamine in striatum and nucleus accumbens. *J Pharmacol Exp Ther* 194:37–46, 1975.
100. Doberauer W: Age, ether narcosis and "weak"-amines. *Experientia* 30:214, 1974.
101. Ordy JM, Brizzee KR, Kaack MB, Claghorn JL: Psychotropic drug-stress interaction effects on the hypothalamic-pituitary-adrenal axis in man and a nonhuman primate, in *Tissue Responses to Addictive Drugs.* New York, Spectrum, 1976, pp 555–588.
102. Geregely I: Aging and adaptation on the molecular level. *Akt Geront* 6:631–633, 1976.
103. Orgel LE: The maintenance of the accuracy of protein synthesis and its relevance to ageing. *Proc Nat Acad Sci* 49:517–521, 1963.
104. Orgel LE: The maintenance of the accuracy of protein synthesis and its relevance to ageing: A correction. *Proc Nat Acad Sci* 67:1476, 1970.
105. Comfort A: The position of aging studies. *Mech Ageing Develop* 3:1–31, 1974.
106. Holliday R, Tarrant GM: Altered enzymes in ageing human fibroblasts. *Nature* 238:26–30, 1972.
107. Holliday R: Ageing of human fibroblasts in culture: Studies on enzymes and mutation. *Humangenetik* 16:83–86, 1972.
108. Holliday R: Senescence of human cells in culture. *Nature* 242:332, 1973.
109. Gershon H, Gershon D: Altered enzyme molecules in senescent organisms: Mouse muscle aldolase. *Mech Ageing Develop* 2:33–41, 1973.
110. Gershon H, Gershon D: Inactive enzyme molecules in aging mice: Liver aldolase. *Proc Nat Acad Sci* 70:909–913, 1973.
111. Gershon H, Zeelon P, Gershon D: Faulty proteins: Altered gene products in senescent cells and organisms, in Kahn A, Shatkay A (eds): *Control of Gene Expression.* New York, Plenum Press, 1974, pp 255–264.
112. Rothstein M: Recent developments in the age-related alteration of enzymes: A review. *Mech Ageing Develop* 6:241–257, 1977.
113. Eisdorfer C, Fann WE (eds): *Psychopharmacology and Aging.* New York, Plenum Press, 1973.
114. Stotsky B: Use of psychopharmacologic agents for geriatric patients, in Mascia AD, Shader RJ (eds): *Clinical Handbook of Psychopharmacology.* New York, J Aronson, 1970, pp 265–278.
115. Stotsky B: Psychoactive drugs for geriatric patients with psychiatric disorders, in Gershon S, Raskin A (eds): *Genesis and Treatment of Psychologic Disorders in the Elderly.* New York, Raven Press, 1975, pp 229–258.
116. Eisdorfer C: Observations on the psychopharmacology of the aged. *J Am Geriatr Soc* 23:53–57, 1975.
117. Prien RF: A survey of psychoactive drug use in the aged at Veterans Administration Hospital, in Gershon S, Raskin A (eds): *Genesis and Treatment of Psychological Disorders in the Elderly.* New York, Raven Press, 1975, pp 143–154.
118. Fann WE: Pharmacotherapy in older depressed patients. *J Gerontol* 31:304–310, 1976.
119. Fann WE, Wheless JC: Effects of psychotherapeutic drugs on geriatric patients, in Usdin E, Forrest J (eds): *Psychotherapeutic Drugs.* Marcel Dekker Press, 1976, pp 545–563.

120. Horita A: Neuropharmacology and Aging, in Roberts J, Adelman RC, Cristofalo VJ (eds): *Pharmacological Intervention in the Aging Process* New York, Plenum Press, 1978, pp 171-185.

121. Barbeau A: Preliminary observations on abnormal catecholamine metabolism in basal ganglia disease. *Neurology* 10:446-451, 1960.

122. Anden NE, Dahlstrom A, Fuxe K, Larsson K: Functional role of the nigrostriatal dopamine neurons. *Acta Pharmacol Toxicol* 24:263-274, 1966.

123. Anden NE, Rubenson A, Fuxe K, Hokfelt T: Evidence for dopamine receptor stimulation by apomorphine. *J Pharm Pharmacol* 19:627-629, 1967.

124. Ungerstedt U: Post-synaptic supersensitivity after 6-hydroxy-dopamine-induced degeneration of the nigro-neostrial dopamine system. *Acta Physiol Scand* 367:69-93, 1971.

125. Costall B, Naylor RJ, Pycock C: The 6-hydroxydopamine rotational model for the detection of dopamine agonist activity: Reliability of effect from different locations of 6-hydroxydopamine. *J Pharm Pharmacol* 27:943-946, 1975.

126. Corrodi H, Fuxe K, Hokfelt T, Lidbrink P, Ungerstedt U: Effect of ergot drugs on central catecholamine neurons: Evidence for a stimulation of central dopamine neurons. *J Pharm Pharmacol* 25:409-412, 1973.

127. Goldstein M, Battista A, Ohmoto T, Anagnoste B, Fuxe F: Tremor and involuntary movements in monkeys: Effect of L-dopa and of a dopamine receptor stimulating agent. *Science* 179:816-817, 1973.

128. Jaton AL, Loew DM, Vigouret JM: CF 25-397 (9, 10-didehydro-6-methyl-8 beta-[2-pyridylthiomethyl] ergoline): A new central dopamine receptor agonist. *Br J Pharmacol* 56:371, 1976.

129. Clemens JA, Smalstig EB, Shaar CJ: Inhibition of prolactin secretion by lergotrile mesylate mechanism action, *Acta Endocrinol* 79:230-237, 1975.

130. Clemens JA, Smalstig EB, Sawyer BD: Studies on the role of the preoptic area in the control of reproductive function in the rat. *Endocrinology* 99:728-735, 1976.

131. Lutterbeck PM, Pryor JS, Varga L, Wenner R: Treatment of non-puerperal galactorrhoea with an ergot alkaloid. *Br Med J* 3:228-229, 1971.

132. Fluckiger E, Dopfner W, Marko M, Niederer W: Effects of ergot alkaloids on the hypothalamic-pituitary axis. *Postgrad Med J* 52:57-61, 1976.

133. Fluckiger E: Pharmacology of prolactin secretion. *Acta Endocrinol* 78: Suppl. 193, 164-165, 1975.

134. Loew DM, Depoortere H, Buerki HR: Effects of dihydrogenated ergot alkaloids on the sleep-wakefulness cycle and on brain biogenic amines in the rat. *Arzneimittel-Forsch* 26:1080-1083, 1976.

135. Loew DM, Vigouret JM, Jaton AL: Neuropharmacological investigations with two ergot alkaloids, hydergine and bromocriptine. Session II. CNS—Effects of ergot alkaloids. *Postgrad Med J* 52:40-46, 1976.

136. Birkmayer W, Hornykiewicz O: Der L-3,4-Dihydroxyphenylalanin (=Dopa) effekt bei der Parkinson-Akinese. *Wien Klin Wschr* 73:787-788, 1961.

137. Cotzias GC, Miller ST, Nicholson AR, Maston WH, Tang LC: Prolongation of the life-span in mice adapted to large amounts of L-dopa. *Proc Nat Acad Sci* 71:2466-2469, 1974.

138. Yahr MD, Duvoisin RC, Schear MY, Barret RE: Treatment of Parkinsonism with levo-dopa. *Arch Neurol* 21:343-354, 1969.

139. Calne DB, Teychenne PF, Claveria LE, Eastman R, Greenacre JK, Petrie A: Bromocriptine in Parkinsonism. *Br Med J* 4:442-444, 1974.

140. Kartzinel R: Bromocriptine and levodopa (with or without carbidopa) in Parkinsonism. *Lancet* 2:272-275, 1976.

141. Kartzinel R, Perlow M, Carter AC, Chase TN, Calne DB: Metabolic studies with bromocriptine in patients with idiopathic Parkinsonism and Huntington chorea. *Arch Neurol* 33:384, 1976.
142. Debono AG, Donaldson I, Marsden CD, Parkes JD: Bromocriptine in Parkinsonism. *Lancet* 2:897-988, 1975.
143. Lieberman A, Miyamoto T, Battista A: Studies on the anti-Parkinsonian efficacy of lergotrile. *Neurology* 25:459-462, 1975.
144. Lieberman AN, Kupersmith M, Vogel B, Goodgold A, Goldstein M: Treatment of Parkinson's disease with bromocriptine. *Clin Res* 24:511, 1976.
145. Lieberman AN, Kupersmith M, Estey E, Goldstein M: Lergotrile in Parkinson's Disease. *Lancet* 2:515-516, 1976.
146. Gilbert JC, Aberdeen UK: Diseases of the central nervous system. Pharmacological basis of treatment. *Br Med J* 4:33-35, 1975.
147. Meyer JS, Welch KMA, Deshmukh VD, Perez FI, Jacob RH, Haufrect DB, Mathew NT, Morrell RM: Neurotransmitter precursor amino acids in the treatment of multi-infarct dementia and Alzheimer's disease. *J Am Geriatr Soc* 25:289-298, 1977.
148. Myres RE: Four patterns of perinatal brain damage and their conditions of occurrence in primates. *Adv Neurol* 10:223-234, 1975.
149. Samorajski TH, Rolsten C, Ordy JM: Changes in behaviour, brain and neuroendocrine chemistry with age and stress in C57 BL/10 male mice. *J Gerontol* 26:168-175, 197.
150. Ordy JM, Schjeide OA: Univariate and multivariate models for evaluating long-term-changes in neurobiological development, maturity and aging, in Ford DH (ed): *Progress in Brain Research*. New York, Elsevier, 1973, pp 25-51.
151. Kogure K, Scheinberg P, Matsumodo K: Catecholamines in experimental brain ischemia. *Arch Neurol* 32:21-24, 1975.
152. Lust WD, Mrsulja BB, Mrsulja BJ, Passonneau JV, Klatzo J: Putative neurotransmitters and cyclic nucleotides in prolonged ischemia in the cerebral cortex. *Brain Res* 98:394-399, 1975.
153. Meyer JS, Welch KMA, Titus JL, Suzuki M, Kim HS, Perex FJ, Mathew NT, Gedye JL, Hrastnik F, Miyakawa Y, Achar VS, Dodson RF: Neurotransmitter failure in cerebral infarction and dementia, in Terry RD, Gershon S (eds): *Neurobiology of Aging*. New York, Raven Press, 1976, pp 121-138.
154. Davison AN: The pathology and biochemistry of the aging brain, in Davison AN, Hood NA (eds): *Action on Ageing*. England, MCS-Consultants, 1976, pp 39-42.
155. Livesley B: Brain failure: Pathogenesis and presentation, in Davison AN, Hood NA (eds): *Action on Aging*. England, MCS-Consultants, 1976, pp 54-56.
156. Domino EF, Davis JM: *Neurotransmitter Balances Regulatory Behaviour.* Edwards Bros, Ann Arbor, Mich, 1975, p 240.
157. Antelman SM, Caggiula AR: Norepinephrine-dopamine interactions and behaviour. *Science* 195:646-653, 1977.
158. Ott EO, Abraham J, Meyer JS, Achari AN, Chee ANC, Mathew NT: Disordered cholinergic neurotransmission and dysautoregulation after acute cerebral infraction. *Stroke* 6:172-180, 1975.
159. Welch KMA, Meyer JS, Teraura T, Hashi K, Shinmaru S: Ischemic anoxia and cerebral serotonin levels. *J Neurol Sci* 16:85-92, 1972.
160. Welch KMA, Chabi E, Buckingham J, Bergin B, Achar VS, Meyer JS: Catecholamine and 5-hydroxytryptamine levels in ischemic brain: Influence of p-chlorophenylalanine. *Stroke* 8:341-346, 1977.
161. Crowell RM, Olsson Y: Focal cerebral ischemia leads to impaired vascular filling. *Neurology* 21:400, 1971.

162. Grote J: Problems of oxygen supply to organs during shock, in Zimmerman WE, Staib J, Jacobson ED (eds): *Shock: Metabolic Disorders and Therapy.* New York, Schattauer-Verlag, 1972, pp 107–120.

163. Siesjo BK, Plum F: Pathophysiology of anoxic brain damage, in Gaull G (ed): *Biology of Brain Dysfunction.* New York, Plenum Press, 1973, pp 319–372.

164. Cohen MM: Animal models of cerebral infarction, in Klawans HL (ed): *Models of Human Neurological Diseases.* Amsterdam, Exerpta Medica, 1974, pp 205–248.

165. Myers RE, Yamaguchi S: Nervous system effects of cardiac arrest in monkeys. *Arch Neurol* 34:65–74, 1977.

166. Gottstein U: Pharmacological studies of total cerebral blood flow in man with comments on the possibility of improving regional cerebral blood flow by drugs. *Arch Neurol Scand* 41:136–141, 1965.

167. Shan Wang H, Busse EW: Heart disease and brain impairment among aged persons, in Palmore E (ed): *Normal Aging II.* Durham, NC, Duke University Press, 1974, pp 160–167.

168. Hossmann KA, Sato K: Recovery of neuronal function after prolonged cerebral ischemia. *Science* 168:375–376, 1970.

169. Hossmann V, Hossmann KA: Return of neuronal functions after prolonged cardiac arrest. *Brain Res* 60:423–438, 1973.

170. Hossmann KA, Takagi S, Sakaki S: Vital microscopy of pial arteries after prolonged cerebral ischemia. *Arzneimittel-Forsch* 26:1233–1234, 1976.

171. Siesjo BK, Nilsson L: The influence of arterial hypoxemia upon labile phosphatase and upon extracellular and intracellular lactate and pyruvate concentrations in the rat brain. *Scand J Clin Lab Invest* 27:83–96, 1971.

172. Ljunggren B, Norberg K, Siesjo BK: Influence of tissue acidosis upon restitution of brain energy metabolism following total ischemia. *Brain Res,* 173–186, 1974.

173. Gygax P, Emmenegger H, Stosseck K: Quantative determination of cortical microflow and EEG in graded hypercapnia, in Langfitt FW, McHenry LC, Reivich M, Wollman H (eds): *Cerebral Circulation and Metabolism.* New York, Springer-Verlag, 1975, pp 371–374.

174. Gygax P, Stosseck K, Emmenegger H, Schweizer A: Influence of anesthetics on cortical mircroflow and EEG in arterial hypotension. Comparison between pentobarbital and $N_2O/O_2$-anesthesia, in Harper M, Jennet B, Miller D, Rowan J (eds): *Blood Flow and Metabolism in the Brain.* New York, Churchill-Livingstone, 1975, pp 11.14–11.15.

175. Kovach AGB, Sandor P: Cerebral blood flow and brain function during hypotension and shock. *Ann Rev Physiol* 39:571–596, 1976.

176. Geiger A: Correlation of brain metabolism and function by the use of a brain perfusion method in situ. *Physiol Rev* 38:9–20, 1958.

177. Emmenegger H, Taeschler M, Cerletti A: Neue Moglichkeit der isolierten Hirndurchstromung. *Helv Physiol Pharmacol Acta* 21:239–244, 1963.

178. Meier-Ruge W, Enz A, Gygax P, Hunziker O, Iwangoff P, Reichlmeier K: Experimental pathology in basic research of the aging brain, in Gershon S, Raskin A (eds): *Genesis and Treatment of Psychologic Disorders in the Elderly.* New York, Raven Press, 1975, pp 55–126.

179. Emmenegger H, Meier-Ruge W: The action of hydergine on the brain. *Pharmacology* 1:65–78, 1968.

180. Cerletti A, Emmenegger H, Enz A, Iwangoff P, Meier-Ruge W, Musil J: Effects of ergot DH-alkaloids on the metabolism and function of the brain. An approach based on studies with DH-ergonine, in Genazzani E, Herken H (eds): *Central Nervous System Studies on Metabolic Regulation and Function.* New York, Springer, 1973, pp 201–212.

181. Gygax P, Schweizer A: The influence of anesthesia on cortical microflow and EEG in arterial hypotension. *Arzneimittel-Forsch* 25:1678, 1975.

182. Gygax P, Wiernsperger N, Meier-Ruge W, Baumann TH: Effect of papaverine and dihydroergotoxine mesylate on cerebral microflow, EEG and $pO_2$ in oligemic hypotension. *Gerontology* 24:14–22, 1978.

183. Hauth H, Richardson B: Cerebral vasodilators. *Ann Rep Med Chem* 12:44–59, 1977.

184. Hunziker O, Emmenegger H, Frey H, Schulz U, Meier-Ruge W: Morphometric characterization of the capillary network in the cat's brain cortex: A comparison of the physiological state and hypovolemic condition. *Acta Neuropath* 29:57–63, 1974.

185. Gygax P, Hunziker O, Schulz U, Schweizer A: Experimental studies on the action of metabolic and vasoactive substances in the brain. *Triangle* 14:80–89, 1975.

186. Kovach AGB: Cerebral blood flow and metabolism in hemorrhagic shock in the baboon, in Harper M, Jennett B, Miller D, Rowan J (eds): *Blood Flow and Metabolism in the Brain.* New York, Churchill-Livingstone, 1975, p 19.

187. Blaustein MP, Ector AC: Barbiturate inhibition of calcium uptake by depolarized nerve terminals in vitro. *Mol Pharmacol* 11:369–378, 1975.

188. Wiernsperger N, Gygax P, Danzeisen M: Cortical $pO_2$-distribution during oligemic hypotension and its pharmacological modifications. *Arzneimittel-Forsch,* 1978.

189. Enz A, Iwangoff P, Markstein R, Wagner H: The effect of hydergine on the enzymes involved in cAMP turnover in the brain. *Triangle* 14:90–92, 1975.

190. Markstein R, Wagner H: The effect of dihydroergotoxine, phentolamine and pindolol on catecholamine-stimulated adenylcyclase in rat cerebral cortex. *FEBS Letters* 55:275–277, 1975.

191. Markstein R, Wagner H: Effect of dihydroergotoxine on cyclic AMP generating systems in rat cerebral cortex slices. *Gerontology* 24:94–105, 1978.

192. Iwangoff P, Meier-Ruge W, Schieweck CH, Enz A: The uptake of DH-ergotoxine by different parts of the cat brain. *Pharmacology* 14:27–38, 1976.

193. Iwangoff P, Enz A, Meier-Ruge W: Incorporation after single and repeated application of radioactive labelled DH-ergot alkaloids in different organs of the cat with special reference to the brain. *Gerontology* 24:126–138, 1978.

194. Iwangoff P, Enz A, Chappuis A: Inhibition of cAMP-phosphodiesterase of different cat organs by DH-ergotoxine in the micromolar substrate range. *IRCS Medical Science* 3:403, 1975.

195. Meier-Ruge W, Iwangoff P: Biochemical effects of ergot alkaloids with special reference to the brain. *Postgrad Med J* 52:47–54, 1976.

196. Iwangoff P, Enz A: The brain specific inhibition of the cAMP-phospho-diesterase (PEase) of the cat by dihydroergotalkaloids in vitro. *IRCS Medical Science:* p 3–4, 3–10–9, 1973.

197. Chappuis A, Enz A, Iwangoff P: The influence of adrenergic effectors on the cationic pump of brain cell membrane. *Triangle* 14:93–98, 1975.

198. Enz A, Iwangoff P, Chappuis A: The influence of dihydroergotoxine mesylate on the low-$K_m$-phosphodiesterase of cat and rat brain in vitro. *Gerontology* 24:115–125, 1978.

199. Goldstein M, Lew JY, Hata F, Liebermann A: Binding interactions of ergot alkaloids with monoaminergic receptors in the brain. *Gerontology* 24:76–85, 1978.

200. Gahwiler BH: Dihydroergotoxine-induced modulation of spontaneous activity of cultured rat purkinje cells. *Gerontology* 24:71–75, 1978.

201. Roubicek J, Geiger CH, Abt K: An ergot alkaloid preparation (hydergine) in geriatric therapy. *J Am Geriatr Soc* 20:222–229, 1972.

202. Arrigo A, Braun P, Kauchtschischwili GM, Moglia A, Tartara A: Influence of treatment on symptomatology and correlated electroencephalographic (EEG) changes in the aged. *Curr Ther Res* 15:417–426, 1973.

203. Matejcek M, Knor K, Arrigo A: Quantitative EEG in geriatric drug research: A working hypothesis, first results and their relation to clinical symptomatology, in Davison AN, Hood NA (eds): *Action on Ageing*. England, MCS-Consultants, 1976, pp 43–47.
204. Rao DB, Norris JR: A double-blind investigation of hydergine in the treatment of cerebrovascular insufficiency in the elderly. *Hopkins Med J* 130:317–324, 1972.
205. Nelson JJ: Relieving select symptoms of the elderly. *Geriatrics* 30:133–139-142, 1975.
206. Rosen HJ: Mental decline in the elderly: Pharmacotherapy (ergot alkaloids versus papaverine). *J Am Geriatr Soc* 23:169–174, 1975.
207. Gaitz CM, Varner RV: Pharmacotherapy of late life organic brain sydromes: Evaluation of hydergine (an ergot derivative) versus placebo using double-blind technique. *Gerontologist* 14:44, 1974.
208. Gaitz CM, Varner RV: A multidisciplinary mental health model. Amer Psych Assoc, Annual Meeting, Anaheim, Calif, May 5-9, 1975.
209. Gaitz CM, Varner RV, Overall JE: Pharmacotherapy of organic brain syndrome in late life. Evaluation of an ergot derivate versus placebo. *Arch Gen Psychiatry* 34:839–845, 1977.
210. Carruthers-Jones DI, Depoortere H, Loew DM: Changes in the rat electrocorticogram following administration of two dihydrogenated ergot derivatives. *Gerontology* 24:23–33, 1978.
211. Hollister LE: Drugs for mental disorders of old age. *JAMA* 234:195–198, 1975.
212. Sathanathan GL, Gershon S: Cerebral vasodilators: A review, in Gershon S, Raskin A (eds): *Genesis and Treatment of Psychologic Disorders in the Elderly*. New York, Raven Press, 1975, pp 155–168.
213. Rossignol P, Boulu R, Ribart M, Paultre C, Bache S, Truelle B: Action de quelques medicaments de l'insuffisance vasculaire cerebrale sur les potentiels primaires somesthesiques evoques au niveau duc cortex et du thalamus chez le chat en etat d'ischemie cerebrale aigue. *Compt Rend Ser D* 274:2027–2029, 1972.
214. Perrault G, Boulu R, Rossignol P: Effet de medicaments de l'insuffisance cerebro-fasculaire chez le chat soumis a des ischemies cerebrales iteratives de breve duree. *J Pharmacol* 6:103, 1975.
215. Perrault G, Liutkus M, Boulu R, Rossignol P: Modification par l'hypoxie ischemique aigue de la response cortico-pyramidale chez le chat. *J Pharmacol* 7:27–38, 1976.
216. Witzmann HK, Blechacz W: Zur stellung von vincamin in der therapie zerebrovaskularer krankheiten und zerebraler leistungsminderung. *Arnzneimittel-Forsch* 27:1238–1247, 1977.
217. Wolthuis OL: Experiments with UCB-6215: A drug, which enhances acquisition in rats: Its effect compared with those of metamphetamine. *Europ J Pharmacol* 16:283–297, 1971.
218. Giurgea C, Lefevre D, Lescrenier C, David-Remacle M: Pharmacological protection against hypoxia-induced amnesia in rats. *Psychopharmacol* 20:160–168, 1971.
219. Giurgea C, Mouravieff-Lesuisse F: Effet facilitateur du Piracetam sur un apprentissage repetitif chez le rat. *J Pharmacol* 3:17–30, 1972.
220. Giurgea CE, Moyersoons FE: On the pharmacology of cortical evoked potentials. *Arch Int Pharmacodyn* 199:67–78, 1972.
221. Platt D, Hering H, Hering FJ: Age-dependent determinations of lysosomal enzyme activities in the liver and brain as well as the measurements of cytoplasmic enzyme activities in the blood of Piracetam pre-treated rats. *Exp Geront* 8:315–324, 1973.
222. Gobert JG: Genese d'un medicament: La piracetam, Metabolisation et recherche biochimique. *J Pharm* 27:281–304, 1972.

223. Gobert JG, Temmerman JJ: Piracetam-induced modification of the brain poly-ribosome content in ageing rats, in Platt D (ed): *Altern*. New York, Schattauer, 1974, pp 143–147.

224. Schulte Am Esch J, Pfeifer G: Volaufige Erfahrungen mit Piracetam in der Intensivtherapie schwerer Schadel-hirn-verletzungen. *Med Klin* 69:1235–1238, 1974.

225. Ulbricht B: Ueber die klinische Anwendung von Piracetam bei chronischem Alkoholiamua und dessen Komplikationen Praedelir und Delir. *Med Welt* 27:1912–1915, 1976.

226. Stegnik AJ: The clinical use of Piracetam, a new nootropic drug: The treatment of symptoms of senile involution. *Arzneimittel-Forsch* 22:975–977, 1972.

227. Faleni R: Clinical trial with Piracetam. *J Pharmacol* 5:30, 1974.

228. Heinitz M: Neue Aspekte zur Therapie der zerebralen Insuffizienz durch Piracetam. *Fortschr Med* 93:293–298, 1975.

229. Bienmuller H, Betz E: Die Regulation der lokalen corticalen Gehirndurchblutung bei Injektion von Noradrenalin, Pentobarbital und Adrenolitico. *Aerztliche Forschung* 4:97–111, 1970.

230. Bienmuller H, Betz E: Wirkung von Nicergolin auf die Hirndurchblutung. *Arzneimittel-Forsch* 22:1367–1372, 1972.

231. Benzi G, Manzo L, De Bernardi M, Ferrara A, Sanguinetti L, Arrigoni E, Berte H: Action of lysergide, ephedrine, nimergoline on brain metabolizing activity. *J Pharm Sci* 60:1320–1324, 1971.

232. Moretti A, Pegrassi L, Suchowsky GK: Effect of nicergoline on some ischemia-induced metabolic changes in the brain of cat, in Genazzani E, Herken H (eds): *Central Nervous System; Studies on Metabolic Regulation and Function*. New York, Springer-Verlag, 1974, pp 213–216.

233. Villa RF: Effect of hypoxia on the cerebral energy state. *Farmaco Ed Sci* 30:561–567, 1975.

234. Montecucchi P: Stimolazione della formazione di AMP ciclico nel cervello di ratto in vitro da parte della nicergolina. *Farmaco Ed Prat* 31:10–17, 1976.

235. Freedman DX: Effects of LSD-25 on brain serotonin. *J Pharmacol Exp Ther* 134:160–166, 1961.

236. Fuxe K, Hokfelt T, Ungerstedt U: Morphological and functional aspects of central monoamine neurons, in Pfeifer CC, Smythies JR (eds): *Intern Rev Neurobiology*. New York, Academic Press, 1970, pp 93–126.

237. Konzett H, Rothlin E: Investigations on the hypotensive effect of the hydrogenated ergot alkaloids. *Br J Pharmacol Chemother* 8:201–207, 1953.

238. Cerletti A: Comparison of abnormal behavioural states by psychotropic drugs in animal and man. *Neuropsychopharmacol* 1:117–123, 1959.

239. Papp RH, Hawkins HB, Share NN, Wang SC: Emesis induced by the intra-cerebrovascular administration of hydergine and mechlorethamine hydrochloride. *J Pharmacol Exper Ther* 154:333–338, 1966.

240. Depoortere H, Loew DM: Alterations in the sleep/wakefulness cycle in rats after administration of (−)-LSD or BOL 48: A comparison with (+)-LSD. *Br J Pharmacol* 44:354–355, 1972.

# CHAPTER 5

# The Use Of Tricyclic Antidepressant Drugs In Geriatric Patients

SHEPARD J. KANTOR
ALEXANDER H. GLASSMAN

Depression is one of the most common psychiatric problems seen in a geriatric population. Its recognition and management can not only enable affected patients to return to their previous level of functioning but can be life saving. The medical management of depressed geriatric patients may be complicated by their inability to tolerate drug side effects, potential adverse interactions between antidepressant medications and other medications they frequently will be taking, or other illnesses from which they may concurrently be suffering. This chapter will outline a rational approach to the use of tricyclic antidepressants in a geriatric population.

## DIAGNOSIS

There are a great many causes for depression, and its optimal management depends upon the ability to recognize these various causes and to match therapy to the cause.

For many years depression was considered to be an illness whose etiology and treatment could be totally explainable in psychological terms. With the introduction of antidepressant drugs, biological etiologies and methods of management of depression have been emphasized. More recently, depression has been recognized as a heterogeneous illness. Some patients who experience depression are in fact suffering the consequences of some undiagnosed medical illness. Other patients manifest depression or depressive symptoms due to an inability to cope with real or symbolic life stresses. Still others seem subject to depressions as a consequence of genetic or biological predispositions. Whereas in the past psychiatrists debated whether depression was a psychological or a biological illness, more recently they have attempted to define criteria which would enable them to distinguish between those patients whose depressions appear to be a consequence of psychological processes and those whose symptoms appear to be biological in origin. A consequence of this has been the emergence of the concept of endogenous depression, major affective disorder, or "endomorphogenic depression".[1,2,3] These terms all describe a syndrome manifested by dysphoric or depressed mood as well as such "vegetative" symptoms as insomnia, anorexia, weight loss, psychomotor retardation or agitation, and diminished sexual interests. Impairment of these "vegetative" functions is thought to be a consequence of central nervous system dysfunction.

Depressions of any origin may be accompanied by feelings of worthlessness, guilt, loss of usual interest in life, or suicidal thoughts or behavior. However, the pervasiveness of dysphoric mood and its unresponsiveness to environmental changes as well as the presence of impairment in the vegetative functions tend to distinguish the endogenous, or biological depressions from those in which psychological processes adequately explain both the origin and perpetuation of the depressed state. The importance of making the distinction between the presence or absence of the syndrome of endogenous depression is that this syndrome identifies the patients most likely to respond to the somatic therapies such as tricyclic antidepressants and electroconvulsive therapy and least likely to respond to psychological or social interventions. However, it should be kept in mind that even the most experienced clinician may at times find it difficult to make this distinction in any given patient. The terms "endogenous depression" or "major depressive disorder" have come to subsume such formerly used diagnostic categories as involutional melancholia, psychotic depression, postpartum depressive psychosis, and manic depressive, depressed. Endogenous depression may at times be confused with other psychiatric disturbances common to geriatric patients. These include involutional paranoid states and organic psychoses that are distinguishable from endogenous depressions in that they are manifested by disturbance of thinking with little or no alteration in mood. These illnesses are unresponsive to tricyclic antidepressants and can be exacerbated by these drugs.

Members of the geriatric population are subject not only to the genetic or biological predispositions to depression to which the general population is at risk, but also to a number of life stresses particular to the elderly. Loss of health, loss of work and parental roles, the dissolution of their families or loss of their spouse, financial concerns, social isolation and alienation, conflicts over their changing self-image, and concerns about death are all major issues which have particular impact on the older population.[4,5]

Patients unable to cope successfully with any or all of these issues who experience depressive feelings but do not develop the endogenous depressive syndrome, are more likely to benefit from social and psychological interventions than from somatic treatments. On the other hand, patients who develop an endogenous depression in this setting will need drug management for their depressive syndrome along with social and/or psychological intervention to enable them to change or better cope with their life situations.

Before undertaking any treatment for the depression of a geriatric patient, it should be kept in mind that serious and life-threatening medical illnesses can masquerade as depression. Any depressed geriatric patient who seeks treatment for his or her depression therefore deserves a thorough medical evaluation.

## DOSE-RESPONSE CHARACTERISTICS OF TCA

Over the past ten years, new techniques and study designs have led to advances in our understanding of the dose-response characteristics of the tricyclic antidepressants (TCA). A knowledge of these dose-response relationships is necessary in order to optimally use these drugs. It should be emphasized that the significant work in this area has been done on patients who have met criteria for endogenous depression. The more a geriatric patient's clinical picture approaches this clinical syndrome, the more likely it is that his response to treatment will parallel the response seen in these studies. A previous history of a tricyclic responsive endogenous depression or ECT responsive depression, or a family history of endogenous depression successfully treated with ECT or TCA, all tend to increase the likelihood of a patient's responding to TCA. However, it should be noted that patients who develop the syndrome of endogenous depression which is accompanied by delusional thinking seem to be less likely to respond to TCA administration than do nondeluded endogenous patients. Such deluded depressed patients seem to respond better to electroconvulsive therapy (ECT) than to tricyclics.[6,7]

For ten years it has been apparent that different individuals given equal

TCA doses will develop different plasma concentrations of these drugs.[8] This is to a large extent the result of genetically determined differences in the rates at which individuals metabolize TCA. These rates of metabolism are also subject to a number of environmental influences (see below). A consequence of this metabolic variation is that plasma TCA concentration and not oral dose has been used in attempting to determine dose-response relationships with TCA.

Sjoqvist and his coworkers from Sweden and Denmark conducted some of the earliest plasma-level studies of TCA. They initially chose to study nortriptyline (NT) because reliable methods for its analysis were available and because it appears to have no active metabolites. To the surprise of many people the initial study by Asberg et al. revealed a curvilinear plasma level-response curve;[9] that is, a poor clinical response was seen at both lower and higher blood levels while a good response was observed only in the middle plasma range.

This result has since been replicated in two further studies. Asberg conducted a more careful replication of her first study in association with Kragh-Sorensen et al. in Denmark[10] and later Kragh-Sorensen et al. conducted a third independent study.[11] In each study the data reveal a curvilinear type of dose-response curve. Drugs with this dose-response characteristic are frequently referred to as having a "therapeutic window"; that is, intermediate plasma concentrations yield a maximal clinical response while lower or higher plasma concentrations show diminished effectiveness. The therapeutic window for nortriptyline appears to be a steady-state level between 50 and 170ng/ml, and the work of Asberg and Kragh-Sorensen has shown that with oral doses of 150mg/day the average plasma steady-state level of nortripyline will fall at the upper end of this therapeutic window. As a result, patients who fail to respond at doses of 150mg/day are more likely to be above the therapeutic window than below it.

Glassman et al. have investigated the dose-response characteristics of imprimine IMI.[12] This drug is slightly more complicated than NT, as IMI is metabolized in the body to desmethylimipramine (DMI), which is itself an active antidepressant. As different patients have different relative concentrations of DMI and IMI, and as these concentrations may vary on a day-to-day basis despite a fixed oral dose of IMI, the results are reported as total amounts of IMI plus DMI at steady-state conditions. Steady-state is the concentration at a time (usually 10 to 14 days after the last dosage adjustment) when the total IMI and DMI concentration remains constant with continued fixed dosage administration of TCA. Their data are somewhat at variance with that obtained in studies of NT. They found that the response rate to IMI therapy is quite low for that sample of the

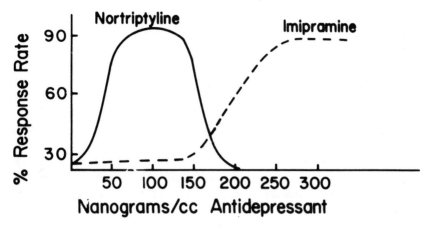

Figure 5-1:   Dose-response characteristics of endogenously depressed patients treated with TCA. The curvilinear curve of nortriptyline, with a therapeutic window between 50 and 170ng/cc (after Kragh-Sorensen), is contrasted with the sigmoid curve of imipramine with maximum response between 150 and 250 ng/cc (after Glassman).

population with blood levels below 150ng/ml. It rises steeply between 150 and 250ng/ml and then, unlike NT, the response rate levels off and remains constant. Recently Gram and his coworkers published a study of 24 patients treated with IMI and, as with Glassman's population, they noted no indication that high plasma concentrations reduced TCA effect.[13] Simpson's reported work done without plasma determinations seems to confirm the work of Glassman and of Gram in that higher doses of IMI were found to be more effective than lower doses.[14]

This type of plasma level-response relationship is very different from the curvilinear relationship that has been described by Asberg et al. and Kragh-Sorensen et al. for NT. Thus, it seems that these two structurally similar tricyclic drugs have very different dose-response characteristics. Furthermore, Glassman's patients were given 3.5mg per kg of IMI, which in men was an average dose of 250mg and women 200mg per day. This is larger than the average dose of TCA generally prescribed. It is of particular significance that even at this dose they found that one-third of their patients obtained plasma concentrations which were inadequate to effectively treat depression.

After several years' investigation of the possible correlations between antidepressant plasma concentrations and clinical effects, two types of dose-response curves have emerged. Secondary amines, such as nortriptyline and protriptyline,[15] show curvilinear relationships with optimum therapeutic ranges of 50 to 170ng/ml and 166 to 237ng/ml, respectively. The study of Gram and his associates and Glassman's work with imipramine show that the relationship with tertiary amines seems to be linear over the usual range of therapeutic plasma levels (see Figure 5-1). Adequate data on DMI or amitriptyline (AMI) are not yet available. This dose-response difference presents the clinician with an unusual and complex situation. When the patient does not respond, the clinician must decide if the patient's lack of improvement is due to his nonresponsiveness to an adequate drug level or to his failure to achieve an appropriate plasma level. If the clinician feels that the patient should respond to a tricyclic drug, in that the correct diagnosis has been made, and that the lack of response is due to an inappropriate IMI blood level, then the data with imipramine suggest that the patient's blood level is probably too low and higher oral doses are needed. In contrast, the typical patient who fails on 150mg/day of nortriptyline probably has too high a blood level and needs a lower oral dose. It should be kept in mind that the nortriptyline patient may fail because his blood level is actually too low although, because of the distribution of blood levels at usual oral doses, this would be less common.

## EFFECTS OF AGING ON PLASMA CONCENTRATION

Unfortunately, most of the TCA dose-response studies have been done in patients well below the geriatric age. The average age in Kragh-Sorenson's NT study was 45 years while Glassman's patients averaged 60 years of age. A number of physiological changes related to aging may affect the ultimate plasma concentration of TCA.[16,17] Diminished GI (gastrointestinal) absorption secondary to decreased GI motility or impaired transport mechanisms might serve to decrease plasma concentration. On the other hand, diminished liver function in the elderly could diminish drug metabolism and induce higher plasma concentration than would be seen in an equal-sized person of a younger age. Diminished plasma proteins to which TCA bind might result in an increased unbound fraction of TCA, which would make a given plasma concentration more potent. A number of investigators have attempted to assess the relationship between age and plasma TCA concentration.

The work of Gram suggests that geriatric patients may develop higher plasma concentrations of IMI and DMI than younger patients given the same mg/kg oral dose.[18] His work must be seen in the light of the observation that on a given mg/kg oral dose of IMI, men tend to develop higher plasma concentrations of IMI + DMI than do women. He found men aged 50 to 59 and men aged 60 to 65 had higher concentrations than women aged 30 to 39. It is uncertain whether these plasma concentration

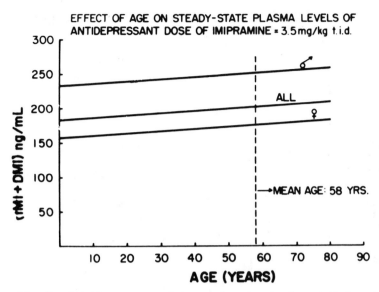

Figure 5-2:   Correlation between age and plasma imipramine plus desmethylimipramine concentration demonstrating that, independent of sex, plasma concentration increases with age in 78 patients given equal mg/kg imipramine doses.

differences are due to sex or age. His data do not allow one to determine whether men in the geriatric age have higher drug concentrations than younger men or if women in the geriatric age have higher concentrations than younger women. However, he did show that women in their fifties do have higher plasma concentration than women in their thirties.

Nies et al. have also investigated the relationship between age and TCA plasma concentrations.[19] Unfortunately, they too did not stratify their patients by sex. They found that geriatric patients develop significantly higher levels of IMI or AMI than younger patients even when younger patients are given larger oral doses of TCA. They also found that IMI, DMI and AMI are more slowly metabolized in geriatric patients than in younger patients. They suggest that the increased incidence of TCA side effects seen in geriatric patients may be due to increased plasma TCA concentrations which may develop as a consequence of diminished drug metabolism. While it is surprising that this should be so, they found NT metabolism to be unaffected by age. If this observation can be replicated, then NT may prove to be a less-complicated TCA to use in geriatric patients.

Perel et al. have data on a large series of IMI-treated patients given equal mg/kg oral medication doses. Their subjects are stratified by both age and sex, and they also find that increasing age is associated with increasing

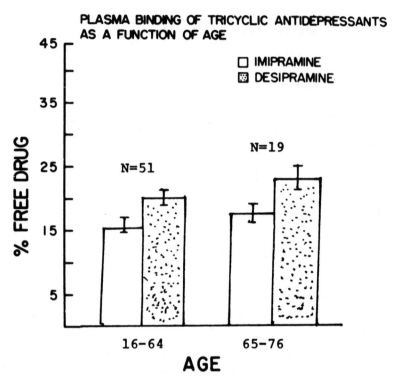

Figure 5-3:   Correlation between age and plasma binding demonstrating that geriatric patients have more unbound drug than younger adults.

TCA plasma concentration (Figure 5-2). They also report that older patients have a higher fraction of free drug than younger patients (Figure 5-3).

Increased TCA plasma levels due to the diminished drug metabolism as well as increased amounts of unbound drug associated with aging would both tend to increase the potency of IMI, DMI and AMI. This would dictate that geriatric patients be given lower mg doses of these TCA than one would give to younger patients of equal weight.

It is recommended that outpatients over 65 be given TCA most cautiously. IMI and AMI may be started in the range of 25 to 40mg/day with further increments at the rate of 25mg/week.[19,20] While younger patients need doses of IMI or AMI in the range of 200 to 300mg/day, considerably smaller doses will usually be adequate for geriatric patients. It should be kept in mind that some geriatric patients, especially those hospitalized for their depression, will need and be able to tolerate significantly higher doses of TCA. The major limitations here would be the patient's ability to tolerate drug-induced side effects. While an adequate treatment trial for younger patients is usually 3 to 4 weeks, geriatric patients may need 4 to 6 weeks to obtain maximal benefit from a given dose of TCA.[19]

Unfortunately, the increased antidepressant potency of TCA given to the elderly produces an increased frequency and intensity of drug-related side effects. It is these side effects which may, in fact, limit the usefulness of TCA in some geriatric patients and to which we now turn.


## SIDE EFFECTS

The ability of TCA to affect the peripheral autonomic nervous system, the central nervous system and the cardiovascular system results in side effects to which all TCA-treated patients may be sensitive but to which geriatric patients are particularly vulnerable.


### Peripheral Autonomic Function

The ability to interfere with the reuptake of norepinephrine by nerve terminals within the central nervous system is the mechanism whereby TCA are thought to reverse severe endogenous depressions. Another property of TCA is that they are able to interfere with acetylcholine (ACh)-mediated synaptic transmission. This is done by blocking ACh receptor sites. This anticholinergic or atropinelike side effect results in a number of peripheral symptoms, including decreased salivation, difficulty in urination, constipation and pupil dilation. Recently, *in vitro* studies have enabled investigators to rank the various TCA in order of anticholinergic potency.[21] Amitriptyline (AMI) is the most anticholinergic. Imipramine is slightly less potent, nortriptyline and doxepin less potent than IMI or AMI, and DMI the least anticholinergic of the TCA tested. An implication of this work is that one could select a TCA with low anticholinergic potency for patients particularly sensitive or vulnerable to the anticholinergic effects of TCA.

Patients with a history of glaucoma are at increased risk from the atropinelike effects of TCA that cause pupil dilation. This dilation results in the iris folding back and blocking the outflow channel from the eye. Patients with narrow-angle glaucoma whose outflow is already impeded may therefore have their condition exacerbated by TCA. Narrow-angle glaucoma can occur at any age. It is somewhat more common in the elderly due to cataract formation, which can also impede outflow. Open-angle glaucoma is more common than narrow-angle glaucoma and is thought to be unaffected by TCA. While patients with glaucoma may be treated with TCA, this should only be done in consultation with an ophthalmologist. A TCA with low anticholinergic potency should be chosen. In general, the concomitant administration of a topical cholinomimetic agent such as pilocarpine would be adequate to overcome this atropinelike effect of TCA.

Patients with a history of prostatic hypertrophy are at risk to develop urinary outflow obstruction when treated with TCA. This is because neurotransmission governing the urinary sphincter is mediated by acetylcholine, and the TCA's ability to interfere with ACh transmission prevents sphincter dilation. Where prostatic enlargement is a concern, agents of low anticholinergic potency should probably be chosen. Any patient developing urinary obstruction while on TCA should have the drug immediately discontinued. In addition to catheterization, obstructed patients may require continuous drains for 24 to 48 hours to enable the bladder to regain its normal tone.

The dry mouth, which is another consequence of the atropinelike effects of TCA, can become a major problem for patients who wear dentures, as diminished salivation may be associated with gum irritation. Again, TCA of low anticholinergic potency may ameliorate this condition. A saliva substitute, VA-OraLube, is also reported to be effective in cases of drug-induced dry mouth.[22]

An alternate method for overcoming the peripheral anticholinergic effects associated with TCA administration is to concomitantly administer a cholinergic medicine. Bethanecol chloride is a peripherally acting cholinomimetic agent which, when administered concomitantly with TCA, is reported to overcome such peripheral symptoms as dry mouth and difficulty voiding.[23] A dose of 25mg tid is recommended. This should not be used in cases where mechanical obstruction of urinary outflow is prominent.

**Central Nervous System**

TCA interfere with ACh-mediated synaptic transmission both in the periphery and in the central nervous system. The central atropinelike activity of TCA can lead to confusion, disorientation, delusions and ataxia. While these symptoms are generally not seen in young or middle-aged adults except in cases of overdose, geriatric patients are particularly vulnerable to these side effects. This may be a consequence of preexisting subclinical organicity, diminished organ reserve or increased end organ sensitivity to ACh blockade. In cases of overdose or in life-threatening situations, the parenteral administration of physostigmine can reverse this syndrome.[24] It does so by increasing the level of ACh in the CNS through inhibition of the effects of naturally occurring acetylcholine esterase. This is the enzyme which normally metabolizes ACh in the CNS. Physostigmine is only available as a parenteral treatment and should be used only in emergency situations. In general, the best treatment for mild organicity or confusional states induced by TCA is reduction of TCA dosage. Switching to a TCA with less anticholinergic potency might also be beneficial.

Patients with Parkinson's disease may exhibit depressive symptoms as part of their illness or as a response to their illness. While TCA may be effective in managing these symptoms, the drugs may exacerbate the difficulties these patients have with balance and postural control as well as underlying or manifest organicity. Postural hypotension and difficulty voiding, both consequences of autonomic dysfunction seen in some Parkinsonian patients, may also be exacerbated by TCA. In general, these problems are not seen when using IMI or AMI in doses of 75mg per day or less, and most Parkinsonian patients tolerate these drugs without difficulty. It should be kept in mind that synergism between the atropinelike effects of TCA and the anticholinergic medications prescribed for Parkinsonian patients may produce toxicity not seen if either agent were used alone. For some geriatric patients, TCA treatment may be precluded if therapeutic drug plasma concentrations are not obtainable without inducing intolerable central nervous system side effects.

**Cardiovascular System**

Shortly after TCA were first introduced, overdose cases demonstrated that they could profoundly affect the cardiovascular system. However, the cardiac effects of therapeutic concentrations of these drugs have only recently become the subject of careful investigation. It is now known that even at therapeutic plasma concentrations, TCA are capable of affecting intracardiac conduction, cardiac rhythm, cardiac contractility and blood-pressure regulation. A knowledge of these effects is of particular importance to the management of depression in geriatric patients, as cardiovascular disease is so common in this population.

The cardiovascular effects of TCA administration must be seen in the context of the dose-response relationships of these drugs (see Figure 5-1, page 113). In addition, preexisting heart disease and circulatory status must be considered when treating geriatric patients with TCA. Unfortunately, most studies of cardiovascular effects of TCA have been done in patients far below the geriatric age, and most have been conducted in populations free from significant cardiovascular disease.

## Intraventricular Conduction

Excessive or toxic NT plasma concentrations have consistently been shown to cause prolongation of intraventricular conduction. In fact, QRS interval prolongation correlates extremely well with plasma concentration of the drug in overdose cases.[25] At plasma concentrations within the therapeutic window, NT does not seem to cause significant conduction disturbances in healthy young and middle-aged adults.[26,27] There is as yet no information about the cardiac effects of NT in older adults or geriatric patients, or in patients with preexisting cardiac disease.

Toxic concentrations of IMI have also been demonstrated to prolong intraventricular conduction. Recent studies demonstrate that IMI in plasma concentrations therapeutic for depression frequently cause prolongation of PR, QRS and QTC intervals.[28] It is currently uncertain whether it is the age or the cardiovascular status of the patients studied or properties instrinsic to IMI which accounts for the apparent differences in cardiac effects between NT and IMI. This is because the IMI patients were significantly older (mean age 59, range 35 to 76) than those studied with NT (mean age 42, range 19 to 57) and also had more preexisting cardiovascular disease than did those studied with NT.

Because TCA are capable of prolonging intraventricular conduction, it might be expected that patients with preexisting disease of the conduction system would be at increased risk when treated with TCA. There has been a report of a patient with preexisting right bundle branch block who, at therapeutic plasma concentrations of IMI, did develop 2:1 heart block, a potentially hazardous cardiac condition.[29] Subsequently, seven other patients with preexisting bundle branch disease who tolerated IMI without adverse effects have been reported.[28] Why some patients with bundle branch disease tolerate TCA well and others do not is uncertain. Patients with preexisting bundle branch disease may be at increased risk for adverse cardiac effects of TCA, and the presence of such a condition would dictate a more cautious use of these drugs. A routine EKG prior to TCA administration would be adequate to detect the presence of this conduction disturbance, and is essential in geriatric patients.

## Cardiac Rhythm

Soon after their introduction, it was demonstrated that toxic concentrations of TCA could cause life-threatening and lethal arrhythmias. It was therefore assumed that the presence of atrial or ventricular arrhythmias were a contraindication to TCA administration. However, it has recently been demonstrated that at concentrations of IMI therapeutic for depression, this drug actually suppresses atrial and ventricular premature contractions.[30] It now appears that some of the arrhythmias which previously had been attributed to TCA administration probably reflected only the chance association between TCA administration and spontaneously occurring cardiac arrhythmic activity. It now seems that IMI may actually benefit patients who have ventricular or atrial premature contractions. The effect of TCA other than IMI on atrial and ventricular premature contractions, or of any TCA on such conditions as atrial fibrillation or atrial flutter, is unknown. Patients in whom arrhythmic activity is of concern, especially those already being treated with antiarrhythmic agents (see Drug Interactions below) should be treated in collaboration with a cardiologist or internist familar with these conditions and their treatment. A routine electrocardiogram would not adequately characterize a patient's arrhythmic activity, and specialized recording techniques would be necessary if arrhythmias were a concern.

**Orthostatic Hypotension**

Orthostatic hypotension is probably the most common cardiovascular effect seen during the routine administration of IMI. In some reported series it is the single most common cause for drug discontinuation.[28] Hayes[31] found all of his 19 TCA patients (mean age 52, range 42 to 64) to have diastolic blood pressure falls of 15mm Hg, with 10 patients having moderate to severe symptoms. Muller[32] found orthostatic hypotension to be a major hazard in geriatric patients (mean age 69) with preexisting cardiac disease, but of minor importance to younger (mean age 39) healthy adults. Whether his findings were related to age, cardiovascular status or properties intrinsic to IMI but not to other TCA must await further studies. Orthostatic hypotension should therefore be kept in mind as a potential problem in patients being TCA treated, especially those whose histories indicate impaired cardiac or cerebral circulation. In an inpatient setting, routine blood-pressure measurements are adequate to define the degree of orthostatic hypotension a TCA patient is experiencing.

Blood pressure should be obtained prior to the initiation of TCA administration and then throughout the treatment period. It should be taken supine and then immediately upon standing at least once a day. In Muller's study of patients with preexisting cardiovascular disease,[32] two patients experiencing both severe dizziness and diastolic blood pressure falls of greater than 20mm Hg suffered myocardial infarctions. Patients experiencing marked dizziness in association with severe blood-pressure falls should therefore have their TCA discontinued.

## Myocardial Contractility

There is as yet little information on the ability of TCA to affect myocardial contractility. Studies in animals[33] and in man[34] suggest that TCA may decrease cardiac output by diminishing cardiac return as a consequence of venous dilatation and by causing a direct decrease in myocardial contractility. While they are preliminary, such findings would dictate an extremely cautious use of TCA in patients with congestive heart failure or poorly compensated cardiovascular function and would contraindicate their use in the immediate postmyocardial infarction period.

## DRUG INTERACTIONS

Elderly patients are often taking one or more medications concomitant with antidepressant drugs. Coadministered medications can interfere or be synergistic with the antidepressant effects of TCA, can exacerbate or diminish TCA side effects or can create toxicity which would not be seen in the absence of coadministered medication or if the coadministered medication were given without the presence of TCA. A basic knowledge of these potential drug interactions is therefore necessary in treating depressed geriatric patients.

### Substances Affecting TCA Metabolism

With a given dose of TCA, the major determinant of TCA plasma concentration is the rate at which the TCA is metabolized by the liver. While the basic rate of metabolism by liver microsomes is genetically determined, a number of drugs have been shown to increase or decrease microsomal enzyme activity and hence affect the TCA plasma concentration.[35] Barbiturates, frequently administered to treat sleep disorders in geriatric patients, are potent inducers of microsomal enzymes, and as a consequence can result in markedly decreased TCA plasma concentrations. As a result, patients given barbiturate sedatives, despite apparently adequate oral doses of TCA, may obtain inadequate TCA plasma concentrations.

Tobacco also seems to stimulate microsomal enzymes, and hence smokers develop lower TCA plasma concentration than do nonsmokers.[36]

While most of the sedative hypnotic drugs have been shown to cause enzyme induction, flurazepam, a commonly used hypnotic, does not seem to affect plasma TCA concentration.[37] This drug would therefore seem to be the drug of choice for patients whose depression is compounded by severe insomnia.

Methylphenidate, a compound which inhibits microsomal enzymes, can be used to increase TCA plasma concentrations.[38] This can be utilized therapeutically by combining methylphenidate with a TCA in patients who appear to be refractory to IMI treatment alone. The table below lists a wide variety of drugs which are capable of affecting hepatic metabolism and hence TCA plasma concentration.

**Table 5-1: Effect of Various Agents on Steady-State Plasma Concentrations of Tricyclic Antidepressants**

| Lowers | No Effect | Raises |
|---|---|---|
| Barbituates | Diazepam | Chlorpromazine |
| Chloral Hydrate | Nitrazepam | Haloperidol |
| Mandrex | Oxazepam | Perphenazine |
| Glutethimide | Flurazepam | Levomepromazine |
| Trihexyphenidyl | Chlordiazepoxide | Chlorprothixene |
| Acid pH (Ammonium | | |
| chloride) | L-triiodothyronine | Thioridazine |
| Smoking | Fluphenazine | Methylphenidate |
| | | Fenfluramine |
| | | Chloramphenacol |
| | | Norethindrone |
| | | Basic pH (Sodium bicarbonate) |
| | | Aging |

## Anticholinergic Drugs

The anticholinergic properties of TCA (see above) are responsible for many of the reported side effects of these drugs. The coadministration of other drugs with anticholinergic or atropinelike properties or side effects would be expected to exacerbate the anticholinergic side effects of TCA. Such drugs would include the phenothiazines or butyrophenone antipsychotic agents, anti-Parkinsonian agents, the belladonna alkaloids or synthetic anticholinergic antispasmodics, such as those agents used for peptic ulcer disease.[39] When possible, such drugs should be discontinued when TCA administration is necessary.

## Cardiovascular Drugs

Patients being treated for cardiovascular disease may be on a variety of

medications, including diuretics, antiarrhythmic agents, antihypertensive
agents, anticoagulants, or be living with permanent cardiac pacemakers.
All of these have significant interactions with TCA.[40]

As mentioned above, orthostatic hypotension is a potentially hazardous
complication associated with TCA administration. It might be expected
that volume-depleting diuretic agents would exacerbate TCA-induced
orthostatic hypotension. In our experience with hospitalized patients, and
in consultation with an internist, we have been able to discontinue diuretic
agents at the time of initiating TCA treatment without loss of blood-
pressure control. However, it should be kept in mind that the hospitalization of hypertensive patients frequently results in normalization of their
blood pressure, and our data are drawn exclusively from hospitalized
patients. Whether these observations about blood-pressure control can be
generalized to outpatients is uncertain.

Antihypertensive agents such as guanethadine, bethanidine and
debrisoquine present another problem. In order to exert their effects, these
drugs must be actively pumped into the adrenergic neurons. TCA inhibit
the effects of this pump and as a consequence inhibit the antihypertensive
properties of these drugs. Therefore, hypertension cannot be controlled
with these agents while TCA are being administered.[41] The effects of
clonidine, another antihypertensive agent, are also inhibited by TCA.[42]
While reserpine and alpha-methyldopa are effective in the presence of
TCA, both these compounds are implicated in precipitating depressions
and would therefore not seem to be appropriate agents in depressed
patients.[43] The optimal management of hypertension in patients treated
with TCA is currently unclear.

Spontaneously occurring atrial and ventricular cardiac arrhythmias are
commonly seen in the geriatric population and are often treated with the
antiarrhythmic agents, quinidine and procainamide. The antiarrhythmic
properties of IMI, as well as its ability to prolong intraventricular
depolarization and repolarization, make it markedly similar in activity to
quinidine and procainamide.[30] Because of this, the coadministration of one
of these agents and IMI might result in toxic effects on the cardiac
conduction system, not seen if either agent were used alone. In close
collaboration with an internist, the dose of antiarrhythmic agent should
probably be decreased in patients being treated for arrhythmias who are,
in addition, in need of IMI. It is currently unknown whether all TCA or
only IMI possess this cardiac property.

Patients with cardiovascular disease are often anticoagulated with oral
agents such as bishydroxycoumarin or warfarinsodium. These drugs are
inactivated through liver metabolism. While TCA are metabolized by the
liver, they are also mild inhibitors of liver microsomal metabolism. TCA

have been shown to prolong the half-life of bishydroxycoumarin, and therefore would have the potential to precipitate excessive bleeding in patients previously stablely anticoagulated with this compound.[44] Anticoagulated patients should therefore have their prothrombin times carefully monitored during TCA treatment, especially when treatment is begun, changed or discontinued.

Increasing numbers of geriatric patients have had their lives prolonged through the placement of permanent ventricular pacemakers. Such pacemakers are usually inserted because of disturbances in the intraventricular conduction system and act by bypassing this system all the time (fixed-rate pacemakers) or when necessary (demand pacemakers). Patients with pacemakers would be protected from TCA's ability to interfere with intraventricular conduction and could therefore be treated safely with TCA despite an impaired conducting system.

## SUMMARY

Depression is a serious and potentially life-threatening condition commonly seen in the geriatric population. The first and most important step in treatment is making an accurate assessment of the nature, degree and apparent causes for the patient's depression. Depressed patients for whom social or psychological interventions would be optimal, or patients needing treatment for occult medical conditions, must be distinguished from those who would seem most likely to respond to TCA administration.

Before starting drug administration, the clinician must be aware of the dose-response characteristics of the TCA being chosen and of the potential interactions between TCA and coexisting medical conditions the patient may have or drugs the patient may concurrently be taking. Extrapolations from studies done in younger patients as well as direct observations in the elderly indicate that on a mg-for-mg basis, geriatric patients are likely to be much more sensitive and vulnerable to the effects of TCA. This is especially true of drug-induced orthostatic hypotension which may be the most important consideration in the TCA treatment of older patients. Doses should be adjusted accordingly.

Keeping the considerations outlined in this chapter in mind should enable the clinician to provide optimal management for severe depressions occurring in the geriatric population.

# REFERENCES

1. Klein DF: Endomorphogenic depression. *Arch Gen Psychiatry* 31:447–54, 1974.
2. Feighner JP, Robbins E, Guze S et al: Diagnostic criteria for use in psychiatric research. *Arch Gen Psychiatry* 26:57–63, 1972.
3. Spitzer RL, Endicott J, Robbins E, et al: Preliminary report of the reliability of research diagnostic criteria applied to psychiatric case records, in Gershon S, Beer R (eds): *Prediction in Psychopharmacology*. New York, Raven Press, 1975.
4. Butler RN: Psychiatry and the elderly: An overview. *Am J Psychiatry* 132:893–900, 1975.
5. Garetz FK: Breaking the dangerous cycle of depression and faulty nutrition. *Geriatrics* 31:73–75, 1976.
6. Glassman AH, Kantor SJ, Shostak M: Depression, delusions and drug response. *Am J Psychiatry* 132:716–719, 1975.
7. Kantor SJ, Glassman AH: Delusional depressions: Natural history and response to treatment. *Br J Psychiatry* 131:351–360, 1977.
8. Hammer W, Sjoqvist F: Plasma levels of monomethylated tricyclic antidepressants during treatment with imipramine-like compounds. *Life Sci* 6:1895–1903, 1967.
9. Asberg M, Cronholm B, Sjoqvist F, et al: Relationship between plasma level and therapeutic effect of nortriptyline. *Br Med J* 3:331–334, 1971.
10. Kragh-Sorensen P, Asberg M, Eggert-Hansen C: Plasma nortriptyline levels in endogenous depression. *Lancet* 1:113–115, 1973.
11. Kragh-Sorensen P, Hansen C, Baastrup P, et al: Self-inhibiting action of nortriptyline's antidepressive effect at high plasma levels. *Psychopharmacologia* 45:305–312, 1976.
12. Glassman AH, Perel JM, Shostak M, Kantor SJ, et al: Clinical implications of imipramine plasma levels for depressive illness. *Arch Gen Psychiatry* 34:197–204, 1977.
13. Gram L, Reisby N, Ibsen I, et al: Plasma levels and antidepressive effect of imipramine. *Clin Pharm Ther* 19:318–324, 1976.
14. Simpson GM, Lee JH, Cuculic Z, et al: Two dosages of imipramine in hospitalized endogenous and neurotic depressives. *Arch Gen Psychiatry* 33:1093–1102, 1976.
15. Whyte S, MacDonald A, Naylor G, et al: Plasma concentrations of protriptyline and clinical effects in depressed women. *Br J Psychiatry* 128:384–390, 1976.
16. Hollister LG: Prescribing drugs for the elderly. *Geriatrics* 32:71–73, 1977.
17. Friedel RO: Pharmacokinetics in the geropsychiatric patient, in Lipton MA, DiMascio A, Killam KF (eds): *Psychopharmacology: A Generation of Progress*. New York, Raven Press, 1978.
18. Gram KF, Sondergaard IB, Christiansen J: Steady state kinetics of imipramine in patients. *Psychopharmacology* 54:225–261, 1977.
19. Nies A, Robinson DS, Friedman MJ, et al: Relationship between age and tricyclic antidepressant plasma levels. *Am J Psychiatry* 134:790–793, 1977.
20. Salzman C, van der Kolk B, Shader RI: Psychopharmacology and the geriatric patient, in Shader RI (ed): *Manual of Psychiatric Therapeutics*. Boston, Little Brown, 1975.
21. Snyder A, Kamamura HI: Antidepressants and their muscarinic acetylcholine receptor. *Arch Gen Psychiatry* 34:236–239, 1977.
22. Fann WE, Shannon I: A treatment for dry mouth in psychiatric patients. *Am J Psychiatry* 134:251–252, 1978.
23. Everett HC: The use of bethanechol chloride with tricyclic antidepressants. *Am J Psychiatry* 132:1202–1204, 1975.
24. Granacher RP: Physostigmine. *Arch Gen Psychiatry* 32:375–380, 1975.
25. Spiker DG, Weiss AN, Chang SS, Ruwitch JE, Biggs JI: *Clin Pharmacol Ther* 18:539–546, 1975.

26. Vohra J, Burrows GD, Hunt D, Sloman G: The effect of toxic and therapeutic doses of tricyclic antidepressant drugs on intracardiac conduction. *Europ J Cardiol* 3/3:219–227, 1975.

27. Ziegler VE, Co BT, Biggs JT: Plasma nortriptyline levels and ECG findings. *Am J Psychiatry* 134:441–443, 1977.

28. Kantor SJ, Glassman AG, Bigger JT Jr, et al: The cardiac effects of therapeutic plasma concentrations. *Am J Psychiatry* 135:534–538, 1978.

29. Kantor SJ, Bigger JT Jr, Glassman AH, Macken DL, Perel JM: Imipramine induced heart block: A longitudinal case study. *JAMA* 231:1364–1366, 1975.

30. Bigger JT Jr, Giardina EG, Perel JM, Kantor SJ, Glassman AH: Cardiac antiarrhythmic effect of imipramine hydrochloride. *N Eng J Med* 296:206–208, 1977.

31. Hayes JR, Born GF, Rosenbaum AH: Incidence of orthostatic hypotension with primary affective disorders treated with tricyclic antidepressants. *Mayo Clin Proc* 52:509–512, 1977.

32. Muller OE, Goodman N, Bellett S: The hypotensive effect of imipramine hydrochloride in patients with cardiovascular disease. *Clin Pharmacol Ther* 2:300–307, 1961.

33. Perel JM, Jandhyala BS, Steenberg ML, et al: Effects of imipramine, chlorimipramine and its metabolites on the hemodynamics and myocardial contractility of anesthetized dogs. *Europ J Pharmacol* 42:403–410, 1977.

34. Muller V, Burckhardt D: Die wirkung tri- und tetrazyklischer antidepressive auf herz und Kreislauf. *Schweiz Med Wochenschr* 104:1911–1913, 1974.

35. Glassman AH, Perel J: The clinical pharmacology of imipramine. *Arch Gen Psychiatry* 28:649–653, 1973.

36. Perel JM, Shostak M, Gann E, et al: Pharmacodynamics of imipramine and clinical outcome in depressed patients, in Gottschalk LA, Merlis S (eds): *Pharmacokinetics of Psychoactive Drugs*. New York, Spectrum, 1976.

37. Robinson DS, Amidon EL: Interaction of benzodiazepines with warfarin in man. Read before the Annual Symposium on Benzodiazepines in Milan, Italy, Nov. 2–4, 1971. To be published.

38. Wharton RN, et al: A potential clinical use for methylphenidate (Ritalin) with tricyclic antidepressants. *Am J Psychiatry* 127:1619–1625, 1971.

39. deGroot MHL: The clinical use of psychotherapeutic drugs in the elderly. *Drugs* 8:132–138, 1974.

40. Bigger JT, Kantor SJ, Glassman AH, Perel JM: Cardiovascular effects of tricyclic antidepressant drugs, in Lipton MA, DiMascio A, Killam KF (eds): New York, Raven Press, 1978.

41. Kaumann A, Basso N, Aramendia P: The cardiovascular effects of desmethylimipramine and guanethidine. *J Pharmacol Exp Ther* 147:54–64, 1965.

42. Briant RH, Reid JL, Dollery CT: Interaction between clonidine and desipramine in man. *Br Med J* 1:522–523, 1973.

43. Simpson FO: Hypertension and depression and their treatment. *Austr New Z J Psych* 7:133–137, 1973.

44. Vesell ES, Passananti T, Greene FE: Impairment of drug metabolism in man by allopurinol and nortriptyline. *N Engl J Med* 283:1484–1488, 1970.

# CHAPTER 6

# Comparative Stereology Of Capillaries In The Cerebral Cortex With Special Reference to Drug Effects

O. HUNZIKER
P. GYGAX

Nowadays the medical practitioner disposes of many drugs in order to treat cerebral insufficiency in old age. Many of them have a vasodilating effect—e.g., the well-known opium-alkaloid papavarine.[1,2,3,4,5] The majority of scientists working today in the field of geriatric research accept a differentiation between vascular[6] and psychoorganic disorders of the aging brain,[7,8,9] the former designated as cerebrovascular insufficiency, the latter as psychoorganic disease of aging. The etiology of cerebrovascular insufficiency is due to a stenosing atherosclerosis of blood vessels—e.g., the carotid and the cerebral basal arteries—whereas the psychoorganic disease of aging is supposed to be a disturbed brain metabolism.[7,10] During the recent past, critical voices came up on the clinical use of vasodilators in old people with dementia.[11] Thereby the general question arises about a beneficial effect of vaso- or metabolically active drugs on cerebral disorders during aging. Concerning an experimental animal model with hypovolemic oligemia, the following chapters may give an explanation of the problem.

Physiological experiments with methods like hydrogen-clearance, EEG and $pO_2$-registration give essential information about the dynamics of microcirculation and cerebral metabolism.[12] Additionally, sterological measurements prove changes of cerebral structures, such as the cortical capillaries. They were quantitatively investigated as an essential part of a functional unit in the cerebral cortex consisting of neurons, astrocytes and the capillary network.[13] Therefore, a better knowledge of the capillary structure leads to a profounder comprehension of neuronal function. In this connection the capillaries were stereologically determined in cat[14] and in man.[15]

## NORMAL CAPILLARY ARCHITECTURE

Since the fundamental descriptions of Craigie,[16,17,18] much work has been done, particularly on animal cerebral capillaries, either light-[19-29] or electron-microscopically.[30-36] In order to get information about the spatial arrangement of capillaries in the cerebral cortex, a three-dimensional reconstruction was performed.[37] The resulting model demonstrated a dense capillary network with predominantly dichotome branching (Figure 6-1). Therewith, the branching pattern of larger cerebral vessels[38] is also maintained on the capillary level. The resulting stable construction as well as an almost complete pericapillary glial sheath[39] do not allow extensive changes of stereological capillary parameters, such as volume or length per unit tissue volume, like in the heart.[40] Consequently, significant deviations from values of the normal cerebral cortex[14] can only occur in a rather finite range. The principle was, for example, demonstrated by comparing the stereological behavior of capillaries in the cerebral cortex of young and aging human subjects. A more comprehensive study of previously published results[15] yielded a moderate but significant increase of capillary diameter, volume and length per unit cortex volume in the precentral gyrus of the parietal lobe (Table 6-1). The specific capillary surface area was decreased. Surprisingly, the minimal intercapillary distances were not significantly altered. Based on an age-dependent decrease of the extracellular space,[41,42] the mentioned results of increased capillary volume and length indicate a condensation of the capillary net in the aging cerebral cortex. In spite of unchanged minimal intercapillary distances, a shorter oxygen-diffusion pathway through the cortical tissue can be expected. As a consequence, the cortical capillary network of the aging human brain is able to adapt to changed blood supply and metabolism. These reflections lead to the main problem of a vascular or metabolic etiology of cerebral insufficiency during old age. The answer to this question is of great importance for the development of a new therapeutic concept. For this purpose the model of hypovolemic oligemia was used to evoke circulatory and metabolic insufficiency in the cat brain.

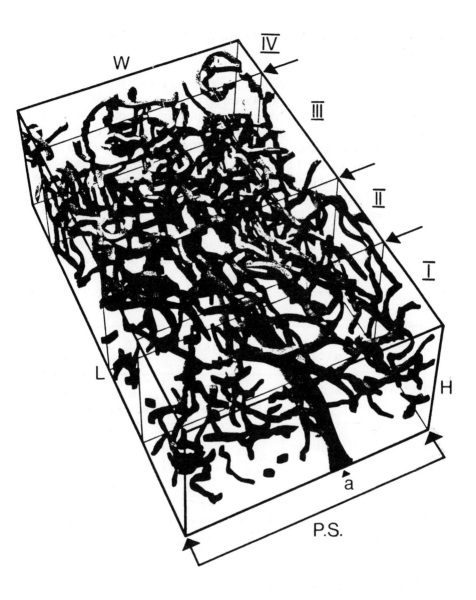

Figure 6-1:    Three-dimensional model of the capillary network in a small tissue block
(volume = 6.2 x 10$^{-2}$mm$^3$) of the cat's cerebral cortex (temporo-parietal suprasylvian gyrus).
a : artery ; P.S. : pial surface.
I - IV : cortical layers.

## AN EXPERIMENTAL ANIMAL MODEL: HYPOVOLEMIC OLIGEMIA

In hypovolemic oligemia (hypovolemic hypotension), the mean arterial blood pressure is lowered to 45mm Hg beyond the autoregulatory threshold of the cerebral cortex. The results are reduction in cerebral microflow and disturbances of the metabolic equilibrium in the brain.[43,44] The situation is characterized by a marked EEG-depression.[45] Obtained by measurements of cerebral blood flow and EEG, the physiological results could be completed and extended in an efficient manner by stereological studies of capillaries in the cerebral cortex of the cat.[13,46] They revealed in the frontal and occipital cortex region of hypovolemic animals a significant diminution of capillary diameter and mean linear distances (Table 6-2). Specific surface area and capillary length per unit cortex volume increased. Apparently, the capillary net responds to a reduced blood pressure and volume. The purpose of this mechanism was supposed to be increased oxygen diffusion and resorption area of the capillary wall together with a

| Stereological | Precentral    Gyrus | |
|---|---|---|
| parameters | young 19−49 years | aged normotonic 66−72 years |
| Diameter (μ) | 5.74 | 6.49 |
| Volume (%) | 2.18 | 3.09 |
| Specific surface area (μ⁻¹) | .476 | .425 |
| Minimal intercapillary distance (μ) | 56.58 | 57.53 |
| Length/unit cortex volume (cm/mm³) | 17.24 | 21.68 |

Table 6-1:   Behaviour of stereological parameters in the human cerebral cortex (precentral gyrus) of young (n = 6) and aged (n = 6) subjects.

higher capillary resistance.[13] Local $pO_2$-measurements[47] have shown that the recorded morphological response on the capillary level is functionally less effective. The $pO_2$-histogram of the frontal suprasylvian gyrus indicated the onset of tissue hypoxia,[47] which caused the mentioned decrease of cerebral electrical activity.[45,48] Therewith, the model of hypovolemic oligemia was proved to be useful for testing cerebral insufficiency.

## DRUG EFFECTS ON STEREOLOGICAL PARAMETERS

Working on the problem of therapeutic influence on cerebral insufficiency, it was of primary interest to investigate the action of the vasodilator papaverine and the neurochemically active drug dihydroergotamine mesylate (DHET; active substance of Hydergine®) under this model situation. Combined with hypovolemic oligemia, additional treatments with papaverine (1mg/kg b.w., i.v.) and DHET

| Stereological parameters | Cat brain- Frontal cortex | |
| --- | --- | --- |
| | Control | Oligemia |
| Diameter (μ) | 5.54 | 3.81 |
| Volume (%) | 3.40 | 3.21 |
| Specific surface area ($\mu^{-1}$) | .24 | .31 |
| Mean linear distances (μ) | 264 | 215 |
| Length/unit cortex volume (cm/mm$^3$) | 39.9 | 62.3 |

Table 6-2: Stereological parameters in the cat's cerebral cortex of controls and animals with hypovolemic oligemia (n = 4).

124 HUNZIKER and GYGAX

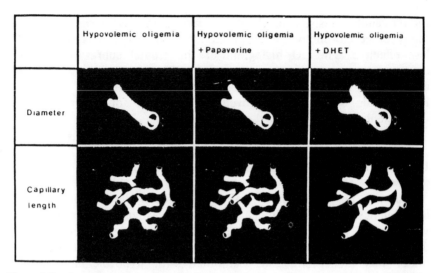

Figure 6-2: Stereological parameters in the cerebral cortex of hypovolemic cats additionally treated with papaverine and DHET.

(0.08mg/kg b.w., i.v.) were provided to investigate a vascular or metabolic etiology of cerebral insufficiency. Together with physiological results, stereological data contributed to clarify the problem.[49] The vasoactive properties of papaverine entailed normalization of cerebral circulation without protecting the EEG.[45,48] Stereological determinations in the cerebral cortex of papaverine-treated hypovolemic animals yielded no significant changes of capillary diameter and length per unit cortex volume (Figure 6-2 center). Thus, papaverine affects dilatation of larger smooth muscle containing blood vessels (diameter $> 8 \mu$m), but does not influence the capillaries (diameter $< 8 \mu$m).[14,49] The drug was assumed to activate arterio-venous shunt mechanisms, causing bypass of oxygen needed by neurons of the cerebral cortex. Based on stereological findings, this assumption was strongly supported by measurements of cerebral $pO_2$-distribution, which revealed an uneven perfusion of cortical tissue with hypoxic and hyperoxic regions.[47,48]

In contrast to the action of papaverine, DHET prevented reduced EEG energies during hypovolemic hypotension.[45] Although total cerebral blood flow was not significantly changed, the stereologically measured capillary diameter and length shifted toward the values measured in animals without oligemia (Figure 6-2, right). The seeming discrepancy between physiological and stereological results has a purely methodological explanation. Whereas measurements of cerebral blood flow with $H_2$-

clearance method[44] record a variety of blood vessels with a diameter larger than $8\mu m$, only capillaries are stereologically determined by means of their alkaline phosphatase activity.[14] The specific surface area of cerebrocortical capillaries was unchanged in DHET-treated animals.[49] This observation suggested a considerable interaction of capillaries with the surrounding astroglia.[25,35] Apparently, DHET influenced only secondarily the capillary net, via the astroglia, and primarily the cerebral metabolism impaired by disturbances of microcirculation.[50] Hence, the effect of DHET in the cerebral cortex sets an example for completing physiological findings with stereological ones: DHET showed physiologically an improving action on the oligemically disturbed cerebral metabolism. The improved situation is reflected in stabilized EEG-energies[45,48] and an improvement of the oxygen supply.[47] The results were stereologically completed by a measured shift of capillary diameter and length toward normal values.[13,14,37]

## CONCLUSIONS

The model of hypovolemic oligemia was demonstrated to evoke signs of CNS deficiency and to simulate to some extent cerebral insufficiency. Drugs like papaverine, dilating larger blood vessels, cause under hypovolemic conditions whether an improvement of the oxygen diffusion area of the capillary wall nor a return of stereological parameters toward normal values. In cerebral insufficiency ergot drugs like DHET influence primarily the disturbed cerebral metabolism and afterward the capillary network by means of the surrounding astroglia. Additionally, neurochemical findings of DHET indicate inhibition of both the norepinephrine-stimulated adenylcyclase- and the low-$k_m$-phosphodiesterase-activity.[51,52] Therewith, the protective action of DHET is to be thought as regulation of the CNS catecholamine turnover.[48] The connection between stereological results of the human aging brain and findings from hypovolemic oligemia helped establish a therapeutic concept: cerebral insufficiency as a consequence of age-dependent involution does not only depend on atherosclerosis of brain vessels, but has a primary metabolic etiology. Consequently, a therapy to influence cerebral age-dependent disturbances in a positive way should go in the direction of compensating metabolic disorders. Quantitative morphological determinations of capillaries in the cerebral cortex contributed importantly to elaborate the abovementioned concept. Together with physiological results, stereology mediates a profounder comprehension of drugs affecting cerebral insufficiency.

# REFERENCES

1. Gottstein U: Pharmacological studies of total cerebral blood flow in man with comments of the possibility of improving regional cerebral blood flow by drugs. *Acta Neurol Scand* (suppl 14) 41:136–141, 1965.
2. McHenry LC, Jaffe ME, Kawamure J, Goldberg HJ: The effect of papaverine on regional cerebral blood flow in focal vascular disease of the brain. *N Engl J Med* 282:1167–1170, 1970.
3. Skinhoj E, Paulson OB: Carbon dioxide and cerebral circulatory control. *Arch Neurol* 20:249–252, 1969.
4. Jayne HW, Scheinberg P, Rich M, Belle MS: The effect of intravenous papaverine hydrochloride on the cerebral circulation. *J Clin Invest* 31:101–114, 1952.
5. Saratikov AS, Usov LA, Gold LI: Papaverine and nospanum hydrochloricum action on the blood supply to the brain. *Pharmakol Toksikol* 32:152–154, 1969.
6. Terry RD, Wisniewski HW: Structural and chemical changes of the aged human brain, in Gershon S, Raskin A (eds): *Aging.* New York, Raven Press, 1975, pp 127–141, vol 2.
7. Meier-Ruge W, Emmenegger H, Gygax P, Iwangoff P, Walliser CH, Cerletti A: About the pathophysiology and therapy of cerebral insufficiency. A contribution to the experimental gerontology of the brain, in Platt D (ed): *Altern.* New York, Schattauer, 1974, pp 153–167.
8. Obrist WD: Influence of circulatory disorders, in Gaitz CM (ed): *Aging and the Brain.* New York, Plenum Press, 1972, pp 117–133.
9. Sokoloff L: Cerebral circulation and metabolism in the aged, in Gershon S, Raskin A (eds): *Aging.* New York, Raven Press, 1975, pp 45–54, vol 2.
10. Meier-Ruge W: Experimental pathology and pharmacology in brain research and aging. *Life Sci* 17:1627–1636, 1975.
11. Sathananthan GL, Gershon S: Cerebral vasodilators: A review, in Gershon S, Raskin A (eds): *Aging.* New York, Raven Press, 1975, pp 155–168, vol 2.
12. Gygax P, Wiernsperger N: Oligemic-hypotension-induced changes in EEG, CBF and $pO_2$ and their pharmacological modifications, in Ingvar DH, Lassen NA (eds): *Cerebral Function, Metabolism and Circulation.* Copenhagen, Munksgaard, 1977, pp 116–117.
13. Hunziker O, Emmenegger H, Frey H, Schulz U, Meier-Ruge W: Morphometric characterization of the capillary network in the cat's brain cortex: A comparison of the physiological state and hypovolemic conditions. *Acta Neuropathol* (Berl) 29:57–63, 1974.
14. Hunziker O, Frey H, Schulz U: Morphometic investigation of capillaries in the brain cortex of the cat. *Brain Res* 65:1–11, 1974.
15. Hunziker O, Abdel'Al S, Frey H, Veteau MJ, Meier-Ruge W: Quantitative studies in the cerebral cortex of aging humans. *Gerontology* 24:27–31, 1978.
16. Craigie EH: On the relative vascularity of various parts of the central nervous system of the albino rat. *J Com Neurol* 31:429–464, 1920.
17. Craigie EH: The vascularity of the cerebral cortex of the albino rat. *J Com Neurol* 33:193–211, 1921.
18. Craigie EH: Postnatal changes in vascularity in the cerebral cortex of the male albino rat. *J Com Neurol* 39:301–324, 1925.
19. Bar Th, Wolff JR: Quantitative relations between the number of ramifications and the length of capillaries in the neocortex of rat during postnatal development. *Z Anat Entw-Gesch* 141:207–221, 1973.
20. Dunning HS, Wolff HG: The relative vascularity of various parts of the central and peripheral nervous system of the cat and its relation to function. *J Com Neurol* 67:433–450, 1937.

21. Horstmann E: Abstand und Durchmesser der Kapillaren im Zentralnervensystem verschiedener Wirbeltierklassen, in Tower DB, Schade JP (eds): *Structure and Function of the Cerebral Cortex.* Amsterdam, Elsevier, 1960, pp 59–63.

22. Kramer J, Lierse W: Die postnatale Entwicklung der Kapillarisation im Gehirn der Maus (Mus musculus L.). *Acta Anat* (Basel) 66:446–459, 1967.

23. Lierse W: Die Kapillarabstande in verschiedenen Hirnregionen der Katze. *Z Zellforsch* 54:199–206, 1961.

24. Lierse W: Die Kapillardichte im Wirbeltiergehirn. *Acta Anat* (Basel) 54:1–31, 1963.

25. Lierse W: Die Hirnkapillaren und ihre Glia. *Acta Neuropath* (Berl) 4:40–52, 1968.

26. Opitz E: Ueber die Sauerstoffversorgung des Zentralnervensystems. *Naturwissenschaften* 35:80–88, 1948.

27. Petren T: Untersuchungen uber die relative Kapillarlange der motorischen Hirnrinde in normalem Zustande und nach Muskeltraining. *Anta Anz* 85: Erg.-H 169–72, 1938.

28. Purves MJ: The physiology of the cerebral circulation. Monographs of the Physiol Society 28, 1972. At the University Press, Cambridge.

29. Vries E de: Laminar injection of brain capillaries in cats. *Psychiat Neurol Bl* (Amst) Feestbundel Kappers, 712–722, 1934.

30. Bar Th, Wolff JR: Development and adult variations of the wall of brain capillaries in the neocortex of rat and cat, in Cervos-Navarro J, et al. (eds): *The Cerebral Vessel Wall.* New York, Raven Press, 1976, pp 1–6.

31. Bennett HS, Luft JH, Hampton JC: Morphological classification of vertebrate blood capillaries. *Am J Physiol* 196:381–390, 1959.

32. Drommer W, Dzuvic A: Zur Feinstruktur der normalen Kapillaren in der grauen Substanz der Grosshirnrinde beim Schwein. *Anat, Histol, Embryol* 4:87–93, 1975.

33. Maynard EA, Schultz RL, Pease DC: Electron microscopy of the vascular bed of rat cerebral cortex. *Am J Anat* 100:409–433, 1957.

34. Wolff JR: Beitrage zur Ultrastruktur der Kapillaren in der normalen Grosshirnrinde. *Z Zellforsch* 60:409–431, 1963.

35. Wolff JR: Ueber die Moglichkeiten der Kapillarverengung im Zentralnervensystem. Eine elektronenmikroskopische Studie an der Grosshirnrinde des Kaninchens. *Z Zellforsch* 63:593–611, 1964.

36. Wolff JR, Bar Th: "Seamless" endothelia in brain capillaries during development of the rat's cerebral cortex. *Brain Res* 41:17–24, 1972.

37. Wiederhold KH, Bielser W, Schulz U, Veteau MJ, Hunziker O: Three-dimensional reconstruction of brain capillaries from frozen serial sections. *Microvascular Res* 11:175–80, 1976.

38. Suwa N, Takahashi T: Morphological and morphometrical analysis of circulation in hypertension and ischemic kidney. Berlin, Urban & Schwarzenberg, 1971.

39. Wolff JR, Bar Th: Development and adult variations of the pericapillary glial sheath in the cortex of the rat, in Cervos-Navarro J, et al (eds): *The Cerebral Vessel Wall.* New York, Raven Press, 1976, pp 7–13.

40. Linzbach AJ: Pathogenese der Herzinsuffizienz bei Hypertonie. *Triangle* 14:17–26, 1975.

41. Bondareff W, Narotzky R: Age changes in the neuronal microenvironment. *Science* 176:1135–1136, 1972.

42. Bondareff W: Extracellular space in the aging cerebrum, in Terry RD, Gershon S (eds): *Neurobiology of Aging.* Raven Press, 1976, pp 167–175.

43. Gygax P, Emmenegger H, Dixon R: Cortical microflow and electrical brain activity (EEG) of the cat in a state of hypovolemic shock (Wigger's model). *IRCS Medical Sciences* 1:20, 1973.

44. Gygax P, Emmenegger H, Dixon R, Peier A: The effect of hypovolemic oligemia on the

cerebral microcirculation and EEG in the cat (Wigger's model), in Cervos-Navarro J (ed): *Pathology of Cerebral Microcirculation*. Berlin, de Gruyter, 1974, pp 386–394.

45. Gygax P, Hunziker O, Schulz U, Schweizer A: Experimental studies on the action of metabolic and vasoactive substances in the brain. *Triangle* 14:80–89, 1975.

46. Bar Th, Wolff JR, Hunziker O: Effects of different hemodynamic conditions on brain capillaries: Alveolar hypoxia, hypovolemic hypotension and ouabain edema, in Penzholz H, Brock M, Hamer J, Klinger M, Spoerri O (eds): *Advances in Neurosurgery — Brain Hypoxia — Pain*. New York, Springer, 1975, pp 10–19.

47. Wiernsperger N, Gygax P, Danzeisen M: Cortical $pO_2$ distribution during oligemic hypotension and its pharmacological modifications. *Arzneimittel-Forsch*, 28:768–770, 1978.

48. Gygax P, Wiernsperger N, Meier-Ruge W, Baumann T: Effect of papaverine and dihydroergotoxine mesylate on cerebral microflow, EEG and $pO_2$ in oligemic hypotension. *Gerontology* 24 (suppl 1):14–22, 1978.

49. Hunziker O, Emmenegger H, Meier-Ruge W, Schulz U: The behaviour of morphometric parameters of cortical capillaries in the brain influenced by DH-ergotoxine and papaverine. *IRCS Medical Sciences* 2:1481, 1974.

50. Meier-Ruge W, Enz A, Gygax P, Hunziker O, Iwangoff P, Reichlmeier K: Experimental pathology in basic research of the aging brain, in Gershon S, Raskin A (eds): *Aging*. New York, Raven Press, 1975, pp 55–126, vol 2.

51. Chappuis A, Enz A, Iwangoff P: The influence of adrenergic effectors on the cationic pump of brain cell membrane. *Triangle* 14:93–98, 1975.

52. Enz A, Iwangoff P, Markstein R, Wagner H: The effect of hydergine on the enzymes involved in cAMP turnover in the brain. *Triangle* 14:90–92, 1975.

# CHAPTER 7

# Quantitative Studies In The Cerebral Cortex Of Aging Persons

O. HUNZIKER
S. ABDEL'AL
H. FREY
M.J. VETEAU
W. MEIER-RUGE

## SUMMARY

The capillary network of the human cerebral cortex was mor-phometrically and stereologically investigated in two age groups: young (19 to 27 years) and aged (66 to 71 years). The latter group was divided into aged and aged hypertonic cases. In the aging cerebral cortex, augmented values of capillary diameter and volume are accompanied by smaller distances between capillaries and an extended length per unit cortex volume. Apparently, the capillary network of the aging brain is able to adapt to a changed metabolism and blood supply. An increased capillary diameter of the aged hypertonic group is probably a direct consequence of high blood pressure. To some extent, the regulating influence of the surrounding astroglia and the extracellular fluid on capillaries seems to be lacking. The presumption is supported by the results of all investigated stereological parameters. In comparison to normotonic brains, higher distances between the capillaries and a decrease of the capillary length were measured.

## Introduction

Since the important investigation of Brody,[1] only a few studies have appeared in the literature concerning age-dependent quantitative changes of neurons in the human brain. As one of few, Treff[2] reported about an age-dependent decrease of the neuronal volume and number in the dentate nucleus of the cerebellum in the ninth and tenth decades. Such quantitative information about the capillary network of the aging brain, which is the subject of this investigation, fails to appear in the literature. As some authors[3,4] dealt with morphometric investigations of cerebral capillaries during maturity of man and rats, it also seemed interesting to study the capillary architecture at the end of life. This paper contributes to the morphological knowledge in gerontology, which is becoming more and more important.

## MATERIALS AND METHODS

The investigation comprises a total of eight brains originating from two young — 19- and 27-years-old men — and an aged group of six cases between 66 and 71 years. Illness or cause of death is listed in Table 7-1. Clinical reports and pathological findings of the remaining four cases of the aged groups revealed hypertension and general arteriosclerosis. Therefore, this group is treated separately (Table 7-1). For the histological procedure, tissue slices were taken from the cortex of the frontal (frontal pole), parietal (anterior and posterior central gyrus), temporal (superior and inferior temporal gyrus) and occipital (occipital pole) lobe (Figure 7-1). Histological serial sections were cut in a cryostat and the cortical capillaries rendered visible by the alkaline-phosphatase reaction.[5] Subsequently they were measured with an optical-electronic image-analyzer, the Leitz-Classimat.[6,7] In our laboratories the Classimat is connected to a computer

### Table 7-1: Listing of investigated cases.

| Investigated cases. Total: 8 brains | | |
|---|---|---|
| Groups | Age | Illness or cause of death |
| Young (n:2) | 19 , 27 | Accidental event (2) |
| Aged (n:6) | without hypertension (n:2)    69 , 72 | Carcinoma of pancreas (1) Congestive cardiac failure (1) |
| | hypertonic (n:4)    66 to 71 | Chronic bronchitis (2) Carcinoma of uterine portio (1) Acute myocardial infarction (1) |

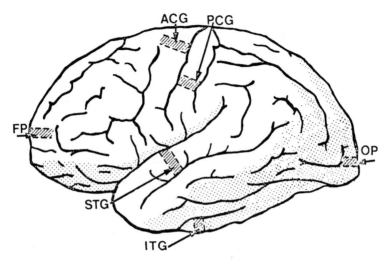

Figure 7-1: Investigated cerebral zones: FP=frontal pole. ACG=anterior central gyrus.
PCG=posterior central gyrus. STG=superior temporal gyrus. ITG=inferior temporal gyrus.
OP=occipital pole.

for interacting with the measuring device and calculating the used
stereological parameters, such as diameter ($\mu$m), projected area (=capillary
volume in %), surface-to-volume ratio (=specific capillary surface area),
mean distance between capillaries in linear direction of TV-lines) ($\mu$m) and
length per unit brain volume (cm/mm$^3$). As a preliminary statistical
analysis the Student-t-test was used to compare the results of the
stereological parameters between the young and aged cases as well as
between the aged and the aged hypertonic group.

## RESULTS

The comparison of the stereological parameters between the young and
the aged group is summarized in Table 7-2. The indicated numbers
represent parametric mean values over all gyri of each group. Compared
with the young group, the capillary diameter of the aged cases was
significantly increased in three gyri (precentral, postcentral and superior
temporal gyrus). The capillary volume (=projected area) of the aged group
tended to augment in all cortex regions and was also significantly larger in
three gyri (precentral, superior temporal gyrus and occipital pole).
Inversely proportional to the diameter, the specific surface area of the
aging brains diminished significantly in the corresponding gyri. The mean
capillary distances also showed a tendency to be reduced in the two aged

Table 7-2: Behavior of stereological capillary parameters in the cerebral cortex of young and aged persons.
(Numbers are mean values over all gyri of each group.)

| Stereological parameters | Precentral gyrus age-dependent-differences | |
|---|---|---|
| | young | aged |
| Diameter ($\mu$) | 6.73 | 7.21 |
| Projected area (%) | 2.32 | 2.97 |
| Specific surface area ($\mu^{-1}$) | .129 | .120 |
| Mean linear distances ($\mu$) | 451 | 373 |
| Length/unit cortex volume (cm/mm$^3$) | 20.65 | 24.05 |

cases. Only the precentral gyrus of the aging brains revealed a significantly elongated capillary length per unit cortex volume. When comparing the two aged groups (Table 7-3), the hypertonic cases showed a significantly increased capillary diameter in four investigated gyri (frontal and occipital pole, precentral and inferior temporal gyrus) and a highly significant increase of the specific surface area. Except the frontal pole, the capillary volume tended to be reduced and was significantly different from the aged cases in the superior temporal gyrus and occipital pole.

In contrast to the other cortical zones, two gyri (superior and inferior temporal gyrus) of the hypertonic group yielded significantly augmented mean distances between capillaries and a shorter length per unit cortex volume.

DISCUSSION

Although the sample number of the investigated young and aged cases is small, the demonstrated tendencies are powerful: as already published for the cat's cerebral cortex,[6] the stereological parameters of cortical capillaries in the human cerebrum are highly correlated regardless of age. A smaller specific surface area is not only accompanied by increased values of diameter and capillary volume, but also followed by shortened mean distances and an increased capillary length.

As published in the literature for other organs, such as kidney, retina and muscle, by Beauchemin et al.[8] a thickening of the capillary basement membrane during aging could contribute to the registered increased

**Table 7-3: Comparison of capillary parameters in the cerebral cortex of young, aged and aged hypertonic cases.**
**(Numbers are mean values over all gyri of each group.)**

| Stereological parameters | Precentral gyrus age-dependent-differences | | |
| --- | --- | --- | --- |
| | young | aged | aged hypertonic |
| Diameter ($\mu$) | 6.73 | 7.21 | 7.51 |
| Projected area (%) | 2.32 | 2.97 | 2.84 |
| Specific surface area ($\mu^{-1}$) | .129 | 120 | .172 |
| Mean linear distances ($\mu$) | 451 | 373 | 434 |
| Length/unit cortex volume (cm/mm$^3$) | 20.65 | 24.05 | 21.75 |

values of diameter and volume. The hypothesis has to be followed up by subsequent electron-microscopical investigations. Bondareff reported recently[9,10] about an age-dependent decrease of the extracellular space as well as of a loss of 27 percent in the number of synapses in the molecular layer of rats. His results fit well with our stereological result of shortened distances between capillaries in the aging human brain.

The data of Bondareff[11] also suggest a decrease in the capacity of the extracellular channels to support neuronal metabolism. Therefore, smaller capillary distances could participate in compensating a decreased transport capacity of the extracellular space.

At first sight the parametrical results of the aged hypertonic cases resemble, with exception of the diameter, those of the young group (Table 7-3). This phenomenon could lead to misinterpretations. Bearing in mind the fact that the investigated cortical tissue is aged, they can easily be avoided: an increased capillary diameter of the hypertonic group is probably a direct consequence of a high blood pressure. To some extent the regulating influence of the astroglia, completely surrounding cortical capillaries, and of the extracellular fluid seems to be lacking. The presumption is supported by the results of longer mean distances between capillaries, a reduced capillary volume and a shortened capillary length per unit cortex volume.

Summing up, the behavior of stereological parameters contributes importantly to the characterization of the capillary network in the cortex of the aging human brain. Especially in age-related hypertension, morphometry and stereology help to set up directives for further investigations of cortical capillaries. The reported morphometric results

argue against the widespread opinion of a decreased blood supply in the
cerebral cortex during aging. Apparently, the capillary network of the
aging brain is able to adapt to a changed metabolism and blood supply.

## REFERENCES

1. Brody H: Organization of the cerebral cortex. III. A study of aging in the human
   cerebral cortex. *J Com Neurol* 102:511–556, 1955.
2. Treff W: Das Involutionsmuster des Nucleus dentatus cerebelli. Eine morphometrische
   Analyse, in Platt D (ed): *Altern*. New York, Schattauer-Verlag, 1974, pp 37–54.
3. Craigie EH: Postnatal changes in the vascularity in the brain stem and cerebellum of the
   albino rat between birth and maturity. *J Com Neurol* 38:27–48, 1925.
4. Diemer K: Capillarisation and oxygen supply to the brain, in Lubbers DW, Luft UC,
   Thews G, Witzleb E (eds): *Oxygen Transport in Blood and Tissue*. Stuttgart, Thieme, 1968,
   pp 118–123.
5. Meier-Ruge W, Bielser, jun W, Wiederhold KH, Meyenhofer M: Incubation media for
   routine laboratory work on enzyme histotopochemistry. *Beitr Path Anat* 142:409–431,
   1971.
6. Hunziker O, Frey H, Schulz U: Morphometric investigations of capillaries in the brain
   cortex of the cat. *Brain Res* 65:1–11, 1974.
7. Kamin G, Kluge N, Muller W, Rzeznik J: Leitz-Classimat. Ein Instrument zur optischen
   Bildatenerfassung. *Leitz-Mitt Wiss u Techn Suppl* 1:1–24, 1970.
8. Beauchemin ML, Antille G, Leuenberger PM: Capillary basement membrane
   thickness: A comparison of two morphometric methods for its estimation. *Microvascular
   Res* 10:76–82, 1975.
9. Bondareff W, Narotzky R: Age changes in the neuronal microenvironment. *Science*
   176:1135–1136, 1972.
10. Bondareff W, Geinisman Y: Loss of synapses in the dentate gyrus of the senescent rat.
    *Am J Anat* 145:129–136, 1976.
11. Bondareff W: Extracellular space in the aging cerebrum, in Terry RD, Gershon S (eds):
    *Neurobiology of Aging*. New York, Raven Press, 1976, pp 167–175.

# CHAPTER 8

# Aging And The Behavioral Effects Of Dopamine Agonists In Rodents

ROBERT C. SMITH

J. RANDOLPH STRONG

JANET STRONG

Age-related changes in catecholamine synthesis and the effects of drugs whose actions may be mediated through these neurotransmitters on their receptors have been documented in both animals and man. For example, recent research has indicated that there is a decrease in catecholamine synthesis,[1,2] an increase in some catecholamine metabolizing enzymes,[3] and decreases in $\beta$-adrenergic receptors with age in both rat and man.[4,5] Decreased potency of drugs, such as propranolol, on blood pressure or cardiac activity has been reported in older-aged humans. Some other drugs, however, have been suggested to have increased physiological or psychological effects in older-aged rats and man. Animal studies have pointed to a lower threshold of greater effect of epinephrine on stimulating locomotor activity and raising blood pressure in the rat and rabbit.[6] Tanner and Domino indicated a greater effect of d-amphetamine on locomotor activity and hyperthermia in older-aged gerbils.[7]

The effects of dopamine agonists on stereotyped behavior in rats have been shown to be mediated primarily by brain dopamine,[8,9] and changes in this behavioral measure have been used to investigate supersensitivity of brain dopaminergic receptors after various pharmacological treatments in rats and mice.[10,11,12,13] Therefore, the current study investigated the

135

interaction of age with the effects of a directly acting dopamine agonist, apomorphine, and two indirectly acting dopamine agonists, d-amphetamine and methylphenidate, on stereotyped and gnawing behavior in rats and mice of various ages.

## METHOD

Fisher 344 rats were obtained from Charles River (Willmington, Massachusetts), which on arrival had designated ages of 2 months (developing), 10 months (mature adults) and 20 months (old). C57BL/10J mice, with designated ages of 4, 14 and 27 months respectively at the beginning of the experiment, were bred at TRIMS from breeder mice originally obtained from the Jackson Laboratories (Bar Harbor, Maine), and some of these mice were further aged at TRIMS. Rats were housed in groups of two, and mice were housed in groups of six, under standard laboratory condition of 72°F, 12-hour light-dark cycle and *ad lib* access to food and water.

Weights of mice were not significantly different in the three age groups (mean weights: 4 month=30.2, 14 month=31.8, 27 month =29.8 grams). Although the young rats weighed about 100 grams less than rats in the two older groups, there were no significant differences in weight between the 10- and 20-month-old rats (mean weights: 2 month=312, 10 month=425, 20 month=421 grams).

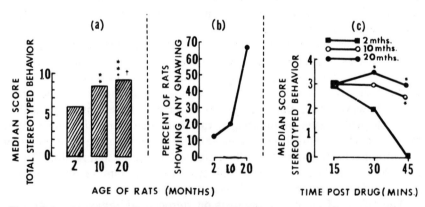

Figure 8-1:    Age and the effects of apomorphine (1mg/kg) on stereotyped behavior in the rat. (a) Median score total stereotyped behavior 0 to 45 minutes post drug. (b) Percent rats showing any gnawing behavior during 45 minutes post-drug. (c) Time course of stereotyped behavior. N = 24 to 52 rats for each group. Statistical significant: between 2 months and other group—* p < .05, ** p < .01, *** p < .001; between 20 month and 10 month animals—† p < .05, †† p < .01.

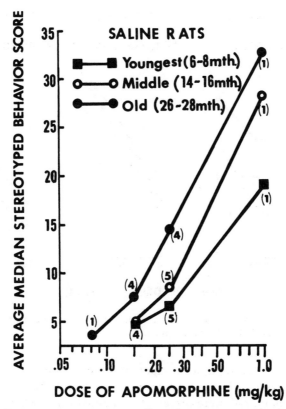

Figure 8-2:   Dose response curves for the effects of age on apomorphine-induced stereotyped gnawing in rats. Each point represents average median gnawing score of 10-12 rats tested with same dose on 1-4 different occasions; each testing occasion separated by at least one week's time.

Rats were administered apomorphine (1mg/kg, i.p.) or d-amphetamine (3.5mg/kg, i.p.). D-amphetamine was administered approximately two weeks after the dose of apomorphine. Animals were scored for stereotyped behavior (SB) at 15-minute intervals for a total of 45 minutes after apomorphine injections and for a total of 90 minutes after d-amphetamine injections. Several specific stereotyped behaviors, including stereotyped sniffing, gnawing, licking, pawing and circling, were scored on a 0 to 5 scale, and total stereotyped behavior was computed as the arithmetic sum of these category scores at a given observational time. Details of the scoring system are presented in our previous publications.[10,11]Some of the rats later participated as a saline control group in another part of the experiment in which they received chronic saline injections for about two months. They were then retested over an eight-

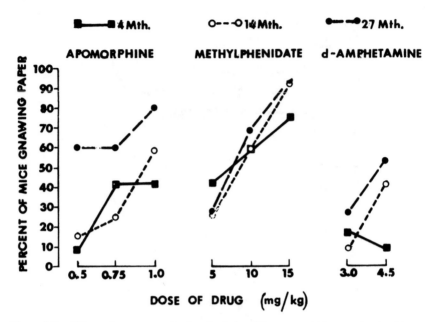

Figure 8-3:   Effects of age on gnawing in mice induced by apomorphine, methyphenidate
and d-amphetamine. N = 8 to 12 for each group.

week period with several doses of apomorphine (.15mg/kg s.c., .25mg/kg
s.c. and 1.0mg/kg i.p.). For evaluation of stereotyped behavior in this part
of the experiment, rats were placed in individual cages which had been
slightly modified from the earlier (pretest) conditions. The same scoring
system was used. Total stereotyped behavior scores and gnawing scores are
utilized in this report.

Mice were administered several doses of apomorphine (0.5, .75, 1.0 mg/
kg), d-amphetamine (1.5, 3.0, 4.5 mg/kg) or methylphenidate (5, 10, 15 mg/
kg) on three different days. Each group received the same order of dosage
administration, which was counterbalanced so that some animals received
the highest dose on the first day and others received the highest dose of
each specific drug on the last day. Mice were placed in individual cages
with corrugated cardboard on the bottom. Stereotyped behavior was
observed at several selected time points throughout a one-hour period;
also, the number of holes bitten in the corrugated paper in one hour was
counted. The latter measure will be used in this report.

Because of the wide variability and skewed distribution of stereotyped
behavior or gnawing scores, statistical tests were performed with
nonparametric procedures. Overall effects for the three age groups were
assessed using the Kruskal-Wallis analysis of variance or $\chi^2$ test, and the

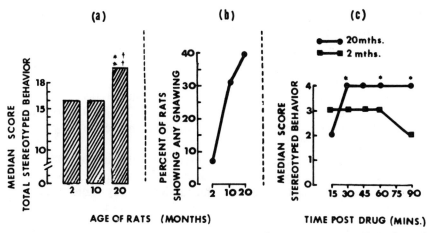

Figure 8-4:   Effects of age on d-amphetamine (3.5 mg/kg) induced stereotyped behavior and gnawing in the rat. (a) median total stereotyped behavior 0-90 minutes after amphetamine. (b) Percent of rats showing any gnawing behavior during 90 minutes. (c) Time course of stereotyped behavior. See Figure 8-1 for explanation of statistical significance and other details.

differences between the specific groups after the Kruskal-Wallis analysis of variance were assessed with the procedures of Dunn.[14]

## RESULTS

Both the direct-acting dopamine agonist, apomorphine, and the indirect-acting dopamine agonists, d-amphetamine and methylphenidate, were found to be more potent in producing their effects on stereotyped behavior in old-aged rats and mice compared to younger rats and mice. Drug effects in middle-aged rats and mice were generally intermediate between the youngest and oldest age groups.

Figure 8-1 shows the effects of 1mg/kg apomorphine (i.p.) on: a) total stereotyped behavior scores during the 45-minute observation period after injection; b) occurrence of gnawing behavior during this observation period; and c) time-course of stereotyped behavior, in rats approximately 2 months, 10 months and 20 months of age. There was a significant effect of age on the total stereotyped behavior induced by 1mg/kg apomorphine ($H_o$ =28.2, df = 2, p < .001) and gnawing behavior ($X^2$ =5.98, df = 2, p < .05) with both 20-month (p < .001) and 10-month (p < .01) rats having higher median stereotyped behavior scores than 2-month-old rats; 20-month rats also had significantly higher (p < .05) scores than 10-month rats. Apomorphine also had a greater effect on inducing stereotyped gnawing in old

(27 months) compared to young (4 months) or middle-aged (14 months) mice (see Figure 8-3). The 2-month rats showed the fastest dissipation of the drug's effect, whereas the 20-month rats showed no substantial decrement in the intensity of stereotyped behavior throughout the 45-minute rating period.

Dose-response curves for apomorphine's effect on stereotyped behavior in rats and mice showed approximately two- to four-fold greater potency of apomorphine on stereotyped behavior in the old compared to the youngest age group (Figure 8-2).

The indirect-acting dopamine agonists, d-amphetamine and methylphenidate, also produced greater stereotyped behavior in older rats and mice. D-amphetamine (3.5mg/kg) induced significantly more intense or frequent stereotyped and gnawing behavior in 20-month-old as compared to 2-month-old rats (Figure 8-4), and the same high level of stereotyped behavior scores was maintained throughout the 90-minute observation in the old rats but not in the younger rats (Figure 8-4). D-amphetamine (4.5mg/kg) also produced a greater frequency of stereotyped gnawing in aged mice, and aged mice tended to show greater gnawing after 15mg/kg methylphenidate (Figure 8-3). Age effects of the direct-acting agonist apomorphine at all doses were slightly greater or more consistent than for the indirect-acting dopamine agonists, d-amphetamine and methylphenidate.

## DISCUSSION

Our results indicate that older-aged rats and mice show increased effects of apomorphine and amphetamine on stereotyped behavior. Also, in the older-aged animals the effect of these dopamine agonists persist at close to their maximum level through the observation period, whereas the young animals showed a more rapid decline of the behavioral effect.

The pharmacological mediation of these increased drug responses in old-aged rats may be related to changes in the sensitivity of dopamine receptors or changes in drug metabolism. Previous research has indicated that the effects of amphetamine and apomorphine on stereotyped behavior in animals are principally mediated by their effect on neurons in the nigra-striatal system, either through a direct stimulation of postsynaptic dopamine receptors hypothesized for apomorphine, or more indirect action through release and blockage of reuptake of dopamine hypothesized for d-amphetamine. Previous research has also provided evidence for a decrease with age in the activity of tyrosine hydroxylase (TH), the rate-limiting enzyme in catecholamine synthesis, especially in the caudate

**Table 8-1: Relationship of Age to Prevalence of Tardive Dyskinesia**

Percentage of Patients with Definite Oral-Buccol Lingual Symptoms of Tardive Dyskinesia

| | | | Age of Patient | | |
|---|---|---|---|---|---|
| 0-20 | 21-30 | 31-40 | 41-50 | 51-60 | 61+ |
| 0 | 3 | 5 | 19 | 24 | 34 |
| (N) | (25) | (163) | (210) | (203) | (220) | (298) |

N = total number of patients in age group. Statistics $_c2$ = 107.49, df = 5, p < .001; $\chi2$ computed from actual number of patients in each cell and its companion, from which percentages shown in Table 8-1 were calculated. Data are from state survey in Illinois. Ratings were done using Smith Tardive Dyskinesia Scale.

nucleus and a decrease in dopamine in some areas of the brain.[1,2] Some authors have suggested that this decrease in TH with age may indicate cell loss in the nigra-striatal system.[3] The resultant decrease in dopaminergic activity of presynaptic neurons may result in functional supersensitivity at the postsynaptic dopamine receptors, which may be expressed in the increased behavioral effects of dopamine agonists on these receptors.

Although supersensitivity of postsynaptic dopamine receptors may be one possible mechanism contributing to the increased stereotyped behavior response of dopamine agonists in old rats and mice, we must consider higher drug concentrations in older-aged animals as an alternative explanation. Higher levels of drugs in some body tissues could result from a decrease in metabolism of the drugs, (which has been documented for several other drugs in both rat and man) and/or decreases in apparent volume of distribution.[15,16] Weight differences per se are unlikely to be the cause of differences in brain concentrations or pharmacokinetics leading to age-related differences in potency, because there were no differences in the weight of mice in all three age groups, or weights of rats in the 10- versus 20-month age group.

If the older-aged human brain was also more sensitive to dopamine agonists, this might provide one explanation for the considerably higher prevalence in older-aged patients of such conditions as tardive dyskinesia (see Table 8-1), whose pathophysiology may involve dopaminergic supersensitivity.[17] However, the relevance of our behavioral findings in rat to the human brain is not clear, since a few early clinical reports and psychological studies done 15 to 30 years ago suggested a decreased effect of amphetamine in older-aged humans.[18,19,20] Because of the relatively unsophisticated methodology and small sample size of these studies, we believe that these findings must be re-evaluated, and additional investigations of the effects of dopamine agonists on psychological and motor function in older-aged man are necessary to clarify the clinical significance of our behavioral findings in older-aged rats.

## ACKNOWLEDGMENT

This research was supported in part by National Institute of Aging Grant 1 R23 AGO725-1. Ms. Linda Talley and Ms. Carolyn Rolsten provided technical assistance.

## REFERENCES

1. McGeer PL, McGeer EG: Enzymes associated with metabolism of catecholamines, acetylcholine, and GABA in human controls and patients with Huntington's chorea. *J Neurochemistry* 26:65–76, 1976.
2. Samarajski T: Age related changes in brain biogenic amines, in Brody A, Honman D, Ordy JM (eds): *Aging*, vol 1. New York, Raven Press, 1975, pp 199–214.
3. Robinson DS, Sourkis TL, Neis A, Harris LS, Sptector S, Barlett DL, Kaye I: Monamine metabolism in the human brain. *Arch Gen Psychiatry* 34:89–91, 1977.
4. Bylund B, Tellez-Inon MT, Hollenberg MD: Age-related parallel decline in beta adrenergic receptors, adenylatecyclase, and phosphodiesterase activity in rat erythrocyte membranes. *Life Sci* 21:403–410, 1077.
5. Schocken DD, Roth GS: Reduced $\beta$-adrenergic receptors concentrations in aging man. *Nature* 267:856–858, 1977.
6. Frolkis VV, Bezrukov VV, Bogatskaya LN, Verkhratsky NS, Zamostian VP, Shevtchuk VG, Shtchegoleua IV: Catecholamines in the metabolism and functional regulation in aging. *Gerontologia* 16:129–140, 1970.
7. Tanner RH, Domino EF: Exaggerated response to (+) amphetamine in geriatric gerbils. *Gerontology* 23:165–173, 1977.
8. Cools AR, Van Rossum JM: Caudal dopamine and stereotyped behavior in the cat. *Arch Int Pharmacodyn* 187:163–173, 1977.
9. Fog R: Stereotyped and catalepsy: Studies of the effects of amphetamines and neuroleptics in rats. *Acta Neurologica, Scandinvaica* (suppl 50):11–65, 1972.
10. Smith RC, Davis JM: Behavioral evidence for supersensitivity after chronic administration of haloperidol, clozapine, and thioridazine. *Life Sci* 19:725–732, 1976.
11. Smith RC, Davis JM: Behavioral supersensitivity to apomorphine and amphetamine after chronic high-dose haloperidol treatment. *Psychopharm Comm* 1:285–293, 1975.
12. Price MTC, Fibger HC: Apomorphine and amphetamine stereotypy after 6-hydroxy dopamine lesions of the substantia nigra. *Europ J Pharm* 29:249–252, 1974.
13. Creese I, Iversen SD: The role of fore-brain dopaminergic systems in amphetamine induced stereotyped behavior in the rat. *Psychopharmacologia* 39:345–357, 1974.
14. Hollander M, Wolfe DA: *Non-parametric Statistical Methods*. New York, John Wiley & Sons, 1973, pp 115–129.
15. Triggs EJ, Nation RL: Pharmacokinetics in the aged: A review. *J Pharmacokinetic and Biopharmaceutics* 3:387–418, 1977.
16. Crooks J, O'Malley K, Stevenson IH: Pharmacokinetics in the elderly. *Clinical Pharmacokinetics* 1:280–296, 1976.

17. Rubovits R, Klawans HL: Implications of amphetamine-induced stereotyped behavior as a model for tardive dyskinesia. *Arch Gen Psychiatry* 27:507–509, 1972.

18. Arnett JH, Harris SE: Effects of small doses of amphetamine in the aged. *Geriatrics* 3:84–88, 1948.

19. Caveness W: Benzedrine sulfate in elderly people, *NY J Med* 47:1003–1005, 1947.

20. Krugman AD, Ross S, Vicino FL, Clyde DJ: A research rate: Effects of d-amphetamine and meprobamate on problem solving and mood of aged subjects. *J Gerontology* 15:419–420, 1960.

# CHAPTER 9

# *Neurochemical Changes In The Aging Human And Nonhuman Primate Brain*

## T. SAMORAJSKI

One of the objectives of aging research is to describe the structural and chemical changes that lead to gradual dysfunction and decreased survival capacity of the individual organism. Aging is considered to be a property of the organism and not of its environment. Biological aging is thought to result from changes that begin at the molecular level and then progress with increasing complexity through systems of cells, tissues and organs to the whole individual.

The period of old age is characterized by changes that are multiple, often rapid in occurrence and with profound effects. As the human being advances in age, hair turns gray, the skin wrinkles, bones become brittle, memory dims, senses become less acute, motor skills diminish and vigor and vitality slowly ebb. Obviously, not all of these changes occur in each person equally, or are of equal consequence or even conducive to mortality. Brain changes are probably the most consistent and of greatest concern to the aged person. The realization of impaired recent memory and mental activity may bring on depression, confusion, restlessness, irritibility and even hostility or withdrawal.[1] Clinical tests of old patients may reveal marked changes in motor performance that seem related to dysfunction of the extrapyramidal system;[2,3] and often require treatment with psychopharmacologic agents.

The recent trend has been to study the structural, chemical and functional changes observed in the brain during the lifespan.[4,5] It is evident from such studies that the mammalian brain undergoes an early period of rapid growth, remains relatively stable during most of adulthood, and then declines in senescence. Most research on the biochemical composition of the brain has focused on the early or "critical" periods of rapid growth, during which the organism is particularly vulnerable to malnutrition and environmental stress.[6,7] Surprisingly few studies have been directly concerned with chemical alterations in the human and nonhuman brain during old age.[8,9,10,11,12,13] It is difficult to understand the paucity of information on the neurochemistry of the brain at advanced ages when one considers the nature and causes of mental diseases and conditions that predominate in the aged.

This paper presents some of our studies in this area and reviews some of the work of others. The results pertain to rhesus-monkey (*Macaca mulatta*) and human brain except when information was available only for other species. Since aging represents a continuation of a developmental lifespan process, major chemical changes associated with development and maturity of the brain have been included where possible as antecedent points of reference. We do not discuss the effect of drugs on the aging process or changes in brain tissue sensitivity that might occur with age in response to a drug at a given blood-level concentration. Information on this aspect of the subject can be found in Bender,[14] O'Malley et al.,[15] Triggs and Nation,[16] Richey and Bender,[17] Bender et al.,[18] and Kormendy and Bender.[19]

## BODY AND BRAIN COMPOSITION

Considering the biochemical aspects of the aging brain is meaningless without taking a look at features that distinguish the nervous system from other organs of the body. Comparisons of approximate composition of the whole body and isolated brain in young and old human beings are shown in Figure 9-1. These results indicate some major quantitative chemical differences between body and brain—the brain containing relatively more water and less lipid, carbohydrate, protein and inorganic substances than the whole body at comparable age levels. In old age, the body gains lipid content; intracellular water, carbohydrate, protein and bone minerals probably are lost. In the brain, the content of lipid, carbohydrate, protein and minerals remains the same or declines slightly with age, whereas water content increases. With advancing old age, water shifts from the brain's intracellular to extracellular compartments. It should be emphasized that these values are only approximations, since the studies do not specify sample size or include a sufficient number of values at different ages to determine the chronologic rate of change. The relative contribu-

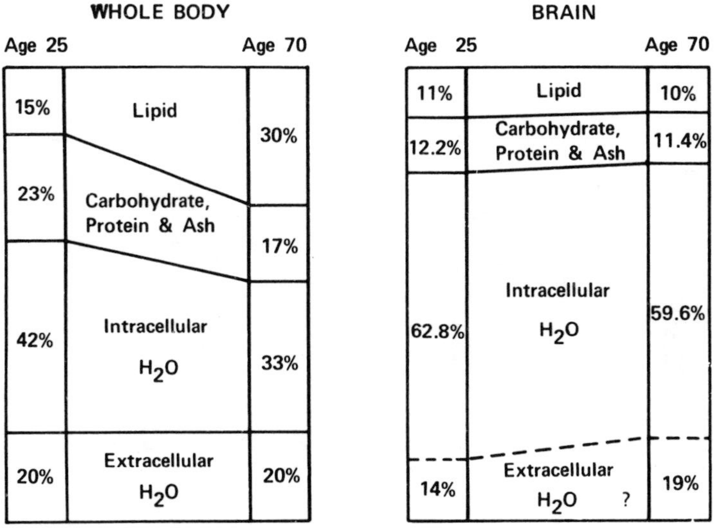

**WHOLE BODY**

| Age 25 | | Age 70 |
|---|---|---|
| 15% | Lipid | 30% |
| 23% | Carbohydrate, Protein & Ash | 17% |
| 42% | Intracellular H₂O | 33% |
| 20% | Extracellular H₂O | 20% |

**BRAIN**

| Age 25 | | Age 70 |
|---|---|---|
| 11% | Lipid | 10% |
| 12.2% | Carbohydrate, Protein & Ash | 11.4% |
| 62.8% | Intracellular H₂O | 59.6% |
| 14% | Extracellular H₂O ? | 19% |

Figure 9-1: Age and distribution of major components of human body and brain. Whole-body values based on males; brain values include male and female averages. [Adapted from Brozek, 1954;[78] Himwich and Himwich, 1959;[9] and Fryer, 1962.[79]]

tion of biological and environmental factors to these changes is unknown. We believe, however, that the data indicate some major differences in the aging process of the brain and other organs of the body. Presumably, the changes that occur with aging in most organs except the brain involve a diminishing potential for cell division and consequently, a gradual replacement of parenchymal cells with connective tissue elements, including a preponderance of fat cells. The brain has no connective tissue (except for blood vessel), and death of the differentiated postmitotic neurons of the mammalian brain is associated with a proliferation of glial cells (gliosis). Both types of change may be characterized overall as degenerative.[20] Therefore, while relatively less quantitative change occurs in the brain with age, the qualitative aspects of the change remain in doubt.

## ORGAN WEIGHTS

Comparing weight changes at different periods of the lifespan may shed some additional light on the wide differences between the brain and other organs. Figure 9-2 illustrates the effect of age on body and organ weights of female rhesus monkeys at 3 to 5, 6 to 10, and 12 to 20 years of age, spans

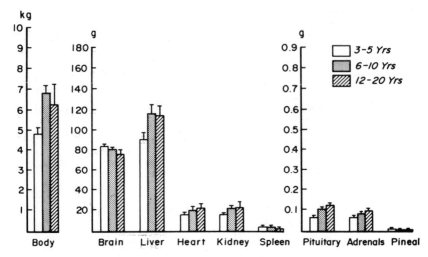

Figure 9-2:    Effect of age on body and organ weights of female rhesus monkeys.

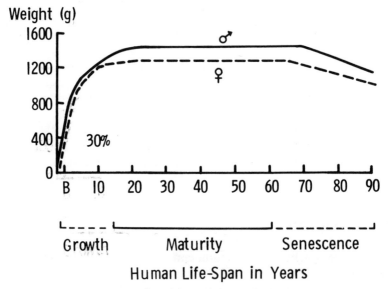

Figure 9-3:    Relationship between brain weight and age throughout the human lifespan.
[Adapted from Ordy, Kaack, and Brizzee, 1975.[5]]

that represent the periods of late development, maturity and old age in this species. It is clear from this illustration that, despite an absence of significant differences in body weight between maturity and old age, the brain and spleen decreased in weight with age whereas the weight of heart, kidney and endocrine glands increased. Each organ may manifest a characteristic change with aging based on its chemical composition, cellular organization and probably the replicating potential of its constituent cells.

As in the aging animal, studies of changes in organ weight of the human brain during development, maturity and old age may also illustrate prominent temporal relations in the lifespan. The major lifespan changes in male and female brain weight are shown in Figure 9-3. The brain weight of human females peaks at an earlier age than that of males and begins to decline slightly earlier. Associated with the decrement in brain weight is a decrease in brain volume relative to skull capacity,[21] which causes the shrunken appearance of the brain often described as a characteristic of advanced age.

## NEUROCHEMISTRY OF AGING

In the past, chemical studies on changes with age in composition and metabolsim of the human brain were often uninterpretable because the time between death and autopsy and the exact area from which tissue was taken were not specified. More recent investigators found that meaningful measures of many constituents such as lipids, amino acids and even neurotransmitter substances and their enzymes could be obtained if the samples were carefully selected and properly prepared and stored. It is possible to obtain uniform results if care is taken to standardize or correct for the time between death and autopsy.[22] From results now available, it is apparent that changes may vary markedly in both rate and time from one gross region of different mammalian species. In the context of these limitations, the seven main chemical constituents of the human brain (Table 9-1) will be briefly summarized.

### Water

Free water comprises the highest proportion of weight of each brain region, ranging from 70 to 90 percent depending on the ratio of white to gray matter. Measurements of water content of mouse, rhesus-monkey and human brain by region indicate that there may be significant species

Table 9-1: Rank order, decline of weight[a], and change in main chemical constituents of average male and female human brain between 25 and 75 years of age.

| | Rank | 25 Years | | 75 Years | |
|---|---|---|---|---|---|
| | | 1320 g | % Weight | 1200 g | % Weight |
| $H_2O$[a] | 1 | 1019.0 | 77.2 | 936.0 | 78.0 |
| Total lipids[b] | 2 | 115.8 | 11.8 | 114.0 | 9.5 |
| Protein, peptides and enzymes[c] | 3 | 118.8 | 9.0 | 86.4 | 7.2 |
| Inorganic salts[d]; cations— Na, K, Ca, Mg anions— Cl, $HCO_3$ metals— Cu, Mn, Zn, Fe, Al | 4 | 16.5 | 1.1 | ? | ? |
| Free amino acids[e] | 5 | 9.2 | 0.7 | 8.4(?) | 0.7(?) |
| Nucleic acids [f] | 6 | 6.3 | 0.48 | 6.4 | 0.54 |
| RNA | | 5.2 | 0.40 | 5.3 | 0.45 |
| DNA | | 1.1 | 0.08 | 1.1 | 0.09 |
| Carbohydrate (glycogen)[g] | 7 | 2.6 | 0.2 | ? | ? |

[a]Burger, 1957 (8).
[b]Calculated from equations of Rouser and Yamamoto, 1969 (25).
[c]Burger, 1957 (8).
[d]Tower, 1969 (45).
[e]Robinson and Williams, 1965, for adult human brain; Davis and Himwich, 1975 (13), for 75-year-old human based on extrapolation from monkey brain.
[f]Samorajski and Rolsten, 1973 (11), based on analysis of frontal cortex.
[g]Kirsch and Leitner, 1967 (77).

differences in water content with increasing age (Figure 9-4). In mouse brain, the water content of the cerebral hemisphere, cerebellum and brain stem decreases with age. In rhesus-monkey and human brain, however, water content in the same regions increases during later life. The decrease in water content with age in the mouse brain may be correlated with progressive formation of myelin membranes and a decreasing extracellular compartment.[23,24] In the human brain the concentration of myelin decreases during aging and extracellular water seems to increase.[21,25]

**Total lipids**

In primates, lipid content increases during development, remains relatively constant during maturity and declines in later life. Marked decreases in lipid metabolism, possibly the result of lowered enzyme activity, also characterize old age.[26] The decline in lipid content and metabolism in old age most probably results from changes in the number

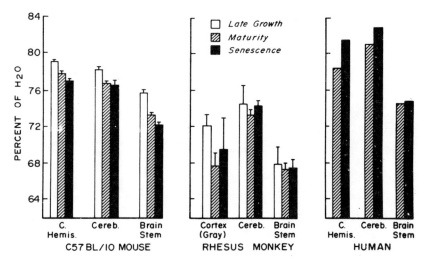

Figure 9-4:   Percentage of water content of mouse, rhesus-monkey and human brain regions.

of neurons and glia present, since each component seems to have a characteristic lipid profile. It is likely that the decrease in lipid concentration in human brain results from death neurons and the consequent degeneration of axons and their associated myelin sheaths. The content of cerebrosides and ethanolamine plasmalogens, which correlates with myelin content, decreases in parallel with the decrease of total brain lipids (Figure 9-5). It appears, then, that in the aging primate brain, as neurons and accompanying myelin are gradually lost, total lipid content decreases.

In addition to the decrease in total lipid content of the human brain during aging, it is evident that significant changes occur in the fatty acids of brain lipids. The most significant age-related differences have been found in the fatty acids of ethanolamine phosphoglyceride (EPG), a major phospholipid of primate brain. In brain myelin of rhesus-monkey and human, a general pattern of change may be seen in the acyl group composition of EPG; a lower proportion of saturated and polyunsaturated acyl groups to a corresponding higher proportion of monounsaturated acyl groups.[23,27] At the same time there is an increase in the chain length of the saturated fatty acids, particularly in the glycolipids,[28] which may impart additional stability to the myelin. This might be another reason for the gradual age-dependent decrease in lipid turnover and total myelin in the primate brain.

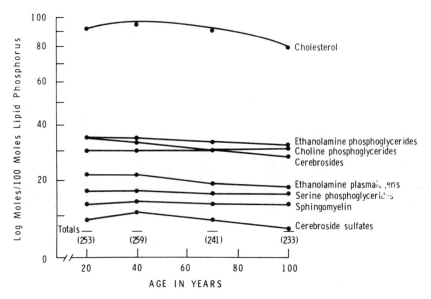

Figure 9-5: Composition of lipids in male human brain as a function of age. [Adapted from Horrocks, Sun and D'Amato, 1975,[26] and based on equations of Rouser and Yamamoto, 1969.[25]]

## Protein, peptides and enzymes

Proteins consist of a vast number of complex molecular structures with diverse functions and an elaborate mechanism for regulating their synthesis. Age-related changes in proteins of the nervous system tend to follow the pattern of many other constituents — namely, increase during development, relative stability during maturity and decline during old age.

MacArthur and Doisey[29] were among the first to study protein content in human brain. They reported that the protein content of brain parts (forebrain, cerebellum and brain stem) and whole brain was about 15 percent lower in a 67-year-old brain than in one 35 years old. Subsequent studies by Burger[8] and Hoch-Ligetti[30] also found protein content in human brain decreased in old age. Studies of the brain of mature and old rhesus-monkeys by Davis and Himwich,[13] from ages 3 to 16, revealed an age-related decrease in protein content in most areas of the brain examined (Figure 9-6). Areas of most significant decline include pons, thalamus, caudate nucleus, hippocampal-amygdaloid complex and occipital cortex. Only white matter showed a slight increase in protein content with age.

Studies of the brain-specific proteins S-100 and 14-3-2 in animal and

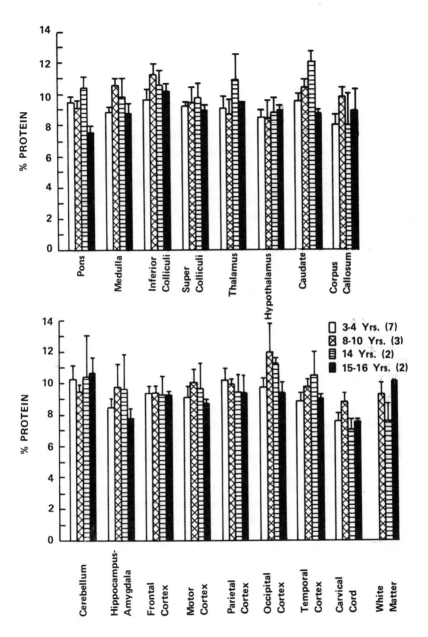

Figure 9-6: Protein levels in discrete areas of the brain and spinal cord of the rhesus monkey at different ages. The number of animals in each group is indicated by the numerals in parenthesis. [Reproduced with permission from Davis and Himwich, 1975[13] and Plenum Press.]

human brain revealed that S-100 protein increased with age in most regions.[10,31] When 14-3-2 was measured in various areas of human brain, no correlation with age was found. Since S-100 is a glial protein and 14-3-2 a neuronal protein, the increase with age of S-100 may represent changes in functions characteristic of the glia—e.g., myelin formation, phagocytic activity and involvement in transport mechanisms and the blood-brain barrier system. It is of interest that both fibrous and protoplasmic astrocytes accumulate filaments and possibly glycogen with age.[32]

Peptides are present in the mammalian brain, and their levels seem to vary between species as well as age. The levels of gluthathione, sarcosine, carnosine, N-acetyl-L-aspartic acid (NAA) and homocarnosine in the brain of mouse, rat, dog and cat are higher in adulthood than at birth.[13] Little is known concerning the metabolic function of these CNS peptides and their distribution in the aged brain of animals and man.

Numerous enzymes associated with subcellular organelles have been measured in brain of several species in relation to age. Reduced enzyme activity was the most frequent finding, although there are some exceptions.[33] Reichlmeier and associates[34] studied the glycolytic and neurotransmitter-associated enzymes of various brain areas from 36 patients ranging from 19 to 92 years of age, all free of neurological disease. An age-dependent decline was found in the activity of cAMP protein kinase and fructose-6-phosphate protein kinase in cortex, acetyl-cholinesterase in putamen, and carbonic anhydrase in cortex and putamen. Hexokinase activity, however, was elevated in the cerebral cortex. In another study of human brain, Nies et al.[35] found monoamine oxidase (MAO) activity increased with age. The meaning of these changes is obscure and may represent disturbances in the regulation of the glycolytic pathway and altered amine metabolism in the aging human brain.

Several studies indicate a decline in oxygen consumption with age[9,36] (for review of studies of whole human brain) which may be the result of neuronal loss rather than lowered metabolism in the surviving cells. In mitochondrial preparations from brain of old rats, respiratory enzymes do not differ significantly from those of young animals.[37]

Changes in some enzymes may be specific to disease states and not to aging in general. Embree and Hess[38] believe, for example, that in Alzheimer's disease a variety of enzymes including acetylcholinesterase and the adenosine triphosphatases are reduced. McGeer and McGeer[39] showed lower than normal levels of striatal tyrosine in persons with Parkinsonism, a disease which is more common and more severe with advancing age. Because of the diversity of enzymes involved in cellular metabolism of the aging brain, only a brief summary can be given here.

However, the reduction with age of many protein enzymes in the human brain closely parallels lower levels of total protein content.

## Inorganic salts

The relatively small proportion of inorganic constituents in brain should not be taken as an indication of their functional importance. Reception, conduction and synaptic transmission of impulses involve changes in ionic permeability that depend on membrane-bound calcium and Na-K transport, together with energy-yielding systems. Nerve-conduction velocity reportedly decreases 13 percent in the ulnar nerve between the ages of 30 and 80.[40] Changes at the membrane level may be responsible for this decrement. We have reported that a decrease in the resistance of membrane-bound synaptasomal Na-K-ATPase to ethanol occurs with age.[41] Changes in the acyl-group composition of phospholipids with age may also affect membrane activity.[42] Another possibility is that a free-radical lipid peroxidation reaction might be propagated through the polyunsaturated fatty acids of the phospholipid in the membrane, leading to membrane damage. Iron and hemeprotein may be some of the most powerful catalysts for initiating lipid peroxidation.[43] In view of such findings, it has been proposed that the cell membranes may be the primary source of aging.[43,44] It is difficult, however, to assess one physiologic parameter like conduction velocity and try to apply it to the spectrum of chemical events that may be associated with it.

The gray matter of most mammalian species contains about 100 $\mu$moles of potassium, 60 $\mu$moles of sodium, 2 $\mu$moles of calcium and 5 $\mu$moles of magnesium per gram of fresh tissue. The total anionic equivalent in gray matter provided by chloride, bicarbonate, sulfates and phosphates is about 60 $\mu$moles per gram of fresh tissue.[45] Few data are available for mineral content of brain regions in relation to aging because of the lack, until recently, of adequate analytic methods. There is, however, an abundance of older data on whole-brain homogenates.[46] These studies have reported decreases in potassium, calcium, magnesium, sulfur and phosphorus; increases in iron and aluminum; and no change in sodium, copper and zinc between maturity and old age.

Lithium is a trace element of particular interest because it is often effective in treatment of manic-depressive illness. Depression affects all age groups, but especially the aged.[1] Although treatment is similar at all ages, several considerations may be important for the older patient. The half-life of lithium in middle-aged groups is about 24 hours, in contrast to 26 to 48 hours for older patients. An older patient, therefore, may reach an adequate dosage level with a smaller amount of drug than a younger person. As is generally true of drug side effects, the old patient is more vulnerable to lithium side effects than the younger one.[47]

## Free amino acids

Free amino acids in the brain participate in protein synthesis, neurotransmission and intermediary metabolism. Amino acids of relatively low concentration, whose main function is the metabolism of protein, include: isoleucine, leucine, threonine, serine, cysteine, methionine, arganine and histidine. The glutamic-acid group, which includes aspartic acid, gamma aminobutyric acid, glutamine, and alanine, comprises about 70 percent of the total amino acid nitrogen pool in the brain and functions as an energy source by way of the tricarboxylic acid cycle. In addition, the glutamic acid family plus alanine and taurine may function as neurotransmitters.[13]

The developmental pattern of these amino acids has been thoroughly studied during early life, and increases in the levels of the brain amino

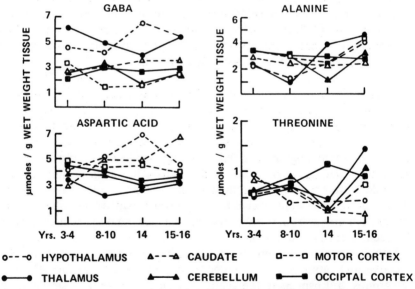

Figure 9-7:   GABA, alanine, aspartic acid, and threonine in monkey brain areas at different ages (3 to 4 years, 7 animals; 8 to 10 years, 3 animals; 14 years, 2 animals; 15 to 16 years, 2 animals). SEM was within 11 percent. [Reproduced with permission from Davis and Himwich, 1975[13] and Plenum Press.]

**Table 9-2: Regional distribution of nucleic acids in brain of rhesus monkey and human during late development (Dev.), maturity (Mat.), and early senescence (Sen.).**

| Region | RNA ($\mu$g/mg wet wt.) | | | DNA ($\mu$g/mg wet wt.) | | | RNA/DNA | | |
|---|---|---|---|---|---|---|---|---|---|
| | Dev. | Mat. | Sen. | Dev. | Mat. | Sen. | Dev. | Mat. | Sen. |
| Rhesus monkey[a] | | | | | | | | | |
| Frontal cortex | 3.43 | 3.59 | 2.92 | 1.25 | 1.43 | 1.33 | 2.83 | 2.51 | 2.20 |
| Caudate | 3.09 | 3.12 | 3.12 | 1.17 | 1.34 | 1.33 | 2.64 | 2.34 | 2.34 |
| Cerebellum | 3.78 | 3.75 | 3.41 | 5.80 | 6.44 | 6.45 | 0.65 | 0.58 | 0.53 |
| Brain stem | 2.14 | 2.00 | 2.09 | 0.93 | 0.94 | 1.17 | 2.30 | 2.13 | 1.79 |
| Human[b] | | | | | | | | | |
| Frontal cortex | 4.28 | 3.95 | 4.37 | 1.22 | 0.94 | 0.88 | 3.51 | 4.20 | 4.96 |
| Caudate | 2.93 | 3.28 | 3.67 | 1.18 | 1.16 | 1.19 | 2.48 | 2.83 | 3.08 |
| Putamen | 3.95 | 3.73 | 3.72 | 1.17 | 1.18 | 1.23 | 3.39 | 3.16 | 3.03 |

Adapted from Samorajski and Rolsten, 1973 (11).
[a]Mean values for five subjects at each age period (i.e. 3 to 5, 6 to 10, and 12 to 18 years representing periods of late development, maturity, and early senescence, respectively).
[b]Based on one subject at the late-development stage (14 years), ten subjects at maturity (46 to 68 years), and six at senescence (70 to 90 years).

acids have been associated with structural and functional maturation. The few studies that have measured changes in amino acids of human brain with age have found relatively little consistent change.[46] Recently, Davis and Himwich[13] investigated the amino acid composition of discrete brain regions of a limited number of young and old cats, dogs, rabbits and rhesus-monkeys. The investigators noted major differences between brain regions and, depending on the brain region examined, found levels of amino acids increased, decreased or unchanged with age. A few typical examples[13] of amino acid levels in selected brain regions of young and old rhesus monkeys are shown in Figure 9-7.

**Nucleic acids**

Although the theory of cell loss with age in the human brain is generally accepted, it is yet to be verified by chemical analyses. Regional variations in DNA and RNA content in relation to age have been examined in animal and human brain, but reports conflict in that they show increases, decreases and no significant change.[10] The results of more recent studies in our laboratory[11] on the regional distribution of nucleic acids in the brain of rhesus-monkey and humans at three age levels representing late development, maturity and old age are shown in Table 9-2. RNA levels in the aged brain of both rhesus monkey and human were normal to slightly depressed. Differences in the concentration of DNA and the RNA/DNA ratio between the periods of maturity and old age were not significant. These results may be interpreted as indicating only minimal neuronal loss or glial proliferations in the brain regions we examined.

Age-associated differences in nucleic acids at the molecular level have also been considered. The available information suggests little or no turnover of DNA in mature neurons and an increase in the stability of nuclear DNA during aging. According to Herrmann,[48] the stability may be imparted by an irreversible crosslinking of chromatin strands. Ermini[49] noted age-related differences in the phosphorylating capability of nuclear histones.

Others have suggested that intracellular changes in RNA levels, turnover and base composition may be a factor in neuronal aging. Hyden[50] found RNA levels in single motor neurons of the human spinal cord increased during development from $402\mu\mu g$/cell to $640\mu\mu g$/cell by age 40 to 60 and then reduced to $420\mu\mu g$/cell by age 80. Animal studies also indicate that RNA turnover in the brain decreases with age.[51] The potential for methylation of nuclear histone and RNA may also decrease with age.[52]

In summary, although there are disagreements, RNA in mammalian brain has been frequently reported to decline with age while the concentration of DNA remains fairly constant. Some observations indicate that nuclear DNA of mature neurons undergoes physical change with age but little if any metabolic turnover. RNA concentration and turnover, on the other hand, may be more labile and highly dependent on a variety of functional states throughout the lifespan.

## Carbohydrates

Glucose is a major carbon source of many brain molecules and normally the sole substrate for its energy metabolism.[53,54] The brain depends on glucose transport from the blood stream, as it has relatively little glucose or stored glycogen reserves. Reported values for the two main carbohydrates of the brain vary widely because of rapid anaerobic glycolysis with cessation of blood flow. Estimates based on rapidly frozen tissue indicate that the glucose content of mammalian brain is about $1.5\mu$moles/g of tissue (27mg/100g). Values reported for glycogen content of young and adult mouse brain are 45 and 40mg/100g of tissue, respectively.[55] Since both of these vital substances are stored in neurons in quantities too small to support neuronal metabolism for more than a few seconds, it is unlikely that quantitative changes with age or disease would have any meaning for the intact cell. Human studies of brain glucose utilization in relation to age have not been reported.

Significant lifespan changes may occur in the concentration and composition of extracellular glycoprotein or glycosaminoglycan (mucopolysaccharide) that may reduce the capacity of the brain to transport vital exogenous metabolites through extracellular channels.[56,57,58] A diminished axonal transport of glycoprotein may be another feature of the senescent brain.[59] The Geinisman group suggests that diminished transport of glycoprotein by the septo-hippocampal pathway may cause loss of synapses observed in the hippocampus of the aged rat brain.[60] Thus, changes in content and macromolecular composition of glycoproteins and glycosaminoglycans may affect a functional decline in the nervous system.

## NEUROTRANSMITTER SUBSTANCES

Of all the events that occur in the aging brain, changes at the synaptic level may be of greatest importance. An imbalance of putative neu-

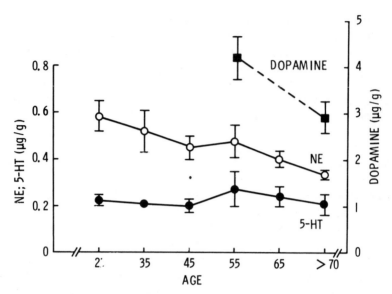

Figure 9-8:    Mean values for norepinephrine (NE) and serotonin (5-HT) in hindbrains from 55 patients [adapted from Nies, et al., 1973.[35]] Values for dopamine (DA) in caudate nuclei are from Bertler (1961[61]) based on two mature persons (52 and 60 years old) and four old ones (74 to 87 years).

rotransmitters may result in greater impairment of information processing than might occur with the loss of neurons. Unfortunately, the analysis of biochemical changes at the synaptic level of the human brain is complicated by the diversity of functions involved and by uncontrolled pre- and postmortem conditions. Nevertheless, some general principles have emerged from the limited data.

Catecholamine systems, particularly dopamine (DA) and its associated enzymes, seem to be the most vulnerable to aging. Age-related decreases in DA content of the caudate nucleus and putamen have been reported by Bertler[61] and Carlsson and Winblad.[62] A small but statistically significant decline in norepinephrine (NE) has also been reported in human hindbrain[35] and in the hypothalamus and brain stem of the rhesus-monkey.[11] Serotonin (5-HT) and 5-hydroxyindole acetic acid (HIAA) content of the human hindbrain does not vary in relation to age.[35] Some of these findings are illustrated in Figure 9-8.

The effect of aging on enzyme systems involved in neurotransmitter synthesis and degradation in human brain has been studied more thoroughly than have the neurotransmitters themselves, because enzymes are more stable and easier to measure. Most enzymes associated with the metabolism of neurotransmitter substances are usually found to decline with age. Dopa decarboxylase (DDC), tyrosine hydroxylase (TH), choline acetyltransferase (CAT) and glutamate decarboxylase (GAD) are among the enzymes most severely affected by age in many regions of the brain.[39,63,64] On the other hand, monoamine oxidase (MAO) activity is elevated with age in several different regions of the brain examined at autopsy.[35,65,66] These studies suggest that aging processes may significantly affect neurotransmitter mechanisms and be a predisposing factor in the development of clinical diseases in man such as depression, Parkinsonism and other disturbances of CNS homeostasis. The altered capacity of the old brain to synthesize neurotransmitter substances might be associated with abnormalities in circulating metabolites, particularly during the later periods of life when cell death, disease and other conditions may further alter neurotransmitter activity.[67]

Knowledge of the chemical changes at the synaptic level in the aging brain is limited, and the functional significance of these changes is virtually unknown. Nevertheless, a variety of drugs is being used to potentiate synaptic transmission by accelerating the synthesis of a relevant neurotransmitter substance or blocking its inactivation.

## LIPOFUSCIN AND CEROID PIGMENT

One of the most consistent alterations in nerve cells of human and other species with increasing age is the accumulation of lipofuscin, or "age" pigment. The progressive accumulation of pigment in postmitotic cells such as neurons has been proposed as a basis for cellular aging.[68] Pathologic conditions such as progeria, alcoholism, senile dementia and Huntington's chorea may also increase the accumulation of intracellular age pigment in the brain.[69,70] The accumulation of age pigment in normal aging and disease is attributed to damage to subcellular membranes, nucleic acids and enzymes by free radicals and/or peroxides.[43]

The enzymes associated with age pigment which have the highest specific activities are acid phosphatase and 2,3 AMP-phosphohydrolase. In addition, significant amounts of neutral lipid and cations such as zinc, iron and calcium are found in the pigment.[70]

Another pigment that may be distinguished in some pathologic states is ceroid. A common feature of both ceroid and lipofuscin pigment is their autofluorescence under ultraviolet light and their origin from lysosomes. They differ markedly, however, in other chemical, physical and biologic properties. Intraneuronal ceroid is found only in Batten-Spielmeyer-Vogt syndrome[71] and Kuf's disease.[72] Further ceroid accumulation is associated with severe cell loss and atrophy. The accumulation of lipofuscin does not

## Table 9-3: Neurochemistry of major neurologic disorders in late life

| Disorder | Effects on Brain | Neurochemical Defect |
|---|---|---|
| Senile dementias | Mental confusion, defective memory | Decreased sulfatides, altered phosphatidyl ethanolamine[a] |
| Affective disorders | Depression, delusions, etc. | Brain amines, trace elements (Li, Na, K), hormonal imbalance[b] |
| Alzheimer's disease | Disorientation, defective memory | *Cortex:* increased cerebroside, hexosamine, acid polysaccharides; decreased ethanolamine phospholipid, [c,d] AChE, ATPase, ganglioside[e] |
| Parkinson's disease | Akinesia, rigidity, tremor | *Basal ganglia:* decreased dopamine, serotonin, and possibly norepinephrine[f] |
| Huntington's chorea | Mental deterioration, progressive movement disorder | *Putamen and caudate:* total protein, lipid, phospholipid, lecithin and GABA reduced; sphingomyelin, cholesterol, RNA and strontium elevated[g,h] |
| Jakob-Creutzfeldt disease | Mental deterioration, motor disturbances | *Cortex:* decreased gangliosides, total phospholipids, hexosamine, RNA; increased proteolipid protein DNA[d,i] |
| Pick's lobar trophy | Intellectual deterioration | *Frontal and temporal lobes:* Sudanophilic and PAS-positive Pick bodies; altered SDH, NADH, ATPase and Acid phosphatase[j] |

Adapted from Embree, Bass and Pope, 1972) and Ordy and Kaack (1975).
Sources: [a]Rouser, Galli, and Kritchevsky, 1965; [b]Weil-Malherbe, 1972; [c]Suzuki, Katzman, and Korey, 1965; [d]Suzuki and Chen, 1966; [e]Shelanski, 1976; [f]Hornykiewicz, 1972; [g]Borri et al., 1967; Embree, Bass, and Pope, 1972; [h]Bird and Iversen, 1974; [i]Pope, Hess, and Lewin, 1964; [j]Roizin et al., 1969.

show atrophy or cell loss to the same degree as ceroid, even in syndromes associated with marked increases of lipofuscin pigment.[73]

It is of some interest that meclofenoxate,[74] chlorpromazine[75] and possibly other therapeutic agents are able to inhibit the accumulation of lipofuscin or, once formed, stimulate its removal from the neuron.[76] Administration of lipofuscin inhibitors such as meclofenoxate, magnesium orotate and kawain may improve sensory-cognitive-motor functions of humans and increase lifespan of experimental animals.[12] However, a direct relation between lipofuscin accumulation and cell function in the aging brain has not been established.

## NEUROCHEMISTRY OF BRAIN DISORDERS

Age-related increases in the incidence of neurologic diseases often make it difficult to differentiate between basic neurological changes with age and pathologic conditions that may be superimposed upon them. Recent advances in neurochemistry, however, have led to an increase in understanding of many neurologic diseases and, in some instances, to effective therapeutic intervention. Successful therapeutic management depends on biochemical information. Table 9-3 summarizes some of the major neurochemical changes in neurologic diseases associated with late life.

## DISCUSSION AND CONCLUSIONS

The neurochemical studies performed to date on age changes in the human brain are very limited because of the difficulties inherent in the use of postmortem tissues, in which the end stage of a disease process is often superimposed on the basic pathology. A more intensive approach is possible with the use of aged experimental animals. The degree of difference that exists between the brain of many animals and human brain is often so great, however, that meaningful comparative studies are difficult to accomplish. Further, many of the neurological diseases of late life are genetically linked and unique to human beings and therefore difficult or impossible to study in animal subjects.

The outstanding neurochemical findings in the aging human brain are summarized in Table 9-4. These findings correlate with extensive neuronal

**Table 9-4: Summary of chemical variations with age in the human brain**

| Increase with age | No change | Decrease with age |
|---|---|---|
| Glycogen content (?) | | |
| Al, Fe | 14-3-2 protein | Intracellular $H_2O$ |
| Monoamine oxidase | Amino acids | Lipid synthesis |
| Lipofuscin (neutral lipid, acid phosphatase, 2, 3, AMP-phosphohydrolase, Zn, Fe, Ca) | Respiratory enzymes | Glycolytic enzymes |
| | Na, Cu, Zn | K, Mg, S, P |
| | DNA | RNA content and synthesis |
| | | Neurotransmitter substances* (DA, NE, DDC, TH, CAT, GAD) |

*Abbreviations: DA, dopamine; NE, norepinephrine; DDC, Dopa decarboxylase; TH, tyrosine hydroxylase; CAT, choline acetyltransferase; GAD, glutamate decarboxylase.

loss and gliosis in some regions of the cortex and damage at the synaptic level. The reduction of most of the tissue constituents raises the possibility of decreased levels of many critical substances that determine the effectiveness of many therapeutic drugs.

Another feature of the aging brain is its increasing susceptibility to disease. Most frequently affected are the cerebral cortex and the basal ganglia. Characteristics of many of the diseases of the brain are further cell loss, astrogliosis and the appearance of plaques, tangles and accumulation of various inclusions and pigment bodies such as ceroid, lipofuscin and amyloid. Senile dementia, Parkinsonism and other diseases of late life add yet an additional echelon of damage to the already accelerating defects of some molecular mechanisms. For these reasons, more multidisciplinary research is needed to delineate the biological factors associated with aging and the diseases of late life.

## ACKNOWLEDGMENTS

The author is indebted to Lore Feldman, Carolyn Rolsten, Les Goekler and Danielle Miller-Soule for their assistance in preparation of the manuscript.

## REFERENCES

1. Gaitz CM: Mental disorders: Diagnosis and treatment, in Busse EW (ed): *Theory and Therapeutics of Aging*. New York, Mecom Press, 1973, pp 72–82.
2. Barbeau A: Aging and the extrapyramidal system. *J Am Geriatr Soc* 21:145–149, 1973.
3. McGeer PL, McGeer EG, Suzuki JS: Aging and extrapyramidal function. *Arch Neurol* 34:33–35, 1977.
4. Timiras PS: *Developmental Physiology and Aging*. New York, Macmillan, 1972, pp 1–692.
5. Ordy JM, Kaack B, Brizzee K: Life-span neurochemical changes in the human and nonhuman brain, in Brody H, Harmen D, Ordy JM (eds): *Aging*. Clinical, Morphological and Neurochemical Aspects in the Aging Central Nervous System. New York, Raven Press, 1975, pp 133–189.
6. Davison AN, Dobbing J: Myelination as a vulnerable period in brain development. *Br Med Bull* 22:40–44, 1966.
7. Dobbing J, Smart JL: Vulnerability of developing brain and behavior. *Br Med Bull* 30:164–168, 1974.
8. Burger M: Die chemische biomorphose des menschlichen gehirns. Abhandlungen der sachsischen akademie der wissenschaften, Leipzig, *Mathematischnaturwissen schafllice Klasse* 45:1–62, 1957.
9. Himwich WA, Himwich HE: Neurochemistry of aging, in Birren JE (ed): *Handbook of Aging and the Individual*. Chicago, University of Chicago Press, 1959, pp 189–215.
10. Perez VL, Moore BW: Biochemistry of the nervous system in aging. *Interdispl Topics Geront* 7:22–45, 1970.

11. Samorajski T, Rolsten C: Age and regional differences in the chemical composition of brains of mice, monkeys and humans, in Ford DH (ed): *Progress in Brain Research,* vol 40: Neurobiological Aspects of Maturation and Aging. New York, Elsevier, 1973, pp 253–265.

12. Ordy JM, Kaack B: Neurochemical changes in composition, metabolism and neurotransmitters in the human brain with age, in Ordy JM, Brizzee KR (eds): *Neurobiology of Aging.* New York, Plenum Press, 1975, pp 253–286.

13. Davis J, Himwich WA: Neurochemistry of the developing and aging mammalian brain, in Ordy JM, Brizzee KR (eds): *Neurobiology of Aging.* New York, Plenum Press, 1975, pp 329–357.

14. Bender AD: The influence of age on the activity of catecholamines and related therapeutic agents. *J Am Geriatr Soc* 18:220–232, 1970.

15. O'Malley K, Crooks J, Duke E, Stevenson IH: Effect of age and sex on human drug metabolism. *Br Med J* 3:607–609, 1971.

16. Triggs EJ, Nation RL: Pharmacokinetics in the aged. A review. *Pharmacokinet Biopharm* 3:387–418, 1975.

17. Richey DP, Bender AD: Pharmacokinetic consequences of aging. *Ann Rev Pharmacol Toxicol* 17:49–65, 1977.

18. Bender AD, Kormendy C, Powell R: Pharmacological control of aging. *Exp Geront* 5:97–129, 1970.

19. Kormendy C, Bender AD: Experimental modification of the chemistry and biology of the aging process. *J Pharm Sci* 60:167–180, 1971.

20. Bourne GH: *Structural Aspects of Aging.* New York, Hafner Publishing, 1969, pp 1–419.

21. Bondareff W: Morphology of the aging nervous system, in Birren JE (ed): *Handbook of Aging and the Individual.* Chicago, University of Chicago Press, 1959, pp 136–168.

22. Bowen DM, Smith CB, White P, Davison AN: Neurotransmitter-related enzymes and indices of hypoxia in senile dementia and other abiotrophies. *Brain* 99:459–496, 1976.

23. Sun GY, Samorajski T: Age changes in the lipid composition of whole homogenates and isolated myelin fractions of mouse brain. *J Gerontol* 27:10–17, 1972.

24. Bondareff W, Narotzky R: Age changes in the neuronal microenvironment. *Science* 176:1135–1136, 1972.

25. Rouser G, Yamamoto A: Lipids, in Lajtha A (ed): *Handbook of Neurochemistry, vol 1: Chemical Architecture of the Nervous System.* New York, Plenum Press, 1969, pp 121–169.

26. Horrocks LA, Sun GY, D'Amato RA: Changes in brain lipids in aging, in Ordy JM, Brizzee KR (eds): *Neurobiology of Aging.* New York, Plenum Press, 1975, pp 359–368.

27. White HB, Galli C, Paoletti R: Ethanolamine phosphoglyceride fatty acids in aging human brain. *J Neurochem* 18:1337–1339, 1971.

28. Dhopeshwarkar GA, Mead JF: Age and lipids of the central nervous system: Lipid metabolism in the developing brain, in Brody H, Harman D, Ordy JM (eds): *Aging.* New York, Raven Press, 1975, pp 119–132.

29. MacArthur CG, Doisey EA: Quantitative chemical changes in the human brain during growth. *J Com Neurol* 30:445–486, 1919.

30. Hoch-Ligetti C: Effects of aging on the central nervous system. *J Am Geriatr Soc* 11:403–408, 1963.

31. Cicero TJ, Ferrendelli JA, Suntzeff V, Moore BW: Regional changes in CNS levels of the S-100 and 14-3-2 proteins during development and aging of the mouse. *J Neurochem* 19:2119–2125, 1972.

32. Raine CS: Neurocellular anatomy, in Siegel GJ, Albers RW, Katzman R, Agranoff BW (eds): *Basic Neurochemistry.* Boston, Little, Brown, 1976, pp 5–33.

33. Bjorksten J: Enzymes and aging, in Martin GJ, Fisch B (eds): *Enzymes in Mental Health.* Philadelphia, J.B. Lippincott, 1966, pp 84–94.
34. Reichlmeier KD, Schlect HP, Ermini M: Enzyme activity changes in the aging human brain. *Gerontologist* 16 (5, abst), 1976.
35. Nies A, Robinson DS, Davis JM, Ravaris CL: Changes in monoamine oxidase with aging, in Eisdorfer C, Fann WE (eds): *Psychopharmacology and Aging.* New York, Plenum Press, 1973, pp 41–54.
36. Kety SS: Changes in cerebral circulation and oxygen consumption which accompany maturation and aging, in Waelsch H (ed): *Biochemistry of the Developing Nervous System.* New York, Academic Press, 1955, pp 208–217.
37. Weinbach EC, Garbus J: Oxidative phosphorylation in mitochondria from aged rats. *J Biol Chem* 234:412–418, 1959.
38. Embree LJ, Hess HH: Microchemistry of ATPases in normal and Alzheimer's disease cortex. *J Neuropath Exp Neurol* 29:136–137, 1970.
39. McGeer PL, McGeer EG: Enzymes associated with the metabolism of catecholamines, acetylcholine and GABA in human controls and patients with Parkinson's disease and Huntington's chorea. *J Neurochem* 26:65–76, 1976.
40. Norris AH, Shock NW, Wagman IH: Age changes in the maximum conduction velocity of motor fibers of human ulnar nerves. *J Applied Physiol* 5:589–593, 1955.
41. Sun AY, Samorajski T: The effects of age and alcohol on Na-K ATPase activity of whole homogenate and synaptosomes prepared from mouse and human brain. *J Neurochem* 24:161–164, 1974.
42. Sun GY, Samorajski T: Age differences in the acyl group composition of phosphoglycerides in myelin isolated from the brain of the rhesus monkey. *Biochem Biophys Acta* 316:19–27, 1973.
43. Tappel AL: Lipid peroxidation and fluorescent molecular damage to membranes, in Trum BF, Arstila A (eds): *Pathobiology of Cell Membranes.* New York, Academic Press, 1975, pp 1–103.
44. Packer L, Deamer DW, Heath RL: Regulations and deterioration of structure in membranes, in Strehler BL (ed): *Advances in Gerontological Research.* New York, Academic Press, 1967, pp 77–120.
45. Tower DB: Inorganic constituents, in Lajtha A (ed): *Handbook of Neurochemistry, vol 1: Chemical Architecture of the Nervous System.* New York, Plenum Press, 1969, pp 1–24.
46. Korenchevsky V: *Physiological and Pathological Aging.* New York, Haffner, 1961, pp 87–159.
47. Prockop LD: Lithium: Research and therapeutic profile in affective disorders, in Hsu JM, Davis RL, Neithamer RW (eds): *The Biomedical Role of Trace Elements in Aging.* St Petersburg, Eckerd College Gerontology Center, 1976, pp 209–219.
48. Herrmann RL: Age-related changes in nucleic acids and protein synthesis, in Ordy JM, Brizzee KR (eds): *Neurobiology of Aging.* New York, Plenum Press, 1975, pp 307–328.
49. Ermini M, Reichlmeier K: Studies on age-related structural channels of chromatin of postmitotic cells by means of in vitro prosphorylation of the histones. *Gerontologist* 16 (5, abstr): 42, 1976.
50. Hyden H: RNA in brain cells, in Quarton GC, Melnechuk T, Schmitt FO (eds): *The Neurosciences: A Study Program.* New York, Rockefeller University Press, 1967, pp 248–266.
51. Balis ME: Nucleic acids and proteins, in Bakerman S (ed): *Aging Life Processes.* Illinois, Charles C. Thomas, 1969, pp 23–51.
52. Moller ML, Miller HK, Balis ME: Effects of amines on macromolecular methylation. *Biochem Biophys Acta* 474:425–434, 1977.

53. Maker HS, Clarke DD, Lajtha AL: Intermediary metabolism of carbohydrates and amino acids, in Siegel GJ, Albers RW, Katzman R, Agranoff BW (eds): *Basic Neurochemistry*. Boston, Little, Brown, 1976, pp 279-307.

54. Sokoloff L: Circulation and energy metabolism of the brain, in Siegel GJ, Albers RW, Katzman R, Agranoff BW (eds): *Basic Neurochemistry*. Boston, Little, Brown, 1976, pp 388-413.

55. Lowry OH, Passonneau JV, Hasselberger FX, Schulz DW: Effect of ischemia on known substances and cofactors of the glycolytic pathway in brain. *J Biol Chem* 239:18-30, 1964.

56. Bondareff W, Breen M, Weinstein HG: Changes in the neuronal microenvironment associated with aging, in Ordy JM, Brizzee KR (eds): *Neurobiology of Aging*. New York, Plenum Press, 1975, pp 485-503.

57. Margolis RU, Margolis RK, Chang LB, Preti C: Glycosaminoglycans of brain during development. *Biochem* 14:85-88, 1975.

58. Margolis RK, Preti C, Lai D, Margolis RU: Developmental changes in brain glycoproteins. *Brain Res* 112:363-369, 1976.

59. Geinisman Y, Bondareff W, Telser A: Diminished axonal transport of glycoproteins in the senescent rat brain. *Mech Ageing Develop*, 6:363-378, 1977.

60. Geinisman Y, Bondareff W, Telser A: Transport of $^3$H-fucose labeled glycoproteins in the septo-hippocampal pathway of young adult and senescent rats. *Brain Res*, 125:182-186, 1977.

61. Bertler A: Occurrence and localization of catecholamines in the human brain. *Acta Physiol Scand* 51:97-107, 1961.

62. Carlsson A, Winblad B: Influence of age and time interval between death and autopsy on dopamine and 3-methoxytyramine levels in human basal ganglia. *J Neural Transmission* 38:271-276, 1976.

63. McGeer PL, McGeer EG: Neurotransmitter synthetic enzymes, in Kerkut GA, Phillips JW (eds): *Progress in Neurobiology*. New York, Pergamon Press, 1973, pp 69-117.

64. McGeer EG, McGeer PL: Age changes in the human brain for some enzymes associated with metabolism of catecholamines, GABA and acetylcholine, in Ordy JM, Brizzee KR (eds): *Neurobiology of Aging*. New York, Plenum Press, 1975, pp 287-305.

65. Robinson DS, Nies A, Davis JM: Ageing, monoamines, and monoamine-oxidase levels. *Lancet* 1:290-291, 1972.

66. Robinson DS: Changes in monoamine oxidase and monoamines with human development and aging. *Fed Proc* 34:103-107, 1975.

67. Samorajski T: Central neurotransmitter substances and aging: A review. *J Am Geriatr Soc*, 25:337-348, 1977.

68. Strehler BL, Barrows CH: Senescence: Cell biological aspects of aging, in Schjeide OA, deJellis J (eds): *Cell Differentiation*. New York, Van Nostrand, 1970, pp 266-283.

69. Reichel W, Garcia-Bunuel R, Dillallo J: Progeria and Werner's syndrome as models for the study of normal human aging. *J Am Geriatr Soc* 19:369-375, 1971.

70. Siakotos AN, Armstrong D: Age-pigment: A biochemical indicator of intracellular aging, in Ordy JM, Brizzee KR (eds): *Neurobiology of Aging*. New York, Plenum Press, 1975, pp 369-400.

71. Zeman W, Donahue S, Dyken P, Green J: The neuronal ceroid-lipofuscinoses (Batten-Vogt syndrome), in Vinken PJ, Bruyn GW (eds): *Handbook of Clinical Neurology*. Amsterdam, North-Holland Publishing, 1970, pp 588-679.

72. Boehme D, Cottrell JC, Leonberg SC, Zeman W: A dominant form of neuronal ceroid-lipofuscinosis. *Brain* 94:745-760, 1971.

73. Siakotos AN, Goebel HH, Patel V, Watanabe I, Zeman W: The morphogenesis and biochemical characteristics of ceroid isolated from cases of neuronal ceroid-

lipofuscinosis, in Volk B, Aronson S (eds): *Sphingolipids, Sphingolipidoses, and Allied Disorders.* New York, Plenum Publishing, 1972, pp 53–61.

74. Nandy K: Further studies on the effects of centrophenoxine on the lipofuscin pigment in the neurons of senile guinea pigs. *J Gerontol* 23:82–92, 1968.

75. Samorajski T, Rolsten C: Chlorpromazine and aging in the brain. *Exp Geront* 11:141–147, 1976.

76. Spoerri PE, Glees P: The mode of lipofuscin removal from hypothalamic neurons. *Exp Geront* 10:225–228, 1975.

77. Kirsch WM, Leitner JW: Glycolytic metabolites and co-factors in human cerebral cortex and white matter during complete ischemia. *Brain Res* 4:358–368, 1967.

78. Brozek J: *Measurement of body compartments in nutritional research.* Washington, D.C., Department of the Army, Office Quartermaster General, 1954.

79. Fryer JH: Studies of body composition in men aged 60 and over, in Shock NW (ed): *Biological Aspects of Aging.* New York, Columbia University Press, 1962, pp 59–78.

# CHAPTER 10

# *Pharmacokinetics In Geriatric Psychopharmacology*

ROBERT HICKS
JOHN M. DAVIS

This chapter concerns itself with the pharmacokinetics of psychotropic medications in the elderly. Pharmacokinetics in general is an area about which there is an ever increasing literature,[1-20] both as the result of more sensitive analytic techniques available and as the result of increasing recognition of pharmacokinetics as a clinically valuable basic science. It is not surprising that the pharmacokinetics of the elderly is also of increasing interest,[21-31] since the older age group constitutes an increasing proportion of the population.[32-35] In addition, there is an increasing concern over drug reactions in general,[36-41] with evidence that the elderly are particularly sensitive.[21,24,26,30,31,36,38,40-43]

Interest in geriatric psychopharmacology (and therefore geriatric pharmacokinetics) is not only a result of the above, but is also related to increasing evidence that psychotropic medications are widely dispensed in both the general population[41,44-51] and (often more so) in the older age groups,[30,31,41,42,44,45,46,48-59] as well as to increasing attention that has been paid to the adverse effects that psychoactive agents may produce when given to the elderly.[21,30,31,41,49,53-55,57,60,61] (The increasing awareness of potential psychotropic drug interactions probably is also a factor, and will be discussed below.)

## DEFINITIONS

*Pharmacokinetics* involves the study of drug *absorption, distribution, biotransformation* (into *inactive* and/or *active metabolites*), and the subsequent *excretion* from the body of the parent drug and/or its metabolites. (Factors affecting drug absorption will be discussed below — see *Chlorpromazine.*) Biotransformation usually occurs in the liver microsomol enzyme systems, although other tissues can contribute. These usually include the soluble portion of the liver, but also the GI (gastrointestinal) tract, kidneys and lungs. In fact, these last three tissues may occasionally be more active than the liver. Minor metabolic activity may occur in the adrenal, brain, heart, muscle, skin and spleen. The gut flora may even metabolize drugs under certain circumstances. Excretion is usually via the kidneys but can occur in other ways (noted in *Clearance* below). (*Metabolism* is usually synonymous with biotransformation, but the term is occasionally used more loosely to include some or all of the other steps in pharmacokinetics just listed.)

*Pharmacodynamics* involves the study of drug *action* (the initial consequence of drug-cell interaction) and *effect* (the subsequent events that follow from this). This is a less widely used term, and it is often subsumed under the general heading of "pharmacokinetics." (Age-related changes in pharmacodynamics will be discussed in this chapter.)

*Elimination (beta) half-life* $(t_{1/2\beta})$ is the half-life of a drug in serum after a distribution equilibrium is obtained. (There are other "half-lives" but this is the most important and thus often referred to simply as the "half-life.")

*Apparent volume of distribution* $(V_d)$ is the total volume of the body compartment(s) into which the drug is distributed. It provides an estimate of the extent of drug distribution through the body fluids and tissues. (As with the half-life, there are various ways of calculation.)

*Clearance* of a drug is the rate of elimination from the body (through biotransformation, renal or fecal excretion, exhalation by the lungs, transudation through the skin, or any combination of these). (When a drug is partly or entirely excreted unchanged from the kidney, its *renal clearance* becomes of great pharmacokinetic importance.)

Clearance of a drug is, therefore, inversely proportional to its elimination half-life $(t_{1/2\beta})$, and directly proportional to the apparent volume of distribution $(V_d)$.

The ultimate pharmacokinetic behavior of a drug involves many physiologic functions that occur simultaneously and which contribute to the determination of drug distribution and elimination. For example, "biotransformation" (or "metabolism" in the strictest sense) refers to many enzymatically mediated chemical transformations. Also, there are large interindividual differences in pharmacokinetics,[18] which may be genetically determined,[1-4,6-12,17,18,20] at least in part. Vesell[10] provided a particularly complete review of the genetic factors. He has recently[18] also discussed the problem of assessing the relative roles of *genetic* and environmental factors in determining these metabolic differences.

Many drugs are lipid-soluble, weak organic acids or bases. They are usually not readily eliminated from the body because of their binding to plasma and tissue proteins, their affinity for body fat, and the ease with which the kidney reabsorbs them (by diffusion through the renal tubular cells). To be excreted, these drugs must be biotransformed into less lipid-soluble metabolites.

Some of these metabolites are pharmacologically active (sometimes more than the "parent" drug), while others are not. If the metabolite is active, termination of action takes place by further biotransformation(s) or by excretion of the active metabolite(s). For a more extensive discussion of pharmacokinetics, the reader is referred to excellent reviews by Drayer[13] and by Greenblatt and Koch-Weser.[14,15] Fingl and Woodberry[62] provide a broader and more comprehensive review, not only of pharmacokinetics, but also of mechanisms of drug action in general.

## GENERAL PRINCIPLES

Triggs and Nation[24] summarize the age-related *physiologic changes in the body which affect pharmacokinetics* as follows:

1. Cardiac output decreases by 30 to 40 percent; renal and splanchnic flow also decrease.
2. Glomerular filtration rate decreases, as does creatinine clearance, although the serum creatinine level may remain normal due to a decrease in body muscle mass.
3. There is direct evidence in animals (and indirect in humans) that hepatic enzyme activity, in both microsomal and soluble portions, also decreases.
4. The concentration of albumin relative to globulins decreases.
5. Sugars, fats and vitamins are less well absorbed by the GI tract.
6. Drug distribution is altered as fat replaces functional tissue in the aging process [according to Novak,[22] the percentage of body fat increases from 18 to 36 percent and 33 to 45 percent in men and women, respectively].

Shader and Greenblatt[31] summarize the *pharmacokinetic effects of age-related changes in bodily function* as:

1. Prolongation of drug elimination half-life ($t_{\frac{1}{2}\beta}$).
2. Reduction in total drug clearance.
3. Inconsistent changes in the volume of distribution ($V_d$).
4. Occasional increases in the unbound drug concentration due to lower serum albumin (although there is no change in affinity of drugs for serum proteins).
5. For drugs excreted by the kidneys, decreased clearance with age.

Crooks, O'Malley and Stevenson[25] state that, while absorption of actively transported substances in the elderly may decrease, many medications are passively absorbed, so there are essentially no age-related changes in absorption. There are, however, studies that suggest the possibility of GI metabolism of chlorpromazine[63,64] and flurazepam.[65] In addition, there is a suggestion that the rate and completeness of diazepam absorption may be decreased in the elderly,[66] and that chlordiazepoxide is absorbed more slowly in the older age group.[67]

Also, there is at least one report[28] suggesting an age-related decrease in the strength of the plasma binding of drugs.

There have been demonstrated age-related changes in the binding of drugs by erythrocytes,[68] but this phenomenon is rarely studied in general, regardless of age,[69] and yields conflicting reports[69,70] in the case of psychotropic agents. It appears that no age-related changes in erythrocyte binding have been demonstrated for a pharmacologic agent. Friedel,[30] in fact, cites the work of Klotz et al.[71] as specifically demonstrating no effect of age on diazepam RBC binding. [However, Klotz's group studied only the effect of age on the plasma: blood distribution ration of this drug, which does not address how much of the drug is bound to the surface of the RBC and how much is actively taken up into the erythrocyte. Also, the data of Klotz's group on the change in this ratio in the elderly (cc = +0.5) could be taken as suggestive of an age-related increase.] Another study[72] obtained data on plasma: blood chlordiazepoxide ratios. This study, however, included only three subjects, 28 to 30 years old, making any conclusion about the effect of aging on these ratios impossible. The ratios found, however, were very small (0, 0.1, 0.24), especially compared to the Klotz data on diazepam (0.58, ±0.16), suggesting strong plasma protein binding of chlordiazepoxide. [Since the aged are prone to have decreased plasma proteins[31] and perhaps decreased plasma drug affinity,[27] one could predict a possible change with aging in this ratio. However, whether this would affect actual RBC binding only can be speculative.] Age-related erythrocyte drug *uptake*—versus binding—may be a different matter; see below, especially *Lithium carbonate*.[116]

Much of the research in geriatric pharmacokinetics—and much of this chapter—has proceeded along these lines, demonstrating how these bodily changes affect absorption, distribution, biotransformation and excretion of psychotropic medications. However, one should always bear in mind that, in addition to *age-related changes in pharmacokinetics,* there are also probable *age-related* changes in receptor-site sensitivity,[9,(see 73,74),17,18,19,-21,22,24,26,29-31,62,73-80] that is, changes in the sensitivity of target organs to a given drug concentration. (In addition, there are specific *drug interactions* that are more likely to occur in the elderly and that can also affect either pharmacokinetics or receptor-site sensitivity, as discussed below.)

The following will concern itself with agents of which the pharmacokinetics have been worked out, which are widely used, or which present special problems in terms of drug interaction.

## PSYCHOTROPIC MEDICATIONS ELIMINATED BY THE KIDNEY

Rowe et al.[81] have demonstrated a 30 percent decrease in creatinine clearance between years 30 and 80 in men. They have also devised a useful nomogram[82] for ascertaining age-(and sex-)adjusted percentile rank in creatinine clearance (see Figure 10-1).

### Lithium carbonate

Lithium carbonate clearance also decreases with age and is directly correlated with creatinine clearance.[83,84] The average half-life of lithium in the body varies with age, from about 18 to 30 hours in younger patients to as long as 36 hours in the elderly.[83] Hewick et al.[85] did a survey of 82 patients which examined the relationship between lithium dose, plasma level and age. They noted that as much as a 50 percent decrease in dose appeared necessary to compensate for changes in the elderly, largely, although not solely, because of decline in lithium clearance. [Fryo et al.[86] reported no correlation between clearance of lithium and aging. However, their data indicate a modest decrease in clearance with age $(r=.28, p<.10)$, although not enough to be statistically significant.]

It should be remembered that lithium has been found to be nephrotoxic, irrespective of age.[84] In a widely noted study, Hestbach et al.[87] recently reported 14 cases of patients on chronic lithium who, on renal biopsy, demonstrated consistent findings of focal atrophy and interstitial fibrosis. They also reported a decrease in creatinine clearance which was statistically related to these pathological changes. These findings were confirmed more recently by Burrows et al,[88] and are suggested by several antecedent studies.[84]

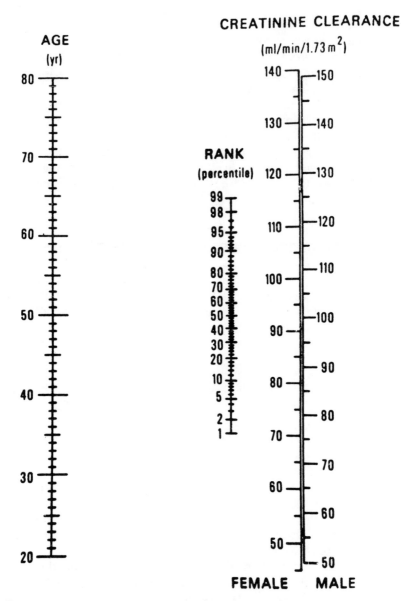

Figure 10-1:   Age- and sex-adjusted percentile rank in creatinine clearance.

From some patients, particularly the elderly, concomitant use of diuretics and lithium is a drug interaction that may further complicate the issue of lithium clearance. Chlorothiazides can produce lithium retention, sometimes resulting in toxic lithium levels.[84] Like sodium, 80 percent of the lithium ion is reabsorbed in the proximal renal tubules,[89] although there is evidence that lithium is also reabsorbed in the loop of Henle.[90] The reabsorption of both sodium and lithium proximally is very similar[84] or "identical.[89] The thiazide diuretics, by producing a distal diuresis of sodium, may increase the fractional reabsorption proximally of sodium,[84,89] and therefore perhaps of lithium.[84] This can produce as much as a 24 percent increase in the reabsorption of lithium in patients chronically treated with thiazide diuretics.[91] This has led clinicians to suggest extreme caution with the concomitant use of lithium and thiazide diuretics,[92] or even a recommendation of discontinuance entirely[93] of lithium in cases where such diuretics are used. Recent studies,[94,95] however, have emphasized the relative safety of the concomitant use of lithium and thiazide diuretics if proper monitoring is carried out. In addition, the use of lithium in patients with actual kidney disease has demonstrated that lithium may be prescribed in the most hazardous situations, providing that the kidneys retain some capacity to excrete lithium and that appropriate precautions are utilized.[95-97] This all has relevance to the elderly patient, who is more likely to suffer from CHF and from renal disease.

As mentioned above, the pharmacokinetics of the drug do not entirely account for its action. Receptor-site sensitivity must also be taken into account, particularly in the case of CNS effects. Foster, Gershell and Goldfarb[98] claim that both therapeutic and toxic CNS effects occur at lower serum levels in the elderly. Baldessarini and Stephens[99] have stated that lithium CNS toxicity is not age-related. Shopsin and Gershon correlated[100] lithium CNS toxicity with preexisting neurologic change rather than age. According to Salzman et al.,[75] this still increases the likelihood of toxicity in the elderly, who are more prone to have CNS impairment. There are many reports of lithium CNS toxicity within the normal therapeutic range; these are well summarized by Rifkin, Quitkin and Klein,[101] who also speculate about preexisting CNS disturbance. Van der Velde[102] reported increased toxicity in 3 out of 12 geriatric patients treated with lithium at levels below 2.0 meq/Li; these were the only instances of toxicity among 150 patients of all ages in this study. Strayhorn and Nash[103] suggested simply that it is impossible to rely solely on serum lithium levels in establishing dosage. They considered evidence for advanced age leading to increased risk for lithium CNS toxicity to be lacking at the time of their review. There have been reports of mild, reversible cognitive changes in normal subjects[104] and patients[105] given lithium. A recent study by

Freidman et al.[106] showed substantially elevated Halstead Impairment indexes among elderly patients on lithium, a phenomenon they did not venture to explain.

Lasagna[107] has recently brought up again the question of toxicity secondary to concomitant lithium carbonate and haloperidol use. This question was first raised in 1974 by Cohen and Cohen,[108] who described four patients on such a regimen (two of whom were over 60 years of age) who developed a severe encephalopathic picture, leaving two with widespread irreversible brain damage and two with persistent Parkinsonism and dyskinesias. Altesman and Cole[109] cite criticisms of this report, and three reviews[110-112] failing to replicate this picture. Of interest here is the work of Pert et al,[113] who recently reported that rats treated concomitantly with lithium and haloperidol failed to develop both the behavioral toxicity to apomorphine and the increased dopamine receptor binding seen with long-term haloperidol treatment. Their study suggested that lithium might actually prevent dyskinesias of the tardive type. [Tardive dyskinesia was noted early by Ayd[114] to occur more often in the elderly, which has been credited[75] as an early report of age-related receptor-site sensitivity.]

Byrd[115] has reported that methyldopa, when administered concomitantly with lithium, can lower serum lithium levels, yet simultaneously enhance lithium CNS toxicity. This would suggest a movement of lithium from extra- to intracellular compartments under the influence of methyldopa. The significance of this interaction is unclear. Schou[89] cites this and another similar report, but states only that the evidence suggests that to combine these agents is "inadvisable."

In our laboratory, Dorus et al.[116] have made the intriguing suggestion that age-related CNS activity in the elderly might be, in part, related to higher intracellular lithium concentration in their erythrocytes.

**Barbital; barbiturate metabolites**

Harvey[117] has written an excellent summary of barbiturate metabolism. Barbiturates not destroyed in the body are excreted in the urine. Only barbital is dependent mainly on renal excretion, with up to 90 percent total dose appearing in the urine unaltered (versus 50 percent for phenobarbital). However, most barbiturates are transformed, principally in the liver, to inactive metabolites. These metabolites are in turn excreted by the urine, although in rats the metabolites of phenobarbital and pentobarbital are excreted into bile in high concentrations. (The thiobarbiturates may be transformed to a small extent in other tissues, especially liver and brain.)

The effect of decreased renal clearance on barbital should be obvious. Decreased renal clearance may also affect the pharmacokinetics of the other barbiturates, even though they are detoxified by the liver. For example, Irvine et al.[118] studied the effect of increasing age on the hydroxylation of amylobarbital. They used a urine and serum assay to measure the metabolite 3'hydroxyamlobarbital for 48 hours after a single oral dose of amylobarbital. The study involved one group of eight subjects, aged 20 to 40 years, and another group of eight, all over 65. At 24 hours, the mean plasma level of the elderly group was significantly greater than the younger. The authors felt this represented decreased hepatic enzyme activity in the elderly. Triggs and Nation[24] criticized the study on the grounds of not having enough data to tell whether the elevated 24-hour plasma levels were due to changes in elimination half-life ($t_{1/2\beta}$), changes in volume of distribution ($V_d$), or both. Triggs and Nation also suggested that, although specific data were not presented, the glomerular filtration rate of the older group was probably lower than that of the younger, and that the slower rate of appearance of the metabolites in the urine of the elderly might be thus simply a result of decreased creatinine clearance. (Changes in creatinine clearance, it should be noted, generally have little effect on the assessment of the pharmacokinetics of most drugs metabolized by the liver.)

## PSYCHOTROPIC MEDICATIONS ELIMINATED BY THE LIVER

The benzodiazepines have received the most attention in terms of the relationship of pharmacologic drugs to aging. In a particularly important study, Klotz et al.[71] studied the effects of age and hepatocellular liver disease on the disposition and elimination of diazepam. There was no correlation between clearance and the subject's age; $V_d$ was age-dependent (i.e., increased) as was $t_{1/2\beta}$ (i.e., decreased). The authors concluded that the prolongation of $t_{1/2\beta}$ was primarily dependent on an increase in the initial $V_d$, and not on a change in metabolism. (However, four elderly patients had a significant reduction in the total plasma clearance, contributing to prolongation of the $t_{1/2\beta}$. The authors suggested that this might represent an age-dependent reduction in hepatic enzyme activity.) They also cautioned that possible changes in receptor-site sensitivity should be taken into account as well. The pharmacokinetic data obtained by Klotz et al. were confirmed by Greenblatt et al.[119] (A somewhat fuller explanation of the increased $V_d$ and the decreased $t_{1/2\beta}$ will be presented below, after discussion of chlordiazepoxide and oxazepam.)

Chlordiazepoxide pharmacokinetics have been well studied,[17,70,72,120,121,122,123,124] especially by Greenblatt and Shader.[67,72,121-124] The $V_d$ appears to increase with age, as does the $t_{1/2\beta}$. In contrast to diazepam, the clearance changes, decreasing with age. According to these studies, this is consistent with decreased hepatic transformation.

Of interest are Greenblatt and Shader's findings[125] that Maalox® (a magnesium and aluminum hydroxide antacid) decreases the rate, although probably not the completeness, of oral chlordiazepoxide absorption [normally 100 percent[72,124]] of chlordiazepoxide. This was correlated with subjective experiences on the part of volunteers. Subjects given chlor-diazepoxide, with or without Maalox, had a slowed or (the normally) rapid absorption of the drug. This, in turn, resulted in slowed or normal attainment of drug plasma levels, presumably leading to delayed or normal attainment of drug equilibrium between plasma and brain tissue. Feelings of "spaciness" and thinking "slowed down" were noted when chlor-diazepoxide was absorbed at the normally rapid rate (without Maalox), suggesting the importance of not only concentration at the receptor-site (and receptor-site sensitivity), but also the rate at which this concentration takes place. A similar delay in the rate, but not completeness, of diazepam absorption has been shown recently by Greenblatt, Shader et al.[127] to occur with the concomitant use of Maalox and Gelusil® (also a magnesium-aluminum hydroxide antacid). Food, however, was shown in this study to decrease the rate of absorption, but to increase the completeness. These findings may be of special relevance to the elderly patient, who is more likely to suffer from any disease, including those that produce GI distress. Also, the geriatric patient may be more sensitive to the CNS side effects of sedative-hypnotics (see *Barbiturates,* below) and thus perhaps to changes in absorption rate and completeness.

It has been demonstrated as far back as 1973 and 1974, respectively, that the intramuscular route of diazepam[66,128,129] and chlordiazepoxide[130,131] results in slower absorption than the oral administration. [In the case of diazepam, a local reaction to its solvent[131] may be the explanation; for chlordiazepoxide, the physiochemical nature of the drug itself may result in precipitation at the injection site.[17,124]] This retardation of action is of obvious concern. The possibility of decreased completeness of absorption, suggested by these studies, has concerned clinicians as well. However, Korttila et al.[132] reported that injections of diazepam deep into the vastus lateralis muscle (in the thigh) resulted in similar absorption (rate and completeness) and comparable clinical effects when contrasted with oral administration. Greenblatt et al.[124] recently reported a slower rate of absorption with intramuscular chlordiazepoxide but similar completeness [86 percent versus 100 percent noted above for oral.[72,124]]

Possible age-related changes in oral GI absorption of diazepam[66] and chlordiazepoxide[67] have been noted above. (It should be noted, however, that both these suggestions are isolated, questionable and unexplained.)

Shull et al,[133] in a study of oxazepam and liver disease, noted no age-related changes in either $t_{1/2\beta}$ or clearance; $V_d$ was either unchanged or minimally elevated in the elderly, depending on the way in which it was calculated. Shull's group concluded that oxazepam metabolism changes the least in terms of age-related pharmacokinetics compared to diazepam and chlordiazepoxide. There appears to be no data as yet on the effects of antacids on oxazepam absorption;[124] one study[134] suggested that food had no effect on absorption. There are no parenteral preparations of oxazepam.

Shull and his group also noted the increased sensitivity of elderly patients to diazepam and chlordiazepoxide cited in the Boston Collaborative Drug Surveillance Program (BCDSP).[60] Shull et al. concluded that, in the case of oxazepam, any increased sensitivity in the elderly would have to involve receptor-site sensitivity, since there appears to be essentially no age-related change in drug disposition. Greenblatt and Shader, however, have suggested that "any differences between various benzodiazepines may in large part be pharmacokinetic rather than neuropharmacologic",[122] although recent work by Castleden et al.[135] on nitrazepam (see below) suggests greater toxicity in the elderly without change in pharmacokinetics. Also, Curry et al.[136] have studied the varying effects on monkey behavior of diazepam and its metabolites, as well as the benzodiazepine clorazepate, also a desmethyldiazepam precursor. They concluded that "differences in the effects of closely related benzodiazepines may not be due solely to their plasma pharmacokinetic properties, but may arise from differences in their intrinsic activity."

It should be noted that the metabolic degradation of diazepam (DZ), chlordiazepoxide (CDX) and oxazepam (OXZ) have similarities.[121,122] Greenblatt and Shader have provided a nice overall summary.[122] DZ and CDX are both broken down initially to active metabolites, desmethyldiazepam (DMDZ) and desmethylchlordiazepoxide (DMCDX). Both also proceed in step-wise fashion to eventually form OXZ, which itself is excreted as an inactive glucoronide. The half-life of CDX [5 to 30 hours[122]] changes markedly with age, while those of DZ [15 to 61 hours[71,119]] and OXZ [4 to 11 hours[137]] exhibit little or no change. This can be explained by the high lipid solubility of DZ, which could also explain the increased $V_d$[71,119] noted above in the proportionately more fatty[22,122] elderly patient. This, in turn, could compensate for the increased $t_{1/2\beta}$, with clearance then remaining the same as in the young. OXZ pharmacokinetics are noted to remain essentially the same in the elderly patient [see Shull et al.,[133] above]; any possible change in $V_d$ would be compensated by the short $t_{1/2\beta}$. Because of this, and because of its shorter half-life,[137] OXZ is less likely to result in toxic plasma levels in the older patient. Largely for these reasons, Ayd,[138] Merlis and Koepke[139] have suggested oxazepam to be the benzodiazepine of choice in the pharmacologic management of anxiety in the geriatric patient.

The pharmacokinetics of flurazepam are unusual.[140] Even after large doses, the drug is barely detectable in the blood. However, its major metabolite, desalkylflurazepam, is immediately detectable and disappears slowly, with a half-life greater than 50 hours. The influence of age on its pharmacokinetics has yet to be worked out in any detail.[141]

Flurazepam toxicity appears low in general [3.1 percent of 2,542 medical inpatients[141]], manifesting itself almost entirely as a minor and easily reversible CNS depression.[141] This CNS depression has been related to both dose ($x^2=11.4$, df=2, p<0.001) and age ($x^2=23.1$, df=2, p<0.001), with unwanted effects found in 39 percent of patients over 70 years of age who were receiving a daily dose of 30mg or more.[141]

Compared to other hypnotics, flurazepam seems to influence REM sleep relatively little;[142,143] also, it has a relative paucity of CNS effects, especially the so-called "paradoxical" excitement (see *Barbiturates, below*). These findings could represent a differential effect on receptor-site sensitivity. Consistent with this are the conclusions of Curry et al.[136] (listed above) and Castleden et al.[135] (described immediately below) about a presumed differential receptor-site response to diazepam and nitrazepam. Against a differential receptor-site action of flurazepam is the Greenblatt and Shader emphasis on the strict relationship between benzodiazepine pharmacokinetics and clinical response[122] (noted under oxazepam, above). Also inconsistent are the similarities to the age-dose relationship of CNS depression reported with diazepam and chlordiazepoxide by the BCDSP.[60] The lack of age-related CNS toxicity, depression *or* excitement, reported by the BCDSP[41] regarding several barbiturates—and the lack of chloral hydrate CNS depression, but not excitement, found in older patients—is hard to relate to this question. Likewise, the unvalidated clinical observations by Greenblatt and Shader,[141] suggesting a lack of CNS toxicity of *any* type "for other nonbenzodiazepine hypnotics such as chloral hydrate, pentobarbital, and secobarbital" are equally hard to relate to the question of a differential effect of flurazepam on receptor-sites compared to other hypnotics. (Flurazepam and other benzodiazepine hypnotics do, however, have a definite advantage, in terms of a relatively lower incidence of drug interactions, over the other sedative-hypnotics, as discussed below, in the Important Drug Interactions section.)

As mentioned, Castleden et al.[135] studied the pharmacologic effect of nitrazepam in the elderly by administering this agent and placebo double-blind, in one dose each, a week apart. They studied two groups of ten patients; one with a mean age of 25.3 years and the other 74.7. Weights of the two groups were "similar"; and all subjects were reported to be "in good health" with "no clinical or biochemical evidence of hepatic, renal or mental disease." However, no specific laboratory data such as liver function tests and creatinine clearance were presented; there was, moreover, no study of plasma binding or other tissue affinity. The nitrazepam was administered as a single 10mg oral dose. Plasma levels were obtained at 12, 36 and 60 hours. Psychomotor testing was performed, and subjective responses were recorded. There was no difference found between the groups in plasma concentration at the three determinations. The $t_{1/2\beta}$ was the same in both groups, as was the $V_d$. The elderly made significantly more mistakes than the young in psychomotor testing, despite the similar pharmacokinetic data. The authors concluded that the difference in nitrazepam effects between the two groups was "due to a change in the ageing brain and not a change in pharmacokinetics."

In a study more epidemiologic than pharmacologic, Greenblatt and Allen[144] noted that nitrazepam CNS toxicity manifested itself as both CNS depression *and* excitement. When manifest as depression of the central nervous system, toxicity correlated strongly ($x^2 > 50$, df=4, p<0.001) with age. The authors noted a clinical similarity to that reported with flurazepam above,[141] as well as to that produced by diazepam and chlordiazepoxide,[60] but a contrast with barbiturate and chloral hydrate CNS depression—supposedly not age-related[41,141]—already discussed (see flurazepam, above). Greenblatt and Allen went on to note a greater incidence of CNS stimulation in nitrazepam when compared to flurazepam. However, the authors interpreted these instances of CNS stimulation as not related to age per se, but more to dose. Greenblatt and Allen admitted, however, that the study did "not establish whether the increased toxicity of nitrazepam in the elderly is due to greater sensitivity of the ageing brain to effects of the drug, or to age-related changes in pharmacokinetics which lead to greater accumulation of the drug in the brain." They cited the Castleden et al. study,[135] but noted the evidence above that, with the other benzodiazepines, pharmacologic activity is largely based on pharmacokinetics. They noted that renal clearance has little to do with nitrazepam clearance, but they did raise the issue of a change in $V_d$ due to altered serum proteins (not considered by the Castleden group).

## Propranolol

This agent has come to be used more widely as anxiolytic of late.[145] One authority in geropsychiatry has reported[146] that it showed promise as an aid to learning in the elderly, but this appears unsubstantiated or ignored. Propranolol, of course, has many nonpsychiatric uses;[147] and, it has been advocated as an agent to reduce tremor, insomnia or agitation produced by tricyclic antidepressants[148] and as an antidote for lithium tremor.[89,149] [This agent may actually *produce* neuropsychiatric disturbances when used medically — e.g., depression,[150,151] confusion and/or hallucinations[145,151] and insomnia.[151]] Greenblatt and Shader[145] have reviewed recent controlled trials of the anxiolytic efficacy of the $\beta$-blockers. They concluded that comparative judgment of these studies, which they summarized as "heterogeneous in design and objective," was "difficult and tenuous." It is not surprising, therefore, that the exact role of propranolol in psychopharmacology, either of the young or the elderly, is yet to be established.[145,147]

The pharmacokinetics of propranolol are interesting.[152-156] Over 90 percent of the circulating drug is bound to proteins.[152] Its biotransformation occurs mostly in the liver.[153] Its hepatic metabolism is not confined to free drug in the circulation;[152] in fact, unlike most drugs, its metabolism might be *accelerated* by binding to elements in the blood, which could actually act as a carrier system to the liver.[154] An active metabolic (4-hydroxypropranolol) has been identified.[155] This appears only after oral administration. The clinical significance of this metabolite is not clear. Greenblatt and Shader[145] note studies showing it to have significant sedative and anticonvulsant properties in animals, while Shand[156] considers it to play only a minor role with chronic administration of its parent, propranolol.

Melander et al.[134] have studied the effect of food on the absorption of propranolol. They found no change in the rate, but an increase in completeness of absorption. They also noted a large interindividual variation in absorption, but not in elimination ($t_{1/2\beta}$= 2 to 3 hours). (Possible mechanisms explaining this phenomenon will be discussed below — see *Chlorpromazine.)*

There is an unresolved question over the site of propranolol's anxiolytic action:[145,157] *peripheral* (by blockade of $\beta$-adrenergic blocking of autonomic feedback) or *central* (by a direct effect on the CNS). Indeed, there has been, and remains, a controversy over the site of anxiety itself, as Lader nicely summarizes.[158] Gottschalk et al.[157] studied the effect of propranolol (60mg in three divided doses over 12 hours), given to 12 "healthy, nonanxious" subjects and a matched placebo group. On a 10-minute stress interview, anxiety scores increased to equal levels in both groups; pulse responses during the interview were significantly lower in the propranolol group. Free fatty acid (FFA) plasma-level responses were not statistically different in the two groups, although lower in the propranolol group. The authors concluded that the findings suggested that "basal or resting" anxiety may be reduced by $\beta$-adrenergic blocking agents, whereas "the magnitude of acutely aroused anxiety is mediated more through the central nervous system." They could not, however, ignore evidence for a CNS effect of propranolol. Greenblatt and Shader[145] have reviewed evidence which suggests "that direct central effects undoubtedly play some role" in the anxiolytic action of this agent.

A study of particular relevance here is that of Castleden et al.[159] His group studied the effect of age on plasma levels of propranolol. After a single dose of 40mg, plasma levels were obtained in serial fashion for up to eight hours, in an elderly and a control group. The propranolol levels in both groups peaked at two hours, but there was a significantly longer "decay" in the elderly group. This was attributed to "substantially reduced first-pass effect." There was, however, no data reported on $V_d$ other than matching for height and weight and "normal" serum proteins. The lack of such data makes these results hard to evaluate, especially if one accepts the suggestion of Evans and Shand[154] that binding of propranolol to elements in the blood might shorten its $t_{1/2\beta}$ by acting as a carrier system to its site of elimination in the liver, and that this all occurs without alteration in $V_d$ or drug clearance. Hence the lack of data in the Castleden study makes it possible to explain the longer "decay" in the elderly as perhaps secondary to the decreased plasma binding of drugs secondary to decreased albumin[31] [or to decreased protein affinity[28]].

Adverse reactions to the $\beta$-blockers are, of course, important for the clinician interested in geriatric pharmacology. Greenblatt and Koch-Weser[151] have provided an excellent review. Adverse reactions to propranolol were found to occur in 8.4 percent of 14,344 hospitalized patients. In a literature survey of 797 outpatients, the authors also found that GI symptoms were the most common (11.2 percent), followed by impairment of cardiac function (6.9 percent) and peripheral arterial insufficiency (5.8 percent). In the hospitalized patients who suffered propranolol-induced cardiac impairment, 20 out of 22 had evidence of preexisting heart disease. Adverse reactions to $\beta$-blockers in general were found by the authors to be more common among the elderly, although the trend was not statistically significant. Sex, hospital, diagnosis, indication for use and concomitant administration of other agents did *not* alter the frequency of adverse reactions. Also, there was a lack of correlation found between adverse reaction and dose, and that half the adverse reactions occurred in patients taking less than 40mg qd. This last is particularly important since the suggested daily anxiolytic dose range is 30 to 120mg qd,[160] and the recommended dose for lithium tremor and tricyclic psychomotor agitation [50 to 80mg[149] and 30 to 40mg qd,[148] respectively] is similar.

The relevance of these findings to anyone treating the geriatric patient should be self-evident, as should the reports of hypoglycemia occurring while on this agent.[151] Abramson et al.[161] reported that propranolol delayed the return of blood glucose levels to normal after insulin-induced hypoglycemia. They also noted a marked diminution in the sympathetic response to hypoglycemia. This is, of course, of major importance to insulin-dependent diabetics, in whom propranolol may obscure the familiar "warning signs" of hypoglycemia, as well as to impair correction of this condition. [Greenblatt and Koch-Weser,[151] however, found that evidence on the interactions between β-blockers and oral hypoglycemics was "unclear," but that clinically important hypoglycemia as a complication of concomitant use of these two groups of drugs was quite rare.]

It is, however, worth noting Shand's reminder[156] that, despite all these reports, propranolol is generally a "safer drug than is generally thought." Shand noted, for example, that in Greenblatt and Koch-Weser's report, only 1.3 percent adverse reactions were life-threatening, and none fatal.

Because of its ability to reduce hepatic blood flow,[162] or for unexplained reasons,[163] propranolol can interfere with the hepatic clearance of other drugs, a phenomenon that Greenblatt and Shader[145] suggest is yet to be fully investigated. The clinical relevance remains to be seen, for young or old.

### Chlorpromazine

Good reviews of the effect of medication on GI absorption,[62,164-166] specifically antacid therapy,[166] are available. Contrary to popular belief, the stomach is not the most important *site* of drug absorption.[165] Basic drugs and drugs absorbed by active transport are not absorbed to any extent by the stomach. Readily diffusable, neutral drugs (such as ethanol) are better absorbed by the greater surface area of the small intestine. Nimmo[165] claims that even weakly acidic drugs, which are largely lipid-soluble at gastric pH (aspirin, barbiturates), are absorbed more slowly from the stomach than from the small intestine. However, the stomach may *influence* absorption greatly. With delayed gastric emptying, absorption is usually either incomplete or delayed. This can be due to increased degradation in the stomach (and possibly intestine), or due to increased time for first-pass effects to take place. Increases in gastrointestinal motility usually increase absorption, but may also decrease absorption if the increase leads to less time for dissolution and adequate contact between the drug and its intestinal absorption site.

Antacids can reduce absorption by binding drugs directly in the GI tract. Antacids with aluminum (and, to some extent, those with magnesium) may delay gastric emptying. Antacids may interfere with absorption by decreasing dissolution in the stomach. However, certain acidic drugs may be better absorbed because of greater dissolution via change in pH around the tablet, as has been suggested[164] for aspirin. Antacids may decrease the urinary excretion of acidic drugs like amphetamines, by raising urine pH[166] (see CNS stimulants, below). The delay in chlordiazepoxide absorption by antacid administration noted above[125,126] was attributed to delayed gastric emptying. The delay in diazepam absorption[127] was partially attributed to a delay in gastric emptying caused by the antacids, as well as to decreased dissolution secondary to buffering of gastric acid.

Ingestion of a meal may enhance absorption by stimulating gastric secretion and/or delaying gastric emptying just enough to allow for greater dissolution and prolonged residence at the intestinal site of absorption.[167] Greater dissolution but delayed gastric emptying were the explanations given for the decreased rate but increased completeness of diazepam absorption.[127] However, the increase in propranolol with meals[134] was suggested to be more related to changes in hepatic blood flow or in first-pass metabolism.[167] This last point is particularly relevant to the elderly, who, as Triggs and Nation[24] have pointed out, have a general decrease in cardiac output and splanchnic blood flow, as well as a decreased capacity for biotransformation of many drugs. It might, therefore, partially explain the longer "decay" of the plasma propranolol levels of the older subjects in the Castleden et al.[159] study above. It might also provide a fuller explanation for the effect of meals on diazepam blood levels noted above,[127] especially since there is evidence of an increase in these levels by meals even when diazepam is given intravenously.[168]

Forrest et al.[169] and Fann et al.[170] noted, respectively, a reduction in urinary and plasma chlorpromazine levels with antacid therapy (Aludrox®, a magnesium trisilicate-aluminum hydroxide compound). The former group found a reduction of urinary CPZ by 55 to 90 percent and the latter a significant lowering of plasma CPZ. Neither study, however, addressed the rate of absorption. Neither addressed whether this effect persisted with high doses over a period of time. Both groups concluded that the decreased absorption was due to actual binding of CPZ by the antacid-gel.

Rivera-Calimlim and her colleagues have noted extensively[171-173] that trihexyphenidyl decreases CPZ absorption, probably by delay in gastric emptying.[173] Rivera-Calimlim also cited the work of Consolo et al.,[174] showing delayed or inhibited absorption of phenylbutazone by desipramine, ascribed to anticholinergic inhibition of gastric emptying by DMI; and work by her own groups[175] felt to show interference with L-dopa absorption by imipramine, explained by the same mechanism. In addition, she cites the work of Leijnse and Van Pragg,[176] who ascribed decreased absorption in the rat of iproniazid as secondary to delayed gastric passage; Mayton and Levy,[177] who claimed impairment of drug absorption in the rat as a result of decreased peristalsis produced by SKF 525–A; and LaVigne and Marchand,[178] who reported inhibition of PAS absorption by diphenhydramine, a structural analogue of SKF 525–A. (It should be noted, however, that studies of the absorption of various drugs are surprisingly few, and LaVigne and Marchand, for example, were not sure of the exact explanation of their findings.)

Rivera-Calimlim[175,179] has also reported low CPZ levels in patients receiving concomitant lithium. She initially suggested[175] that either lithium or the patient's clinical state could alter CPZ absorption, metabolism or excretion; she also presented, with Kerzner,[179] evidence for changes in gastric emptying.

[Possible metabolism of CPZ by the GI tract itself[63,64] has been mentioned above.] Since older patients are more likely to have GI disturbances, these studies on CPZ may be relevant.

Rivera-Calimlim et al.[180] studied the effect of age on CPZ plasma levels. They found that younger age, chronicity of disturbance and prolonged drug treatment were associated with decreased plasma levels. Her group felt that this effect was possibly the result of impaired gut absorption or accelerated metabolism of CPZ.

This, however, does not necessarily imply greater clinical efficacy in the older patient, who, this one study suggests, may have higher plasma levels. Curry[181] has found no correlation between plasma levels and clinical response, although Alfredsson[70] has at least well correlated CPZ plasma and CSF levels (r=0.91).

We[182] have recently summarized the problems of assessing CPZ (and other antipsychotic) plasma levels in terms of relation to clinical effect. In this summary, we also stressed the importance of the interaction of the drug and/or its metabolites with the receptor-site giving, as an example, the work of Maxwell et al.

Maxwell's group[183] studied the plasma disappearance and cerebral effects of CPZ in 24 patients with compensated cirrhosis versus a matched control group. No pharmacokinetic differences between the two groups were found (although the levels of only the parent drug were obtained). Drowsiness and EEG slowing were found in all subjects. However, in three of four patients who had a history of prior encephalopathy, mild confusion and deterioration of visual-motor testing were found. These three also exhibited the greatest EEG slowing (to 4 cps). The authors concluded that the susceptibility of some patients with cirrhosis to CPZ probably reflects increased CNS sensitivity, rather than difference in hepatic drug metabolism.

Maxwell's study suggests that Bender's early conclusion[21] that the "central nervous system is perhaps the system most sensitive to alterations in drug activity with age" is relevant. It also suggests that Hamilton's early conclusion[184]—that the neuronal loss due to aging is "the primary manifestation responsible for the altered reactivity and sensitivity of the aged to neurogenic drugs"—is, while perhaps oversimplified, equally relevant. It suggests that both Bender and Hamilton were aware early of the importance of addressing age-related changes in receptor-site sensitivity (versus pharmacokinetic changes) with aging.

To return to our own review,[182] we also noted the complex nature of chlorpromazine metabolism, and the suggestion that the pharmacokinetic study of another antipsychotic drug with a simpler metabolism—such as butaperazine—might be more fruitful. We also reviewed evidence that the study of erythrocyte drug uptake might be more fruitful than plasma levels. We suggested that some of the mechanisms in the distribution of the drug across the RBC membrane might mimic those governing the passage of the drug through the blood-brain barrier to the brain receptor-sites. These directions could prove fruitful some day in the understanding of drug effects in the elderly.

### Thioridazine

Martensson and Roos[185] noted increased serum levels of thioridazine in elderly patients. Axelsson and Martensson[186] also reported lower levels with age in a group of patients treated with thioridazine alone, but higher levels in a group comprised of patients treated concomitantly with other medications. The latter study did not address the issue of drug interaction.

### Haloperidol

Forsman and Ohman[187] reported no age-related changes in serum haloperidol.

### Tricyclic antidepressants

Tricyclic antidepressants have been, as noted, reported to delay gastric emptying,[167,171–175] a fact of possible relevance to treatment of the elderly.

A more important interaction, however, is that between the tricyclics and various neuroleptics, usually with the latter inhibiting TCA metabolism,[188] although the opposite has been reported.[189] Since depression is so prevalent in the elderly,[190,191] often accompanied by psychosis,[191] the chance of such a combination is quite high and should be kept in mind.

Alexander Nies et al.[192] have recently reported a correlation between age and elevated steady-state serum imipramine, desipramine and amitriptyline in patients treated with imipramine and amitriptyline (nortriptyline levels were found to be unchanged). The authors suggested decreased liver enzyme activity as the cause. They encouraged lowering the TCA dosage by a third to a half in the elderly.

## OTHER IMPORTANT DRUG INTERACTIONS

The increasing interest and recent proliferation of literature on drug interactions [contained in various references in the Introduction, especially the report by the BCDSP,[41] and elsewhere below,[89,93,95,107,108,115,125-127,151,161-167,169-180,187-189] et al.] is continuing to grow at a rate which has been termed an "explosion".[193] Literature on interactions between all pharmacologic agents,[193-197] with specific reference to the elderly,[198] is prolific, as is literature on psychotropic drug interactions in general,[93,199,200] and on psychoactive drug interactions among the geriatric population.[201] Shader, Greenblatt et al. have also provided a nice review of interactions of drugs for seizures and other brain disorders.[202]

There is also a growing literature on "polypharmacy",[203] especially with regard to psychotropic agents in the elderly [see Winstead, Blackwell, et al.[51] and Whanger[55] below] and the well-known work of Fracchia, Shepperd and Merlis (e.g.,[203,204]). There is concern about the escalating use of multiple psychotropic drugs in the elderly, especially in view of the study by Ingman et al.,[57] which noted that the greatest number of prescriptions in a long-term care facility were given to the patients with the *least* physical and mental impairment. This has prompted Ayd[205] to criticize this practice and to demand a more "rational" approach. Eisdorfer[206] suggests that psychoactive drugs per se are "not necessarily being over-used," but that "the administration of psychotropic agents should be based on a rational approach," with "awareness of the actions of these drugs." Shader,[207] however, suggests that the pejorative connotation of "polypharmacy" is not always justified, especially in conditions that involve symptoms not amenable to treatment by one drug alone.

Many potential interactions have been discussed; others of relevance not mentioned will be listed briefly.

## Chloral hydrate

This old and widely used agent may (via its metabolite trichloracetic acid) displace acidic drugs from plasma proteins. This can result in a sudden increase in the free blood levels of these displaced agents and shortening of their elimination half-lives (e.g., warfarin, diphenylhydantoin).[208]

With warfarin, however, this phenomenon may be of more academic than clinical significance. Clear documentation of prothrombin-time prolongation by chloral hydrate exists,[209] but actual relevance of this to practice is questionable.[107,210] Likewise, a clinically significant interaction in the case of diphenylhydantoin (phenytoin, DPH) and chloral hydrate does not appear to have been demonstrated.[202,208]

## Barbiturates

Barbital was mentioned above because of its unique pharmacokinetic properties that set it apart from the other barbiturates (see above,[117]). Also, the study on amylobarbital by Irvine et al.,[118] with the criticism of it by Triggs and Nation,[24] was presented to illustrate some of the problems in attempting a full explanation of a drug's pharmacokinetics without complete data.

Hexobarbital was one of the first drugs to be studied from the standpoint of pharmacokinetics.[1] Consequently, the metabolism of it and other barbiturates is well understood [as reviewed by Harvey,[117] above]. In general, however, the use of these agents has fallen into disrepute, especially in the elderly. This is partly because of the so-called "paradoxical" excitement[211] alleged to occur with hypnotics, especially this group.[75,212] One should recall, however, the BCDSP data on chloral hydrate and several barbiturates[41] suggesting little or no age-related change in CNS side effects with these agents. Also worth recall are Greenblatt and Shader's clinical observations[141] to the same effect. In addition, the suppression of REM sleep seen with these agents[213] [and much less with flurazepam[142,143]] might be the cause of so-called "rebound" nightmares and insomnia.[213] Moreover, the high risk of addiction[117,208,214] and gravity of an overdose with these agents[208,215,216] [especially when compared to flurazepam[208]] has further discredited their value. This has helped lead to a widely publicized condemnation[217] of them as "archaic" in 1973, and to the subsequent ascendance of flurazepam as the most prescribed hypnotic in the United States and Canada.[141]

This is, however, not the only cause for concern with the use of these agents. Perhaps more important is the ability of these agents to induce microsomal enzyme activity markedly.[1,3,202,208] This can affect plasma levels of warfarin, often with catastrophic results. The greatest danger occurs when a barbiturate is suddenly stopped in a patient on concomitant anticoagulants (which may have previously been increased to compensate for the faster metabolism by the hypnotic-induced hepatic enzymes).

Antipsychotic[169,218] and antidepressant[219,220] medications may be more rapidly metabolized with concomitant use of barbiturates. Actual clinical significance of these interactions has not yet been documented, nor has the report[187] that barbiturates (and DPH) lower haloperidol levels.

The interactions between the antipsychotics and phenobarbital may be of special interest, since many patients on anticonvulsant medications often come to the attention of the psychiatrist later in life, especially in the cases of behavioral dysfunction associated with temporal lobe epilepsy (TLE), specifically the schizophrenia-like psychosis described by Slater and Beard[221] (a "schizophreniform" psychosis, often paranoid, but usually with a more available affect than schizophrenia itself) and/or the bizarre "interictal personality" of TLE described by Waxman and Geschwind[222] (hypergraphia, hyperreliogiosity, "viscosity" of personality, and occasionally hyposexuality). Also of interest is the possiblity that DPH, itself a weak enzyme inducer,[3,202,223] might induce the metabolism of psychotropic agents. However, Shader et al.[202] have reviewed this possibility exhaustively with no findings of clinically important interactions. Shader et al.[202] and Lasagna[107] also reviewed the interaction between phenobarbital and DPH, with the same conclusion of no important clinical effect.*

**Glutethimide**

This agent may be grouped with the barbiturates in terms of enzyme induction, potential for abuse, gravity of overdosage and REM deprivation.[208]

---

*The relevance of phenobarbital (and/or DPH) on antipsychotic treatment of TLE-related behavioral dysfunction is clouded not only by these conclusions but also by the fact that there appears to be no widely accepted dose ranges for these disturbances (N Geschwind, personal communication, 1978). In fact, R.H. has successfully treated a case of TLE "interictal personality" in a 50-year-old white female (whose diagnosis was confirmed in conference by Geschwind) with haloperidol 6mg qd, despite concomitant treatment with DPH and primidone (a phenobarbital precursor).

## Other hypnotics and sedatives

Enzyme induction by methaqualone and ethchlorvynol has been suggested,[208] but this does not appear to be of significance. Chloral hydrate and flurazepam do not seem to cause clinically significant enzyme induction,[208] nor does meprobamate[224] or other benzodiazepine hypnotics and sedatives.[202,224] There are many scattered reports to the contrary, especially about the benzodiazepines, but these are described aptly by Shader, Greenblatt et al.[202] as "weak" and/or anecdotal. An example of such reports is that by Dugal et al.[225] on DZ and AMI, which reviews the literature with little question and which itself is vague in its findings, conclusion and clinical relevance. There is some evidence[208] that food and/ or antacids can delay the absorption of many hypnotics, leading the patient to take more of the drug than usual. The absorption is ultimately, however, complete, thus resulting in a delayed reaction, with excessive and prolonged sedation. For the elderly, who might be more sensitive to hypnotics,[75,211,212] this is of particular relevance.


## Anticholinergic agents

Essentially all "anti-Parkinsonian" agents, the tricyclic antidepressants and phenothiazines possess anticholinergic properties. Many of the antihistamines, often prescribed for sleep, do so as well. In the elderly one must, therefore, be concerned about paralytic ileus, urinary retention, glaucoma, tachycardia and confusional states.

Confusional states are especially relevant, since these agents alone, or in combination, can produce an atropine psychosis, especially in the case of the older patient, whose cerebral function may already be compromised.[21,61,75,184] Also, the agitated confusion produced by these agents may be misinterpreted by overworked nursing-home or state-hospital staff as a worsening of the condition for which these drugs were given in the first place. Our group has demonstrated[226] that an atropine psychosis produced by the combination of a phenothiazine, tricyclic and/or anti-Parkinsonian can be reversed by physostigmine. Physostigmine can be particularly useful in diagnosing and treating these toxic states.[227] [The differential potency of anticholinergic psychotropic agents in binding to clinically important receptors is shown in Table 10-1, compiled by Baldessarini.[228]]

It is worth noting that amantadine, an anti-Parkinsonian agent suggested as having no anticholinergic activity,[229] has recently been demonstrated to have caused a delirium reversed by physostigmine.[230] Of interest also is the suggestion that the benzodiazepines may have some

## Table 10-1: Table 10-1: Differential potency of anticholinergic psychotropic agents in receptor binding.

| Agent | EC$_{50}$(nM)[a] | K$_d$(nM)[b] |
|---|---|---|
| Scopolamine | 0.3 | – |
| Atropine | 0.4 | 2 |
| Trihexyphenidyl (Artane) | 0.6 | – |
| Benztropine (Cogentin) | 1.5 | – |
| Amitriptyline (Elavil, etc.) | 10 | 100 |
| Doxepin (Sinequan) | 44 | 300 |
| Nortriptyline (Aventyl) | 57 | 1,000 |
| Imipramine (Tofranil, etc.) | 78 | 400 |
| Protriptyline (Vivactil) | – | 2,000 |
| Desipramine (Norpramin, etc.) | 170 | 2,000 |
| Clozapine (Leponex) | 26 | 3 |
| Thioridazine (Mellaril) | 150 | 60 |
| Promazine (Sparine) | 650 | 60 |
| Chlorpromazine (Thorazine, etc.) | 1,000 | 2,000 |
| Triflupromazine (Vesprin) | 1,000 | – |
| Acetophenazine (Tindal) | 10,000 | 4,000 |
| Perphenazine (Trifalon) | 11,000 | 4,000 |
| Fluphenazine (Prolixin) | 12,000 | 2,000 |
| Trifluoperazine (Stelazine) | 13,000 | 20,000 |
| Haloperidol (Haldol) | 48,000 | 7,000 |
| Iproniazid (Marplan) | 100,000 | – |
| Nialamid (Niamid) | 100,000 | – |
| Phenelzine (Nardil) | 100,000 | – |

a. Data are half-maximally effective concentrations (EC$_{50}$) of drugs which compete for the binding to tissue of the labeled test agent, $^3$H-QNB—an avid and selective muscarinic antagonist, [$^3$H]-3-quinuclidinylbenzilate—as estimated in rat brain homogenates. Concentrations are in units of nM (nanomolar, or $10^{-9}$M). Adapted from Baldessarini, 1977 (A), based on data of Snyder, Yamamura, and Greenberg, 1974 (B) and 1977 (C).

b. From data of Richelson and Divinetz-Romero, 1977 (D), based on the potency of the test drugs in blocking the formation of cyclic guanosine-3′,5′—cyclic-monophosphate (cyclic GMP) by carbonylcholine (a stable acetylcholine analogue), using cultured mouse neuroblastoma cells. Data are reported as dissociation constants (K$_d$ in units of nM). The two units are best compared by the fank-order of potencies, disregarding the absolute values obtained.

(A) Baldessarini RJ: *Chemotherapy in Psychiatry*. Boston, Harvard University Press, 1977, p 103.

(B) Snyder SH, Greenberg D, Yamamaura HI: Antischizophrenic drugs and brain cholinergic receptors: Affinity for muscarinic sites predicts extra pyramidal effects. *Arch Gen Psychiatry* 31:58–61, 1974.

(C) Snyder SH, Yamamura H: Antidepressants and the muscarinic acetylcholine receptor. *Arch Gen Psychiatry* 34:236–239, 1977.

(D) Richelson E, Divinitz-Romero S: Blockade of psychotropic drugs of the muscarinic acetylcholine receptor in cultured nerve cells. *Biol Psychiatry* 12:771–785, 1977.

anticholinergic activity as well,[231,232,233,234] especially since the package insert for Valium® (diazepam) contains a warning about possible precipitation of glaucoma.

## MAO inhibitors

The MAO inhibitors have the potential for a number of adverse drug and/or food interactions, which can be catastrophic for the elderly, whose cardiovascular system is more likely to be compromised. Baldessarini[235] has put together an excellent table of drug interactions involving the MAO inhibitors (see Table 10-2). The Massachusetts General Hospital Psychopharmacology Clinics have an inclusive instruction list[236] to patients outlining foods and beverages that contain tyramine and over-the-counter (OTC) drugs which contain substances, especially sympathomimetics, that can react with the MAOIs (see Table 10-3). [No list of OTC medications is, of course, ever up to date. The reader is referred elsewhere[237] for a more comprehensive list that might include relevant medications not in the MGH list.] Of interest is Guttman's finding[59] that 69 percent of 447 elderly patients studied used OTC medications [versus 10 percent in the general adult population.[46]] Physicians were consulted about the use of these agents by only one-sixth of this group. Chien et al.[238] found a similar pattern for drug use in the elderly with OTC agents constituting 40 percent of the medications used.

### Tricyclic antidepressants and hypertensive medications

The adverse reactions that occur between these agents are also summarized by Baldessarini in Table 10-2. The most notable interaction is the antagonism of guanethidine by the tricyclics (including doxepin) which can lead to ever-increasing doses of guanethidine in a patient on tricyclic medication. [We have shown[239] that chlorpromazine can have a similar interaction with guanethidine.] It is worth mentioning that the more recently introduced clonidine (Catapres®) has been reported to lead to hypotension when used concomitantly with desipramine,[240] which is at variance with Table 10-2. (A complete review of the literature on this — and all the potential drug interactions in this table — is beyond the scope of this chapter, yet is of obvious relevance to geriatric pharmacology. It is suggested, therefore, to the reader that this table is only a guideline, and that there is no substitute for a continuing review of the most recent literature on these drug interactions, which are in many cases potentially fatal, especially for the elderly patient.)

## Table 10-2: Drug interactions involving MAO inhibitors.

Modified from: Baldessarini R.J. *Chemotherapy in Psychiatry.* Cambridge, MA: Harvard University Press, 1977, pp 109–111.

| Agent | Tricyclic Antidepressants | MAO Inhibitors |
|---|---|---|
| Alcohol, anxiolytics, antihistamines | More sedation and anticholinergic effects | More sedation, decreased metabolism |
| Anesthetics | Cardiac arrhythmias (?) | Potentiate |
| Barbiturates | More sedation and anticholinergic, increased metabolism of antidepressant | More sedation, decrease metabolism of MAO inhibitors |
| Narcotics, especially meperidine | Some potentiation | Dangerous CNS depression or excitation and fever |
| Anticonvulsants | Make less effective | CNS depression |
| Anticholinergics, antiparkinson agents, spasmolytics | Potentiate each other, more anticholinergic effects | Potentiate, CNS intoxication; decrease metabolism of MAO inhibitors |
| L-dopa | Decrease absorption | May induce hypertension |
| Stimulants, anorexics | Potentiate, induce hypertension, decrease metabolism of tricyclics | CNS excitation hypertension, fever |
| Reserpine | Acutely, hypertension; later some inhibition; arrhythmias(?) | Paradoxical hypertension and CNS excitation acutely |
| Alpha-methyldopa | May antagonize | Paradoxical hypertension |
| Alpha-methyltyrosine | — | — |
| Guanethidine, bethanidine debrisoquine | Antagonize, severe withdrawal hypotension[c] | Potentiate: acute hypertion with guanethidine |
|  | — | More hypotension |
| Alpha-adrenergic blockers (e.g., phentolamine, phenoxybenzamine) | Antagonize | Antagonize |
| Beta-adrenergic agonists (e.g., epinephrine, isoproterenol) | Potentiate | Potentiate[b] |
| Beta-adrenergic blockers | Antagonize | Antagonize acutely, potentiate later |
| Anticoagulants (e.g., coumarins and indanediones) | Minimal potentiation | Probably potentiate |
| Cardiac agents (e.g., quinidine, digitalis) | May potentiate | ? |
| Steroids | Unpredictable | ? |
| Insulin and Oral hypoglycemics | Unpredictable, may potentiate | Potentiate |
| Oral alkalis (e.g., Amphojel®, and resins (e.g., Cholestyramine, Questran®) | Absorption of trycyclics decreased | ? |

## Table 10-2 (continued)

a. Unless otherwise stated, effects are those of the antidepressants on actions of the medical agents in the first column. Dash (−) indicates no effect known; question mark (?) indicates no effects clearly demonstrated, but should be suspected.

b. Beware of administering dental preparations of procaine (Novocain®) containing epinephrine (adrenalin) to patients receiving MAO inhibitors.

c. Addendum (R.H. and J.M.D.):
It was once suggested that doxepin was an exception to the TCA-guanethidine interaction. This interaction was shown, however, to occur when doxepin was administered in doses equipotent to other trycyclics. (Fann W.E., Cavanaugh J.H., Kaufmann J.S., Griffith J.D., Davis J.M., Janowsky D.S., and Oates J.A. Doxepin: Effects on transport of biogenic amines in man *Psychopharmacologia 22:* 111–125, 1971).

## CNS stimulants

Since stimulants are often given to geriatric patients, it is worth noting that methylphenidate has been reported to inhibit hepatic microsomal enzymes.[241] This is especially opposite to the effect of barbiturates,[202] yet no clinically significant interaction between these two agents has been confirmed.[202]

Pharmacologically, amphetamine is a very complex drug.[241] It may exert its pharmacologic action through a variety of mechanisms:[241] release of at least two neurotransmitters, dopamine and norepinephrine; inhibition of uptake of a wide variety of neurotransmitters; action as a MAO inhibitor; direct action on receptor-sites; and possible action as a false transmitter through some of its metabolites.

As we have summarized,[241] many drugs may potentiate amphetamine action by blocking metabolism in the brain. These drugs include tricyclics and CPZ and other phenothiazines. CPZ prolongs GI hypermotility caused by amphetamine in the rat, while elevating and prolonging amphetamine levels. Studies have suggested that CPZ may also decrease urinary excretion of an amphetamine metabolite. Yet CPZ is an effective agent in treating amphetamine psychosis, as is haloperidol. However, the latter does not prolong the sojourn of amphetamine in the body, suggesting it as the drug of choice for amphetamine psychosis. (Barbiturates are ineffective as antidotes for amphetamine psychosis.)

By raising the urinary pH, sodium bicarbonate reduces the urinary excretion of amphetamine, a basic drug.[166] "Nonsystemic" antacids (of the magnesium-aluminum hydroxide type) raise urine pH, but there is little data on the effect of this on urinary amphetamine excretion.[166]

## Ethanol

Much recent attention has been focused on alcoholism in the elderly.[242,243] Also the use of alcohol, as a facilitator of social and

# Table 10-3: Substances which react with MAO inhibitors.

From the *Massachusetts General Hospital Psychopharmacology Clinics (PPC)**

## MAO INHIBITOR INSTRUCTION LIST**

**FOODS AND BEVERAGES**  To avoid serious and potentially dangerous reactions, you should not eat or drink any of the following while taking MAO-inhibitor:

1. *Aged or strong cheeses*, such as: Camambert, Cheddar, Gruyere, Stilton, Boursalt, Emmenthal, Brie, Cracker Barrel, Bleu, Roquefort, Romano. *Permitted in small amounts* are: American cheese, Gouda, Parmesan. *Permitted* are: cottage cheese, cream, "farmer", "cream". *If you are uncertain* about a cheese, *do not eat it.*
2. *Yeast 1 extract and food supplements (such as Ovaltine and Bovril, used mostly in England). Baked products raised with yeast are allowed.*
3. Yogurt (in excess of 1 cup per meal); *sour cream.*
4. Liver especially chicken (and spreads prepared from liver).
5. *Canned or processed fish*, such as herring, canned sardines, anchovies, and lox.
6. *Canned or processed meats*, especially sausages and salami.
7. *Game*, such as rabbit, pheasant, goose, duck, game hens, venison (deer).
8. *Broad beans* (English bean and Chinese pea pod) or *fava beans.*
9. *Canned figs, raisins.*
10. More than one *banana* or *avocado* per day.
11. *Pickles; sauerkraut.*
12. *Soy sauce.*
13. *Beer, ale, sherry; red wine (especially Chianti);* one or two glasses of white wine per day can be permitted, but this should be discussed first.
14. Beverages including *caffeine,* such as coffee, tea, or cola may be consumed in moderation. We suggest that you not exceed 4 cups of caffeinated beverages per day.

**MEDICATIONS†**  Do not take any other medication without checking first with me. This includes especially *over-the-counter drugs,* examples of which are listed below (which is by no means complete):

| *Analgesics (pain medication)* | Bronkaid Mist | Vicks Formula 44 | Contac |
| Empirin | Medihaler-Epi | | Coricidin |
| Percogesic | Primatene Mist | *Nasal Decongestants* | Coricidin D |
| Vanquish | Vaponefrin | *(Drops and Sprays)* | Coricidin Demilets |
| Zumarin | | Alcon-Efrin | Coricidin Medilets |
| | *Liquid Decongestants,* | Contac Spray | Dristan |
| | *Cough Suppressants* | Coricidin Mist | Ornex |
| *Sleeping Aids* | Chericold | NTZ | Sinutab |
| Dormin | Coldene | Neo-Synephrine | Super Anahist |
| Nytol | | | |

| | | | |
|---|---|---|---|
| Sleep-Eze | Novahistine | Privine | Triaminicin |
| Sominex | Novahistine-DH | Sinex | Ursinus |
| | Nyquil | Dristan | |
| *Inhalation Products* | Super Anahist Syrup | Vicks Va-Tra-Nol | *Other* |
| Adrenalin | Triaminic | | Tedral |
| Asthmanephrin | Triaminicol | *Nasal Denongestants (pills)* | |
| Breatheasy | Trind | Allerest | |

*Jerrold F. Rosenbaum (Acting Director).

**Prepared by Robert Hicks, M.D. (Former Director), 1977; modified by Ross J. Baldessarini, M.D. (Chief Consultant), 1977; modified from Appendix G: Restricted substances for patients on MAO inhibitors. In *Psychiatric Drugs: A Desk Reference* (2nd ed) (Honigfeld G, Howard A, eds, New York, Academic Press, 1978.

†(See reference 237 in text)

interpersonal interactions, is well established in geriatrics.[244,245] It is, therefore, worth noting here the work of Vestal et al.,[246] who studied the alcohol pharmacokinetics in a group of 50 healthy subjects, ranging in age from 21 to 81, by ethanol infusion. Rates of ethanol elimination were not noted to be changed in older patients. There was, however, an increased peak concentration level in the elderly. This was demonstrated to be secondary to decreased $V_d$ in association with decreased lean body mass. The authors concluded that this suggested that age-related changes in pharmacokinetics would be relevant in assessing the pharmacological effects of alcohol in the elderly patient.

It should be noted that alcohol is an inducer of hepatic microsomal enzyme activity in the chronic user.[195] It, however, can inhibit this activity if alcohol is still in the blood.[195] Obviously, if alcohol damages the liver markedly, metabolic biotransformation is decreased, although the degree of hepatic impairment often has to be marked for this to occur.[8]

Of possible relevance here is the recent controversy over the effects of alcohol on diazepam absorption. Hayes et al.[247] compared plasma diazepam levels between one group given this drug with water and another given the drug with ethanol. They reported significantly higher levels of plasma diazepam (taken serially from one to four hours) in the group concomitantly given ethanol.

Greenblatt, Shader et al.,[248] on the other hand, found that coadministration of an ethanol cocktail ("screwdriver") containing low ethanol concentrations (about 10 percent by volume) and diazepam resulted in both delayed and lowered peak diazepam concentrations. They attributed their findings to delayed gastric emptying due to the direct effect of ethanol on gastrointestinal motility. They explained the findings of Hayes et al. as the result of high ethanol concentration (50 percent by volume) used (versus their own "real life" cocktail). They suggested that the 50 percent concentration of ethanol might disrupt the "barrier" function of the gastric mucosa, possibly facilitating permeability to drugs. They also noted that Hayes and his group suspended and/or dissolved powdered diazepam tablets in the ethanol before administration. This, they conjectured, possibly aided the dissolution of the poorly water-soluble drug, thereby circumventing the time usually required for dissolution in the GI tract. They cautioned that their study "by no means established that coadministration of diazepam and ethanol is without potential hazard." They went on to suggest, however, that if a synergistic action between the two drugs exists, it is probably not based on changes in pharmacokinetic absorption. In support of the findings of Greenblatt and Shader's group is the report of Linnoila et al.,[249] that ingestion of diazepam with pure ethanol (0.8g/kg body weight) did not significantly increase plasma levels followed over four hours, and that exactly the same procedure with chlordiazepoxide appeared to reduce the rate of absorption of the drug (with plasma levels followed for only five hours, thus not permitting a full assessment of the completeness of absorption).

Paul and Whitehouse[250] studied the effects of ethanol and diazepam combination in mice. They found that ethanol reduced OXZ levels but increased DMDZ levels, suggesting an inhibition of the biotransformation of DZ to OZ. (The pathways of diazepam metabolism have been discussed above; see *Benzodiazepines.*) They also noted an accumulation of DMDZ in the brains of ethanol pretreated mice, which they suggested was a possible explanation for the supra-additive effect of the combination of ethanol and diazepam on motor coordination.

These findings may have special relevance to the older person taking alcohol by prescription or through abuse. Since the elderly CNS is likely to be more sensitive to drug effect, good judgment would suggest care in the administration of alcohol to the geriatric patient, especially with the concomitant administration of CNS sedatives [even though there is evidence, not controlled for age, that the supra-additive effects of ethanol taken with other CNS depressants is generally of minor clinical relevance.[208]]

## Analgesics

Analgesics are relevant here in that hypochondriasis is often the presenting symptom of depression in the aged.[251] Consistent with this are the findings that 55.4 percent of the OTC drugs in the Guttman sample[59] were analgesics. Also, Bozzetti and MacMurray[242] have called attention to the "hidden menace" of drug abuse in the elderly. In addition, Capel and Peppers[252] have summarized data showing that the proportion in the older opiate addicts is on the increase (while the proportion of younger addicts is decreasing)— direct evidence that the concept of addicts "maturing out" of narcotic use is not a realistic one.

The effect of age on the pharmacokinetics of various analgesics is reviewed by Shader and Greenblatt.[31] They cite evidence for a decrease in erythrocyte and plasma binding of meperidine with increasing age, but also work that either is faintly suggestive or completely negative for other age-related pharmacokinetic changes. They note work showing acetaminophen to have a prolonged $t_{1/2\beta}$, reduced clearance, but unchanged $v_d$ with increase in age. Their review also includes several studies of phenylbutazone that essentially show no consistent age-related change in pharmacokinetics.

Problems attendant with opiate use, specifically GI effects, take on a special significance in the elderly. Constipation is often a problem in the older patient, which can only be made worse by such agents. Gastrointestinal slowing produced by opiates might also delay gastric emptying and possibly impair GI absorption, already usually compromised with regard to certain vitamins[24] and possibly some drugs such as diazepam[66] and chlordiazepoxide.[67]

The clinician is reminded also of the potential for a reaction of many analgesics, especially meperidine,[241] with MAO inhibitors (see Table 10-2). This suggests another reason beyond cardiovascular concerns for caution in prescribing MAOIs to the elderly.

## CONCLUSION

It would be desirable to be able to summarize all the above material on changes in pharmacokinetics with aging. However, as Shader and Greenblatt have recently stated,[31] "no cohesive model or theory is yet predictive of the rate and/or extent of changes in pharmacokinetics that occur with age."

One can, however, suggest caution in the use of psychotropic agents in the elderly. More specifically, the clinician should keep in mind the following points:

1. The elderly patient is more likely to be sensitive to drug effects, regardless of any change in pharmacokinetics.
2. Such a patient is thus more likely to suffer from adverse drug interactions, because of not only his or her intrinsic sensitivity to drug effects, but also because (s)he is more likely to be on more than one medication, often a self-administered over-the-counter agent.
3. It is, therefore, imperative to obtain a complete record of all medications, keeping in mind that:
a) the patient may be unable or unwilling to comply with this data collection because of a dementing process and/or depression;
b) (s)he might not regard certain agents (especially OTC type) as important enough to mention;
c) (s)he may conceal the use of an agent (such as an analgesic or sedative) with which (s)he does not understand the risks;
d) (s)he may be prone to abuse alcohol and/or drugs.
4. The clinician should keep medications at a minimum.
5. The clinician should err on the side of caution and assume that the patient may have an impaired capacity to metabolize and/or excrete any drug.

6. Appropriate laboratory testing is essential and should be carried out before administration of an agent, unless the clinical situation is so dire that this is not feasible. (It should be emphasized that creatinine clearance is the only reliable measure of the GFR, since the serum creatinine may remain normal long after its renal clearance has diminished.)

It should be kept in mind, however, that the aging process varies from individual to individual, and from one organ system to another within the same individual. Therefore, the concept of the "geriatric" individual as a homogeneous entity, demarcated by some age-related cutoff line, is simplistic. Lamy and Kitler[253] suggest a direction away from the automatic classification of persons over 65 years of age as "elderly" or "geriatric," and away from the equation of "aging" with "illness." They also point out that there is not necessarily a correlation between "chronologic" and "biologic" age.

## ACKNOWLEDGMENTS

The authors wish to thank Doctors Richard J. Shader (of the Massachusetts Mental Health Center) and, especially, David J. Greenblatt (of the Massachusetts General Hospital), Harvard Medical School, for their generous supply of material—much as yet unpublished—to serve as a guide and/or for actual use in this manuscript. The similar generosity of Dr. Ross J. Baldessarini (of The McLean Hospital and also the Massachusetts General Hospital Psychopharmacology Clinics, Harvard Medical School) is also appreciated, especially his contribution to the tables and figure.

We are especially grateful to Ms. Suzanne Simenson for her help in the enormous task of organizing this manuscript.

## REFERENCES

1. Quinn GP, Axelrod J, Brodie BB: Species, strain, and sex differences in metabolism of hexobarbitone, amidopyrine, antipyrine and aniline. *Biochem Pharmacol* 1:152–159, 1958.
2. Brodie BB: Physiochemical and biochemical aspects of pharmacology. *JAMA* 202:600–609, 1967.
3. Conney AH: Pharmacological implications of microsomal enzyme induction. *Pharmacol Rev* 19:317–366, 1967.
4. Remmer H: The role of the liver in drug metabolism. *Am J Med* 49:617–629, 1970.
5. Gibaldi M, Boyes RN, Feldman S: Influence of first-pass effect on availability of drugs in oral administration. *J Pharm Sci* 60:1338–1340, 1971.

6. Vesell ES, Passananti GT: Utility of clinical determinations of drug concentrations in biological fluids. *Clin Chem* 17:851–866, 1971.
7. Gillette JR: Factors affecting drug metabolism. *Ann NY Acad Sci* 178:43–66, 1971.
8. Williams RT: Hepatic metabolism of drugs. *Gut* 13:579–585, 1972.
9. Davies DS, Prichard PNC (eds): *Biologic Effects of Drugs in Relation to their Plasma Concentration.* Baltimore, University Park Press, 1973.
10. Vesell ES: Advances in pharmacogenetics, in Stein AG, Bearn AG (eds): *Progress in Medical Genetics vol 9.* New York, Grune & Stratton, 1973, pp 291–367.
11. Koch-Weser J: Implications of blood level assays of therapeutic agents. *Clin Pharmacol Ther* 16:129–288, 1974.
12. Vesell ES: Relationship between drug distribution and therapeutic effects in man. *Ann Rev Pharmacol Toxicol* 14:249–270, 1974.
13. Drayer DE: Pathways of drug metabolism in man. *Med Clin N Am* 49:927–944, 1974.
14. Greenblatt DJ, Koch-Weser J: Clinical pharmacokinetics (I). *N Engl J Med* 193:702–705, 1975.
15. Greenblatt DJ, Koch-Weser J: Clinical pharmacokinetics (II). *N Engl J Med* 293:964–969, 1975.
16. Greenblatt DJ, Koch-Weser J: Intramuscular injection of drugs. *N Engl J Med* 295:542–546, 1976.
17. Gottschalk LA: Pharmacokinetics of the minor tranquilizers and clinical response, in Lipton MA, DiMascio A, Killam KF, (eds): *Psychophamacology: A Generation of Progress.* New York, Raven Press, 1978, pp 975–985.
18. Vesell ES: Factors causing individual variations of drug concentrations in blood. *Clin Pharmacol Ther* 16:135–148, 1977.
19. Dvorchik BM, Vesell ES: Significance of error associated with use of the one-compartment formula to calculate clearance of thirty-eight drugs. *Clin Pharmacol Ther* 23:617–623, 1978.
20. Gibaldi M, Levy G, McNamara PJ: Effect of plasma protein and tissue binding on the biologic half-life of drugs. *Clin Pharmacol Ther* 24:1–4, 1978.
21. Bender AD: Pharmacologic aspects of aging: A survey of the effect of increasing age on drug activity in adults. *J Am Geriatr Soc* 12:114–134, 1964.
22. Novak LP: Aging, total body potassium, fat-free mass, and cell mass in males and females between ages 18 and 85 years. *J Gerontol* 27:438–443, 1972.
23. Bender AD: Pharmacodynamic principles of drug therapy in the aged. *J Am Geriatr Soc* 13:192–198, 1974.
24. Triggs EJ, Nation RL: Pharmacokinetics in the aged: A review. *J Pharmacokin Biopharm* 3:387–418, 1975.
25. Crooks J, O'Malley K, Stevenson IH: Pharmacokinetics in the elderly. *Clin Pharmacokin* 1:280–296, 1976.
26. Lamy PP, Vestal RE: Drug prescribing for the elderly. *Hosp Prac* 11:111–118, 1976.
27. Ritschel WA: Pharmacokinetic approach to drug dosing in the aged. *J Am Geriatr Soc* 24:344–354, 1976.
28. Wallace S, Whiting B, Runcie J: Factors effecting drug binding in plasma of elderly patients. *Br J Clin Pharmacol* 3:327–330, 1976.
29. Ritchey DP, Bender AD: Pharmacokinetic consequences of aging. *Ann Rev Pharmacol Toxicol* 17:49–65, 1977.
30. Friedel RO: Pharmacokinetics in the geropsychiatric patient, in Lipton MA, DiMascio A, Killam KF (eds): *Psychopharmacology: A Generation of Progress.* New York, Raven Press, 1978, pp 1497–1503.
31. Shader RI, Greenblatt DJ: Pharmacokinetics and clinical drug effects in the elderly. *Psychopharm Bull,* in press.

32. Brotman HE: Who are the aging?, in Busse EW, Pfieffer E (eds): *Mental Illness and Later Life*. American Psychiatric Association, Washington, DC, 1973, pp 19–39.
33. Ostfeld AM, Gibson DC (eds): *Epidemiology of Aging*. US Government Printing Office, Washington DC, 1975.
34. Butler RN: *Why Survive? Being Old in America*. New York, Harper & Row, 1975.
35. Bureau of Census. *Demographic Aspects of Aging and the Older Population in the United States*. US Government Printing Office, Washington, DC, 1976.
36. Seidl LG, Thornton GF, Smith JW, Cluff LE: Studies on the epidemiology of adverse drug reactions: III. Reactions in patients on a general medical service. *Bull Johns Hopkins Hosp* 119:299–315, 1966.
37. Smith JW, Seidl LG, Cluff LE: Studies on the epidemiology of adverse drug reactions: V. Clinical factors influencing susceptibility. *Ann Int Med* 65:629–640, 1966.
38. Hurwitz N: Predisposing factors in adverse reactions to drugs. *Br Med J* 1:536–539, 1969.
39. Hurwitz N: Admissions to hospital due to drugs. *Br Med J* 1:539–540, 1969.
40. Caranassos GJ, Stewart RE, Cluff LE: Drug induced illness leading to hospitalization. *JAMA* 228:713–717, 1974.
41. *Drug Effects in Hospitalized Patients: Experiences of the Boston Collaborative Drug Surveillance Program, 1966–1975*. New York, John Wiley & Sons, 1976.
42. Peterson DM, Thomas CW: Acute drug reactions among the elderly. *J Gerontol* 30:552–556, 1975.
43. Brunaud M: Toxicite et pharmacodynamie des medicaments chez les animaux ages. *Therapie* 30:321–329, 1975.
44. Parish PA: The prescribing of psychotropic drugs in general practice. *J Roy Coll Gen Prac* 21(suppl 4), 1971.
45. Stolley PD, Becker HH, McElliva JD, Lasagna L, Gainer M: Drug prescribing and use in an American community. *Ann Int Med* 76:537–540, 1972.
46. Parry HJ, Balter MB, Mellinger GD, Cisin IH, Manheimer DI: National patterns of psychotherapeutic drug use. *Arch Gen Psychiatry* 28:769–783, 1973.
47. Rowe IL: Prescription of psychotropic drugs by general practitioners: I. General. *Med J Austr* 1:589–593, 1973.
48. Rowe IL: Prescriptions of psychotropic drugs by general practitioners: II. Antidepressants. *Med J Austr* 1:642–644, 1973.
49. Learoyd BM: Psychotropic drugs — Are they justified? *Med J Austr* 4:474–479, 1974.
50. Greenblatt DJ, Shader RI, Koch-Weser J: Psychoactive drug use in the Boston area: A report from the Boston Collaborative Drug Surveillance Program. *Arch Gen Psychiatry* 32:518–521, 1975.
51. Winstead DK, Blackwell B, Eillers MK, Anderson A: Psychotropic drug use in five city hospitals. *Dis Nerv Sys* 39:504–509, 1975.
52. Barton R, Hurst L: Unnecessary use of tranquilizers in elderly patients. *Br J Psychiatry* 112:989–990, 1966.
53. Dawson-Butterworth K: The chemotherapeutics of geriatric sedation. *J Am Geriatr Soc* 18:97–114, 1970.
54. Learoyd BM: Psychotropic drugs and the elderly patient. *Med J Austr* 1:1131–1133, 1972.
55. Whanger AD: Drug management of the elderly in state hospitals, in Fann WE, Maddox GL (eds): *Drug Issues in Geropsychiatry*. Baltimore, Williams & Wilkins, 1974, pp 103–109.
56. Prien RF, Haber PA, Caffey EM: The use of psychoactive drugs in elderly patients with psychiatric disorders: Survey conducted in twelve Veteran's Administration hospitals. *J Am Geriatr Soc* 23:104–112, 1975.

57. Ingman SR, Lawson IR, Pierpaoli PG, Blake P: A survey of the prescribing and administration of drugs in a long-term care institution for the elderly. *J Am Geriatr Soc* 23:309–316, 1975.
58. Chapman SF: Psychotropic drug use in the elderly: Public ignorance or indifference? *Med J Austr* 2:64–68, 1976.
59. Guttman D. Patterns of legal drug use by older Americans. *Addic Dis* 3:337–355, 1977.
60. Boston Collaborative Drug Surveillance Program: Clinical depression of the central nervous system due to diazepam and chlordiazepoxide in relation to cigarette smoking and age. *N Engl J Med* 288:277–280, 1973.
61. Salzman C, Shader RJ, Pearlman M: Psychopharmacology and the aged, in Shader RI, DiMascio A (eds): *Psychotropic Drug Side Effects: Clinical and Theoretical Perspectives.* Baltimore, Williams & Wilkins, 1969, pp 261–279.
62. Fingl E, Woodberry DM: General principles of basic pharmacologic principles, in Goodman LS, Gilman A (eds): *The Pharmacological Basis of Therapeutics* 5th ed. New York, Macmillan, 1975, pp 1–46.
63. Hollister LE, Curry SH, Derr JE, Kanter SL: Studies of delayed-action medication: V. Plasma levels and urinary excretion of four different dosage forms of chlorpromazine. *Clin Pharmacol Ther* 17:48–59, 1970.
64. Curry SH: Chlorpromazine: Concentrations in plasma, excretion in urine and duration of effect. *Proc Roy Soc Med* 64:285–289, 1971.
65. Mahon WI, Ineba T, Stone RM: Metabolism of flurazepam by the small intestine. *Clin Pharmacol Ther* 22:228–233, 1977.
66. Garattini S, Marcucci F, Morselli PL, Mussini E: The significance of measuring blood levels of benzodiazepines, in Davies DS, Prichard BNC (eds): *Biological Effects of Drugs in Relation to Their Plasma Concentration.* Baltimore, University Park Press, 1973, pp 211–225.
67. Shader RI, Greenblatt DJ, Harmatz JS, Franke K, Koch-Weser J: Absorption and disposition of chlordiazepoxide on young and elderly male volunteers. *J Clin Pharmacol* 17:709–718, 1977.
68. Chan K, Kendall MJ, Mitchard M, Wells WDE, Vickers MD: The effect of aging on plasma pethidine concentration. *Br J Clin Pharmacol* 2:297–302, 1975.
69. Bickel MH: Binding of chlorpromazine and imipramine to red cells, albumin, lipoproteins and other blood components. *J Pharm Pharmacol* 27:733–738, 1975.
70. Alfredsson G, Wade-Helgodt B, Sedvall G: A mass fragmentographic method for the determination of chlorpromazine and two of its active metabolites in human plasma and CSF. *Psychopharmacology* 48:123–131, 1976.
71. Klotz U, Avant GR, Hoyumpa A, Schenker S, Wilkinson GR: The effects of age and liver disease in the disposition and elimination in adult man. *J Clin Invest* 55:347–359, 1975.
72. Greenblatt DJ, Shader RI, Franke K, MacLaughlin DS, Ransil BJ, Koch-Weser J: Kinetics of intravenous chlordiazepoxide: Sex differences in drug distribution. *Clin Pharmacol Ther* 22:893–903, 1977.
73. Brodie BB, Mitchell JR: The value of correlating biological effects of drugs with plasma concentration, in Davies DS, Prichard BNC (eds): *Biological Effects of Drugs in Relation to Their Plasma Concentration.* Baltimore, University Park Press, 1973, pp 1–12.
74. Sjoquist F, Bertilsson L: Plasma concentrations of drugs and pharmacologic response in man, in Davies DS, Prichard BNC (eds): *Biological Effects of Drugs in Relation to Their Plasma Concentration.* Baltimore, University Park Press, 1973, pp 25–40.
75. Salzman C, Shader RI, Harmatz JS: Response of the elderly to psychotropic drugs: Predictable or idiosyncratic?, in Gershon S, Raskin A (eds): *Aging, vol 2.* New York, Plenum Press, 1975, pp 259–272.

76. Snyder SH, U'Prichard DC, Greenberg DA: Neurotransmitter receptor binding in the brain, in Lipton MA, DiMascio A, Killam KF (eds): *Psychopharmacology: A Generation of Progress.* New York, Raven Press, 1978, pp 361–370.
77. Kuhar MJ: Autoradiographic localization of receptor sites in the CNS *in vivo,* in Lipton MA, DiMascio A, Killam KF (eds): *Psychopharmacology: A Generation of Progress.* New York, Raven Press, 1978, pp 371–376.
78. Creese I, Snyder SH: Behavioral and biochemical properties of the dopamine receptor, in Lipton MA, DiMascio A, Killam KF (eds): *Psychopharmacology: A Generation of Progress.* New York, Raven Press, 1978, pp 377–388.
79. Lefkowitz RJ: Identification and regulation of adrenergic receptors, in Lipton MA, DiMascio A, Killam KF (eds): *Psychopharmacology: A Generation of Progress.* New York, Raven Press, 1978, pp 389–396.
80. Haefely WE: Behavioral and neuropharmacological aspects of drugs used in anxiety and related states, in Lipton MA, DiMascio A, Killam KF (eds): *Psychopharmacology: A Generation of Progress.* New York, Raven Press, 1978, pp 1359–1374.
81. Rowe JW, Andres R, Tobin JD, Norris AH, Shock NW. The effect of age on creatinine clearance in men: A cross-sectional and longitudinal study. *J Gerontol* 31:155–163, 1976.
82. Rowe JW, Andres R, Tobin JD, Norris AH, Shock NW: Age-adjusted standards for creatinine clearance. *Ann Inter Med* 84:567–569, 1976.
83. Schou M: Lithium in psychiatric therapy and prophylaxis. *J Psychiat Res* 6:69–95, 1968.
84. Jefferson JW, Greist JH: Lithium and the kidney. *Seminars in Psychiatry,* in press
85. Hewick DS, Newbury P, Hopwood S, Naylor G, Moody J: Age as a factor affecting lithium therapy.' *Br J Clin Pharmacol* 4:201–205, 1977.
86. Fyro B, Petterson U, Sedvall G: Pharmacokinetics of lithium in manic-depressive patients. *Acta Psychiat Scand* 49:237–247, 1973.
87. Hestbach J, Hansen HE, Andisen A, Olsen S: Chronic renal lesions following long-term treatment with lithium. *Kidney International* 12:205–213, 1977.
88. Burrows GD, Davies B, Kincaid-Smith P: Unique tubular lesions after lithium. *Lancet* 1:1310, 1978.
89. Schou M: Pharmacology and toxicology of lithium. *Ann Rev Pharmacol Tox* 16:231–243, 1976.
90. Steele TH, Budgeon RL, Larmore CK: Pharmacological characterization of lithium reabsorption in the rat. *J Pharmacol Exper Ther* 196:188–193, 1976.
91. Peterson V, Hvidt S, Thomsen K, Schou M: Effect of prolonged thiazide treatment on renal lithium clearance. *Br Med J* 3:143–145, 1974.
92. Baldessarini RJ, Lipinski JF: Lithium salts: 1970–1975. *Ann Inter Med* 83:527–533, 1975.
93. Fann WE: Some clinically important interactions of psychotropic drugs. *South Med Sch J* 66:661–665, 1973.
94 Himmelhoch, Poust RI, Mallinger AG, Hanin I, Neil JF: Adjustment of lithium dose during lithium chlorthiazide therapy. *Clin Pharmacol Ther* 22:222–227, 1977.
95. Ayd FJ: Broadening the clinical uses of lithium: Co-administering lithium and thiazide diuretics. *Inter Drug Ther News* 12:25–27, 1977.
96. McNelly WV, Tupin JP, Dunn M: Lithium in hazardous circumstances with one case of toxicity. *Comprehen Psychiatry* 11:279–286, 1970.
97. Procci WR: Mania during maintenance hemodialysis successfully treated with oral lithium carbonate. *J Nerv Ment Dis* 164:355–358, 1977.
98. Foster JR, Gershell WJ, Goldfarb AI: Lithium treatment in the elderly. *J Gerontol* 32:299–302, 1977.
99. Baldessarini RJ, Stephens JH: Lithium carbonate for affective disorders: I. Clinical pharmacology and toxicology. *Arch Gen Psychiatry* 22:72–77, 1970.

100. Shopsin B, Gershon S: Pharmacology-toxicology of the lithium ion, in *Lithium: Its Role in Psychiatric Research and Treatment*. New York, Plenum Press, 1973, pp 107–147.

101. Rifkin A, Quitkin F, Klein DF: Organic brain syndrome during lithium carbonate treatment. *Comprehen Psychiatry* 14:251–254, 1973.

102. Van der Velde CD: Toxicity of lithium carbonate in elderly patients. *Am J Psychiatry* 127:1075–1077, 1971.

103. Strayhorn JM, Nash JL: Severe neurotoxicity despite "therapeutic" serum lithium levels. *Dis Nerv Syst* 38:107–110, 1977.

104. Judd LL, Hubbard B, Janowsky DS, Hucy LY, Takahashi KI: The effect of lithium carbonate on the cognitive functions of normal subjects. *Arch Gen Psychiatry* 34:355–357, 1977.

105. Kusumo KS, Vaughn M: Effects of lithium salts on memory. *Br J Psychiatry* 131:453–457, 1977.

106. Freidman MJ, Culver CM, Ferrell RB: On the safety of long-term treatment with lithium. *Am J Psychiatry* 134:1123–1126, 1977.

107. Lasagna L: Some adverse reactions with other drugs, in Lipton MA, DiMascio A, Killam KF (eds): *Psychopharmacology: A Generation of Progress*. New York, Raven Press, 1978, pp 1005–1008.

108. Cohen WJ, Cohen NH: Lithium carbonate, haloperidol and irreversible brain damage. *JAMA* 230:1283–1287, 1974.

109. Altesman RI, Cole JO: Lithium therapy: A practical review. *McLean Hosp J* 3:106–121, 1978.

110. Baastrup PC, Hollnagel P, Sorenson R, Schou M. Adverse reactions in treatment with lithium carbonate and haloperidol. *JAMA* 236:2635–2646, 1976.

111. Juhl RP, Tsuang MT, Perry PJ: Concomitant administration of haloperidol and lithium carbonate in acute mania. *Dis Nerv Sys* 38:675–676, 1977.

112. Krisha NR, Taylor MA, Abrams R: Combined haloperidol and lithium carbonate in treating manic patients. *Comprehen Psychiatry* 19:119–120, 1978.

113. Pert A, Rosenblatt JE, Sivit C, Pert C, Burrey WE: Long-term treatment with lithium prevents the development of dopamine receptor sensitivity. *Science* 201:171–173, 1978.

114. Ayd FJ: Tranquilizers and the ambulatory geriatric patient. *J Am Geriatr Soc* 8:909–914, 1960.

115. Byrd GJ: Methyldopa and lithium carbonate: Suspected interaction. *JAMA* 233:320, 1975.

116. Dorus E, Pandey GN, Schumacker R, Davis JM: Age-related variation in the red blood cell lithium/plasma ratio and lithium side-effects. Unpublished manuscript.

117. Harvey SC: Hypnotics and sedatives, in Goodman LS, Gilman A (eds): *The Pharmacological Basis of Therapeutics* 5th ed. New York, Macmillan, 1975, pp 102–125.

118. Irvine RE, Grove J, Toseland PA, Trounce JR: The effect of age of the hydroxylation of amylobarbitone sodium in man. *Br J Clin Pharmacol* 1:41–43, 1974.

119. Greenblatt DJ, Harmatz JS, Shader RI: Factors influencing diazepam pharmacokinetics: Age, sex and liver disease. *Inter J Clin Pharmacol* 16:177–179, 1978.

120. Schwartz MA, Postma E, Gaut Z: Biological half-life of chlordiazepoxide and its metabolite, demoxepam, in man. *J Pharm Sci* 50:1500–1503, 1971.

121. Randall LO, Kappell B: Pharmacological activity of some benzodiazepines and their metabolites, in Garattini S, Mussini E, Randall LO (eds): *The Benzodiazepines*. New York, Raven Press, 1973, pp 27–51.

122. Greenblatt DJ, Shader RI: Detection and quantification, in *Benzodiazepines in Clinical Practice*. New York, Raven Press, 1974, pp 17–32.

123. Greenblatt DJ, Hartmatz JS, Stanski DR, Shader RI, Franke K, Koch-Weser J: Factors

influencing blood concentrations of chlordiazepoxide: A use of multiple regression analysis. *Psychopharmacology* 54:277–282, 1977.

124. Greenblatt DJ, Shader RI, Macleod SM, Sellers EM: Clinical pharmacokinetics of chlordiazepoxide: A review. *Clinical Pharmacokin,* in press.

125. Greenblatt DJ, Shader RI, Harmatz JS, Franke K, Koch-Weser J: Influence of magnesium and aluminum hydroxide on chlordiazepoxide absorption. *Clin Pharmacol Ther* 19:234–239, 1976.

126. Greenblatt DJ, Shader RI, Harmatz JS, Franke K, Koch-Weser J: Absorption rate, blood concentrations, and early response to oral chordiazepoxide. *Am J Psychiatry* 134:559–562, 1977.

127. Greenblatt DJ, Allen MD, MacLaughlin DS, Harmatz JS, Shader RI: Diazepam absorption: Effect of antacids and food. *Clin Pharmacol Ther,* in press.

128. Gamble JAS, Mackey JS, Dundee JV: Plasma levels of diazepam. *Br J Anaesthesia* 45:1085, 1973.

129. Hillested L, Mansen T, Melsom H, Drivenes A: Diazepam metabolism in normal man: I. Serum concentrations and clinical effects after intravenous, intramuscular and oral administration. *Clin Pharmacol Ther* 16:479–484, 1974.

130. Gottschalk LA, Biener R, DiNovo EC: Effects of oral and intramuscular routes of administration on serum chlordiazepoxide levels and the prediction of these levels from predrug fasting serum glucose concentrations. *Res Comm Chem Path Pharmacol* 8:697–702, 1974.

131. Greenblatt DJ, Shader RI, Koch-Weser J, Franke K: Slow absorption of intramuscular chlordiazepoxide. *N Engl J Med* 291:1116–1118, 1974.

132. Korttila K, Sothman A, Andersson P: Polyethylene glycol as a solvent for diazepam: Bioavailability and clinical effects after intramuscular administration, comparison of oral, intramuscular and rectal administration, and precipitation from intravenous solutions. *Acta Pharmacol Toxicol* 31:104–107, 1975.

133. Shull HG, Wilkinson GR, Johnson R, Schenker S: Normal disposition of oxazepam in acute viral hepatitis and cirrhosis. *Ann Inter Med* 84:420–425, 1976.

134. Melander A, Danielson K, Schersten B, Wahlin E: Bioavailability of oxazepam: Absence of influence of food intake. *Acta Pharmacol Toxicol* 40:584–588, 1977.

135. Castleden CM, George GF, Mercer D, Hallett C: Increased sensitivity to nitrazepam in old age. *Br Med J:* 1:10–12, 1977.

136. Curry SH, Whelpton R, Nicholson AN, Wright CM: Behavioral and pharmacokinetic studies in the monkey *(Mucatta mulatta)* with diazepam, nordiazepam, and related 1, 4-benzodiazepines. *Br J Pharmacol* 61:325–330, 1977.

137. Greenblatt DJ, Shader RI, Koch-Weser J: Pharmacokinetics in clinical medicine: Oxazepam versus other benzodiazepines. *Dis Nerv Syst* 36(supplement 2):6–13, 1975.

138. Ayd FJ: Oxazepam: An overview. *Dis Nerv Syst* 36(supplement 3):14–15, 1975.

139. Merlis S, Koepke HH: The use of oxazepam in elderly patients. *Dis Nerv Syst* 36(supplement 6):1975.

140. Kaplan SA, DeSilva JAF, Jack ML, Alexander K, Strojny N, Weinfield RE, Puglisi CV, Weissman L: Blood level profile in man following chronic oral administration of flurazepam hydrochloride. *J Pharmaceut Sci* 62:1932–1935, 1973.

141. Greenblatt DJ, Allen MD, Shader RI: Toxicity of high-dose flurazepam in the elderly. *Clin Pharmacol Ther* 21:355–361, 1977.

142. Dement WC, Zarcone VP, Hoddes E, Smythe H, Carskadon M: Sleep laboratory and clinical studies with flurazepam, in Garrattini S, Mussini E, Randall LO (eds): *The Benzodiazepines.* New York, Raven Press, 1973, pp 599–611.

143. Kales A, Scharf MB: Sleep laboratory and clinical studies of the effects of benzodiazepines on sleep: Flurazepam, diazepam, chlordiazepoxide, and RO 5-4200, in

Garrattini S, Mussini E, Randall LO (eds): *The Benzodiazepines.* New York, Raven Press, 1973, pp 577–598.

144. Greenblatt DJ, Allen MD: Toxicity of nitrazepam in the elderly: A report from the Boston Collaborative Drug Surveillance Program. *Br J Clin Pharmacol* 5:407–413, 1978.

145. Greenblatt DJ, Shader RI: Pharmacotherapy of anxiety with benzodiazepines and β-adrenergic blockers, in Lipton MA, DiMascio A, Killam KF (eds): *Psychopharmacology: A Generation of Progress.* New York, Raven Press, 1978, pp 1381–1390.

146. Eisdorfer C, Howlin J and Wilkie F: Improvement in learning in the aged by modification of autonomic nervous system activity. *Science* 170:1327–1329, 1970.

147. Inderal®: *Physicians' Desk Reference,* 32nd ed. Medical Company, Oradell, NJ, 1978, pp 603–605.

148. Greenblatt DJ, Shader RI: Rational use of psychotropic drugs: IV. Antidepressants. *Am J Hosp Pharm* 32:59–64, 1975.

149. Kirk L, Baastrup PC, Schou M: Propranolol treatment of lithium-induced tremor. *Lancet* 2:1086–1087, 1973.

150. Waal HJ: Propranolol-induced depression. *Br Med J* 2:50, 1967.

151. Greenblatt DJ, Koch-Weser J: Adverse reactions to β-adrenergic receptor blocking drugs: A report from the Boston Collaborative Drug Surveillance Program. *Drugs* 7:118–129, 1974.

152. Evans GH, Niss AS, Shand DG: The disposition of propranolol: III. Decreased half-life and volume of distribution as a result of plasma binding in man, monkey, dog and rat. *J Exper Pharmacol Ther* 186:114–122, 1973.

153. Evans GH, Wilkinson GR, Shand DG: The disposition of propranolol: IV. A dominant role for tissue uptake in the dose-dependent extraction of propranolol by the perfused rat liver. *J Exper Pharmacol Ther* 186:447–454, 1973.

154. Evans GH, Shand DG: Disposition of propranolol: VI. Independent variation on steady-state circulating drug concentrations and half-life as a result of plasma drug binding in man. *Clin Pharmacol Ther* 14:494–500, 1973.

155. Fitzgerald JD, O'Donnell SR: Pharmacology of 4-hydroxy-propranolol, a metabolite of propranolol. *Br J Pharmacol* 43:222–235, 1971.

156. Shand DG: Propranolol: Resolving problems in usage. *Drug Ther (Hosp):* 52–60, August 1978.

157. Gottschalk LA, Stone WN, Goldine CG: Peripheral versus central mechanisms accounting for antianxiety effects of propranolol. *Psychosom Med* 36:47–55, 1974.

158. Lader M: Current psychophysiological theories of anxiety, in Lipton MA, DiMascio A, Killam KF (eds): *Psychopharmacology: A Generation of Progress.* New York, Raven Press, 1978, pp 1375–1380.

159. Castleden CM, Kaye CM, Parsons RL: The effect of age on plasma levels of propranolol and practolol in man. *Br J Clin Pharmacol* 2:303–306, 1975.

160. Appendix II: Pertinent data on sedative drugs (antianxiety agents), in Shader RI (ed): *Manual of Psychiatric Therapeutics: Practical Psychopharmacology and Psychiatry.* Boston, Little, Brown, 1975, p 316.

161. Abramson EA, Arky RA, Woeber KA: Effect of propranolol on the hormonal and metabolic responses to insulin-induced hypoglycaemia. *Lancet* 2:1386–1389, 1966.

162. Wilkinson GR, Shand DG: A physiological approach to hepatic drug clearance. *Clin Pharmacol Ther* 18:377–390, 1975.

163. Greenblatt DJ: Impairment of antipyrene clearance in humans by propranolol. *Clin Pharmacol Ther* 21 (abstr): 104–105, 1977.

164. Koch-Weser J: Bioavailability of drugs (I). *N Engl J Med* 291:233–237, 1974.

165. Nimmo WJ: Drugs, diseases and altered gastric emptying. *Clin Pharmacokin* 1:189–203, 1976.

166. Hurwitz A: Antacid therapy and drug kinetics. *Clin Pharmacokin* 2:269–280, 1977.
167. McLean AJ, McNamara PJ, duSouch P, Gibaldi M, Lalka D: Food, Splanchic blood flow, and bioavailability of drugs subject to first-pass metabolism. *Clin Pharmacol Ther* 24:5–10, 1978.
168. Korttila K, Kangas L: Unchanged protein binding and the increase of serum diazepam levels after food intake. *Acta Pharmacol Toxicol* 40:241–245, 1977.
169. Forrest FM, Forrest IS, Serr MT: Modification of chlorpromazine metabolism by some other drugs frequently administered to psychiatric patients. *Biol Psychiatry* 2:53, 1970.
170. Fann WE, Davis JM, Janowsky DS, Sekerke HJ, Schmidt DM: Chlorpromazine: Effects of antacids on its gastrointestinal absorption. *J Clin Pharmacol* 13:388–390, 1973.
171. Rivera-Calimlim L, Castaneda L, Lasagna L: Effects of mode of management on plasma chlorpromazine in psychiatric patients. *Clin Pharmacol Ther* 14:978–986, 1973.
172. Rivera-Calimlim L, Nasrallah H, Strass J, Lasagna L: Clinical response and plasma levels: Effect of dose, dosage schedules, and drug interactions on plasma chlorpromazine levels. *Am J Psychiatry* 133:646–652, 1976.
173. Rivera-Calimlim L: Impaired absorption of chlorpromazine in rats given trihexyphenidyl. *Br J Pharmacol* 56:301–305, 1976.
174. Consolo S, Morselli PL, Zaccala M, Garattini S: Delayed absorption of phenylbutazone caused by desmethylimipramine in humans. *Europ J Pharmacol* 10:239–242, 1970.
175. Morgan JP, Rivera-Calimlim L, Sundareson PR, Trabert N: Imipramine-medicated interference with levodopa absorption for the gastrointestinal tract in man. *Neurology* 25:1029–1034, 1975.
176. Leijnse B, Van Pragg HM: The influence of iproniazid on the absorption from the gastrointestinal tract in rats. *Arch Inter Pharmacodyn Ther* 150:582–590, 1964.
177. Mayton WL, Levy G: Effects of SKF 525-A on drug absorption in rats (I). *Life Sci* 10:691–697, 1971.
178. Lavigne JG, Marchand C: Inhibition of the gastrointestinal absorption of p-aminosalicylate (PAS) in rats and humans by diphenhydramine. *Clin Pharmacol Ther* 14:404–412, 1973.
179. Kerzner B, Rivera-Calimlim L: Lithium and chlorpromazine (CPZ) interaction. *Clin Pharmacol Ther* 19 (abstr): 109, 1976.
180. Rivera-Calimlim L, Nasrallah H, Gift T, Kerzner B, Greisbach PH, Wyatt RJ: Plasma levels of chlorpromazine: Effect of age, chronicity of disease, and duration of treatment. *Clin Pharmacol Ther* 21 (abstr):115–116, 1977.
181. Curry SH: Metabolism and kinetics of chlorpromazine in relation to effect, in Sedvall G, Uvnas B, Zotterman Y (eds): *Antipsychotic Drugs: Pharmacodynamics and Pharmacokinetics.* Oxford, Pergamon Press, 1976, pp 343–352.
182. Davis JM, Erickson S, Dekirmenjian H: Plasma levels of antipsychotic drugs and clinical response, in Lipton MA, DiMascio A, Killam KF (eds): *Psychopharmacology: A Generation of Progress.* New York, Raven Press, 1978, pp 905–915.
183. Maxwell JD, Carella M, Parkes JD, Williams R, Mould GP, Curry SH: Plasma disappearance and cerebral effects of chlorpromazine in cirrhosis. *Clin Sci* 43:143–151, 1973.
184. Hamilton LD: Aged brain and the phenothiazines. *Geriatrics* 21:131–138, 1966.
185. Martensson E, Roos B-E. Serum levels of thioridazine in psychiatric patients and healthy volunteers. *Europ J Clin Pharmacol* 6:181–186, 1973.
186. Axelsson R, Martensson E: Serum concentration and elimination from serum of thioridazine in psychiatric patients. *Curr Therapeutic Research* 19:242–264, 1976.
187. Forsman A, Ohman R. Applied pharmacokinetics of haloperidol in man. *Curr Ther Res* 21:396–411, 1977.

188. Gram LF, Overo KF: Drug interaction: Inhibiting effect of neuroleptics on metabolism of tricyclic antidepressants in man. *Br Med J* 1:463–465, 1970.
189. El-Yousef MK, Menier DM. Tricyclic antidepressants and phenothiazines. *JAMA* 229:1419, 1974.
190. Myers JM, Sheldon D, Robinson SS: A study of 138 elderly first admissions. *Am J Psychiatry* 120:244–249, 1963.
191. Pfeiffer E, Busse EW: Mental disorders in later life—Affective disorders; paranoid, neurotic, and situational reactions, in Busse EW, Pfeiffer E (eds): *Mental Illness and Later Life.* Washington, DC, American Psychiatric Association, 1973, pp 107–144.
192. Nies A, Robinson DS, Freidman MJ, Green R, Cooper TB, Ravaris CL, Ives JO: Relationship between age and tricyclic antidepressant plasma levels. *Am J Psychiatry* 134:790–793, 1977.
193. Burns JJ, Conney AH: Drug interactions: Historical aspects and perspectives, in Morselli PL, Garattini S, Cohen SN (eds): *Drug Interactions.* New York, Raven Press, 1974, pp 7–9.
194. Cohen SN, Armstrong MF (eds): *Drug Interactions: A Handbook for Clinical Use.* Baltimore, Williams & Wilkins, 1974, pp 7–9.
195. Nies AS: Drug Interactions. *Med Clin N Am* 58:965–979, 1974.
196. *Evaluations of Drug Interactions,* 2nd ed. Washington, DC, American Pharmaceutical Association, 1976.
197. Karch FE, Lasagna L: Toward the operational identification of adverse drug reactions. *Clin Pharmacol Ther* 21:247–254, 1977.
198. Bressler R, Palmer J: Drug interactions in the aged, in Fann WE, Maddox GL (eds): *Drug Issues in Geropsychiatry.* Baltimore, Williams & Wilkins, 1974, pp 49–60.
199. Greenblatt DJ, Shader RI: Drug interactions in psychopharmacology, in *Manual of Psychiatric Therapeutics: Practical Psychopharmacology and Psychiatry.* Boston, Little, Brown, 1975, pp 269–293.
200. Ban TA: Drug interactions with psychoactive drugs. *Dis Nerv Syst* 36:164–166, 1975.
201. Fann WE: Interactions of psychotropic drugs in the elderly. *Postgrad Med* 55:132–186, 1973.
202. Shader RI, Weinberger DR, Greenblatt DJ: Problems with drug interactions in treating brain disorders. *Psychiat Clin N Am* 1:51–69, 1978.
203. Sheppard C, Beyel V, Fracchia J, Merlis S: Polypharmacy in psychiatry: A multi-state comparison of psychotropic drug combinations. *Dis Nerv Syst* 35:183–189, 1974.
204. Fracchia J, Sheppard C, Merlis S: Combination medications in psychiatric treatment: Patterns in a group of elderly hospital patients. *J Am Geriatr Soc* 19:301–307, 1971.
205. Ayd FJ: Rational Pharmacotherapy: Once-a-day drug dosage. *Dis Nerv Syst* 34:371–377, 1973.
206. Eisdorfer C: Observations on the psychopharmacology of the aged. *J Am Geriatr Soc* 24:53–57, 1973.
207. Shader RI: Problems of polypharmacy in depression. *Dis Nerv Syst* 38:30–34, 1976.
208. Greenblatt DJ, Miller RR: Rational use of psychotropic drugs: I. Hypnotics. *Am J Hosp Pharm* 31:990–995, 1974.
209. Sellers EM, Koch-Weser J: Potentiation of warfarin-induced hypoprothrombinemia by chloral hydrate. *N Engl J Med* 283:827–831, 1970.
210. Griner PF, Raisz LG, Rickles FR, Wiesner FJ, Oderoff CL: Chloral hydrate and warfarin interaction: Clinical significance? *Ann Inter Med* 74:540–543, 1971.
211. Stotsky S: Use of psychopharmacologic agents for geriatric patients, in DiMascio A, Shader RI (eds): *Clinical Handbook of Psychopharmacology.* New York, Science House, 1970, pp 266–278.

212. Gibson II JM: Barbiturate delirium. *Practitioner* 197:345–347, 1966.

213. Kales A, Kales JD: Sleep disorders: Recent findings in the diagnosis and treatment of disturbed sleep. *N Engl J Med* 280:487–499, 1974.

214. Wikler A: Diagnosis and treatment of drug dependence of the barbiturate type. *Am J Psychiatry* 125:758–765, 1968.

215. Davis JM, Bartlett E, Termini B: Overdose of psychotropic drugs: A review (II). *Dis Nerv Syst* 29:246–256, 1968.

216. Greenblatt DJ, Shader RI: Psychotropic drug overdosage, in *Manual of Psychiatric Therapeutics: Practical Psychopharmacology and Psychiatry.* Boston, Little, Brown, 1975, pp 237–267.

217. Koch-Weser J, Greenblatt DJ: The archaic barbiturate hypnotics. *N Engl J Med* 291:790–791, 1973.

218. Curry SH, Davis JM, Janowsky DS, Marshall JHL: Factors affecting chlorpromazine plasma levels in psychiatric patients. *Arch Gen Psychiatry* 22:209–215, 1970.

219. Alexanderson B, Evans DAP, Sjoquist F: Steady-state plasma levels of nortriptyline in twins: Influence of genetic factors and drug therapy. *Br Med J* 5:764–768, 1969.

220. Burrows GD, Davies B: Antidepressants and barbiturates. *Br Med J* 4:113, 1971.

221. Slater E, Beard AW: The schizophrenia-like psychoses of epilepsy: i. Psychiatric aspects. *Br J Psychiatry* 109:95–112, 1963.

222. Waxman SG, Geschwind H: The interictal behavior syndrome of temporal epilepsy. *Arch Gen Psychiatry* 32:1580–1586, 1975.

223. Morselli PL, Rizzo M, Garattini S: Interaction between phenobarbital and diphenylhydantoin in animals and in epileptic patients. *Ann NY Acad Sci* 179:88–107, 1971.

224. Greenblatt DJ, Shader RI: Rational use of psychotropic drugs: II. Antianxiety agents. 31:1077–1080, 1974.

225. Dugal R, Caille G, Albert J-M, Cooper: Apparent pharmacokinetic interaction of diazepam and amitriptyline in psychiatric patients: A pilot study. *Curr Ther Res* 18:679–686, 1975.

226. El-Yousef MK, Janowsky DS, Davis JM, Sekerke JH, Dreyfuss R: Reversal by physostigmine of anti-parkinsonian drug toxicity: A controlled study. *Am J Psychiatry* 130:141–145, 1973.

227. Granacher RP, Baldessarini RJ: Physostigmine: Its use in acute anticholinergic syndrome with antidepressant and anti-parkinsonian drugs. *Arch Gen Psychiatry* 32:375–380, 1975.

228. Baldessarini RJ: The clinical pharmacology and toxicology of antipsychotic drugs. Part II: Actions and neurological side effects. *Weekly Psychiatry Update Series* 2 (lesson 40): 1–8, 1978.

229. Gelenberg AJ: Amantadine in the treatment of benztropine-refractory extrapyramidisorders induced by antipsychotic drugs. *Curr Ther Res* 23:375–380, 1978.

230. Casey DE: Amantadine intoxication reversed by physostigmine. *N Engl J Med* 298:516, 1978.

231. Schallek W, Schlosser W, Randall LO: Recent developments in the pharmacology of the benzodiazepines. *Adv Pharmacol Chemother* 10:119–183, 1972.

232. DiLiberti J, O'Brien ML, Turner T: The use of physostigmine as an antidote in accidental diazepam intoxication. *J Pediatrics* 86:106–107, 1975.

233. Blitt CD, Petty WC: Reversal of lorazepam delirium by physostigmine. *Anesthes Analges* 54:607–608, 1975.

234. Van der Kolk BA, Shader RI, Greenblatt DJ: Autonomic effects of psychotropic drugs, in Lipton MA, DiMascio A, Killam KF (eds): *Psychopharmacology: A Generation of Progress.* New York, Raven Press, 1978, pp 1009–1020.

235. Baldessarini RJ: *Chemotherapy in Psychiatry.* Cambridge, Mass, Harvard University Press, 1977, 109–111.
236. Massachusetts General Hospital, Psychopharmacology Clinics (PPC) *MAO Inhibitor Instruction List.* Boston, 1976.
237. *Handbook of Non-Prescription Drugs,* 5th ed. American Pharmaceutical Association, 1977.
238. Chien C-P, Townsend EJ, Ross-Townsend A: Substance use and abuse among the community elderly: The medical aspect. *Addic Dis* 3:357–372, 1978.
239. Janowsky DS, El-Yousef MK, Davis JM, Fann WE: Antagonism of guanethidine by chlorpromazine. *Am J Psychiatry.* 130:808–812, 1973.
240. Briant RH, Reid JL, Dollery CT: Interaction between clonidine and desipramine in man. *Br Med J* 1:522–523, 1973.
241. Davis JM, Sekerke J, Janosky DS: Drug interactions involving the drugs of abuse. *Drug Intel Clin Pharm* 8:120–141, 1974.
242. Bozzetti LP, MacMurray JP: Drug misuse among the elderly: A hidden menace. *Psychiatric Ann* 7:95–107, 1977.
243. Schuckt MA, Morrissey ER, O'Leary MR: Alcohol problems in elderly men and women. *Addict Dis* 3:405–427, 1978.
244. Kastenbaum R: Wine and fellowship in aging: An exploratory action program. *J Human Rel* , 1965.
245. Chien CP, Stotsky BA, Cole JO: Psychiatric treatment for nursing home patients: Drug, alcohol, and milieu. *Am J Psychiatry* 130:543–548, 1973.
246. Vestal RE, McGuire EA, Tobin JD, Andres R, Norris AH, Mezey E: Aging and ethanol metabolism. *Clin Pharmacol Ther* 21:343–354, 1977.
247. Hayes SL, Pablo G, Radomski T, Palmer RF: Ethanol and oral diazepam absorption. *N Engl J Med* 296:186–189, 1977.
248. Greenblatt DJ, Shader RI, Weinberger DR, Allen MD, MacLaughlin DS: Effect of a cocktail on diazepam absorption. *Psychopharmacology* 57:199–203, 1978.
249. Linnoila M, Otterstrom S, Anttila M: Serum chlordiazepoxide, diazepam and thioridazine concentrations after the simultaneous ingestion of alcohol or placebo drink. *Ann Clin Res* 6:4–6, 1974.
250. Paul CJ, Whitehouse LW: Metabolic basis for the supra-additive effect of the ethanol-diazepam combination in mice. *Br J Pharmacol* 60:83–90, 1977.
251. de Alarcon R: Hypochondriasis and depression in the aged. *Gerontologica Clinica* 6:266–277, 1964.
252. Capel WC, Peppers LG: The aging addict: A longitudinal study of known abusers. *Addic Dis* 3:389–403, 1978.
253. Lamy PP, Kitler ME: Drugs and the geriatric patient. *J Am Geriatr Soc* 19:23–33, 1971.

# CHAPTER 11

# The Cyclic Nucleotide System In The Brain During Development And Aging

M.J. SCHMIDT
G.C. PALMER
G.A. ROBISON

The discovery of abnormalities in the brain during advanced aging would be an important first step in the design of rational therapeutic approaches for treating the mental dysfunction that often accompanies old age. Our current understanding of the biology of the brain allows alternative explanations for the behavioral abnormalities of senescence. It would be logical to assume that since nerve cells are not replaced when lost, mental dysfunction occurs due to a decrease in the number of brain cells with advancing age.[1,2] But widespread cell loss is not seen in many brain regions.[3,4,5] Furthermore, many structural studies have now been questioned on technical grounds, and the "neuronal fallout" theory of aging is in dispute.[6,7] There also is no generalized loss of basic cell constituents such as RNA, DNA or protein in the aged brain.[8,9] Although significant declines in cardiac contractility and cardiac output are seen with advancing age,[10] basal rates of blood flow in the brain may not be markedly different in older humans[11] or animals.[12]

Alternatively, ultrastructural changes in synaptic morphology[13,14,15] or neurochemical abnormalities might account for the functional defects in the aged. A sizable number of enzymes have been studied in aged brains, but in old age the activity of most brain enzymes varies only slightly from that observed in young.[9,16,17,18] This has also been the case with human studies.[17] Reductions in important brain enzymes have been reported,[17,18] but most of the decline occurs in the first two decades of life and does not correlate with the psychological manifestations of the aging process.

The fact that there is no general deterioration of brain cells with age suggests that subtle changes in neuronal functioning may take place. Considerable evidence indicates that information transfer in the brain occurs through chemical coupling between adjacent neurons. Neurotransmitters synthesized and stored in presynaptic nerve endings are released upon demand and interact with specialized postsynaptic receptors on the external surface of neuronal membranes. This causes molecular perturbations in the membranes which not only excite the cell, but also produce substances within the cell that alter the neurochemistry of the neuron. These intracellular changes can be fleeting or of considerable duration; ionic flux can be altered or protein synthesis increased and enzymes induced. Therefore, age-related alterations in transmitter levels, receptor activity or in the secondary intracellular processes of information transfer could play an important role in the aging process in the central nervous system.

There have been many studies in which neurotransmitter concentrations have been measured in the brains of aged animals and man. In general, transmitter levels were not found to be lower in most brain areas.[9,19] Using more refined dissection techniques, several workers have reported reductions in norepinephrine in the hypothalamus,[20] dopamine in the corpus striatum,[9] and serotonin in several discrete brain nuclei.[21] Thus, some loss of mental function during aging may be attributable to these losses in key neurotransmitter substances in vital brain regions. The motor disturbances of Parkinsonism are probably an example of this, reflecting an age-related loss of dopamine in the corpus striatum.[22]

Equally as important as the transmitter substances themselves are those cellular components with which the transmitters interact. The receptor concept has done much to advance the understanding of the biochemistry of synaptic transmission. At this time, however, there have been few attempts to study receptor function in the brain during aging. Roth[23] examined steroid receptor binding in the brains of aged rats and found decreased binding of dexamethasone in the cerebral cortex of aged rats. Reduced binding of estradiol also occurs in the aged brain.[24]

Methods are now available to study the receptor binding affinities of the chemicals involved in synaptic transmission, but as yet extensive studies have not been conducted in brains of aged animals. One group[25] measured cholinergic receptor binding (atropine binding) in samples of the cerebral cortex of humans after death. A progressive decline (25 percent) in the number of binding sites was seen in normal subjects between the ages of 60 and 90. Quinuclidinyl benzilate binding was reduced in the temporal lobe of elderly patients with Pick's disease. However, Davies and Verth[26] did not detect a decrease in muscarinic receptor sites in the brains of aged humans.

The concentration of beta-adrenergic receptors in mononuclear cells is lower in aged humans.[27] Membranes from erythrocytes of 15-month-old rats also have fewer beta-receptors,[28] but these same workers could detect no change in the number or characteristics of beta ligand binding in the brains of old rats. Preliminary evidence (Schmidt and Enna, unpublished observations) also indicates no differences in dihydroalprenolol binding in several brain regions of Wistar rats 3, 12 and 24 months of age. Binding in the cerebral cortex of humans also has shown no consistent change with age. Further studies of transmitter binding in the brain during aging will be of interest in assessing this initial event in synaptic transmission.

Binding of a neurotransmitter to postsynaptic membrane sites is not thought to be sufficient to transmit signals to the interior of the cell. In some cases it would appear that intracellular second messengers, synthesized in response to the transmitter, function in this capacity. Cyclic AMP and cyclic GMP are among the leading candidates as the intracellular messengers for several transmitters in the central nervous system. Norepinephrine increases cyclic AMP accumulation in many brain regions of animals[29] and man.[30,31] Glutamate[32] and acetylcholine[33] increase cyclic GMP in some brain regions. Dopamine stimulates cyclic AMP synthesis in the striatum[34] and other dopamine-rich regions of the brain.[35] The evidence that cyclic AMP functions as an intracellular messenger for many putative neurotransmitters in the brain is now substantial.[36]

A change in the concentration of cyclic AMP or cyclic GMP might be only one of several steps in the cellular response to transmitter stimulation. Once cyclic AMP or cyclic GMP is synthesized in the cell, two things may happen: each can be rapidly catabolized to 5'-AMP or 5'-GMP by phosphodiesterases, specific for cyclic nucleotides.[37] This appears to be the major route for eliminating cyclic nucleotides from the neuron. Alternatively, either of the cyclic nucleotides can attach themselves to certain protein-phosphorylating enzymes, collectively referred to as protein kinases. These enzymes are considered to be the intracellular effectors for most if not all of the physiologically important effects of cyclic AMP—i.e., it is the cyclic nucleotide-dependent enzyme, rather than cyclic AMP itself, which triggers cell processes.[38] Once protein kinase is activated, it can phosphorylate a number of neuronal proteins, including brain ribosomes[40] and synaptic membrane proteins.[41,42] At this time there is no evidence that phosphorylation of any of these components alters brain function. But there is clear evidence in peripheral tissues that

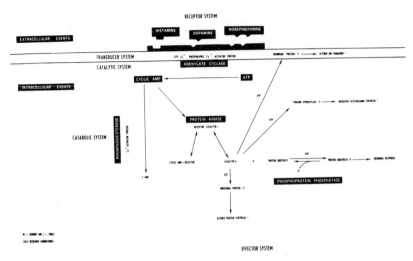

Figure 11-1:   The components of the cyclic AMP system in the brain.

phosphorylation can alter enzyme activity.[43] By analogy, one might expect
that phosphorylation of neuronal proteins would alter their activity.

The final component of the cyclic nucleotide system is the enzyme
phosphoprotein phosphatase. This enzyme removes the phosphate group
from kinase-phosphorylated proteins, thereby returning the system to the
native state.[43,44] Relatively little is known about this enzyme at the present
time, and it has not been extensively studied as a function of age in any
system.

A theoretical diagram of our view of the role of the cyclic nucleotide
system in the biochemistry of synaptic transmission is shown in Figure
11-1. The remainder of this review will concentrate on the components of
the cyclic nucleotide system as they relate to development and aging in the
brain.


## THE CYCLIC NUCLEOTIDE SYSTEM IN THE DEVELOPING BRAIN

### Cyclic Nucleotide Concentrations In The Developing Brain

*Cyclic AMP Concentration in the Brain in vivo*

The steady-state concentration of cyclic AMP and cyclic GMP has been
estimated in the brains of rats, mice, rabbits and chickens during late
gestation and early adulthood. In fetal chicks, small amounts of cyclic
AMP were detected in the neural tube and Henson's node, embryonic

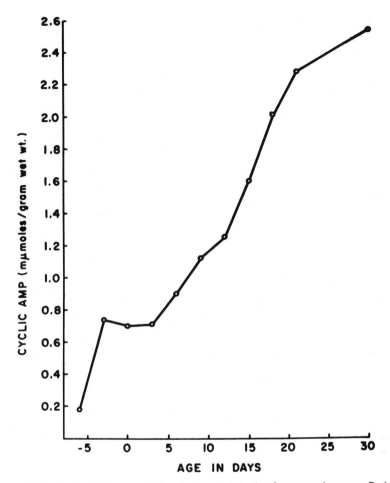

Figure 11-2:   Cyclic AMP concentrations in the whole brain of rats at various ages. Brains were removed from the heads of rats which had been quick-frozen in liquid nitrogen. Each point represents data from at least 4 rats. From Schmidt et al.[47]

structures which give rise to the central nervous system.[45] The level of cyclic AMP in the brain of chickens appears to be highest during the late embryonic period, with a continual decline in amounts in the cerebral cortex during the first 28 days posthatching.[46] In these studies, rapidly frozen tissue was used.

Schmidt et al.[47] measured the level of cyclic AMP in the whole brain of 6- to 30-day-old rats sacrificed by rapid freezing. Levels were lowest six days prior to birth, increased threefold before birth, and remained constant during the first week postnatal. Then a linear increase in the level of cyclic AMP continued through 20 to 30 days of age. The change between birth and 30 days old was nearly threefold (Figure 11-2). A similar pattern was noted in the brain stem and forebrain of mice killed by freezing.[48] In the cerebellum, however, cyclic AMP concentrations did not change significantly between birth and adulthood.

Examination of cyclic AMP content of fetal human brain revealed approximately 9 picomoles per mg protein.[49] Amounts in 3-day to 3-month-old humans (autopsy material) were in the same range.[50] Much higher levels (76 picomoles per mg protein) were found in gray matter from the frontal lobe of middle-aged humans.[30] Values in white matter were approximately one-third that of gray matter. Therefore, lack of regional definition in sampling might have influenced the previously reported studies on whole brain from fetal and neonatal material.

A potentially confounding factor in studies of cyclic AMP concentrations in the brain *in vivo* is the fact that cyclic AMP levels are markedly affected by anoxia and ischemia. Decapitation and delayed tissue fixation produce large elevations of cyclic AMP in all brain regions.[48,51] The decapitation effect in rats occurs throughout the brain development period with little difference across age in the magnitude of the response.[47] It is possible that the lower levels of cyclic AMP in the brains of very young rats or chicks may merely reflect the more rapid tissue fixation that is possible in small animals with thinner skulls and a smaller brain mass. The use of microwave irradiation as a means of tissue fixation should aid in determining steady-state concentrations of cyclic AMP in the brain *in vivo*.[52] As yet, regional levels of cyclic nucleotides have not been determined in rats during the brain development period using this rapid tissue fixation technique.

*Cyclic AMP Concentration in the Brain in vitro*

Another approach for estimating the steady state concentration of cyclic AMP in the brain is to measure nucleotide levels in tissue slices of brain during incubations *in vitro* in the absence of receptor stimulants. *In vitro*, basal levels of cyclic AMP have been found not to change appreciably during the course of development in whole brain,[47] in the cerebral cortex,[53,54,55,56] in various areas of the neonatal rabbit,[53] or in cultures of dissociated fetal brain cells.[57]

The lack of difference across age in cyclic AMP concentration in slices of developing brain *in vitro* is in contrast to the marked increases in nucleotide levels seen *in vivo*. This indicates that *in vivo* estimates of cyclic

AMP levels in the brains of mature rats may, in fact, reflect a certain influence of anoxia in the older, more slowly fixed samples. As previously noted, a revaluation of the steady-state concentration of cyclic AMP in the brain during the neonatal period using more appropriate methods of tissue fixation is needed.

### Cyclic GMP Concentrations in the Brain in vivo

The concentration of cyclic GMP in the brain does not change significantly in the initial moments following anoxia.[48] Therefore, levels found in frozen tissue probably represent valid estimates of actual concentrations existing in the brain *in vivo*. No change in cyclic GMP was found between birth and 20 days of age in the brain stem or forebrain of mice sacrificed by rapid freezing.[48] A marked rise in cyclic GMP did take place in the cerebellum beginning at 12 days of age. The difference between cerebellar levels at ten days of age and in adults was over sixfold. A similar trend was reported by Spano *et al*.[58] and Govoni *et al*.,[59] who used microwave irradiation as a means of tissue fixation. However, these workers found that cerebellar cyclic GMP increased between twenty- to thirtyfold between birth and adulthood.

### Adenylate Cyclase Activity in the Developing Brain

The changes in cyclic nucleotide concentrations in the brain during development could result from an elevated amount or increase in the activity of adenylate cyclase, the membrane-bound enzyme responsible for the conversion of ATP to cyclic AMP.[60] Adenylate cyclase activity in the brain is higher than in most organs, and activity varies between brain regions.[61] A thorough review of this enzyme has appeared.[62]

Adenylate cyclase activity has been detected in the brain at the earliest stages of development. Cyclase activity was found in 15-day-old chick embryos[46] and in the brains of rats one day before birth.[63] Initially we reported[47] that adenylate cyclase activity in the absence of stimulants increased fourfold during the first nine days postpartum and then markedly declined during the next two weeks. Several other groups have also reported dramatic increases in cyclase activity during the first weeks of life in all brain regions examined.[46,55,63,64,65,66,67]

A decline in adenylate cyclase activity following days 9 to 20 has been observed in the whole brain,[47] the cerebral cortex[55,65,67] and in the brain stem.[63,65] There is reason to believe that the fall in activity in some of these cases was more apparent than real, reflecting the presence of uncontrolled ATPase activity in the assay system. The maintenance of optimal concentrations of ATP is required for accurate estimation of adenylate cyclase activity. ATPase activity increases fourfold during the second two weeks of life in the rat brain, and it was at this time that cyclase activity appeared to decrease. Adding sodium fluoride to the reaction to inhibit ATPase maintained high ATP concentrations during the reaction (Schmidt and Robison, unpublished observations) and markedly increased cyclic AMP synthesis in brain homogenates.[62] The depletion of ATP probably accounts for the near total loss of adenylate cyclase activity which we initially reported to occur in whole-brain experiments.[47] However, others have also reported a decline in basal cyclase activity during maturation, even though ATP-regenerating systems were included in the reaction mixture.[55,60,63] It would appear, therefore, that a measurable decline in basal adenylate cyclase activity begins to take place in the brain after the second postnatal week.

Sodium fluoride appears to act on the catalytic component of adenylate cyclase to directly stimulate the enzyme, quite apart from its ability to inhibit ATPase activity. Activation of adenylate cyclase by fluoride also appears to be age-dependent. The enzyme from newborn rat brain is only marginally stimulated by fluoride,[47,55,56,63,65,67] but significant activation is seen between 7 and 16 days of age, and the greatest percentage of stimulation occurs in the adult brain. However, the greatest absolute level of cyclic AMP synthesis is present in the 10- to 20-day-old brain. A similar developmental pattern is seen in the pineal gland.[65]

Von Hungen et al.[63] observed that calcium also stimulated cyclic AMP synthesis in homogenates of the developing cerebral cortex, with the activation pattern resembling that seen for fluoride.

Some differences in the developmental timetable were seen in regional studies of fluoride-sensitive adenylate cyclase in the developing brain. The peak of activity occurred at 9 days in the whole brain,[47] at 16 to 19 days in the cerebral cortex,[55,56,63,65,67] at 10 days in the brain stem,[65] and at 30 days in the cerebellum.[65] The late development of adenylate cyclase in the cerebellum may reflect the fact that a significant amount of cell proliferation and maturation occurs in the rat cerebellum during the postnatal period.[68]

A limited number of studies has been conducted with human brain. Adenylate cyclase activity was detected in the brains of 12- to 14-week-old fetuses.[49,69] No direct comparison was made to older subjects, but specific activity was significantly lower than that reported for adult brain.[30,70]

## Guanylate Cyclase Activity in the Developing Brain

There has been only one report on guanylate cyclase activity in the brain during the postnatal developmental period. Activity in the 100,000g supernatant fraction from the rat cerebellum declined 66 percent between eight days of age and adulthood.[58] This decline in synthetic capacity is in contrast to the twenty-fivefold rise in cyclic GMP levels in the cerebellum during this same time period.[59]

## Cyclic Nucleotide Phosphodiesterases in the Developing Brain

Cyclic nucleotide concentrations in cells are regulated by the rate of catabolism as well as synthesis. The conversion of cyclic nucleotides to the corresponding 5'-mononucleotide is the only known means by which the cyclic nucleotides are metabolized. This reaction, which is catalyzed by a family of relatively specific phosphodiesterases, is probably the principal means by which intracellular cyclic nucleotide levels in brain are lowered (the others being suppression of adenylate cyclase activity and loss of the nucleotide into the extracellular space). Excellent recent reviews covering phosphodiesterase activity in general[71] and brain phosphodiesterase in particular[72,73] are available. Changes in phosphodiesterase activity during fetal and postnatal development were previously summarized by Weiss and Stradar,[49] and the following represents a brief update on this subject.

Phosphodiesterase activity exists in at least three distinct forms, differing from each other in kinetic behavior, substrate specificity and other properties. Almost all cells, including both neural and glial elements from different brain regions, have been found to contain two or more of these forms. Overall activity in brain tissue is high, relative to the activity found in most other tissues,[72,73] with perhaps greater activity in postsynaptic structures than elsewhere.[61] Histochemical techniques have also localized phosphodiesterase in postsynaptic structures.[74,75] In rat brain, highest enzyme activity is present in gray matter. The ratios of one form of phosphodiesterase to another seem to vary in different types of cells, although the significance of this is presently obscure.[71]

One major form of phosphodiesterase, sometimes referred to as the "high $K_M$" enzyme, has a lower affinity (higher apparent $K_M$) for cyclic AMP than for cyclic GMP, although the $V_{max}$ is higher for cyclic AMP than for cyclic GMP. This is the enzyme originally discovered and thought for many years to be the only phosphodiesterase responsible for the metabolism of cyclic AMP. The kinetic properties of this enzyme now suggest that it might be more importantly involved in the metabolism of cyclic GMP than cyclic AMP. It is further characterized by its sensitivity to a calcium-dependent activator protein which occurs in brain.[76] In fact, the activity of this form of the enzyme is very low in the absence of the activator, which suggests that the activator protein might play an important regulatory role. Both the enzyme and the activator are soluble proteins found predominantly in the supernatant fraction of tissue extracts. The activator has been detected in the cerebrum, brain stem and cerebellum of newborn rats.[49]

A second major form of the enzyme, sometimes referred to as the "low $K_M$" form, has a higher affinity for cyclic AMP than for cyclic GMP and is not sensitive to the calcium-dependent activator. It is often found in association with particulate fractions containing fragments of the cell membrane, although it can be easily solubilized. Importantly, the activity of this phosphodiesterase in some cells has been found to change in response to hormones.[71,77]

A third form of the enzyme, distinctly different from the other two, is characterized by the ability to be activated by low concentrations of cyclic GMP, leading to increased hydrolysis of low concentrations of cyclic AMP.[71] In the case of the previously discussed forms, the two cyclic nucleotides compete for the same catalytic site in a manner predictable from their individual $K_M$s.

Still other forms of the enzyme may exist in some cells. For example, six different fractions of phosphodiesterase activity can be isolated from brain tissue by a variety of separation techniques.[49, 78] It is possible, however, that some of these fractions represent preparative artifacts arising from proteolysis or other causes[79] rather than separate forms existing and functioning intracellularly *in vivo*.

Early experiments with the developing rat brain, in which phosphodiesterase activity in both soluble and particulate fractions was measured,[47] disclosed a sharp increase in activity in both fractions between birth and 24 days postpartum. No developmental changes in the properties of either fraction, such as susceptibility to inhibition by methylxanthines, could be detected.[47] Generally similar results were obtained by others,[49,67,80] although an apparently different pattern of development was reported by Hommes and Beere.[64] The latter discrepancy can be understood in terms of inadequate methodology, since these investigators used an assay designed for the measurement of 2, '3'-phosphodiesterase activity rather than the cyclic nucleotide phosphodiesterase being discussed here.

Regional differences in the ontogeny of rat-brain phosphodiesterase activity were reported by Weiss and Stradar and their colleagues[49,65,81] and some prostaglandins, dopamine and serotonin.[36,73] However, norepinephrine was incapable of eliciting an increase in cyclic AMP others.[67] Total activity in homogenates of cerebral cortex and brain stem developed in a manner similar to that seen in the whole-brain experiments.[47] However, activity in cerebellar homogenates was high at birth and actually declined with increasing age.[65] The increase in phosphodiesterase activity in the cerebral cortex was due almost exclusively to an increase in a "high $K_M$" form of the enzyme, whereas in the cerebellum the ratio of this form to other forms did not change with age.[81] Another difference between regions was that the calcium-dependent activator was initially low in the cerebellum and increased with age, whereas in the other brain areas it was initially high and then decreased with age.[81]

Davis and Kuo[82] studied the development of phosphodiesterase activity in guinea-pig brains. The "low $K_M$" form using cyclic AMP as substrate remained constant from 13 days before birth through parturition and puberty. Conversely, the activity of a form having high affinity for cyclic GMP was considerably lower in the fetus and progressively increased to the adult level.

Different forms of phosphodiesterase activity have also been measured in human fetal tissue.[83] The ratio of the "high $K_M$" form to the "low $K_M$" form was about 2:1, similar to the ratio found in newborn rat brains.[49] In the cerebral cortex, total activity against either cyclic AMP or cyclic GMP was generally found to be greater in preparations obtained from mature brains than from fetal tissue, and there seems to be an interesting shift at maturity from the soluble to the particulate fraction.[83]

Adinolfi and Schmidt,[75] using histochemical techniques, observed that the appearance of phosphodiesterase in the developing cerebral cortex coincided with the appearance of postsynaptic junctions during the second postnatal week. The ability of neurotransmitters to stimulate cyclic AMP synthesis follows much the same developmental sequence.

## Neurohumoral Stimulation of Adenylate Cyclase in the Developing Brain

### Cyclic AMP Accumulation in Tissue Slices in Vitro

Neurotransmitter-stimulated accumulation of cyclic nucleotides is hypothesized to be one means of transferring information at the synapse. Cyclic AMP concentrations increase in tissue slices from most regions of the mature rat brain in response to norepinephrine, epinephrine, isoproterenol, glutamate and adenosine; and to a lesser extent to histamine,

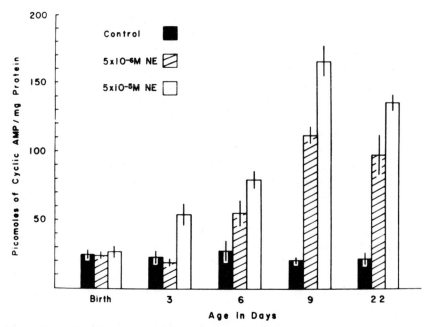

Figure 11-3:    Norepinephrine-stimulated accumulation of cyclic AMP in whole brains of
rats. Brains were chopped, suspended in buffer and incubated at 37° for 50 min., with
norepinephrine present during the final 6 min. Each bar represents the mean ± s.e.m. of 3
to 6 brains. From Schmidt et al.[47]

accumulation in tissue slices of whole brain from newborn rats.[47] The first
detectable stimulation of cyclic AMP synthesis by norepinephrine was
seen at three days of age, while at nine days old the response reached its
zenith. A slight decline in hormonal response occurred during the next
two weeks of life (Figure 11-3). Perkins and Moore[55] examined the
ontogenesis of adenylate-cyclase sensitivity to norepinephrine, isoproterenol and adenosine in the rat cerebral cortex. Adenosine did not
elevate cyclic AMP in cortical slices until the eighth day after birth. The
magnitude of the response to adenosine increased gradually to maximal
levels by day 15. In contrast, an enhanced accumulation of cyclic AMP by
the catecholamines was not apparent until 11 to 12 days postpartum.
    However, the catecholamines and adenosine acted synergically and,
when added together, could elicit an accumulation of cyclic AMP as early
as day 5. It would appear that norepinephrine is capable of elevating cyclic
AMP in the newborn rat brain if the proper conditions are present.
Perhaps the coupling of catecholamine receptors to adenylate cyclase is
not fully developed in the newborn.
    Histamine increases cyclic AMP accumulation in slices of the cerebral

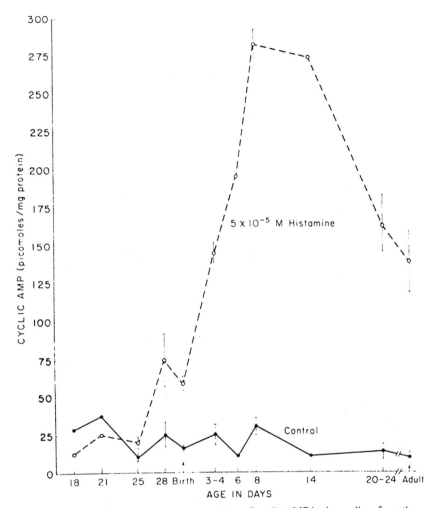

Figure 11-4:   Histamine-stimulated accumulation of cyclic AMP in tissue slices from the cerebral cortex of rabbits. Tissues were incubated for 50 min. with 5 x 10⁻⁵M histamine present during the final 6 min. Each point represents the mean ± s.e.m. of 3-6 animals. From Palmer et al.[54]

cortex of adult rabbits, but norepinephrine is only marginally active.[84] The first detectable histamine-induced stimulation of cyclic AMP synthesis was seen at fetal day 25, and from fetal day 28 to birth the response increased four- to fivefold.[54] A maximal elevation in cyclic AMP was observed at 8 to 14 days postpartum, and by 20 days of age the response had decreased to adult levels (Figure 11-4).

Although histamine increased cyclic AMP levels over tenfold in

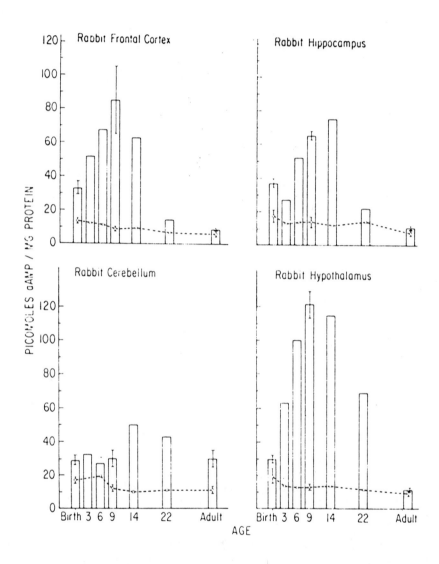

Figure 11-5:   Norepinephrine-stimulated accumulation of cyclic AMP in tissue slices from various areas of the rabbit brain. Tissues were incubated for 50 min., with 5 x 10⁻⁵M norepinephrine present during the final 6 min. Each bar represents the mean ± s.e.m. of 2 to 6 animals. The dashed line represents cyclic AMP levels in the tissue in the absence of norepinephrine. From Schmidt and Robison.[53]

cortical slices from adult rabbits,[54] the effect of norepinephrine was barely detectable.[53,84] However, early during postnatal development nor-epinephrine was capable of producing dramatic elevations in cyclic AMP accumulation in cortical tissue slices,[53] as illustrated in Figure 11-5. The hypothalamus and hippocampus were other regions of the rabbit brain which showed this pattern of development: a lack of stimulation in the adult and marked increases during early development. An exception was the cerebellum, where there was a significant norepinephrine response in the adult as well as the neonate.[53,85]

A thorough study of the development of the cyclic AMP generating system in the chicken has been conducted by Patton et al.[46] They found that neither histamine nor isoproterenol stimulated cyclic AMP ac-cumulation in slices of the cerebral cortex of chicks three to five days before hatching. Adenosine, however, stimulated cyclic AMP synthesis at all times examined. Just prior to hatching and during the three days posthatching, all compounds elicited the greatest increases in cyclic AMP.

During the first postnatal month, the effects of all agents diminished approximately 50 percent. These studies were extended in vivo, relying on the lack of blood-barrier in the young chick to facilitate passage of histamine and isoproterenol into the brain. Again, it was noted that both amines activated the system to the greatest extent immediately after birth. During the first postnatal month the response *in vivo* to histamine decreased 50 percent and the response to isoproterenol declined 75 percent.

The development of the cyclic AMP system in the chicken appears earlier than in the rat or rabbit, but the chick is approximately ten days ahead of the rodents in terms of brain development—i.e., chicks are fully mobile and visually competent at birth, whereas the rat reaches this stage at approximately 13 to 14 days of age. Therefore, the development of the response to stimulants appears to coincide with the maturation of the central nervous system. This was clearly shown in studies in which the effects of norepinephrine on cyclic AMP accumulation were compared in the brain of newborn and 25-day-old guinea pigs. This species is born neurologically mature, fully mobile and visually complete following a 60-day gestational period. In this animal, hormone sensitivity was the same in the newborn as in the adult.[47]

*Cyclic GMP Accumulation During Development*

Little work has been done on the characteristics and responses of the cyclic GMP system in the developing brain. As previously mentioned, levels of cyclic GMP *in vivo* in the cerebellum are markedly lower in neonatal than in adult rats. It was also found that while harmaline increased and diazepam decreased the level of cyclic GMP in the cerebellum of adult rats *in vivo,* no such changes occurred in newborn rats.[58,59]

Diazepam decreases cyclic GMP levels only in the cerebella of adult rats, but GABA is equally effective in lowering cyclic GMP in both the young and adult animal. Spano and Govoni and their colleagues[58,59] speculated that the absence of drug effects in the newborn may reflect the absence of complete neurological connections and cell types in the immature cerebellum. The effect of GABA, however, indicates that those cells which are responsible for cyclic GMP synthesis are fully capable of responding to appropriate stimuli prior to innervation.


*Cyclic AMP Synthesis in Cell-free Homogenates*

Most tissues, when homogenized, lose considerable hormone-stimulated adenylate cyclase activity. The brain is especially labile in this respect. Incubation of norepinephrine ($10^{-4}$M) with homogenates of whole brain did not change cyclic AMP synthesis at any age between birth and 30 days of age.[47] However, in these same preparations, stimulation by fluoride was readily detected. Similarly, no catecholamine response was detected in homogenates of human fetal brain.[69] Due to the intricate coupling between hormone receptors and adenylate cyclase in the neuronal membrane, it is not difficult to imagine that mechanical perturbation during homogenization might lead to malfunctioning of the system. However, in some regions of the brain (such as the cerebral cortex, dopamine-rich areas of the CNS and the pineal gland) adenylate cyclase retains measurable hormone sensitivity.

The pineal gland was studied during the neonatal period by Weiss.[65] He reported that pineal homogenates did not respond to norepinephrine until two days after birth. A maximal response was elicited at 20 days of age.

Hormone-sensitive adenylate cyclase has been extensively studied in the developing cerebral cortex and "subcortex" by von Hungen *et al.*[63] Small stimulations by norepinephrine, dopamine and serotonin were detected in both regions at all ages between birth and one year of age. Elevations were 20 to 60 percent in the cerebral cortex and 10 to 40 percent in the remaining portion of the brain. The total increase in cyclic AMP concentration in the presence of norepinephrine or dopamine was highest at ten days of age, but basal adenylate cyclase also increased with age. Therefore, the percentage effect of the dopamine was attenuated somewhat. Although the norepinephrine-stimulated accumulation remained the same through development,[86] the response to dopamine decreased and the effect of serotonin was barely detectable in the mature animals.[63]

Recently, regionally specific dopamine-sensitive adenylate cyclases have been localized in dopamine-rich areas of the brain and have been equated by some investigators with the dopamine receptor.[84] Makman et al.[88] examined the effects of dopamine on cyclic AMP synthesis in the retina of monkeys and rats during the postnatal period. Dopamine stimulation was 63 percent of maximum at birth, while apomorphine and isoproterenol were as active in newborn monkeys as in adults. However, low doses of isoproterenol were without effect in the newborn. Dopamine did not stimulate cyclic AMP synthesis in the retina of newborn rats, but a dramatic increase in stimulation took place between 6 and 14 days postpartum. Between 14 and 29 days of age, the ability of dopamine to stimulate cyclic AMP synthesis decreased 50 percent.

A 50 percent decline in apomorphine-sensitive adenylate cyclase activity was reported to occur in the striatum of rats between 15 and 60 days of age.[89] Both the affinity of apomorphine for adenylate cyclase and the magnitude of the reaction were lower in the caudates of adult rats. On the other hand, dopamine stimulation was found to be constant across age at several different concentrations of amine. Spano and his coworkers[89] speculated that dopamine and apomorphine might be interacting with different types in the developing caudate, with the apomorphine-sensitive cell type regressing during maturation. However, Coyle and Campochiaro[66] reported that dopamine stimulation of cyclic AMP synthesis in caudate homogenates fell 50 percent between eight days of age and adulthood. These workers also found that total dopamine-sensitive adenylate cyclase activity was only 20 percent of the adult potential at birth and that basal cyclase activity increased tenfold during the first weeks of life.

The appearance and developmental time course of catecholamine-sensitive cyclic AMP accumulation in brain slices or homogenates can also be demonstrated in brain cells in tissue culture. Gilman and Schrier[57] reported that brain cultures from 21-day gestational rats were not responsive to isoproterenol, analogous to the lack of effect seen in slices of whole brain at birth.[47] The first response was detected after three days of culture and a maximal response seen at 14 days of culture. In fetal mouse brain cultures, responses to isoproterenol and norepinephrine did not appear until 9 days in culture.[90]

Tissue-culture experiments are important, for they illustrate that hormone receptor sensitivity can develop in the absence of peripheral influences. Interestingly, the development of dopamine-sensitive adenylate cyclase precedes the appearance of biochemical evidence of presynaptic terminals[66] or haloperidol binding to striatal membranes.[91] This casts further doubt on the importance of presynaptic input for the development of hormone-stimulated cyclic AMP accumulation.

A comparison of the developmental patterns of various components thought to be involved in synaptic transmission is shown in Table 11-1. It

### Table 11-1: Developmental Sequence of Systems Involved in Noradrenergic Transmission in the Brain

| System | First Appearance | Maximum Activity | Reference |
|---|---|---|---|
| 1. Norepinephrine synthesis | Detected 15 Fetal days | 40–60 days | (178) |
| 2. Amine storage capacity | Birth | Birth | (179) |
| 3. Levels of norepinephrine | Birth | 60 Days | (56) |
| 4. Amphetamine-induced release of catecholamine | Birth | – | (180) |
| 5. Amine reuptake | Birth | Birth | (179) |
| 6. Density of norepinephrine innervation | First visualized at 1–2 weeks | 40–60 days | (178, 179) |
| 7. Adenylate cyclase activity | Birth | 15 days followed by a decline | (47) (47, 55) |
| 8. NaF Stimulation of cyclic AMP synthesis | 5 days | | |
| 9. Stereospecific binding of ligands to *beta* receptors | 7 days | 12–14 days | (56) |
| 10. Norepinephrine-sensitive adenylate cyclase | 5 days | 5–12 days followed by a decline | (47, 55, 56) |
| 11. Cyclic AMP phosphodiesterase activity | Birth | 20 days | (47, 49) |
| 12. Cyclic AMP dependent protein kinase | 3 days (almost adult activity) 6 days prior to birth | 6–21 days Birth | (110) (108) |
| 13. Phosphorylation of phosphoprotein I | Birth 3 days | Birth 3 days | (42, 117) |

is clear that the systems do not develop in concert. The postsynaptic components (adenylate cyclase, adenylate cyclase activation, transmitter binding) appear before reuptake and transmitter synthesis systems, which are markers for presynaptic nerve endings. There is electrophysiological evidence for this also. Woodward *et al.*[92] reported that electrical activity of Purkinje cells can be modulated by iontophoresis of transmitter substances onto cerebellar cells of neonatal rats before there is evidence of presynaptic input into the cerebellum. In fact, the Purkinje cells appear to be hypersensitive to transmitter substances, analogous to the hyperactivity of the adenylate cyclase system during the 9 to 15 days period postpartum.

These studies suggest that presynaptic input is not required for the development of transmitter receptors. This was shown directly by Weiss,[65] who disrupted the adrenergic input into the pineal gland by removing the superior cervical ganglion in newborn rats. Following recovery, there was no detectable difference in norepinephrine-sensitive adenylate cyclase activity in pineal homogenates from adult animals. Extending these studies, Weiss and Stradar[49] found that disruption of presynaptic input by immunosympathectomy or by administration of 6-hydroxydopamine to newborn rats also did not retard the development of catecholamine-stimulated cyclic AMP accumulation in the pineal gland. In fact, the system became supersensitive, as is usually the case in mature rats following transmitter depletion.[36,93] These phenomena have been replicated in the rat brain[94,95,96] and chick brain *in vitro* and *in vivo.*[97] Nahorski[97] reported that under conditions where isoproterenol-stimulated accumulation of cyclic AMP was enhanced by catecholamine depletion, the response to histamine or adenosine was not changed. Therefore, the alteration in receptor sensitivity was specific.

Mollinoff[96] observed that coincidental with the increase in adenylate cyclase stimulation following neonatal amine depletion in rats, there was an increase in the number of transmitter receptors in the cerebral cortex. No change in [$^3$H] Propranolol binding was detected in chick brain.[97]

It is thus clear that hormone receptors can develop normally in the absence of presynaptic input. Cyclic AMP generating systems can appear and mature in the complete absence of synaptic stimulation during the developmental period. It is also apparent that the immature receptors can compensate for the lack of presynaptic input by increasing their sensitivity, in a manner similar to that seen in the mature nervous system.

However, receptors in the developing brain appear to have some unique characteristics. For example, it seems more than coincidental that in almost all brain regions there is an exaggerated cyclic AMP response to stimulants during the 8- to 15-day period after birth. This phenomenon is seen in both rabbits and rats, with norepinephrine, adenosine or histamine, and can be observed to varying degrees in all studies of the cyclic AMP system in the developing brain published to date. Synaptic development is progressing rapidly during this time; synaptic specialization is occurring and cell-cell interactions multiplying rapidly. One might speculate that at this time postsynaptic receptor sites are hypersensitive or relatively nondiscriminative with respect to transmitter-receptor interaction. We have recently observed that cortical slices from the brains of two- to four-day-old humans (autopsy material) seem to be more responsive to norepinephrine than do adult samples.[50] However, at this time the sample number is too small to permit definitive conclusions.

One of the most striking changes that occurs in the cortex of the rat during the first weeks of life is the extensive proliferation of synaptic elements. Assuming that norepinephrine is acting on a postsynaptic site to elicit the rise in cyclic AMP levels,[61,98] it seems possible that as more synapses appear the density of norepinephrine receptors would likewise increase. Studying the anatomical development of the rat cortex, Eayrs and Goodhead[99] found that few axons and little dendritic branching were present at birth. An increase in the number of dendrites occurred between 6 and 12 days of age, while extensive arborization and interneuronal interaction did not approach maturity until 18 days. Caley and Maxwell[100] found similar results stating that no real synapses (based on electron microscopic studies) could be detected in the cortex until the end of the first week. A dramatic increase in the number of stainable synaptic junctions in the rat parietal cortex during the third week of life was reported by Aghajanian and Bloom.[101] The concentration of norepinephrine in the brain, only 20 percent of adult levels at birth, also increases during the first weeks of life.[102] The culmination of these changes is the appearance of electrical activity in the brain. Little activity is seen until 7 days of age,[103] but by 10 days the mature pattern is present in the rat.[104] Thus, the beginning of functionality in the brain coincides with the appearance of those components associated with synaptic transmission. The levels of endogenous cyclic AMP, adenylate cyclase and phosphodiesterase activities, and norepinephrine sensitivity all increase during this period. This further suggests an important role for cyclic AMP in synaptic transmission.

Based upon studies of the rat brain, the paucity of synaptic profiles, the low levels of norepinephrine, and the inability of norepinephrine to stimulate the production of cyclic AMP in brain slices from immature rats all could account for the low levels of cyclic AMP in the neonatal rat brain *in vivo*.

At the time when the norepinephrine response does emerge, lipid begins to be rapidly deposited in the brain.[105] It is possible that such lipid deposition is necessary for the construction of functional synaptic membranes, or, more specifically, the neurohormonal receptors. It has been suggested[62,106] that adenylate cyclase might be deeply embedded in a lipoprotein matrix within the cell membrane, with unique regionally specific components dictating transmitter specificity. It is possible that during the early stages of brain development these critical components have not yet been synthesized and deposited in the membrane, thereby precluding the proper orientation of the regulatory subunit which faces the synaptic cleft. In this way norepinephrine sensitivity would be lacking until these components appear. If this were the case, interneuronal interaction would await the development of those elements which play a role in the neurochemical phase of brain function.

If transmitters communicate between cells by altering the level of cyclic AMP in adjacent neurons, the inefficiency of the cyclic AMP generating system in the brain during early life would contribute to the marginal functioning of the nervous system during this time. However, other components of the cyclic nucleotide system are equally important in translating synaptic messages to the interior of the neuron. These systems might also be rate-limiting for brain development.

## Protein Kinase and Protein Phosphorylation during Brain Development

### Protein Kinase Activity in the Developing Brain

It is generally accepted that cyclic AMP exerts many of its intracellular effects by activating the enzyme protein kinase (ATP: protein phosphotransferase, E.C.2.7.1.37) with the cell.[38,107] Cyclic GMP-dependent kinases are also present in the brain. Once activated, protein kinase phosphorylates many cellular proteins and in so doing probably alters their activity.[38,39]

High levels of cyclic AMP-dependent and cyclic AMP-independent protein kinase activity are present in the immature brain. We were not able to detect significant protein kinase activity in homogenates of whole brain, and so used a semipurified preparation ($[NH_4]_2SO_4$ fractionated) for study of protein kinase during the postnatal period.[108] Significant activity was present in the brain six days before birth, and the enzyme was fully active at this time. No change in activity in the presence or absence of cyclic AMP was detected throughout the postnatal development period and continuing to one year of age. Cyclic AMP ($5 \times 10^{-6}$M) increased activity approximately 250 percent at all ages.

Measurement of soluble brain protein kinase using casein as the phosphate acceptor revealed that activity was constant between 5 and 30 days of age.[109] However, when histane was used as the substrate, activity assayed in the absence of cyclic AMP increased between 5 and 30 days of age while the activity of the cyclic AMP-stimulated kinase remained constant during this time period. Gaballah et al.[110] also observed a greater increase in cyclic AMP-independent protein kinase activity during development than in the cyclic AMP-dependent form of the enzyme. Interestingly, Takahashi et al.[109] found that cyclic AMP binding activity in the soluble fraction (presumably to the receptor unit of protein kinase) declined 50 percent during the 5- to 17-day period postpartum. These observations indicate that protein kinase may be more sensitive to stimulation by cyclic AMP during the early postnatal period, although we have found no evidence of this in our own studies.[40, 108]

Protein kinase has been studied in subcellular fractions from the brain during the postnatal period. Histone kinase activity was present and stimulated by cyclic AMP in all fractions at all ages.[109,110] Greatest activity was found in the mitochondrial and supernatant fractions at all ages between -3 and 70 to 90 days of age. Both cyclic AMP-dependent and cyclic AMP-independent kinase activities were found to increase during the early postnatal period in all fractions except the nuclear fraction. Most of the change occurred within the first six days postpartum. The greatest change took place in the mitochondrial fraction. Gaballah et al.[110] found that microsomal protein kinase increased 150 percent during the first six days postpartum, but we[40] did not detect a difference in microsomal kinase activity between newborn and 30-day-old rats. The manner in which Gaballah et al.[110] expressed their results probably accounts for this discrepancy.[40]

Soluble brain protein kinase has been thoroughly studied by Takahashi et al.[109] These investigators purified the enzyme from the brains of rats 4, 9 or 30 days of age during DEAE cellulose chromatography. Multiple peaks of kinase activity were detected. Four-day-old rats had four peaks of activity, 9-day-old rats had five peaks, and 30-day-old animals had only three major peaks of histone kinase activity. In all cases, only one peak was activated by cyclic AMP, this being the final active fraction eluted from the column. Only three major peaks of casein kinase activity were detected in the brains of 9- or 3-day-old rats, and only the final fraction was stimulated by cyclic AMP. There were no differences noted in the protein profiles across age in these studies. It is difficult to assess the meaning of these findings, since protein kinase is easily dissociated during preparation and appears to be able to dissociate and reassociate freely in solution.[43] Therefore, the differences in peaks between ages might be artifactual.

## Protein Phosphorylation During Brain Development

The tissue-specific response to an alteration in cyclic nucleotide concentration within the cell appears to result from the phosphorylation of intracellular and membrane proteins.[38,39] It has been proposed that protein phosphorylation is the means by which cyclic AMP exerts its intracellular effects on neuronal function.[111] Proteins present in nervous tissue which are phosphorylated include brain microsomes and ribosomes,[40] synaptic membrane proteins,[112] neurotubule-associated protein,[113] cholinergic receptor proteins[114] and other undefined proteins.[41,108]

It is hypothesized that phosphorylation alters the configuration or behavior of intracellular proteins, and cellular dynamics are altered (e.g., phosphorylation of synaptic membranes might be involved in the ionic fluxes and current changes that accompany an action potential). Interestingly, electrical stimulation of tissue slices of the cerebral cortex enhances membrane phosphorylation,[115] and Ehrlich et al.[116] found that training increased the incorporation of phosphate into select proteins in synaptic membranes in several brain regions. Thus, age-related changes in protein phosphorylation might have widespread effects on brain function.

Only a limited number of investigators have studied the substrates for protein kinase during development. Incubation of the 27,000g supernatant from rat brain with radioactive ATP led to the phosphorylation of proteins endogenous to the brain.[108] Between six days prior to birth and 15 days postpartum there was a significant increase in the amount of phosphate incorporated into TCA-precipitatable material, and incorporation was increased in the presence of cyclic AMP. Endogenous phosphorylation did not change between 15 and 40 days after birth. These results indicated that either the amount of endogenous protein kinase substrate or the propensity of the substrates for phosphorylation increased during early postnatal brain development. No attempt was made to define the nature of the proteins phosphorylated. Schmidt and Sokoloff[40] attempted to determine if alterations in the phosphorylation of ribosomal proteins changed during brain development. They theorized that differential rates of ribosomal phosphorylation in the neonate might account for the decline in protein synthetic ability of the brain during the early postnatal period.[117] Purified ribosomes could serve as substrates for protein kinase at all times between birth and one year of age, but there were no differences in the degree of phosphate incorporated across age. No significant protein kinase activity was detected in the ribosomes from the brains at any age. Further, it was found that phosphorylation of brain ribosomes caused only a 10 to 15 percent decrease in in vitro protein synthesis with no differences noted between young and mature animals (Schmidt and Sokoloff, unpublished observations).

There have been several other recent references to changes in protein phosphorylation during brain development. Protein kinase phosphorylates two specific proteins found in synaptic membranes. These are designated protein I and II.[42] Protein I is of special interest, for this substrate has not been detected in any nonneural tissues examined[42] and is present in the cerebrum of newborn rats in only small amounts. The amount of this protein increases markedly during the 2- to 3-week period postnatal.[111] Ehrlich et al.,[117] on the other hand, were unable to detect the presence of protein I in the brains of 1-day-old rats. At the present time we have no idea of the physiological function of protein I, but its: a) uniqueness to the nervous system, b) susceptibility to phosphorylation and c) appearance during the time when synaptic transmission appears in the brain suggest a potentially important role for this protein in brain function.

The studies discussed above indicate that the protein kinase–protein phosphorylation system in the brain changes little during the neonatal development period. Unlike the receptor system, it would appear that the phosphorylation system is almost fully operational shortly after birth. However, it is important to remember that although the kinase system is potentially fully operational during the early period postpartum, the rate-limiting factor is the amount of cyclic AMP available to activate the kinase. As discussed earlier, the number of hormone receptors, the coupling of receptors to adenylate cyclase, and adenylate cyclase activity per se are only low during this time. Therefore, one would predict that the cyclic nucleotide system would not operate at adult potential until 10 to 20 days after birth.

Several studies have shown that the brain is especially vulnerable to insult during the neonatal period. This is probably due to the fact that many systems, including the cyclic nucleotide system, are undergoing rapid development in the brain during this time period. Neonatal thyroidectomy and malnutrition result in widespread damage to the developing brain. Since the cyclic nucleotide system might play a pivotal role in brain function, it seemed possible that the effects of these insults might manifest themselves through aberrant development of the components of this system. We found that neonatal thyroidectomy did not affect the levels of cyclic AMP, the ability of norepinephrine to stimulate cyclic AMP accumulation in brain slices, adenylate cyclase or phosphodiesterase activities, or cyclic AMP-dependent or independent protein kinase activities.[108] Thus, although many enzyme systems in the brain are affected by neonatal thyroidectomy,[118] the cyclic AMP system appears to be refractory.

Conversely, administration of thyroid hormone during the postnatal period leads to precocious neurophysiological development in the rat. However, administration of thyroxine or triiodothyronine during the first six days of life did not affect basal microsomal protein kinase activity or the stimulation of the enzyme by cyclic AMP in the brains of the rats at ten days of age.[119]

The effect of neonatal undernutrition on adenylate cyclase in the cerebral cortex was studied by Kauffman et al.[67] Enzyme activity in cortical homogenates from 3- 10- or 19-day-old animals was not affected by undernourishment.

These findings, coupled with the evidence that postsynaptic hormone-sensitive adenylate cyclase activity develops in the absence of presynaptic input, indicate that the cyclic AMP system is developmentally programmed and refractory to insult.

**Summary**

Five major generalizations can be drawn from the studies on the development of the cyclic nucleotide system in the brain:

1. The system does not develop as a complete unit; rather, transmitter binding develops at one rate, adenylate cyclase and phosphodiesterase at another rate, and hormone-stimulated cyclic AMP synthesis at yet another rate. Protein kinase changes little during the postnatal period.
2. The presence of synaptic input or monoamine transmitters during development is not required for receptors coupled to adenylate cyclase to develop properly.
3. During "adolescence," receptors appear to be supersensitive and perhaps relatively nondiscriminative.
4. The development of the system is not influenced by insults such as undernutrition or thyroid hormone imbalance.
5. The system is genetically programmed.

**THE CYCLIC NUCLEOTIDE SYSTEM IN THE BRAIN DURING AGING**

Studies of the cyclic nucleotide system during development have shown that cyclic nucleotide concentrations, transmitter-stimulated cyclic nucleotide accumulation, and adenylate and guanylate cyclase activities

change in the brain during the neonatal period of rapid brain development. Some studies indicated that the system might be more active in the
brains of young animals.[47,53,54,55,56] Therefore, a logical assumption was that
declines in the cyclic nucleotide system might continue into old age and
contribute to the mental dysfunction that often accompanies senescence.

## Cyclic Nucleotide Concentrations in the Brain During Aging

The level of cyclic AMP in sections of the cerebral cortex was found to
be lower in rats six months of age and older than in young Fisher–344
rats.[120] No differences were seen between 6 months and 24 months of age,
however, indicating that this reflects a maturational phenomenon rather
than an aging decline. A complicating factor in the above studies is the fact
that the rats were killed by decapitation prior to the fixation of the tissues.
Decapitation elevates cyclic AMP concentrations in all brain regions,[51] and
it is possible that the cyclic AMP generating system of old rats responds
differently following decapitation. The level of cyclic AMP in the striatum
of 24- and 30-month-old rats killed by microwave irradiation was found by
Puri and Volicer[121] to be similar to concentrations in young animals. At
this time these are the only studies which have attempted to estimate *in
vivo* cyclic AMP concentrations in the brain during advanced aging. No
studies on cyclic GMP levels *in vivo* in the aged brain have been reported.

Another estimate of the steady-state level of cyclic nucleotides in the
brain can be obtained by measuring the "basal" or resting levels of cyclic
AMP and cyclic GMP in tissue slices during *in vitro* experiments. In such
studies, brain regions from young and adult rabbits contained the same
concentrations of cyclic AMP, although slight declines were noted
between birth and old age in the frontal cortex, hippocampus and
hypothalamus.[53] Palmer *et al.*[54] also found little difference in basal levels of
cyclic AMP during *in vitro* incubations of slices of the cerebral cortex of
large adult rabbits. Unfortunately, in both the latter studies the exact ages
of the "adult" animals were unknown. More recently, *in vitro* experiments
have been conducted using brain slices from Wistar rats at 3, 12 and 24
months of age.[122] No differences between the ages were detected in the
cyclic AMP content of the hippocampus, hypothalamus, brain stem,
limbic forebrain region or the cerebral cortex during *in vitro* incubations
(Table 11-2). A significant reduction in the level of cyclic AMP was noted
in the cerebellum of rats 24 months old, but differences were not
statistically significant at 12 months of age. Cyclic GMP concentrations
were determined in these same tissues during *in vitro* incubations in the
absence of stimulants. Again, no significant differences were seen in any
region other than the cerebellum of 24-month-old rats (Table 11-2).

## Table 11-2: Resting Levels of Cyclic Nucleotides in Vitro in Brain Regions of Rats of Various Ages

| | (picomoles cyclic GMP/mg protein) | | |
| | 3 month | 12 month | 24 month |
|---|---|---|---|
| Brain stem | 0.42 ± 0.008 (4) | 0.33 ± 0.03 (4) | 0.35 ± 0.05 (4) |
| Cerebral cortex | 0.31 ± 0.05 (6) | 0.46 ± 0.05 (7) | 0.40 ± 0.05 (4) |
| Hippocampus | 0.45 ± 0.06 (9) | 0.47 ± 0.06 (8) | 0.39 ± 0.04 (9) |
| Hypothalamus | 0.44 ± 0.03 (4) | 0.50 ± 0.05 (4) | 0.55 ± 0.14 (4) |
| Cerebellum | 24.11 ± 3.24 (11) | 19.83 ± 2.11 (11)* | 12.25 ± 1.71 (11)* |

| | (picomoles cyclic AMP/mg protein) | | |
| | 3 month | 12 month | 24 month |
|---|---|---|---|
| Brain stem | 10.8 ± 1.2 (13) | 15.9 ± 2.3 (12) | 6.6 ± 0.6 (4) |
| Cerebral cortex | 11.5 ± 1.6 (10) | 12.9 ± 1.9 (10) | 15.2 ± 2.2 (10) |
| Hippocampus | 9.4 ± 1.2 (8) | 8.2 ± 0.7 (8) | 12.2 ± 1.0 (8) |
| Hypothalamus | 11.6 ± 2.5 (8) | 16.2 ± 5.9 (5) | 17.1 ± 2.0 (8) |
| Cerebellum | 26.7 ± 4.9 (8) | 16.9 ± 2.3 (7) | 15.1 ± 1.4 (8)* |

Brain regions from individual rats were sliced and incubated *in vitro* with buffer. Concentrations of cyclic GMP and cyclic AMP were determined in tissues after a 30–120 min. Equilibration period. Values represent the mean ± s.e.m. of the indicated number of determinations, each of which was assayed in duplicate for cyclic GMP and cyclic AMP. Statistically significant differences across age are indicated (*). (From Schmidt and Thornberry, 1978.)

Assessing the gerontological relevance of "basal" levels of cyclic nucleotides in young and old animals is difficult because it is not yet clear exactly what determines the resting level of cyclic AMP or cyclic GMP in the brain. Most treatments which affect transmitter-stimulated cyclic nucleotide accumulation *in vitro* or *in vivo* do not alter the "basal" concentrations of nucleotides — e.g., amine depletion,[29] antipsychotics[123] or antidepressants.[124] It is possible that "basal" levels of cyclic AMP represent a compartmentalized ·pool which is not metabolically labile. It has also been shown that the binding of cyclic AMP to protein kinase protects the nucleotide from catabolism via phosphodiesterase.[125] Therefore, it may be that those molecules of cyclic AMP which represent the "basal" level of cyclic nucleotide in the cell are, in fact, physiologically inert. It seems unlikely that "basal" cyclic AMP levels are due to the continued release of transmitters and activation of synthesis of nucleotide, in a manner analogous to the miniature end-plate potential recorded at the neuromuscular junctions. If this were so, receptor blocking agents would reduce cyclic AMP levels in non-stimulated tissues.

The reduction in the resting level of cyclic AMP and cyclic GMP which occurs in the cerebellum of aged rats is best explained by an age-related loss of Purkinje cells in this brain region.[126,127,128] Histofluorescence staining has localized a major portion of cerebellar cyclic AMP in the Purkinje cell layer,[129] and Mao et al.[130] proposed that the Purkinje cell synthesizes cyclic GMP in response to stimulation by glutamate. Therefore, a loss of Purkinje cells might account for the reductions in cyclic nucleotides seen in this brain region. In line with this, a significant reduction in cyclic GMP levels was found in vivo[131] and in vitro[132] in a mutant strain of mice[133] which have only 10 percent of the normal number of Purkinje cells.

Studies in progress in our laboratory have not detected an age-related difference in cyclic AMP levels in samples of the cerebral cortex and cerebellum of humans 6 to 16 hours after death.[50] Amounts of cyclic AMP in the urine are lower in elderly patients,[134] but since the source of urinary cyclic AMP is unknown and affected by environmental variables,[135] the relevance of this observation is unknown.

### Adenylate Cyclase Activity in the Brain During Aging

Adenylate cyclase activity has been measured in homogenates from several brain regions in rats as old as 30 months. Walker and Walker[136] reported that adenylate cyclase activity in the caudate and cerebellum of two-year-old Sprague-Dawley rats was significantly increased, while no change in activity was found in the cerebral cortex and hippocampus. We found that cyclase activity in the hippocampus, cerebellum (Schmidt and Truex, unpublished observation) and striatum[122] remained the same between three months and 24 months of age in Wistar rats. Others have also detected no change in basal adenylate cyclase activity in the striatum[59] or other dopamine-rich brain areas[59] of 20 to 30-month-old rats. The activity of adenylate cyclase in homogenates of the cerebral cortex was studied in depth by Zimmerman and Berg.[137] They were unable to detect a change in either the $K_m$ for ATP or the $V_{max}$ of the enzyme in old Fisher rats.

Exposure of adenylate cyclase to sodium fluoride (NaF) is known to stimulate the enzyme, although little is known of the mechanism involved.[138] The fluoride-stimulated activity is not reduced in the cerebral cortex([136,137] and unpublished observations), hippocampus[136] or cerebellum[136] of two-year-old rats. In contrast, Walker and Walker[136] found adenylate cyclase in the caudate nucleus of aged rats to be less responsive to NaF than that of three-month old rats, although Puri and Volicer[121] were unable to confirm this finding.

In summary, it appears that the resting and fluoride-stimulated activities of brain adenylate cyclase are not markedly different in rats which are considered to be senescent (older than 24 months). Adenylate cyclase in other organs seems to be more susceptible to the effects of aging for significant declines in adenylate cyclase, and guanylate cyclase activities were found in the liver, lung, heart and muscle of rats 300 days old.[139] Basal and NaF-stimulated adenylate cyclase activity in isolated fat cells also decline between 3 and 6 months of age,[140,141] and cyclase in erythrocytes is much less active in 74 compared to 372-day-old rats.[142] The lack of change in adenylate cyclase activity with increasing age is consistent with the stability of the "basal" level of cyclic AMP observed *in vivo* and *in vitro* in the brains of aged rats as discussed above.

**Cyclic Nucleotide Phosphodiesterases in the Brain During Aging**

Zimmerman and Berg[137] found that when phosphodiesterase was assayed in the presence of high levels of cyclic AMP there was no difference in diesterase activity between animals 1 to 3 months old and 6 to 24 months of age. However, when micromolar amounts of substrate were used, the hydrolysis was 30 percent lower in the cortical preparations from the rats in the older group. Puri and Volicer[121] found a decline only in the high affinity enzyme in homogenates of the striatum prepared from aged rats. The fall in activity was 16 percent at 24 months of age and 25 percent at 30 months when compared to 4- or 12-month-old controls. We found (Schmidt and Toomey, unpublished observations) that cyclic AMP hydrolysis in preparations of the hippocampus or cerebellum from 24-month-old rats was not different than that in 3-month-old animals. Both the high and low affinity enzymes were examined. No one has measured the cyclic GMP phosphodiesterase in the brains of aged rats, although it was found to increase in the guinea pig brain[82] and in the human brain[83] during maturation.

Another difference found by Zimmerman and Berg[143] was that the phosphodiesterase activator from old rats was more active than that of young, 4-month-old animals. However, the magnitude of this difference was small (15 to 25 percent) and only occurred in assays where the concentration of cyclic AMP hydrolyzed was in the micromolar range. However, it seems possible that the decline in phosphodiesterase activity in the aged brain is perhaps compensated for by an elevation in the activity of the activator. It is interesting that age-related changes were detected only when the enzyme was assayed at low substrate concentrations. Since the brain levels of cyclic AMP are in the micromolar range,[52] the differences found might be of physiological relevance. But it is difficult to explain why the concentrations of cyclic AMP in the cerebral cortex *in vivo* are reduced when the catabolic activity in the system is also reduced and adenylate cyclase activity does not decline.

Studies on peripheral organs revealed a significant decline in cyclic AMP phosphodiesterase only in the hearts of 300-day-old rats, but marked reductions in cyclic GMP hydrolysis were observed in the liver, lung and skeletal muscle as well as the heart.[139] On the other hand, cyclic AMP catabolism in adipose tissue doubles between the ages of 5 weeks and 24 weeks.[140]

In brain tissue, then, the synthetic and degradative components of the cyclic nucleotide system appear relatively intact and unaffected by the process of aging. Cyclic AMP synthesis through adenylate cyclase does not decrease with age, the hydrolysis of large amount of cyclic AMP by phosphodiesterase is not different in aged rats, and catabolism of physiological levels of cyclic AMP is only reduced 30 percent in aged rats. *In toto,* these results predict that the resting steady-state levels of cyclic AMP in the brains of young and old rats should not differ. This is what has been found in the striatum *in vivo*[121] and in most brain regions *in vitro.*[122] However, one might expect the greatest effects of aging to be observed under conditions requiring the system to respond to stimuli.

## Neurohumoral Stimulation of Cyclic Nucleotide Accumulation in the Brain During Aging

Age-related declines in hormone-stimulated accumulation of cyclic AMP have been reported to occur in a number of peripheral tissues including lymphocytes,[144] erythrocytes,[142] adipose tissue[140,141] and the liver.[145] Changes in hormone-stimulated cyclic AMP accumulation also occur in brain. We found that norepinephrine-stimulated accumulation of cyclic AMP in whole rat brain peaked at 15 days of age.[108] Similarly, the cyclic AMP increase in response to adenosine or adenosine plus norepinephrine was maximal in slices of the cerebral cortex of rats at this time, and then declined after 45 days of age.[55] Histamine-induced elevations of cyclic AMP in the rabbit cerebral cortex were highest in the 10- to 14-day time period after birth, following which levels progressively decline into adulthood.[54] This was even more pronounced in the frontal cortex, hypothalamus and hippocampus of rabbits when norepinephrine was used as the stimulant.[53] In the latter experiments no significant elevation of cyclic AMP occurred in "old" rabbits, although the increase seen at 9 days of age ranged from 6.5- to twelvefold in the various regions (Figure 11-5). Application of norepinephrine to the surface of the cerebral cortex of anesthesized rats elicited a reduced accumulation of cyclic AMP in rats 6 months or older compared to 1- to 3-month old rats.[146]

Thus, there are numerous instances in which stimulated accumulation of cyclic AMP declined with age in peripheral organs as well as the central nervous system. However, in almost all cases the declines occurred during the developmental period and therefore reflect maturational changes rather than changes accompanying the organ dysfunction seen in senility. Experiments designed to study hormone-receptor interaction in the brain after maturation and into old age *per se* are limited.

We reported[53] that the age-related declines in norepinephrine-stimulated cyclic AMP accumulation which occurred in the rabbit brain were regionally selective. Although all areas were most responsive to norepinephrine during the 9- to 14-day-old period, a significant fall in cyclic AMP synthesis occurred in the hypothalamus, hippocampus and cerebral cortex, but not in the cerebellum of rabbits 22 days of age (Figure 11-5). Then, a further decline was seen in adult rabbits approximately 3 years old. The lifespan of the rabbit is five to six years, which would make the animals used in these studies approximately middle-aged. It can be seen that the greatest postdevelopment fall in cyclic AMP accumulation occurred in the hypothalamus, while little significant change took place in the cerebellum or frontal cortex. There was no significant fall in histamine-induced cyclic AMP synthesis in the cerebral cortex of rabbits between 22 days and 2- to 3-year-old time point (Figure 11-4).

The postmaturational declines in norepinephrine and histamine-elicited accumulations in cyclic AMP synthesis in the rabbit brain indicated that similar changes in receptors might occur in the rat brain. A decrease in the number of muscarinic receptors in the frontal cortex of humans[25] and reduced glucocorticoid[23] binding in the cortex of the rat suggested that receptor dysfunction may be widespread in the aged brain. In fact, Berg and Zimmerman[146] did observe a reduction in cyclic AMP accumulation when norepinephrine was applied to the surface of the rats older than 6 months. However, it is difficult to interpret these studies due to the methods employed. For example, surface application of norepinephrine *in situ* makes it difficult to control dose-response relationships or to quantitate the amount of compound reaching the brain. Also, anesthesia reduces cyclic AMP levels[52,146] and in general depresses metabolic activity. Furthermore, the rats were killed by decapitation prior to tissue fixation and concentrations of cyclic AMP rise in the brain in response to this trauma,[51] thereby perhaps masking or otherwise influencing the hormone-induced component of the response. But most importantly, even if the reduction in norepinephrine-induced cyclic AMP

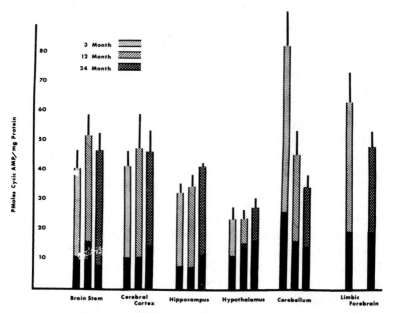

Figure 11-6:　Resting and norepinephrine-stimulated accumulation of cyclic AMP in slices of brain regions from young, old and aged rats. Tissues were incubated for optimal periods of time in the presence or absence of $10^{-5}$M norepinephrine (except the cerebellum where $10^{-4}$M norepinephrine was used). The reaction was terminated at the time of maximal cyclic AMP accumulation in each area: brain stem and hippocampus — 6 min.; hypothalamus and limbic forebrain — 10 min.; cerebellum — 15 min.; and cerebral cortex — 20 min. Hatched bars represent the mean ± s.e.m. of 4 to 8 animals. Solid bars depict cyclic AMP concentrations in the slices in the absence of norepinephrine. From Schmidt and Thornberry.[122]

accumulation is real, the decrement occurs between 3 and 6 months of age with no further decline thereafter. Therefore, this difference again represents a maturational change which becomes apparent before the behavioral manifestations of aging are seen.[147]

We conducted a survey study of cyclic nucleotide accumulation in the presence of norepinephrine using tissue slices from a number of brain regions. Experiments were conducted *in vitro* to give greater control over the system. Animals at 3, 12 and 24 months of age were chosen for study based on the suggestion of C. Finch (personal communication) that animals at the age of 50 percent survival approximate humans 70 to 80 years old. Rats in our colony are at the 50 percent mortality point when they are 24 months of age, and this was the oldest group used. Rats 3 months of age are sexually mature and past the rapid-growth phase of brain development, and these animals were classed as "young adults." A

**Table 11-3: Resting and Norepinephrine-Stimulated Accumulation of Cyclic AMP in Slices of Brain from Adult and Aged Rats**

| | *3 Month* | *12 Month* | *24 Month* |
|---|---|---|---|
| | Brain stem | | |
| $H_2O$ | 10.8 ± 1.2 (13) | 15.9 ± 2.3 (12) | 6.6 ± 0.6 (4) |
| Norepinephrine,$10^{-5}M$ | 41.0 ± 5.8 (7) | 52.5 ± 6.8 (7) | 47.1 ± 5.5 (5) |
| Norepinephrine, $10^{-3}M$ | 53.0 ± 5.4 (4) | 54.1 ± 7.7 (3) | 69.8 ± 11.3 (5) |
| | Cerebellum | | |
| $H_2O$ | 26.7 ± 4.9 (8) | 16.9 ± 2.3 (7) | 15.1 ± 1.4 (8) |
| Norepinephrine, $10^{-4}M$ | 83.0 ± 12.0 (7) | 45.7 ± 8.4 (7) | 35.4 ± 4.0 (9) |
| | Hypothalamus | | |
| $H_2O$ | 11.6 ± 2.5 (8) | 16.2 ± 5.9 (5) | 17.1 ± 2.0 (8) |
| Norepinephrine, $10^{-5}M$ | 23.1 ± 4.3 (5) | 23.9 ± 3.1 (4) | 28.1 ± 2.7 (5) |
| Norepinephrine, $10^{-4}M$ | 111.7 ± 28.3 (3) | 100.4 ± 16.8 (2) | 80.2 ± 7.8 (3) |
| | Limbic forebrain | | |
| $H_2O$ | 20.5 ± 3.1 (7) | — | 19.6 ± 2.5 (8) |
| Norepinephrine, $10^{-5}M$ | 64.0 ± 10.3 (7) | — | 48.8 ± 4.8 (8) |
| Norepinephrine, $10^{-4}M$ | 122.8 ± 18.7 (8) | — | 107.4 ± 12.7 (8) |
| | Cerebral cortex | | |
| $H_2O$ | 11.5 ± 1.6 (10) | 12.9 ± 1.9 (10) | 15.2 ± 2.2 (10) |
| Norepinephrine, $10^{-5}M$ | 41.8 ± 5.0 (7) | 48.2 ± 11.5 (8) | 47.0 ± 6.6 (8) |
| Norepinephrine, $10^{-3}M$ | 66.1 ± 7.8 (12) | 71.4 ± 5.6 (12) | 90.8 ± 9.8 (13) |
| | Hippocampus | | |
| $H_2O$ | 9.4 ± 1.2 (8) | 8.2 ± 0.7 (8) | 12.2 ± 1.0 (8) |
| Norepinephrine, $10^{-5}M$ | 33.0 ± 2.9 (8) | 35.0 ± 4.4 (8) | 42.3 ± 1.0 (8) |
| Norepinephrine, $10^{-4}M$ | 68.0 ± 11.8 (8) | 80.2 ± 10.1 (8) | 63.6 ± 6.0 (8) |
| Norepinephrine, $10^{-3}M$ | 72.8 ± 7.2 (7) | 66.8 ± 7.7 (8) | 61.5 ± 6.3 (7) |

Values represent the mean ± S.E.M. of the indicated number of determinations, each of which was assayed in duplicate for cyclic AMP concentration. Preincubation times and the time of exposure to norepinephrine varied with the region and are indicated in Methods. Points which differ significantly ($P < 0.05$) from the 3-month-old rats are underlined.

group of 12-month-old rats were included in most studies to establish if any changes represented senility (12 versus 24 months), maturation (3 versus 12 months) or an age-related continuum (3 versus 12 versus 24).

Our results indicate that in most brain areas there is no age-related decrement in norepinephrine-stimulated accumulation of cyclic AMP (Figure 11-6). Regions examined include the cerebral cortex, hippocampus, hypothalamus, limbic forebrain, cerebellum and the brain stem. Therefore, "vegative" lower brain areas as well as more highly developed regions were studied. The possibility existed that changes in receptor sensitivity or maximal response might occur independently, and therefore norepinephrine concentrations were selected in most cases to examine the lower as well as the higher points on the dose/response curve. However, neither sensitivity nor maximal response parameters changed during the 3- to 24-month period (Table 11-3). Similarly, the concentration of cyclic

AMP in the brain following electrical stimulation was found to be the same in young and older rats.[146] However, since the basal level of cyclic AMP was significantly lower in the older rats, the percentage increase was greater in the aged animals.

Our findings indicated that in many brain regions there was no decrement in transmitter-receptor interaction during aging as evidenced by monitoring cyclic AMP accumulation in brain slices *in vitro*. As with all neurochemical studies, it is possible that measuring biochemical changes in gross brain regions obscured actual differences which are present in discrete areas of the CNS. It is also possible that the dysfunction of individual neurons is compensated for by adjacent cells which serve the same function. Therefore, if the number of responsive cells is large enough in a particular brain region, defects occurring in a small number of cells might not be noticeable when the whole region is assayed. But in anatomically discrete brain regions with restricted inputs or outflows, and in areas where there is little functional redundancy, it might be expected that age-related defects would be most noticeable. The cerebellum might be considered one such area, since the outflow system of the cerebellum occurs solely through Purkinje cells. Any loss of Purkinje cells with aging might have a dramatic effect on both biochemistry and function of the cerebellum. As mentioned, there have been several reports of Purkinje cell loss with age in humans and other vertebrates.[126,127,128]

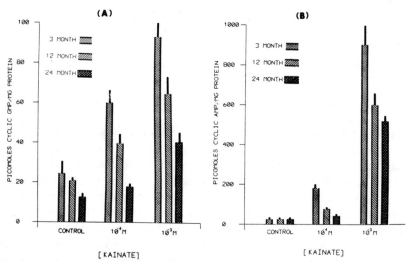

Figure 11-7:   Resting and kainic acid-stimulated accumulation of cyclic GMP (A) and cyclic AMP (B) in cerebellar slices from young, old and aged rats. Tissues were incubated for 2 hrs. and 30 min. with kainate present during the final 15 min. Values represent the mean ± s.e.m. of 9 to 13 animals. From Schmidt and Thornberry.[122]

Incubation of slices of the cerebellum with norepinephrine produced an elevation in cyclic AMP levels at all ages, but the increment in the aged rats was considerably less than at other ages (Figure 11-6). We showed[148] that kaninic acid, a cyclic analogue of glutamic acid, elevated cyclic AMP and cyclic GMP concentrations in the cerebellum *in vitro*. Addition of kaninic acid *in vitro* also revealed an age-related decrement in cyclic GMP as well as cyclic AMP accumulation (Figure 11-7). Similar changes were seen in the cerebella of "nervous" mice which have a reduced number of Purkinje cells as a result of a genetic defect.[132] The data suggest that localized alterations in neuronal populations or receptor activity may occur in select brain regions. These neurochemical defects in the cerebellum might account for some of the physiological dysfunctions seen in old age. For example, motor incoordination and the ability to maintain body temperature in response to a lowering of the environmental temperature[149] might depend on an intact cyclic GMP synthesizing system. Guidotti et al.[150] reported that the shivering and tremorogenic response in rats exposed to the cold correlated with an elevation of cyclic GMP in the cerebellum.

The cerebellum receives noradrenergic input from the locus coeruleus. Norepinephrine-elicited increases in cyclic AMP levels probably mediate the inhibition of spontaneous discharge which occurs in the Purkinje cells following stimulation of the coeruleus.[98] Recently a similar pathway has been described in the hippocampus,[151] and it appears that it might be an analogous system in which noradrenergic input causes an elevation of cyclic AMP in the hippocampus, thereby reducing the spontaneous discharge of hippocampal pyramidal cells (F. E. Bloom, personal communication). Activation of this pathway enhances self-stimulation,[152] perhaps indicative of positive reinforcement. Since we found that cyclic nucleotide synthesis was lower in the cerebellum from aged rats, it seemed possible that a similar situation might exist in the hippocampus. However, the degree of stimulation of cyclic AMP accumulation in slices of the hippocampus was not different across the ages at any concentration of norepinephrine (Table 11-3). It is possible that the measurements made in our system using whole hippocampus were not discrete enough to detect aberrant functioning, since the noradrenergic terminals impinge selectively on hippocampal pyramidal cells.[152]

Another brain region with limited anatomical and functional redundancy is the corpus striatum. Reduced synthesis and concentration of dopamine have been observed in this brain region in aged mice.[9] One of the main pathways to the striatum employs dopamine as the transmitter substance. Kebabian et al.[34] proposed that activation of striatal dopamine-sensitive adenylate cyclase might be the means by which dopamine exerts its effects in the striatum.

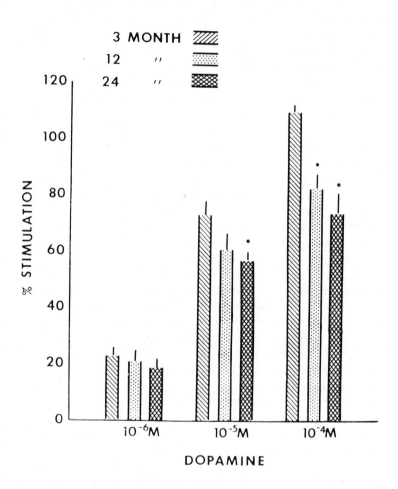

Figure 11-8:    Dopamine stimulation of cyclic AMP accumulation in homogenates of the corpus striatum from young, old and aged rats. The striatum from individual rats was dissected and homogenized. Adenylate cyclase activity was estimated by monitoring the conversion of $[^{32}P]\alpha$-ATP to $[^{32}P]c$AMP during 3 min. incubations. Values represent the mean percent increases in cAMP synthesis $\pm$ s.e.m. of 9 individual determinations, each of which was assayed in duplicate for adenylate cyclase activity. Values which differ significantly from the 3-month-old rats are indicated (*); $P < 0.05$, Student's t-test. Basal activities did not differ significantly with age: 3 month $-$ 162.8 $\pm$ 18.7; 12 month $-$ 148.7 $\pm$ 22.7; 24 month $-$ 120.3 $\pm$ 15.2 pmoles of cAMP synthesized/mg protein/min. at 37°C. From Schmidt and Thornberry.[122]

Walker and Walker[136] found that dopamine did not stimulate cyclic AMP synthesis in the striatum of two-year-old rats. We found that although dopamine stimulation of cyclic AMP synthesis in the striatum declined with age, dopamine was able to significantly elevate cyclic AMP levels in tissue preparations from rats at all ages (Figure 11-8). In our studies basal activity was also slightly lower in the homogenates from aged rats, but Walker and Walker[136] reported that nonstimulated adenylate cyclase activity was greater in preparations from older rats. There are a number of reasons to suspect that the results from the earlier experiments might be atypical: 1) the biphasic dopamine and norepinephrine dose-response relationships reported by Walker and Walker have not been seen by us or other investigators measuring adenylate cyclase activity in the striatum; 2) anesthetized rats were used in the studies; 3) norepinephrine inhibition of striatal adenylate cyclase and cerebellar activation of adenylate cyclase has not been observed by us or others; and 4) homogenates were frozen prior to assay, which has been shown to partially reduce dopamine stimulation of cyclic AMP synthesis. Our data derived from homogenates from three-month-old rats agree with basal activity and the degree of dopamine stimulation of cyclic AMP synthesis reported by others.[153] Pharmacological studies with our system[154] also agree with the findings of others in terms of the specificity of the dopamine response in this region.

Recently Puri and Volicer[121] examined dopamine-stimulated cyclic AMP synthesis in homogenates of the striatum of Fisher–344 rats between the ages of 4 and 30 months. They found no significant elevation of adenylate cyclase activity in animals older than 24 months. These findings are similar to those of Walker and Walker,[136] but different from Schmidt and Thornberry.[122] However, the degree of stimulation in the four-month-old rats reported by Puri and Volicer was significantly less than we have seen and than reported by others monitoring adenylate cyclase activity in young animals.[34,153] Since the basal activity reported by Puri and Volicer is almost exactly what we found (170 pmole cyclic AMP synthesized/mg protein/min), it would appear that they were not eliciting a maximal effect in their cyclase assay system — i.e., 50 percent maximal activation versus 120 percent activation. This is probably due to the high concentration of $Mg^{++}$ that was used. Bockhaert et al.[153] found that increasing the level of $Mg^{++}$ in the assay reduced the degree of stimulation by dopamine.

Dopamine-stimulated adenylate cyclase activity also is lower in the striatum of 20- to 24-month-old Sprague-Dawley rats.[59] Again, basal values were not different across ages, but stimulation by dopamine or apomorphine was lower by about 60 percent. Activity was also lower in the nucleus accumbens, olfactory tubercle and substantia nigra, other areas of the brain that receive dopaminergic terminals. Interestingly, the ability of dopamine to stimulate retinal adenylate cyclase was increased in the old rats. The authors speculated that this phenomenon might reflect the development of supersensitive receptors due to light deprivation in the old animals.

The differences between laboratories in terms of the magnitude of the reduction in dopamine-sensitive adenylate cyclase activity during senescence might well reflect differences in the way in which the assay was conducted.[87] Alternatively, strain differences in hormonal responsivity might account for the disparities.[155]

The 20 to 60 percent decline in dopamine-stimulated cyclic AMP synthesis in dopamine-rich brain areas during advanced aging indicates that postsynaptic receptor systems partially fail in this area. In line with this, J. Joseph (personal communication) has found a 30 percent reduction in haloperidol binding in the striatum of 24-month-old Wistar rats. That caudate tyrosine hydroxylase is 18 percent lower in aged Wistar rats[156] indicates that presynaptic elements are also affected. Such changes in the dopaminergic transmitter system in this region probably contribute significantly to the functional declines observed in aged individuals, and may explain the reduced sensitivity of aged rats[157] and humans[158] to the stimulatory effects of amphetamine.

There are also reports indicating that receptors become supersensitive to transmitter stimulation with advanced aging.[159,160] It is well documented that noradrenergic neurons adapt to changes in the levels of stimulation by altering the synthesis of transmitters.[161] Also surgical[93] or chemical[29,93,162,163] denervation enhances postsynaptic elevation of cyclic AMP synthesis. It might have been predicted, then, that since the level of dopamine falls in the striatum of aged rats[9] and dopamine synthesis is reduced in the striatum of humans,[17] dopamine-sensitive adenylate cyclase activity would increase. Instead, basal activity is not changed and the transmitter-stimulated component of adenylate cyclase is actually decreased with increasing age. Attempts to detect denervation supersensitivity in the striatum have also failed in most[93,165] but not all cases.[164] As mentioned previously, the dopamine-sensitive adenylate cyclase in the retina does become hyperactive in aged rats.[59]

There are several components in hormone-receptor systems which, if defective, could account for the decrements in cyclic AMP and cyclic GMP accumulation in the striatum and cerebellum. Hormone action involves 1) binding to select sites on cell membranes, 2) activation of adenylate cyclase and synthesis of cyclic AMP, 3) cyclic nucleotide accumulation and degradation within the target organ, 4) activation of cyclic AMP-dependent protein kinase, and ultimately 5) phosphorylation of intracellular molecules responsible for the physiological event characteristic of the organ. In the studies summarized to this point we have shown that not all areas of the brain show a defect in the initial stages of the transmitter response encompassing hormone binding, activation of adenylate cyclase and accumulation of cyclic AMP within the tissue. Preliminary evidence indicates that alprenolol binding to beta-adrenergic receptors is only reduced in the cerebellum of aged Wistar rats (M. J. Schmidt and S. J. Enna, unpublished observations). Nonetheless, alterations at points beyond cyclic nucleotide accumulation might occur and lead to tissue dysfunction. This appears to be the case in blood vessels where the decline in the ability to relax in response to isoproterenol[166] appears not to be due to a reduced capacity to synthesize and accumulate cyclic AMP.[167,168] This suggests that aberrations in protein kinase or phosphorylation patterns might occur during aging.

### Cyclic AMP-dependent Protein Kinase Activity and Protein Phosphorylation in the Brain During Aging

Protein kinase activity has been studied in the cortex of cattle four months to eight years of age.[169] Kinase activity in the absence of cyclic AMP was not different across age in the crude homogenate or the synaptosomal or nuclear fraction. Kinase activity in the presence of 5 $\mu$M cyclic AMP was enhanced in all fractions and at all ages. In the synaptosomal and nuclear fractions of animals one or eight years of age, cyclic AMP-stimulated kinase activity was reduced approximately 25 percent compared to four-month-old stock. There was no difference in protein kinase activity between the one-year-old and the eight-year-old animals. The modest declines in cyclic AMP-dependent protein kinase activity are already present in cattle one year of age, which are adolescent at most. Therefore the fall noted seems to represent a maturational effect.

We studied protein kinase activity in the 20,000g supernatants prepared from the cerebral cortex, hippocampus, striatum and cerebellum of rats 3 and 24 months of age.[170] No significant differences across age were observed in the cerebral cortex (Figure 11-9) or other areas (data not shown) at any concentration of cyclic AMP. At both ages the maximal activation occurred at $10^{-6}$M cyclic AMP, and the shape of the curves was identical. However, at all points, preparations from aged rats were 10 to 25 percent less active. Activity in the absence of cyclic AMP was also the same at 3 and 24 months of age.

We have also studied protein kinase in the human brain during aging.

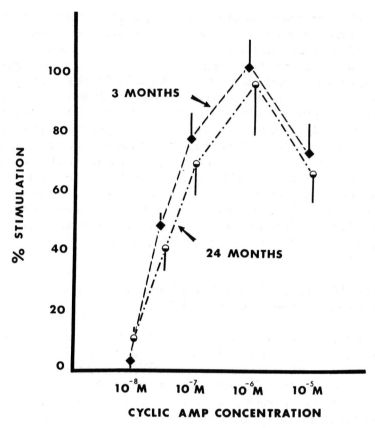

Figure 11-9:    Cyclic AMP-dependent protein kinase activity in the cerebral cortex of young, old and aged rats. Points represent the percent stimulation of histone phosphorylation by protein kinase as a function of cyclic AMP concentration. Basal levels of activity (no added cyclic AMP) were 184 ± 6.0 and 168 ± 16.3 pmoles Pi/mg protein/min. in the cerebral cortex of 3 and 24-month-old rats, respectively. Protein kinase activity was measured in triplicate by incubating 20-30 ugm of 27,000 g supernatant protein together with 50 mM TES buffer, 10 mM Mg (Ac)$_2$ 100 ugm thymus histone, 5 uM ($\delta$-$^{32}$P)-ATP, and varying concentrations of cyclic AMP. Incubations lasted 5 min. Each point represents the mean ± s.e.m. of 5 enzyme preparations. From Schmidt et al.[170]

Protein kinase was present in the cerebral cortex of humans at all ages, and the enzyme was activated three- to fivefold in the presence of a maximally stimulating concentration of cyclic AMP.[50] There were no significant or consistent differences in kinase activity in the cortex between the ages of 2 days and 81 years. Representative data are shown in Figure 11-10.

These data, as well as those of Reichlmeier,[169] indicated that cyclic AMP-dependent and independent protein kinase activities in the brain do

# PROTEIN KINASE IN HUMAN CORTEX

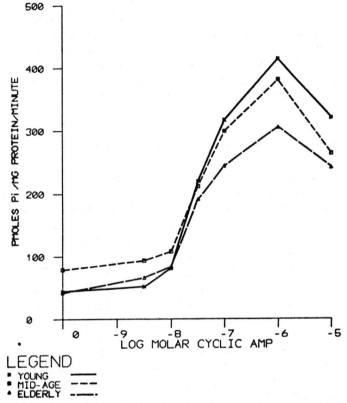

LEGEND
- YOUNG ———
- MID-AGE — — —
- ELDERLY —·—·—

Figure 11-10:   Cyclic AMP-dependent protein kinase activity in the cerebral cortex of young (2 days to 2 yrs., N=7), mid-aged (42 to 59 yrs., N=4) or elderly (63 to 82 yrs., N=4) humans. Points represent protein kinase activity in the presence or absence of varying concentrations of cyclic AMP. Protein kinase activity was measured in triplicate by incubating 20-50 ugms of 27,000 g supernatant protein as indicated in the legend to Figure 9. From Schmidt and Ghetti.[50]

not lose significant activity with advanced aging, and the sensitivity of the enzyme to stimulation by cyclic AMP also does not change. There have been no determinations of protein kinase activity during aging in peripheral tissues at this time, such that one cannot say of the stability of the brain enzyme during aging is unique. Cyclic GMP-dependent protein kinases have not been studied in brain as a function of age.

It was important to determine if critical substrates of protein kinase were lost or altered during aging, and we now have some data bearing on this point. Incubation of synaptosomal membrane fragments with radioactive ATP and cyclic AMP leads to the labeling of many protein bands.[42,112] In a series of studies with aging rats, no differences were detected in the qualitative or quantitative patterns of phosphorylation in rats 3, 12 or 24 months of age.[170] Regions examined included the cerebral cortex, cerebellum, hippocampus and the caudate nucleus. Therefore, it appears that the major proteins which are phosphorylated by cyclic AMP-dependent protein kinase remain intact in the rat brain during advanced aging. Experiments with human brain are underway.

## Phosphoprotein Phosphatase Activity in the Brain During Aging

The final component in the cyclic nucleotide system is the enzyme phosphoprotein phosphatase. This enzyme exists in several forms in peripheral tissues[43] as well as in the brain.[44] Phosphoprotein phosphatases remove the phosphate from proteins which were phosphorylated by protein kinases. In this way proteins are returned to their native state and the physiological response terminated.

We measured protein phosphatase activity by monitoring the dephosphorylation of histone in the presence of the 27,000g supernatant fraction from the striatum and cerebral cortex of rats at 3 and 24 months of age. There was no difference in phosphatase activity between the ages (L. T. Truex and M. J. Schmidt, unpublished observations).

To summarize, animal studies have shown that the steady-state levels of cyclic AMP and cyclic GMP in the brain do not change during aging. Similarly, adenylate cyclase, the enzyme responsible for the production of cyclic AMP, is unaffected by aging. The binding of norepinephrine and the ability of this neurotransmitter to stimulate the accumulation of cyclic AMP remains intact in most brain regions of aged rats. Small reductions in the catabolism of low levels of cyclic AMP do occur, at least in the cerebral cortex. The intracellular effector of cyclic AMP, the enzyme protein kinase, remains stable during aging, as does the pattern and extent of phosphorylation of synaptosomal proteins in brain regions of old rats, and as does the enzyme phosphoprotein phosphatase. However, significant decrements have been found in some brain regions with some transmitters or stimulants. Dopamine-stimulated synthesis of cyclic AMP is reduced in the striatum of old rats, although the magnitude of decline is questionable. The cerebellum also appears to be affected by aging, in that accumulations of cyclic AMP and cyclic GMP are lower in cerebellar tissue exposed to either norepinephrine or a metabolically stable glutamate analogue, kaninic acid. These cerebellar effects might be due to the loss of Purkinje cells in the cerebellum with age.

The experiments to date indicate a remarkable stability of the cyclic nucleotide system in the central nervous system during advanced aging of rodents. Preliminary studies on human brain[50] have also failed to detect marked differences in the cyclic nucleotide levels or protein kinase activity in cortical tissue obtained at autopsy from patients as old as 82 years.

**Summary and Conclusions**

What then are the implications of these findings for geriatric psychopharmacology and therapeutics? First, a universal decline in transmitter-receptor interactions appears not to occur in the brain during aging. It might have been suspected that if the "protein error" hypothesis of Orgel[171,172] or the "free-radical and membrane cross-linking" theory of Harman[173] were correct and applicable to brain tissue, then one or more of the components of the cyclic nucleotide system would have shown "errors" in function. This appears not to be the case on any widespread scale, based on the experimental data accumulated thus far. What the striatal and cerebellar findings indicate, however, is that in labile brain regions the receptor components of the system can fail while the remaining elements remain intact. Therefore, restoration of function might be possible by potentiating existing rudimentary responses (e.g., by the administration of phosphodiesterase inhibitors) or by circumventing the cyclic AMP-generating system and triggering cellular reactions by directly activating protein kinase (e.g., through the administration of cyclic nucleotide analogues). It is possible that the reduced synthesis of cyclic AMP in the striatum and cerebellum is not due to loss of neurons or receptors, but rather to alteration in the nature of membrane receptors. If this is the case, substituting synthetic transmitter analogues for the natural transmitters might restore function by providing "altered transmitters" to fit "altered receptors."

The fact that receptor systems appear to function normally in most brain regions indicates that clinically active psychoactive substances should produce much the same activity in elderly subjects as in young adults. Notable exceptions, however, might be agents that affect the striatal dopaminergic system. One might expect the incidence of tardive dyskinesia following antipsychotic administration to be increased in the elderly due to the fact that dopamine receptors in the striatum are already compromised 30 to 60 percent in the aged brain. Also the lack of effect or partial effectiveness of L-dopa therapy in elderly Parkinsonism patients may be due to the inability of the caudate to convert the precursor (L-dopa) to dopamine as a result of the decline in the activity of catecholamine synthetic enzymes in the aged striatum. For this reason, direct-acting dopamine stimulants might be most appropriate. These would be effective since the receptor systems are probably largely intact (at least 40 to 70 percent) in the brains of aged rats.

The situation in the cerebellum is different, however. According to several reports there is a marked decline in transmitter-receptor activation with age. Restoration of transmitter efficacy in this region might best be accomplished by phosphodiesterase inhibitors which would potentiate the diminished cyclic AMP response. Interestingly, Shimamoto et al.[174] reported that three patients with presenile and senile dementia, and seven patients with cerebellar degeneration, showed signs of clinical improvement following four to ten months' treatment with Phthalazinol, a phosphodiesterase inhibitor. Papaverine, often used in geriatric medicine as a cerebral vasodilator, might owe some of its activity to its ability to inhibit phosphodiesterase in brain.[175,176] Some beneficial effects of papaverine in mild senile organic brain syndrome have been reported.[177] Many studies have implicated cyclic AMP as an important regulator of striatal function,[87] suggesting that phosphodiesterase inhibitors might also be of use in Parkinsonism as well.

The studies summarized here represent only the beginnings of programs designed to thoroughly examine transmitter-receptor function in the brain during aging. Further experimentation may disclose labile points in the transmitter-intracellular messenger system in the aged brain. Our hope is that this research will eventually enable us to design new therapeutic agents that can be used to prolong and restore the functioning of the central nervous system in old age.

## ACKNOWLEDGMENTS

We wish to acknowledge the expert technical assistance of Lew L. Truex and John F. Thornberry, who were instrumental in accumulating much of the recent data on the cyclic nucleotide system in the brain during aging. Dr. Bernidino Ghetti was helpful in obtaining human brain tissue. We especially thank Ms. Ruth Leonard for her diligence and help during the typing and editing of the manuscript.

# REFERENCES

1. Wright EA, Spink JM: A study of the loss of nerve cells in the central nervous system in relation to age. *Gerontologia* 3:277–287, 1959.
2. Brody H: Structural changes in the aging nervous system. *Interdiscipl Topics Geront* 7:9–21, 1970.
3. Brody H: Aging of the vertebrate brain, in Rockstein M (ed): *Development and Aging in the Nervous System.* New York, Academic Press, 1973, pp 121–133.
4. Brizzee DR, Sherwood N, Timiras PS: A comparison of cell populations at various depth levels in cerebral cortex of young adult and aged Long-Evans rats. *J Gerontol* 23:289–297, 1968.
5. Brody H, Vijayashankar A: Anatomical changes in the nervous system, in Finch CE, Hayflick L (eds): *Handbook of the Biology of Aging.* New York, Van Nostrand Reinhold, 1977, pp 241–261.
6. Hanley T: "Neuronal fall-out" in the aging brain: A critical review of the quantitative data. *Age and Ageing* 3:133–151, 1974.
7. Howard Evelyn: DNA content of rodent brains during maturation and aging, and autoradiography of postnatal DNA synthesis in monkey brain, in Ford DH (ed): *Prog. Brain Research.* New York, Elsevier, pp 91–144, 1973.
8. Franks LM, Wilson PD, Whelan RD: The effects of age on total DNA and cell number in the mouse brain. *Gerontologia* 20:21–16, 1974.
9. Finch CE: Neuroendocrine and automatic aspects of aging, in Finch CE, Hayflick L (eds): *Handbook of the Biology of Aging.* New York, Van Nostrand Reinhold, 1977, pp 262–280.
10. Kohn RR: Heart and cardiovascular system, in Finch CE, Hayflick L (eds): *Handbook of the Biology of Aging.* New York, Van Nostrand Reinhold, 1977, pp 282–317.
11. Oldendorf WH, Kitano M: Isotope study of brain blood turnover in vascular disease. *Arch Neurol* 12:30–38, 1965.
12. Haining JL, Turner MD, Pantall RM: Local cerebral blood flow in young and old rats during hypoxia and hypercapnia. *Am J Physiol* 218:1020–1024, 1970.
13. Geinisman Y, Bondareff W: Decrease in the number of synapses in the senescent brain: a quantitative electron microscopic analysis of the dentate gyrus molecular layer in the rat. *Mech Ageing Develop* 5:11–23, 1976.
14. Feldman ML, Dowd C: Loss of dendritic spines in aging cerebral cortex. *Anat Embryol* 148:279–301, 1975.
15. Scheibel ME, Lindsay RD, Tomiyasu U, Scheibel AB: Progressive dendritic changes in the aging human limbic system. *Expt Neurol* 53:420–430, 1976.
16. Hollander J, Barrows CH: Enzymatic studies in senescent rodent brains. *J Gerontol* 23:174–179, 1968.
17. McGeer E, McGeer PL: Neurotransmitter metabolism in the aging brain, in Terry RD, Gershon S (eds): *Neurobiology of Aging.* New York, Raven Press, 1976, pp 389–403.
18. Roberts J, Goldberg PB, Baskin SI: Biochemical changes in the central nervous system with age in the rat. *Exp. Ageing Res* 2:61–74, 1976.
19. Timiras PS, Hudson DB, Oklund S: Changes in central nervous system free amino acids with development and aging, in Ford DH (ed): *Prog in Brain Research: Neurological Aspects of Maturation and Aging.* New York, Elsevier, 1973, pp 267–275.
20. Miller AE, Shaar CJ, Riegle GD: Aging effects on hypothalamic dopamine and norepinephrine content in the male rat. *Exp Ageing Res* 2(5):475–480, 1976.
21. Meek JL, Bertilsson L, Cheney DL, Zsilla G and Costa E: Aging-induced changes in acetylcholine and serotonin content of discrete brain nuclei. *J Gerontol* 32:129–131, 1977.

22. Hornykiewicz O: Abnormalities of nigrostriatal dopamine metabolism: neurochemical, morphological, and clinical correlations. *J Pharmacol S (suppl)* 64, 1974.

23. Roth GS: Reduced glucocorticoid binding site concentration in cortical neuronal perikarya from senescent rats. *Brain Res* 107:345-354, 1976.

24. Roth GS, Adelman RC: Age related changes in hormone binding by target cells and tissues; possible role in altered adaptive responsiveness. *Exp Geront* 10:1-11, 1975.

25. White P, Goodhardt MJ, Keef JP, Hiley CR, Carrasco LH, Williams IEI: Neocortical cholinergic neurons in elderly people. *Lancet* (March 26):668-671, 1977.

26. Davies P, Verth AH: Regional distribution of muscarinic acetylcholine receptor in normal and Alzheimer's-type dementia brains. *Brain Res* 138:385-392, 1978.

27. Schocken DD, Roth GS: Reduced B-adrenergic receptor concentrations in ageing man. *Nature* 267:856-858, 1977.

28. Bylund DB, Tellez-Inon MT, Hollenberg MD: Age-related parallel decline in beta-adrenergic receptors adenylate cyclase and phosphodiesterase activity in rat erythrocyte membranes. *Life Sci* 21:403-410, 1977.

29. Palmer GC, Sulser F, Robison GA: Effects of neurohumoral and adrenergic agents on cyclic AMP levels in various areas of the rat brain *in vitro*. *Neuropharmacology* 12:327-337, 1973.

30. Kodama T, Matsukado Y, Shimizu H: The cyclic AMP system of human brain. *Brain Res* 50:135-146, 1973.

31. Shimizu H, Tanaka S, Suzuki T, Matsukado Y: The response of human cerebrum adenyl cyclase to biogenic amines. *J Neurochem* 18:1157-1171, 1971.

32. Ferrendelli JA, Chang MM, Vinscheif DA: Elevation of cyclic GMP levels in central nervous system by excitatory and inhibitory amino acids. *J Neuroche M,* 22:535-540, 1974.

33. Lee T-P, Kuo JP, Greengard P: Role of muscarinic cholinergic receptors in regulation of guanosine 3':5'-cyclic monophosphate content in mammalian brain, heart muscle and intestinal smooth muscle. *Proc Nat Acad Sci* 69:3287-3291, 1972.

34. Kebabian JW, Petzold GL, Greengard P: Dopamine-sensitive adenylate cyclase in caudate nucleus of rat brain and its similarity to the "Dopamine Receptor." *Proc Mat Acad Sci* 69:2145-2149, 1972.

35. Clement-Cormier YC, Tobison GA: Adenylate cyclase from various dopaminergic areas of the brain and the action of antipsychotic drugs. *Biochem Pharmacol* 26:1719-1722, 1977.

36. Daly J: *Cyclic Nucleotides in the Nervous System.* New York, Plenum Publishing, 1977.

37. Appleman MM, Thompson WJ, Russell TR: Cyclic nucleotide phosphodiesterases. *Adv Cyclic Nucleotide Res* 3:65-98, 1973.

38. Greengard P: Phosphorylated proteins as physiological effectors. *Science* 199:146-152, 1978.

39. Williams M, Rodnight P: Protein phosphorylation in nervous tissue: Possible involvement in nervous tissue function and relationship to cyclic nucleotide metabolsim. *Prog Neurobiol* 8:183-250, 1977.

40. Schmidt MJ, Sokoloff L: Activity of cyclic AMP-dependent microsomal protein kinase and phosphorylation of ribosomal proteins in rat brain during postnatal development. *J Neurochem* 21:1193-1205, 1973.

41. Johnson EM, Maeno H, Greengard P: Phosphorylation of endogenous protein of rat brain by cyclic adenosine 3',5'-monophosphate dependent protein kinase. *J Biol Chem* 246:7731-7739, 1971.

42. Ueda T, Maeno H, Greengard P: Regulation of endogenous phosphorylation of specific proteins on synaptic membrane fractions from rat brain by adenosine 3',5'-monophosphate. *J Biol Chem* 248:8295-8305, 1973.

43. Nimmo HG, Cohen P: Hormonal control of protein phosphorylation, in Greengard P, Robison GA (eds): (cf2 Adv. Cyclic Nucleotide Research. New York, Raven Press, 1977 vol 8, pp 146–247.
44. Maeno H, Greengard P: Phosphoprotein phosphatases from rat cerebral cortex: Subcellular distribution and characterization. *J Biol Chem* 247:3269–3277, 1972.
45. Reporter M, Rosenquist GC: Adenosine 3′,5′-monophosphate: Regional differences in chick embryos at the head process stage. *Science* 178:628–630, 1972.
46. Patton MW, Nakorski SR, Rogers KJ: Regulation of cyclic adenosine 3′,5′-monophosphate concentration in chick cerebral hemispheres during development. *J Neurochem* 27:807–812, 1976.
47. Schmidt MJ, Palmer EC, Dettbarn WD, Robison GA: Cyclic AMP and adenyl cyclase in the developing rat brain. *Develop Psycholbiol* 3:53–67, 1970.
48. Steiner AL, Ferrendelli JA, Kipnis DM: Radioimmunoassay for cyclic nucleotides: Effects of ischemia, changes during development and regional distribution of adenosine 3′,5′-monophosphate and guanosine 3′,5′-monophosphate in mouse brain. *J Biol Chem* 247(4):1121–1124, 1972.
49. Weiss B, Strader SJ: Adenosine 3′,5′-monophosphate during fetal and postnatal development, in Boreus L (ed): *Fetal Pharmacology.* New York, Raven Press, 1973, pp 205–235.
50. Schmidt MJ, Ghetti B: Studies on the cyclic AMP system in human brain during aging. Society for Neuroscience Abstracts Vol. III Seventh Annual Meeting, 1977.
51. Schmidt MJ, Schmidt DE, Robison GA: Cyclic adenosine monophosphate in brain areas: Microwave irradiation as a means of tissue fixation. *Science* 173:1142–1143, 1971.
52. Schmidt MJ, Hopkins JT, Schmidt DE, Robison GA: Cyclic AMP in brain areas: Effects of amphetamine and norepinephrine assessed through the use of microwave radiation as a means of tissue fixation. *Brain Res* 42:465–477, 1972.
53. Schmidt MJ, and Robison GA: The effect of norepinephrine on cyclic AMP levels in discrete regions of the developing rabbit brain. *Life Sci* 10:459–464, 1971.
54. Palmer GC, Schmidt MJ, and Robinson GA: Development and characteristics of the histamine-induced accumulation of cyclic AMP in the rabbit cerebral cortex. *J Neurochem* 19:2251–2256, 1972.
55. Perkins JP, Moore MM: Regulation of the adenosine cyclic 3′,5′-monophosphate content of rat cerebral cortex: Ontogenetic development of the responsiveness to catecholamines and adenosine. *Mol Pharmacol* 9:774–782, 1973.
56. Harden TK, Wolfe BB, Sporn JR, Perkins JP, Molinoff PF: Ontogeny of β-adrenergic receptors in rat cerebral cortex. *Brain Res* 125:99–108, 1977.
57. Gilman AG, Schrier BK: Adenosine cyclic 3′,5′-monophosphate in fetal rat brain cultures. 1. Effect of catecholamines. *Mol Pharmacol* 8:410–416, 1972.
58. Spano PF, Kumakura K, Govoni S, Trabucchi M: Post-natal development and regulation of cerebellar cyclic guanosine monophosphate system. *Pharmacol Res Comm* 7:223–237, 1975.
59. Govoni S, Loddo P, Spano PF, Trabucchi M: Dopamine receptor sensitivity in brain and retina of rats during aging. *Brain Res* 138:565–570, 1977.
60. Sutherland EW, Rall TW, Menon T: Adenyl cyclase. I. Distribution, preparation, and properties. *J Biol Chem* 237:1220–1227, 1962.
61. Weiss B, Costa E: Regional and subcellular distribution of adenyl cyclase and 3′,5′-cyclic nucleotide phosphodiesterase in brain and pineal gland. *Biochem Pharmacol* 17:2107–2116, 1968.
62. Perkins JP: Adenyl cyclase, in Greengard P, Robison GA (eds): *Adv Cyclic Neucleotide Research.* New York, Raven Press, 1973, vol 3, pp 1–64.

63. Von Hungen K, Roberts S, Hill DE: Developmental and regional variations in neurotransmitter-sensitive adenylate cyclase systems in cell-free preparations from rat brain. *J Neurochem* 22:811–819, 1974.
64. Hommes FA, Beere A: The development of adenyl cyclase in rat liver, kidney, brain and skeletal muscle. *Biochem Biophys Acta* 237:296–300, 1971.
65. Weiss B: Ontogenetic development of adenyl cyclase and phosphodiesterase in rat brain. *J Neurochem* 18:469–477, 1971.
66. Coyle JT, Campochiaro P: Ontogenesis of dopaminergic-cholinergic interactions in the rat striatum: A neurochemical study. *J Neurochem* 27:673–678, 1976.
67. Kauffman FC, Harkonen MHA, Johnson EC: Adenyl cyclase and phosphodiesterase activity in cerebral cortex of normal and undernourished neonatal rats. *Life Sci* 11:613–621, 1972.
68. Jacobson M: *Developmental Neurobiology*. New York, Holt Rinehart and Winston, 1970, pp 42–59.
69. Menon KMJ, Giese S, Jaffe RB: Hormone- and fluoride-sensitive adenylate cyclases in human fetal tissues. *Biochem Biophys Acta* 304:203–209, 1973.
70. Williams RH, Little SA, Ensinck JW: Adenyl cyclase and phosphodiesterase activities in brain areas of man, monkey, and rat. *Am J Med Sci* 258:190–202, 1969.
71. Wells JN, Hardman JG: Cyclic nucleotide phosphodiesterases, in Greengard P, Robison GA (eds): *Adv Cyclic Neucleotide Research*. New York, Raven Press, 1977, vol 8, pp 119–143.
72. Kebabian JW: Biochemical regulation and physiological significance of cyclic nucleotides in the nervous system, in Greengard P, Robison GA (eds): *Adv Cyclic Neucleotide Research*. New York, Raven Press, 1977, vol 8, pp 421–508.
73. Nathanson JA: Cyclic nucleotides and nervous system function. *Physiol Rev* 57:157–256, 1977.
74. Florendo NT, Barnett RJ, Greengard P: Cyclic 3',5'-nucleotide phosphodiesterase: Cytochemical localization in cerebral cortex. *Science* 173:745–747, 1971.
75. Adinolfi AM, Schmidt SY: Cytochemical localization of cyclic nucleotide phosphodiesterase activity at developing synapses. *Brain Res* 76:21–31, 1974.
76. Brostrom CO, Wolff DJ: Calcium-dependent cyclic nucleotide phosphodiesterase from brain. *Arch Biochem Biophys* 172:301–311, 1976.
77. Van Inwegan RG, Robinson GA, Thompson WJ, Armstrong KJ, Stouffer JE: Cyclic nucleotide phosphodiesterases and thyroid hormones. *J Biol Biochem* 250:2452–2456, 1975.
78. Pledger WJ, Stancel GM, Thompson WJ, Strada SJ: Separation of multiple forms of phosphodiesterase activity from rat brain by isoelectrofocusing. *Biochem Biophys Acta* 370:242–248, 1974.
79. Van Inwegan RG, Pledger WJ, Strada SJ, Thompson WJ: Characterization of cyclic nucleotide phosphodiesterases with multiple separation techniques. *Arch Biochem Biophys* 175:700–709, 1976.
80. Gaballah S, Popoff C: Cyclic 3',5'-nucleotide phosphodiesterase in nerve endings of developing rat brain. *Brain Res* 25:220–222, 1971.
81. Strada SJ, Uzonor P, Weiss B: Ontogenetic development of a phosphodiesterase activator and the multiple forms of cyclic AMP phosphodiesterase of rat brain. *J Neurochem* 23:1097–1103, 1974.
82. Davis CW, Kuo JF: Ontogenetic changes in levels of phosphodiesterase for adenosine 3',5'-monophosphate and guanosine 3':5'-monophosphate in the lung, liver, brain and heart from guinea pigs. *Biochem Biophys Acta* 444:554–562, 1976.
83. Kang ES: Cyclic nucleotide phosphodiesterase activities of the fetal and mature human cerebral cortex. *Pediatr Res* 11:655–663, 1977.

84. Kakiuchi S, Rall TW: Studies on adenosine 3′,5′-phosphate in rabbit cerebral cortex. *Mol Pharmacol* 4:379–388, 1968.

85. Kakiuchi S, Rall TW: The influence of chemical agents on the accumulation of adenosine 3′,5′-phosphate in slices of rabbit cerebellum. *Mol Pharmacol* 4:367–378, 1968.

86. Kohrman AF: Patterns of development of adenyl cyclase activity and norepinephrine responsiveness in the rat. *Pediatr Res* 7:575–581, 1973.

87. Schmidt MJ: New perspectives on dopamine-sensitive adenylate cyclase in the brain, in Palmer GC (ed): *Neuropharmacology of Cyclic Nucleotides*. Baltimore, Urban and Schwarzenberg, in press, 1978.

88. Makman MH, Brown JH, Mishra RK: Cyclic AMP in retina and caudate nucleus: Influence of dopamine and other agents, in Drummond GI, Greengard P, Robison GA (eds): *Adv Cyclic Nucleotide Research*. New York, Raven Press, 1975, vol 5, pp 661–679.

89. Spano PF, Kumakora K, Govoni S, Trabucchi M: Ontogenetic development of neostriatal dopamine receptors in the rat. *J Neurochem* 27:621–624, 1976.

90. Seeds NW, Gilman AG: Norepinephrine stimulated increase of cyclic AMP levels in developing mouse brain cell cultures. *Science* 174:292, 1971.

91. Pardo JV, Creese I, Burt DR, Snyder SH: Ontogenesis of dopamine receptor binding in the corpus striatum of the rat. *Brain Res* 125:376–382, 1977.

92. Woodward DJ, Hoffer BJ, Siggins GR, Bloom FE: The ontogenic development of synaptic functions, synaptic activation on responsiveness to neurotransmitter substances in rat cerebellar Purkinje cells. *Brain Res* 34:73–97, 1971.

93. Dismukes RK, Daly JW: Adaptive responses of brain cyclic AMP-generating systems to alterations in synaptic input. *J Cyclic Neucleotide Res* 2:321–336, 1976.

94. Palmer GC and Scott HR: The cyclic AMP response to noradrenalin in young adult rat brain following post-natal injections of 6-hydroxydopamine. *Experientia* 30:520–521, 1974.

95. Perkins JP: Regulations of adenyl cyclase activity by neurotransmitters and its relation to neural function, in Tower DB, Brady RO (eds): *The Nervous System*, vol 1. The Basic Neurosciences. New York, Raven Press, 1975, pp 381–394.

96. Mollinoff PB: Role of beta adrenergic receptors in regulating responsiveness to catecholamines in rat cerebral cortex. *Adv Cyclic Neucleotide Research*. New York, Raven Press, 1978, in press.

97. Nahorski SR: Altered responsiveness of cerebral beta adrenoceptors assessed by adenosine cyclic 3′,5′-monophosphate formation and [³H] propranolol binding. *Mol Pharmacol* 13:679–689, 1977.

98. Siggins GR, Hoffer BJ, Bloom FE: Cyclic adenosine monophosphate: possible mediator for norepinephrine on cerebellar Purkinje cells. *Science* 165:1018–1020, 1969.

99. Eayrs JT, Goodhead B: Postnatal development of the cerebral cortex in the rat. *J Anatomy* 93:385–402, 1959.

100. Caley DW, Maxwell DS: An electron microscopic study of neurons during postnatal development of the rat cerebral cortex. *J Com Neurology* 133:17–44, 1968.

101. Aghajanian and Bloom FE: The formation of synaptic junctions in developing rat brain: a quantitative electron microscopic study. *Brain Res* 6:716–727, 1967.

102. Karki N, Kuntzman R, Brodie BB: Norepinephrine and serotonin brain levels at various stages of ontogenic development. *Fed Proc* 19:282, 1960.

103. Deza L, Elidelberg E: Development of cortical electrical activity in the rat. *Exp Neurol* 17:425–438, 1967.

104. Crain SM: Development of electrical activity in the cerebral cortex of the albino rat. *Proc Exp Biol Med* 81:49–51, 1952.

105. McIlwain H: *Biochemistry and the Central Nervous System.* Boston, Little, Brown, 1966.
106. Robinson GA, Butcher RW, Sutherland EW: Adenyl cyclase as an adrenergic receptor. *Ann NY Acad Sci* 139:703–723, 1967.
107. Walsh DA, Perkins JP, Krebs EG: An adenosine 3',5'/monophosphate-dependent protein kinase from rabbit skeletal muscle. *J Biol Chem* 243:3763–3774, 1968.
108. Schmidt MJ, Robinson GA: The effect of neonatal thyroidectomy on the development of the adenosine 3',5'-monophosphate system in the rat brain. *J Neurochem* 19:937–947, 1972.
109. Takahashi T, Matsuzaki S, Nunez J: Modification in soluble protein kinase and cyclic AMP binding capacity of developing rat brain. *J Neurochem* 24:303–304, 1975.
110. Gaballah S, Popoff C, Sooknenden G: Changes in cyclic 3',5'-adenosine monophosphate-dependent protein kinase levels in brain development. *Brain Res* 31:19–21, 1971.
111. Greengard P: Possible role for cyclic nucleotides and phosphorylated membrane proteins in post-synaptic actions of neurotransmitters. *Nature* 260:101–108, 1976.
112. Routtenberg A, Ehrlich YH: Endogenous phosphorylation of four cerebral cortical membrane proteins: Role of cyclic nucleotides, ATP and divalent cations. *Brain Res* 92:415–430, 1975.
113. Sloboda RD, Rudolph SA, Rosenbaum JL, Greengard P: Cyclic AMP-dependent endogenous phosphorylation of a microtubule-associated protein. *Proc Nat Acad Sci* 72:177–181, 1975.
114. Teichberg VI, Sobel A, Changeux J: Phosphorylation of acetylcholine receptor by endogenous membrane protein kinase in receptor-enriched membranes of *Torpedo Californica. Nature* 167:540–542, 1977.
115. Williams M, Rodnight R: Stimulation of protein phosphorylation in brain slices by electrical pulses: speed of response and evidence for net phosphorylation. *J Neurochem* 24:601–603, 1975.
116. Ehrlich YH, Rabjohns RR, Routtenberg A: Experiential input alters the phosphorylation of specific proteins in brain membranes. *Pharmacol Biochem Behav* 6:169–174, 1977.
117. Ehrlich YH, Davis LG, Gilfoil T, Brunngraber EG: Distribution of endogenously phosphorylated proteins in subcellular fractions of rat cerebral cortex. *Neurochem Res* 2:533–548, 1977.
118. Schmidt MJ: The cyclic AMP system in the developing rat brain and the effects of neontal thyroidectomy. PhD thesis, Vanderbilt University, 1971.
119. Schmidt MJ: Effects of neonatal hyperthyroidism on activity of cyclic AMP-dependent microsomal protein kinase. *J Neurochem* 22:469–471, 1974.
120. Zimmerman I, Berg A: Levels of adenosine 3',5' cyclic monophosphate in the cerebral cortex of aging rats. *Mech Ageing Develop* 3:33–36, 1974.
121. Puri SK, Volicer L: Effect of aging on cAMP levels and adenylate cyclase and phosphodiesterase activities in the rat corpus striatum. *Mech Ageing Develop* 6:53–58, 1977.
122. Schmidt MJ, Thornberry JF: Cyclic AMP and cyclic GMP accumulation *in vitro* in brain regions of young, old and aged rats. *Brain Res* 139:169–177, 1978.
123. Palmer GC, Robinson GA, Manian AA, Sulser F: Modification by psychotropic drugs of the cyclic AMP response to norepinephrine in the rat brain *in vitro. Psychopharmacologia (Berl)* 23:201–211, 1972.
124. Vetulani J, Sulser F: Action of various anti-depressant treatments reduces reactivity of noradrenergic cyclic AMP-generating system in limbic forebrain. *Nature* 257:495–496, 1975.
125. O'Dea RF, Haddox MK, Goldberg ND: Interaction with phosphodiesterase of free and kinase-complexed cyclic adenosine 3',5'-monophosphate. *J Biol Chem* 246:6183–6190, 1971.

126. Ellis RS: Norms for some structural changes in the human cerebellum from birth to old age. *J Com Neurol* 32:1–33, 1920.
127. Hall TC, Miller AKH, Corsellis JAN: Variations in the human Purkinje cell population according to age and sex. *Neuropath Appl Neurol* 1:267–292, 1975.
128. Inukai T: On the loss of Purkinje cells, with advancing age, from the cerebellar cortex of the albino rat. *J Com Neurol* 45:1–28, 1928.
129. Siggins GR, Battenberg EF, Hoffer BJ, Bloom FE, Steiner AL: Noradrenergic stimulation of cyclic adenosine monophosphate in rat Purkinje neurons: An immunocytochemical study. *Science* 179:585–588, 1973.
130. Mao CC, Guidotti A, Costa E: The regulation of cyclic guanosine monophosphate in rat cerebellum: Possible involvement of putative amino acid neurotransmitters. *Brain Res* 79:510–514, 1974.
131. Mao CC, Guidotti A, Landis S: Cyclic GMP: Reduction of cerebellar concentration in "nervous" mutant mice. *Brain Res* 90:335–339, 1975.
132. Schmidt MJ, Nadi NS: Cyclic nucleotide accumulation *in vitro* in the cerebellum of "nervous" neurologically mutant mice. *J Neurochem* 29:87–90, 1977.
133. Sidman RL, Green MC: "Nervous" a new mutant mouse with cerebellar disease, in Sadourdy M (ed): *Les Mutants Pathologiques chez l'animal*. Paris, CNSR, 1970, pp 69–79.
134. Gennari C, Galli M, Montagnani M: Urinary cyclic adenosine monophosphate in young adults and elderly subjects. *J Clin Pathol* 29:69–72, 1976.
135. Broadus AE: Clinical cyclic nucleotide research, in Greengard P, Robison GA (eds): *Adv Cyclic Neucleotide Research* New York, Raven Press, 1977, pp 509–548.
136. Walker JB, Walker JP: Neurohumoral regulation of adenylate cyclase activity in rat striatum. *Brain Res* 54:386–390, 1973.
137. Zimmerman ID, Berg AP: phosphodiesterase and adenyl-cyclase activities in the cerebral cortex of the aging rat. *Mech Ageing Develop* 4:89–96, 1975.
138. Maguire ME, Ross EM, Gilman AG: β-Adrenergic receptor: Ligand binding properties and the interaction with adenyl cyclase. *Adv Cyclic Neucleotide Res* 8:1–83, 1977.
139. Williams RH, Thompson WJ: Effect of age upon guanyl cyclase, adenyl cyclase, and cyclic nucleotide phosphodiesterase in rats. *Proc Soc Exp Biol Med* 143:382–387, 1973.
140. Forn J, Schonhofer PS, Skidmore IF, Krishna G: Effect of aging on the adenyl cyclase and phosphodiesterase activity of isolated fat cells of rat. *Biochem Biophys Acta* 28:304–309, 1970.
141. Cooper B, Gregerman RI: Hormone-sensitive fat cell adenylate cyclase in the rat. *J Clin Invest* 57:161–168, 1975.
142. Sheppard H, Burghardt CR: Age-dependent changes in the adenylate cyclase and phosphodiesterase activity of rat erythrocytes. *Biochem Pharmacol* 22:427–429, 1973.
143. Zimmerman ID, Berg AP: An effect of age on the phosphodiesterase activator protein of rat cerebral cortex. A brief note. *Mech Ageing Develop* 6:67–71, 1977.
144. Makman MH: Properties of adenylate cyclase of lymphoid cells. *Proc Nat Acad Sci* 68:885–889, 1971.
145. Bitensky MW, Russell V, Blanco M: Independent variation of glucagon, and epinephrine responsive components of hepatic adenyl cyclase as a function of age, sex and steroid hormones. *Endocrinology* 86:154–159, 1970.
146. Berg A, Zimmerman ID: Effects of electrical stimulation on norepinephrine on cAMP levels in the cerebral cortex of the aging rat. *Mech Ageing Develop* 4:377–383, 1975.
147. Gold PE, McGaugh J: Changes in learning and memory during aging, in Ordy JM and Brizzee KR (eds): *Advances in Behavioral Biology.* New York, Plenum Press, 1975, vol 16, pp 145–158.
148. Schmidt MJ, Thornberry JF, Molloy BB: Effects of kainate and other glutamate

analogues on cyclic nucleotide accumulation in slices of rat cerebellum. *Brain Res* 121:182–189, 1977.

149. Finch CE, Foster JR, Mirsky AE: Ageing and the regulation cell activities during exposure to cold. *J Gen Physiol* 54:690–712.150, 1969.

150. Mao CC, Guidotti A, Costa E: Interactions between $\alpha$-amino butyric acid and guanosine 3',5'-monophosphate in rat cerebellum. *Mol Pharmacol* 10:736–745, 1974.

151. Segal M, Bloom FE: The action of norepinephrine in the rat hippocampus. II. Activation of the input pathway. *Brain Res* 72:99–114, 1974.

152. Segal M, Bloom FE: The actions of norepinephrine in the rat hippocampus. IV. The effects of locus coeruleus stimulation on evoked hippocampal unit activity. *Brain Res* 107:513–525, 1976.

153. Bockhaert J, Premont J, Glowinski J, Thierrry AM, Tassin JP: Topographical distribution of dopaminergic innervation and of dopaminergic receptors in the rat striatum. II. Distribution and characteristics of dopamine adenylate cyclase-interaction with dopaminergic receptors. *Brain Res* 107:303–315, 1976.

154. Schmidt MJ, and Hill LE: Effects of ergots on adenylate cyclase activity in the corpus striatum and pituitary gland. *Life Sci* 20:789–798, 1977.

155. Sattin A: Cyclic AMP accumulation in cerebral cortex tissue from inbred strains of mice. *Life Sci* 16:903–914, 1975.

156. McGeer EG, Fibiger HC, McGeer PL, Wickson V: Aging and brain enzymes. *Exp Gerontol* 6:391–396, 1971.

157. Verzar F: The age of the individual as one of the parameters of pharmacological action. *Acta Physiol Acad Sci Hung* 19:313–318, 1961.

158. Nathanson MH: The central action of beta-aminopropyl benzene (benzedrine). *JAMA* 108:528–531, 1937.

159. Bender AD: The influence of age on the activity of catecholamines and related therapeutic agents. *J Am Geriatr Soc* 18:220–232, 1970.

160. Frolkis VV: The autonomic nervous system in the aging organism. *Triangle* 8:322–328, 1969.

161. Fuller RW, Steinberg M: Regulation of enzymes that synthesize neurotransmitter monamines, in Weber G (ed): *Advances in Enzyme Regulations*. Oxford, Pergamon Press, 1976, vol 14, pp 347–390.

162. Palmer DS, French SW, Marod MI: Noradrenergic subsensitivity and supersensitivity of the cerebral cortex after reserpine treatment. *J Pharmacol Exp Ther* 196:167–171, 1976.

163. Kalisker A, Rutledge CO, Perkins JP: Effect of nerve degeneration by 6-hydroxydopamine on catecholamine-stimulated adenosine 3',5'-monophosphate formation in rat cerebral cortex. *Mol Pharmacol* 9:619–629, 1973.

164. Mishra RK, Gardner EL, Katzman R, Makman MH: Enhancement of dopamine-stimulated adenylate cyclase activity in rat caudate after lesions in substantia nigra: evidence for denervation supersensitivity. *Proc Nat Acad Sci* 71:3883–3887, 1974.

165. Gnegy M, Vzunov P, Costa E: Participation of an endogenous $Ca^{++}$-binding protein activator in the development of drug-induced supersensitivity of striatal dopamine receptors. *J Pharm Exp Ther* 202:558–564, 1977.

166. Fleisch JH, Maling HM, Brodie BB: Beta-receptor activity in aorta: variations with age and species. *Cir Res* 26:151–162, 1970.

167. Cohen ML, Berkowitz BA: Age-related changes in vascular responsiveness to cyclic nucleotides and contractile agonists. *J Pharm Exp Ther* 191:147–155, 1974.

168. Cohen ML, Blume AS, Berkowitz BA: Vascular adenylate cyclase: Role of age and guanine nucleotide activation. *Blood Vessels* 14:25–42, 1977.

169. Reichlmeier KD: Age related changes of cyclic AMP-dependent protein kinase in bovine brain. *J Neurochem* 27:1249–1251, 1976.

170. Schmidt MJ, Truex LT, Conway R, Routtenberg AY: Cyclic AMP-dependent protein kinase activity and synaptosomal protein phosphorylation in the brains of aged rats. *J Neurochem,* in press, 1978.

171. Orgel LE: The maintenance of accuracy of protein synthesis and its relevance to aging. *Proc Nat Acad Sci* 49:517–521, 1963.

172. Orgel LE: Ageing of clones of mammalian cells. *Nature* 243:441–445, 1973.

173. Harman D: Aging: A theory based on free radical and radiation chemistry. *J Gerontol* 11:298–300, 1956.

174. Shimamoto T, Murase H, Numano F: Treatment of senile dementia and cerebellar disorders with phthalazinol. Cyclic AMP-increasing agent, phthalazinol, in therapeutic trials in hitherto incurable morbid conditions (I). *Mech Ageing Develop* 5:241–250, 1976.

175. Adachi K, Numano F: Phosphodiesterase inhibitors: Their comparative effectiveness *in vitro* in various organs. *Jap J Pharmacol* 27:97–103, 1977.

176. Weiss B, Hiat WN: Selective cyclic nucleotide phosphodiesterase inhibitors as potential therapeutic agents. *Ann Rev Pharmacol Toxicol* 17:441–477, 1977.

177. Branconnier RJ, Cole JO: Effects of chronic papaverine administration on mild senile organic brain syndrome. *J Am Geriatr Soc* 25:458–462, 1977.

178. Coyle JT: Development of the central catecholaminergic neurons, in Schmitt FO and Worden FG (eds): *The Neurosciences Third Study Program.* Cambridge, Mass, MIT Press, 1974, pp 877–884.

179. Coyle JT, Molliver ME: Major innervation of newborn rat cortex by monoaminergic neurons. *Science* 196:444–447, 1977.

180. McGeer EG, Fibiger HC, Wickson B: Differential development of caudate enzymes in the neonatal rat. *Brain Res* 32:433–440, 1971.

# Index

acetaminophen, 199
acetylcholine, 107–109, 154, 215
adenosine, 154, 223, 224, 227, 231, 232
adenylate cyclase, 20, 21, 24–26, 28, 36, 38,
    40, 41, 71, 82, 84, 86, 125, 219–221, 223,
    224, 228–233, 236, 237, 240–242, 247,
    249–251, 254
adipose tissue, 242
adrenaline, 70
agitation, 100, 192
albumin, 183
alcoholism, 84, 161, 195
alkaline phosphatase, 125
alpha adrenergic blockers, 29, 32, 135,
    181–185, 231
alpha adrenergic receptors, 38
alpha methyldopa, 114
alprenolol, 251
Alzheimer's disease, 9, 69, 74, 154
amantadine, 191
amino acids, 148, 156, 158
amitriptyline, 104–107, 109, 188, 191
amphetamine, 135–141, 185, 195, 250
amphetamine psychosis, 195
amylobarbital, 177, 189
amyloid, 164
anaerobic glycolysis, 164
analgesics, 199, 200
anisomycine, 72
anorexia, 100
anoxia, 218, 219
antacids, 178, 184, 185, 191, 195
anticholinergics, 107, 108, 115, 191
anticoagulants, 114, 190
anticonvulsants, 182, 190
antihistamines, 191
antihypertensives, 114, 193
antiparkinsonians, 191
antipsychotics, 190, 239
anxiety, 7, 8, 10, 180, 182
apomorphine, 74, 136–140, 176, 229, 249
arteriosclerosis, 119, 125, 130
aspirin, 184, 185
ATP, 14, 15, 22, 28, 29, 32, 36, 82, 219, 220,
    233, 235, 254
ATPase, 18, 19, 24, 28, 29, 32, 36–41, 71, 155,
    220

atropine, 107, 108, 113, 214
atropine psychosis, 191
autolytic behavior, 18
aversive stimuli, 51
avoidance, 50–54, 57–62

barbital, 176, 177, 189
barbiturates, 79, 112, 176–178, 180, 181, 184,
    189, 190, 195
Batten-Spielmeyer-Vogt syndrome, 161
benzodiazepines, 177, 179–181, 191, 199
beta adrenergic blockers, 24, 25, 29, 182,
    183, 184
beta adrebergic receptors, 135, 215, 251
bicarbonate, 19
biogenic amines, 72
blood brain barrier, 187
blood pressure, 135
bromocriptine, 74, 83
butaperazine, 187
butyrophenones, 113
    *see also* haloperidol

calcium, 28, 220, 222, 223
capillaries, 119–125, 129–134
carbohydrates, 146, 159
carbon dioxide, 19, 20
carbonic acid, 19
carbonic anhydrase, 19, 20
cardiac rhythm, 110, 111
cardiovascular function, 9
casein kinase, 234
catabolism, 70
catecholamines, 19, 24, 26, 28, 29, 32, 36, 38,
    40, 41, 66, 70, 71, 72, 79, 82, 125, 135,
    140, 160, 224, 228, 229, 231, 256
cationic pump, 19
cerebral bloodflow, 1, 2, 5, 76, 78, 80, 84, 122,
    124, 218
cerebral cortex, 67, 68, 120, 122, 124, 125,
    129, 132, 134, 154, 164, 214, 215, 219,
    220, 223–225, 227, 228, 232, 235, 237,
    238, 240–245, 251, 252, 254
cerebral insufficiency, 69, 75, 76, 85, 119,
    120, 123–125
cerebral ischemia, 83
ceroids, 161, 162, 164